VOICES
of COLOR

For Aspi, my partner and friend
For my sons, Romil and Zubin
For my parents, Vir Bala and Balram Rastogi

M.R.

For Social Justice Activists around the world
For Mental Health Professionals committed to working at the margins

L.W.

VOICES of COLOR

First-Person Accounts of
Ethnic Minority Therapists

EDITORS

MUDITA RASTOGI

Illinois School of Professional Psychology,
Argosy University, Chicago

◆

ELIZABETH WIELING

University of Minnesota, St. Paul

SAGE Publications
Thousand Oaks ■ London ■ New Delhi

For information:

Sage Publications, Inc.
2455 Teller Road
Thousand Oaks, California 91320
E-mail: order@sagepub.com

Sage Publications Ltd.
1 Oliver's Yard
55 City Road
London EC1Y 1SP
United Kingdom

Sage Publications India Pvt. Ltd.
B-42, Panchsheel Enclave
Post Box 4109
New Delhi 110 017 India

Printed in the United States of America on acid-free paper.

Library of Congress Cataloging-in-Publication Data

Voices of color: first-person accounts of ethnic minority therapists/edited by Mudita Rastogi and Elizabeth Wieling.
    p. cm.
Includes bibliographical references and index.
  ISBN 0-7619-2890-1 (pbk.)
1. Psychotherapy—Cross-cultural studies. 2. Psychiatry, Transcultural.
3. Cross-cultural counseling. 4. Cultural psychiatry. I. Rastogi, Mudita.
II. Wieling, Elizabeth.
RC455.4.E8V65 2005
616.89—dc22

2004003254

04   05   06   07   08   09   10   9   8   7   6   5   4   3   2   1

Acquiring Editor:	Arthur T. Pomponio
Editorial Assistant:	Veronica Novak
Project Editor:	Claudia A. Hoffman
Copy Editor:	Jamie Robinson
Typesetter:	C&M Digitals (P) Ltd.
Indexer:	Molly Hall
Cover Designer:	Janet Foulger

Contents

Acknowledgments

We are deeply grateful to the editorial team at Sage Publications. Art Pomponio, our editor, believed in this project from its inception and guided us at each step. We would like to thank him immensely for his help. Veronica Novak, Claudia Hoffman, Jamie Robinson, and others with Sage were knowledgeable, efficient, and always available to us.

It was a pleasure to work with the authors who contributed to this volume. Their courage and willingness to share their experiences have made the book what it is. Our thanks also to reviewers Priscilla A. Gibson of the University of Minnesota, Maria Senour of San Diego State University, and Carole Woolford-Hunt of Argosy University.

I (M.R.) would like to thank the following people:

Dr. Liz Wieling, my coeditor, friend, and colleague, has been a partner in the evolution of this book. Her creativity and warmth make her a joy to collaborate with. Without her insights and passion, this book would not have been possible.

Dr. Karen Wampler has taught me much of what I know and continues to be an inspiration. I feel truly lucky to have her in my life. I am also grateful to Drs. Satish Saberwal, Gwen Sorrell, and Richard Wampler for all that I have learned from them about critical thinking, diversity, and social justice.

My colleagues and students, too numerous to name individually, and my therapy clients, have constantly challenged me to grow and become a better teacher, therapist, and researcher. For this, I am deeply indebted.

I am thankful to my extended family and friends in India, including Vir Bala and Balram Rastogi, Arnawaz and Jimmy Havewala, and Manish, Meenal, Neha, and Riya Rastogi, for being my anchors, despite the miles between us. Their support means a lot to me.

Aspi Havewala, my husband and partner, deserves vastly more thanks than I am able to express. His love, caring, and sense of humor sustained me through the months I worked on this book. Aspi willingly did extra housework and childcare to free up my time. Romil and Zubin, my sons, brought me joy, laughter, and balance. They always help me see what is important and what is not. For these gifts, I will be grateful forever.

—Mudita Rastogi

I (L.W.) have been transformed by an array of gifts received by others in the forms of love, courage, respect, social, feminist and political activism, and compassion. I humbly thank all the people who have believed in me and supported me throughout my personal and professional development. I am particularly indebted to the people in my everyday life who push me to experience the present in mindful and meaningful ways. These are my students, clients, neighbors, teachers, mentors, family, and friends.

My dearest friends, Robert Schneiders, Amy Hermsen, Kevin Swanson, Karen and Richard Wampler, Steven Harris, Maha ElObeid, and Mona Mittal, motivate and support me in pursuing my dreams. My parents, Edwin and Maria Wieling, and my brothers, David Wieling and Ed Wieling, affirm who I am and fuel the passion that drives me. My dear colleague and friend, Mudita Rastogi, provides me with endless inspiration. Collaborating with Mudita over the years has been the most enjoyable journey of my academic career.

—Liz Wieling

1

Introduction

Mudita Rastogi and Elizabeth Wieling

Voices of Color emerged from a serendipitous meeting. We (the coeditors) were introduced to each other at the AAMFT (American Association for Marriage and Family Therapy) Research Conference in Chicago in 1999, and we realized immediately that we had several common interests. When we later talked on the phone to discuss collaboration, the name of AALANAMFT (African American, Latino/a, Asian and Native American Marriage and Family Therapists) emerged as a logical venue to explore our interests. We had met some of the members of the group and were impressed by their mission and convictions. This online group is a community comprised primarily of MFTs (marriage and family therapists) of color who actively discuss topics ranging from members' personal updates to their professional struggles. The group members also meet in person at the annual AAMFT conferences. Both of us became members of AALANAMFT (which is also called just AALANA), and later we did a pilot study on the experiences of the group's members (Rastogi & Wieling, 2000; Wieling & Rastogi, 2001, 2003). AALANA became important to us because it gave us a community within which to discuss issues that are significant to us and sorely underrepresented in the field. We found AALANA a very supportive environment, with a communication style and group process which differ from those of other professional groups that communicate via a listserv. Our study documented the voices of MFTs of color, a small minority group in the field of marriage and family therapy and the mental health profession in general. We were interested in the members' perceptions of their ethnic identity and their experiences in graduate school, in work settings, and in the AAMFT.

In conducting the pilot study, our literature search revealed that, barring a few exceptions, a strong, first-person voice of therapists of color was missing from the literature (Wieling & Rastogi, in press). When we presented this finding at conferences and discussed it further with the AALANA members, a consensus emerged that

(a) Therapists of color have unique experiences related and relevant to their profession.

(b) These therapists, while by no means a homogeneous group, have certain consistent experiences by virtue of being persons of color within a U.S. context.

(c) The constructs of ethnicity, racism, and oppression often help therapists of color organize and give meaning to their experiences.

(d) The perspectives of these therapists are valuable, rich, and complex. They add to the current knowledge and literature in the field of mental health and contribute to our understanding of ethnicity, cultural differences, and diversity.

(e) This discourse, in the therapists' own voices, needs to be an integral part of the mental health field.

(f) Therapists of color, like other mental health professionals, can and do foster positive social change through their personal and professional interactions with other people.

We wanted to record and disseminate these perspectives by documenting the experiences of therapists of color. Given the diversity of professional training in the field, we invited all ethnic minority mental health professionals—including psychologists, social workers, counselors, and marriage and family therapists—to contribute to this venture. When we floated our ideas for this book to colleagues and listservs for mental health professionals, we found ourselves flooded with email from interested authors. Even in our most optimistic moments we had not imagined that so many therapists of color wanted to have their voices heard. Clearly, this topic is very important and speaks to the burning issues of minority therapists. A number of mental health professionals who have given us feedback on this book say that its contents are intuitively and intellectually meaningful to them. The narratives included here capture the experiences of therapists of color, which range from ethnic identity development to struggling and thriving in agencies, universities, and classrooms to challenging our supervisees, our clients, and ourselves to grapple with oppression. *Voices of Color* shows us that therapists of color live these issues every day. Their stories and analyses give us a unique perspective on the arena of ethnic and cultural differences in the mental health field.

Both of us identify as women of color *and* as international persons, educators, and therapists. I (M.R.) received my doctoral degree in Marriage and Family Therapy in the United States, but I was born and raised in India and as an adult have lived in India and Hong Kong as well as the United States. In college and for a few years afterward, I worked with grassroots organizations, in economically oppressed communities, and on gender-related issues in India. My current teaching, clinical, and research interests include exploring how gender and culture intersect with family and couple relationships, issues of bicultural and bilingual clients, access to mental health for minority communities, and social justice. I (E.W.) identify as multiethnic and am a citizen of both the United States and Brazil. My clinical research interests include the development of culturally effective and efficacious preventive and clinical interventions, methodological considerations in cross-cultural research, intercultural couple relationships, and issues related to the status of women—including women's mental health, family relationships, education, economic well-being, and political influence in the United States and abroad. We would like to acknowledge up front that since neither of us grew up in the United States, we understand that our experiences around race, ethnicity, and culture are likely to be different from those of ethnic minority MFTs who were born and raised in this country. However, we also believe that as MFTs of color we share many points of connection in our experience of being "othered" within the dominant White U.S. culture.

While teaching courses that focus on diversity and during clinical discussions on topics addressing multiculturalism, we found that when students relate concepts like oppression, racism, and discrimination to real-life situations, they seem to "get it"—they are able to more readily grasp concepts such as White privilege, internalized racism, patriarchy, and so on. Therefore, among our primary goals for this book is to help students to become sensitive to differences and similarities, increase their self-awareness, question their own values and beliefs, and eventually integrate a thorough and complex understanding of culture and ethnicity in their work as clinicians, educators, supervisors, researchers, and administrators. We utilize our own stories and those of our clients and students to generate lively discussion in classes and in supervision. We hope that this book will serve as a resource for exploring the multiple meanings of diversity. Several of the chapters detail the authors' struggles with racism in the therapy room, within institutions, and with peers. The collection of writings here speaks to the multiple ways in which mental health professionals can be agents of social change. We hope that our readers will ponder this aspect of their professional role as well.

Finally, we would like to underscore the complexity of language usage and discuss the terms we employ to signify diversity. We believe that all the terms used here have political undertones and that ultimately our use of language will include and exclude particular groups in ways that might obscure, be offensive, or be hurtful. We do not know how to avoid this language trap, but we would like to encourage our readers to deconstruct the terms and their multiple implications. We see this issue—language—as one of the challenges that we must continue to think through as teachers, researchers, and clinicians so that we can develop more acceptable, appropriate, and respectful ways to refer to ourselves and others as we communicate and interact. Our contributors have used different terms to refer to diverse peoples. We have chosen to use the terms *therapists of color* and *ethnic minority* with the recognition of some of the inherent pros and cons of this terminology. The former term carries with it the connotation of solidarity among a group of people by virtue of their common experiences, but it erroneously implies that European Americans do not have "color" or ethnicity. The latter, the term *ethnic minority,* could be applied to any ethnic group, but it emphasizes the underprivileged status of these groups. Yet another factor to consider regarding the language used to refer to diversity is that although the focus of this book is the experiences of populations of color, other forms of diversity such as gender, social class, sexual orientation, religion, national origin, and physical ability or disability are an integral part of discussions on diversity. In fact, it is critical that the points of intersection between multiple "diversities" be acknowledged and understood in all their complexity.

Many of the chapters in the book discuss the intersection of ethnicity with gender, religion, social class, nationality, immigration history, and disability. However, in the spirit of accountability, we would like to mention an unfortunate omission in this book. Like many other books on ethnicity, *Voices of Color* does not discuss issues related to sexual and/or romantic orientation in depth. We recognize the importance of the perspectives and lived experiences of the various subgroups that identify as gay, lesbian, bisexual, and transgendered, to list a few, and that there are a vast range of ways in which sexuality and love are expressed and intersect with other dynamics of diversity. We could report that we were simply unable to easily secure submissions on these topics, but we realize now that we could have been more aggressive in seeking contributions in these areas.

Voices of Color is divided into three sections. Section I of the book, "Identity and Professional Development of Therapists of Color," contains accounts by trainees and therapists of their own growth and ethnic identity development. Section II, "Ethnicity and Race in the Therapy Room and in the Classroom," contains chapters by clinicians, supervisors, and academics. Often referring to real cases, they write about their memorable and painful moments and help us look at the dynamics of race and ethnicity in clinical settings, in academic institutions, and in the supervisor-trainee relationship. Section III, "Theory- and Research-Based Interventions and Approaches," consists of chapters that bring together research and clinical practice to present culturally sensitive models that are relevant to specific populations. A brief note about each chapter follows.

Chapter 2 is an account by Monika Sharma of her life as an Asian Indian woman and a psychologist. She documents in painful detail the struggles she faced growing up in a primarily White neighborhood, her ethnic identity development, and her entry into the psychology profession. Sharma weaves into her story the issue of gender; as a woman of Asian Indian origin, it's an issue that's never too far away. She also confronts her internal racism and discusses the lessons she learned about herself in the classroom and in the therapy room.

Three Latino therapists from different countries of origin, Luis Antonio Rivas, Edward A. Delgado-Romero, and Kelly Ramón Ozambela, provide a superb account of their "narratives" as they converge language, professional, and identity issues. This chapter is an exemplar in its articulation of the multiple complexities of being bilingual and bicultural within White dominant culture. Each of the authors describes a personal journey and manages to weave into it important theoretical, clinical, and research considerations. The authors accomplish their purpose of sharing their experiences with a strong sense of *personalismo* and genuineness.

Janet M. Derrick contributes a remarkable chapter depicting her clinical and professional perspectives as a Metis woman of Mohawk ancestry living in Canada. This chapter is submitted to the reader in a poetic yet highly informative manner. Derrick illustrates her experiences with rich stories and provides important definitions, a literature review, and a case study to further illustrate current Native family dynamics in a clinical context.

Shalonda Kelly and Nancy Boyd-Franklin's chapter explores the relational dynamics among African American clients, therapists, and supervisors. The chapter does a superb job of describing how racial, cultural, and familial factors become manifest across these difference roles. Case examples are used to illustrate relational dynamics within parallel processes that lead to personal empowerment in each of these three levels.

The chapter by Larry Jin (Kwok Hung) Lee is very powerful due to his sensitivity and honesty. A social worker by training, Lee says he was taught to leave all references to racism outside the therapy room door. By using vignettes of difficult exchanges he had with clients and colleagues, he compels the reader to enter into a discourse about the "unmentionable." Lee's chapter shows us that racism can be, and often is, a presenting problem. Mental health professionals cannot *not* deal with it.

The chapter by Saba Rasheed Ali, Jonathan R. Flojo, Krista M. Chronister, Diane Hayashino, Quincy R. Smiling, Danielle Torres, and Ellen Hawley McWhirter resulted from a conference presentation. These seven authors discuss situations where the therapist of color is on the receiving end of racism. How do we react to and address racism directed at us by our clients, supervisors, and supervisees? Each of the authors describes a vignette of a powerful experience with racism, as well as how he or she responded to it and perhaps resolved it. The last part of the chapter includes excellent suggestions for educators, supervisors, and program directors to use to plug the hole in training regarding multicultural issues.

As a child, Debra A. Nixon dreamt of becoming a teacher, but she imagined all her students and colleagues as Black. She is now teaching at a predominantly White university. Her chapter describes specific interactions with students and colleagues around issues of ethnicity and race and the difficulties faced by female faculty of color. She also discusses her approaches to teaching diversity courses and to teaching itself. As a Black scholar, she embraces a certain pedagogical style that matches her values and culture. Nixon shows us how she does an effective job of getting her students to have difficult dialogues.

The chapter by Azmaira H. Maker is timely and offers unique insights regarding a highly sensitive and political topic within the current milieu. Maker dares to share her experiences as a Muslim woman and therapist in the United States. She accomplishes the task of opening the space for dialogue around stereotypic notions of Muslim families. She challenges assumptions of differences between therapists and clients based on race, religion, nationality, and culture, and she concludes by sharing accounts of how she uses her "self" in the clinical context to dismantle long-held negative assumptions that often interfere with therapeutic progress.

In her chapter exploring urban and rural landscapes of ethnicity and gender, Laurie L. Charlés provides a thorough and insightful account of her experiences as a Latina supervisor and educator. In addition to sharing personal accounts, Charlés provides a case example and proceeds to engage in a dialogue that involves her perspectives and experiences and moves from upholding a culture of sameness, to developing a metacultural awareness, to what she refers to as "changing colors in a tiny village in Togo." She concludes the chapter by proposing questions related to her case example.

Carmen Aguirre, Judith Maria Bermúdez, J. Ruben Parra Cardona, Jorge Antonio Zamora, and Nenetzin Angelica Reyes provide an exemplary and thought-provoking account of their journeys, as individuals and as a group, as they deconstructed the processes involved in integrating language, context, and meaning making as bilingual and bicultural therapists. The chapter describes their challenges as they engaged in the process of actively co-constructing more authentic bicultural selves. The authors provide helpful suggestions and propose important questions that may be used by mental health providers and supervisors in clinical training settings.

Mudita Rastogi and Carole Woolford-Hunt provide a compelling and deeply personal account of their experiences as "academic sojourners" in the United States. Anyone who was raised in another country and later entered the United States for academic and professional pursuits is likely to find validation and affirmation in this chapter. The authors provide insightful discussions on "internationals" as a neglected category within the diversity discourse, identity struggles of persons with international and/or dual citizenship status, the lack of knowledge surrounding the experiences of foreigners in the United States, issues around role overload, experiences of isolation, and professional issues specific to persons with international status. The chapter concludes with a list of helpful hints for international faculty and institutional administrators.

In their chapter about South Asians in the United States, Amaira H. Maker, Mona Mittal, and Mudita Rastogi provide an in-depth account of the current status of this much neglected population within the mental health clinical and research literature. The authors document the immigration history and changing demographics of the subgroups that comprise South Asians. Next, they provide a discussion on acculturation and ethnic identity issues, followed by a thorough literature review on clinical issues for this population. A significant contribution of this chapter is its introduction of a theoretical model that includes multiple assessment levels for working systemically with South Asian families in the United States. Each level is accompanied by a set of guiding questions for mental health practitioners to consider.

Denise D. McAdory's personal and professional experience with domestic violence led her to propose a therapeutic model for working with Black female victims and perpetrators of domestic violence. Her model is unique in that it takes into account the history and social experiences of the Black community in the United States. McAdory intersperses her writing with accounts of her own experiences with oppression. One can see how her deep understanding of domestic violence and Black culture make her model extremely effective.

The chapter by Narumi Taniguchi examines the notion of self based on the Japanese word *jibun*. Taniguchi explains that in Japanese culture one's "self" is considered part of a group. She then proceeds to use Social Constructionist and Bowenian theories to illustrate the differences between how Japanese and middle-class White Americans might decipher terms like *differentiation* and *self*. Her therapy and supervision examples further bring to life the intriguing notion of *jibun*.

Martha Adams Sullivan has written a compelling Afrocentric analysis of Black families. It is her contention that systems ideas and the traditional beliefs of Black families are highly compatible. Sullivan also brings in her own values as a feminist to discuss the intersection of gender and ethnicity. She uses this framework to understand the difficulties of Black families and the resources they possess to cope with their problems.

Nithyakala Karuppaswamy and Rajeswari Natrajan have written about family therapy from the perspective of Hindu women from India. They incorporate the issues of spirituality, ethnicity, international student status, gender, and disability in their analyses. Karuppaswamy and Natrajan have provided summaries of clinical cases in which they used their Hindu world-view to understand and work with clients and thus were provided with an alternate and unique look at their own lives. Their chapter is rich and complex, as well as full of new insights.

Melanie Domenech-Rodríguez and Elizabeth Wieling take the position that the lack of conceptual and methodological frameworks that appropriately position families and communities of color within a historical, political, and socioeconomic context has led to gross disparities in mental health services. They discuss problems related to the lack of evidence-based models in preventive and clinical interventions with populations of color and provide recommendations based on their current work that may aid scholars and clinicians alike in achieving both efficacy and effectiveness.

The chapter by J. Ruben Parra Cardona, Richard S. Wampler, and Dean M. Busby provides a heartfelt narrative of each author's personal journey and development regarding cultural identity and awareness of issues related to diversity, privilege, and oppression. The authors propose a theoretical framework for reconceptualizing how we understand and apply concepts of acculturation and cultural identity within a clinical context. This chapter contributes new sensibilities to the array of experiences persons from diverse backgrounds encounter as they enter a new cultural context, and it provides specific theoretical guidelines to clinicians about how to think through and interact with these complexities.

We hope that this book will be helpful both as a text for a course in the area of diversity and as a collection of essays that are relevant to the daily lives of our readers. We see it being read by graduate students, educators, clinicians, supervisors, trainees, and administrators. Each of the chapters is structured to include (a) a personal narrative by the author or authors, (b) references to the existing literature, and (c) a section of reflections, questions, and exercises on the material in the chapter. The latter may be used individually by readers to further their understanding of the chapter, discussed in small groups of students, assigned by instructors, or used to expand the conversation in supervision.

We found the task of working on *Voices of Color* to be enriching, growth inducing, and at times painful. This project also challenged us to consider the ways in which we could pursue the goal of social justice in our multiple roles. It is our hope that you, the reader, will similarly find this book to be transformative, both professionally and personally. We welcome your comments and feedback. Please contact us at MuditaRastogi@hotmail.com and lwieling@che.umn.edu.

References

Rastogi, M., & Wieling, E. (2000, November). *AALANA speaks: The voices of MFTs of color*. Workshop presented at the annual conference of the American Association for Marriage and Family Therapy, Denver, CO.

Wieling, E., & Rastogi, M. (2001, October). Multiculturalism and MFT: A dialogue among stakeholders. In E. Wieling (Chair), *Cultural issues panel*. Workshop conducted at the annual conference of the American Association for Marriage and Family Therapy, Nashville, TN.

Wieling, E., & Rastogi, M. (2003). Voices of marriage and family therapists of color: An exploratory survey. *Journal of Feminist Family Therapy, 15*(1), 1–20.

SECTION I

Identity and Professional Development of Therapists of Color

2

Emerging Identity

An Asian Indian Female
Psychologist's Perspective

Monika Sharma

I spent most of my childhood wishing I were invisible. Being the only brown-skinned girl among the standard white-skinned faces, this was not possible for me. At times, I was painfully self-conscious trying to navigate my Asian Indian background in a mostly White America. At other times, I managed to feel like I blended in and was in blissful denial of my difference.

It was not until I entered graduate school in clinical psychology that I was challenged to critically examine my history, relationships, and beliefs in an effort to deepen my self-awareness. It was there that I learned to appreciate the important part my ethnicity has played throughout my life. Whether I chose to embrace it, ignore it, or push it away, it has always been a powerful force within me. Even now, I often struggle to comprehend who I am, where I belong, and the choices I make. Still, being Asian Indian American will remain a vital part of my identity.

Personal Background

When my parents came to the United States in 1971 for my father to practice medicine here, they knew only a handful of Asian Indian families.

13

The Immigration Act of 1965 allowed foreigners holding or pursuing professional degrees to immigrate to the United States (Agarwal, 1991). Prior to this act, very few Indians had succeeded in immigrating to the United States. During the first few years after the Immigration Act, a small number of Indians, like my parents, departed from their family networks in India so that they might carve a life in America that was rich with possibilities for themselves and their children. These were the Indian pioneers who moved away from traditional lifestyles and rooted themselves in a new country without any rules or role models to follow. My parents had no map of where to go or what to expect of their lives in America. Along with their fellow Indian immigrant families, my parents were in the position to chart the way for future immigrant families and generations.

Being Indian became something I observed in my parents, not something that I carried within me. My parents talked to each other in Hindi but spoke to my younger brother and me in English. I never bothered trying to learn the meaning of their Hindi words since I would not have understood the content of my parents' grown-up discussions anyway. My brother and I occupied ourselves with *Sesame Street* and Legos™ while my mother conducted her daily prayers. I was not taught the Hindu religion, nor was I included in its daily rituals. We took a trip to India when I was 3 years old. I do not have any memories of it, but photographs tell me I was there. Being Indian was foreign to me.

It was not until I was 7 years old and my family moved to a middle-class, White suburban neighborhood that I realized it was not only my parents who were different from others—it seemed that I was different, too. My peers treated me as a foreigner and frequently called me "brownie," "nigger," and "Gandhi's girlfriend." I was taunted daily. After school at the bus stop, other children often ripped my belongings from my hands and ran away with them. I would chase them, crying, while my books and papers were strewn all over the lawn. Gym and recess were agonizing periods for me. I was usually the last one picked for teams and was rarely thrown the ball. During recess, I would often sit against the wall alone while watching my classmates play together. The few times I had ventured to join them, I was immediately scorned and told "Go away!" Up to this point in my life, I had thought that I was like all the other children in America. Apparently, I had thought wrong.

I blamed my appearance for my exclusion from the mainstream. In turn, I blamed my parents for passing down these superficial differences to me. I had felt like an outsider to the Indian community and now I felt like an outsider to American society, too. Every morning when I looked in the mirror, I prayed to see a reflection of a fair-skinned girl. I believed my skin color was my chief barrier to being accepted as an American.

When I was in seventh grade, an African American family moved into the neighborhood. They had five children; the youngest, Michelle, was a girl in my grade. I heard all of the neighbors talking about this family moving in and about their fear that "soon Black people will take over the neighborhood." I was nervous. Until then, I had been considered a "nigger" by my neighborhood peers and dreaded being associated with this "true" Black family. I made a conscious effort to affiliate myself with my White neighbors and classmates by joining them in bad-mouthing Michelle and her family. My White peers allowed me into their circle of conversations about "us" versus "them." Within a year of moving into the neighborhood, Michelle and her family moved away. I remember feeling some guilt that we did not bother to give Michelle a chance—she would sit alone on the bus, eat her lunch alone, and disappear after school within the safety of her home and family. I also remember another feeling being stronger in me than my guilt—relief that I had been included in the "us" group.

High school offered me a new experience—one that involved less struggle and desperation to belong. I studied and played alongside several Asian Indian, African American, Latino, East Asian, European, and mainstream American White students at a private college preparatory school. I felt safe identifying myself as Asian Indian, and I was supported to explore my cultural heritage for the first time.

When I began college, I was anxious that the ethnic utopia of high school would no longer exist. Striving to belong, I sought out White friends and avoided members of the college's Indian Student Association. I did not want to be segregated in any way. I wanted to be part of the mainstream. I could not understand why Indians wanted to associate exclusively, it seemed, with other Indians, and I viewed them with disdain. I perceived them as a threat to my assimilation and openly attempted to disassociate myself from them. I believed these Indians to be "nerds," unattractive, and embarrassing compared to my American counterparts. I openly referred to them as *desis* (countrymen) and *FOBs* (fresh off the boats), terms that were considered derogatory at that time. The two Indian friends I had were the "cool" ones, the exceptions to what I believed was the general rule. I later learned that many FOBs had their own condescending label for Indians like me who grew up in America—*ABCDs* (American-born confused desis). Today, *desis* is no longer considered a disparaging term, and Indians raised both in India and in America use it to connote solidarity. Even ABCD is now used humorously to capture some of the real confusion experienced by second-generation Indians.

When I was in college, I remember having a conversation with one of my Indian friends about identity. A White friend had asked us if we identified ourselves as Indian or as American. Without hesitation, I replied "American."

My Indian friend was surprised and stated that she considered herself to be first Indian, then American. I defended my self-identification by saying that I was born in America, I speak English, and I live my days more as a part of American society than as a member of the Indian community. To me, India was where my parents came from; America was where I came from.

I graduated college having majored in psychology and also having fulfilled premed course requirements and earned a certificate in criminal justice. My first job out of college was as a childcare worker in a residential facility for children involved with the Illinois Department of Children and Family Services (DCFS). Most of the residents were African American and Latino boys. This was my first experience working with people in minority groups. I saw myself as attempting to lead them out of their harsh realities and toward a healthier life. However, I did not appreciate the complexity of their lives from their point of view, and I became frustrated that these boys did not operate the way I assumed people operated. It had not occurred to me that I would have more success connecting with these boys by respecting them on their platform instead of asking them to meet me on mine—my platform being guided by middle-class White society.

Next, I worked with foster families from mostly African American and Latino backgrounds. At that time, in the early 1990s, DCFS was quick to investigate cases in which children were discovered living with family members other than a biological parent, such as grandparents, aunts, and uncles. The biological parents of these children were considered guilty of "neglect," and DCFS brought these families into their system. As a case manager, I helped families meet the living and childcare standards set forth by DCFS, a governmental institution that was composed largely of White men and women. Working with these families helped me to appreciate some of their cultural differences that I could not appreciate in working solely with the boys on the residential unit. For the first time, I got to know these minority families in the context of their neighborhood, poverty, and pressures. I saw the strengths of grandparents and women in African American families and respected the strict male head of household in Latino families. I learned more about the meaning of "healthy" adaptation from these families than I did from DCFS's policies and standards.

Working with ethnic minority foster families provided me with an escape from dealing with my own confusion regarding my identity and purpose. I experienced a great sense of pride and accomplishment from being in a helping position and focusing on other people's difficulties. I felt safe there; I knew my place. One day, I found this sense of place unexpectedly challenged. During the weekly Teen Support Group for the adolescent foster children, the teenagers turned their discussion to the topic of "race wars" between Blacks and Whites. A heated debate ensued among the teenagers regarding where I belonged—was I Black or White? In graduate school, when I reflected back on this event, I realized that I had created my own version of a race war in my mind. I had divided the world into White and Other, and during my childhood I had made a choice about on which side I wished to belong.

Graduate School and Training: A Turning Point

I both dreaded and looked forward to the required class called "Assessment and Treatment Issues with Racial, Ethnic, and Culturally Diverse People of Color." It seemed that students either loved it or hated it. It was an experiential class that met over two weekends and involved heavy reflection and dialogue with peers. I registered to take the class during the fall semester of my second year in graduate school. Up to that point, very little attention had been paid in my classes to the issue of cultural diversity.

It was a difficult class for me to experience, largely because it brought to the surface some of my unconscious attitudes that I preferred to believe I did not own. It pushed me to examine and admit that as a case manager, I unwittingly participated in institutionalized racism. I had not realized that "the use of the White middle-class yardstick has resulted in inappropriate and even destructive service delivery to persons of certain backgrounds" (Pinderhughes, 1989, p. 14). I came to understand that I had imposed White middle-class standards on people from non-White, non-middle-class backgrounds. The guise of "child welfare" was being used to coerce stable and culturally traditional families to conform to the White notion that the nuclear family structure is healthiest. Understanding this caused me to place many of America's institutions in question.

In addition to examining how racism is perpetuated by our society's collective beliefs and values, students in the class were asked to inspect their personal attitudes toward minority groups. The most surprising and powerful concept introduced to me in this context was *internalized racism*, which refers to a minority person's internalization and acceptance of negative messages of the dominant group about their minority culture. Internalized racism "manifests as an embracing of 'whiteness' (use of hair straighteners and bleaching creams, stratification by skin tone within communities of color, and 'the white man's ice is colder' syndrome); self-devaluation (racial slurs as nicknames, rejection of ancestral culture, and fratricide); and resignation, helplessness, and hopelessness" (Jones, 2000, p. 1213).

The class discussed internalized racism in the African American population, but it dawned on me that this concept accurately captured my feelings, thoughts, and behaviors toward my own Indian traits. Many people in my

Indian community envied Indians with lighter skin and devalued Indians with darker skin. I had perceived Indians as a source of personal embarrassment, rejection, and shame. In contrast to how I viewed Indians, I believed that White people were sophisticated and attractive. My actions toward Indians and toward White people had been guided by these perceptions, which were shaped by my biased exposure to White versus Indian cultures and personal experiences of racism. I rejected other Indians as I had attempted to reject the Indian parts of myself.

I was able to recognize and own up to my personal biases and achieve greater self-awareness through the experiential format of this class. Pinderhughes (1989) advocated using the experiential group encounter for participants to acknowledge and identify their biases, grapple with them privately, reveal them to the group, and discover the origin of these feelings and perceptions. The group format helps participants to recognize how these biases influence each participant's behaviors toward culturally different others and to explore new ways of thinking and behaving. The experiential group setting increases clarity concerning cultural identity, respect for differences in people, and comfort in cross-cultural interactions. Participants can come to understand the importance of taking responsibility for their values and biases on both personal and societal levels. A critical component of this honest self-exploration in the class I took was the safe environment created by our instructor, an African American man. Through his respect, nonjudgmental attitude, and encouragement, students were able to share deeply buried thoughts that were often connected to feelings of shame, vulnerability, and disgust.

Once the door to this personal journey was opened, I felt compelled to continue. I took elective classes that included "Cross-Cultural Issues of Empowerment" and "Cultural Development: Child and Adolescent Issues." For me, the most powerful learning tools in these classes were the experiential components and reflective writing exercises. The class on child and adolescent issues in cultural development was especially evocative for me because I was able to revisit how my childhood and adolescent experiences with ethnicity shaped me, my goals, and my relationships.

One of my instructors was an Asian Indian woman in her mid-30s who later served as the chair for my clinical research project and proved to be a wonderful mentor. She taught in the family minor, the specialization that I chose to pursue. During my first year at school, I had not initiated any contact with her. My "Treatment Issues" instructor (a Black man) confronted me with this observation after I completed his class during my second year. Until then, I did not realize that my instructors made such observations. Apparently, people still viewed me as an ethnic minority and assumed I would have reached out to this instructor because of our similar background.

I naively believed that ethnicity was a trait I could wear or discard; I thought that I had successfully assimilated. After my instructor shared his observation, I acknowledged that I was very self-conscious around this Indian instructor *because* of our shared culture. I had imagined that she expected more from me than from other students and was afraid of disappointing her. My ethnicity and associated presumptions continued to influence my actions, through times of both acceptance and denial.

The family minor involved a high level of exploration of personal family history, generational patterns of values and behaviors, and reflection. The head of the family minor, a White male instructor in his 60s, became a second mentor to me. I took most of my upper level classes with these two mentors. They encouraged students to examine the messages they received from their family and society about race, gender, age, ethnicity, religion, immigration history, socioeconomic status, and sexual orientation. This was accomplished through genograms and in-class role-plays. I learned that as clinicians we could not assume we knew everything about any individual or family we were treating based on any single one of the above diversity factors. We also could not assume diversity issues did not exist for a White, heterosexual, middle-class person. It was important for us to help our clients explore the messages they received and to honor their perspectives and experiences.

As a graduate student in clinical psychology, I was required to complete a diagnostic practicum, a therapy practicum, and an internship. Through these various training experiences, my attitude toward people of color was tested in real situations rather than hypothetical ones. I thought that I could be objective, given my motivation to be sensitive to diversity issues. However, I realized that my automatic thoughts are so deeply ingrained in me that they often appear without my awareness and I must always work to keep them in check.

During my diagnostic practicum, I was asked to assess a White mother who was being investigated for possible child abuse. Her daughter was diagnosed with possible shaken baby syndrome. When the mother arrived for her appointment, she was dressed professionally in a business suit. The mother was highly educated, worked in a corporate office, and lived in a wealthy Chicago neighborhood. I assumed that she would know better than to violently shake her baby. I remember feeling internal discomfort and incongruence with the idea that this mother could have been guilty of child abuse. Prior to beginning any tests, I believed the parents' claim that the baby must have suffered a series of falls and assumed the parents to be innocent. A thorough history and test results suggested it was very likely that the mother could have shaken her baby. The baby had several serious medical issues from birth, demanded significant attention and care, and reportedly cried often. The mother's psychological profile suggested that she was a perfectionist, had a low tolerance for frustration, and was prone to verbal and physical outbursts. I later heard that the court found the parents guilty of abuse and that the baby was made a ward of the DCFS.

I was shocked that I had assumed the best of this mother based on her appearance and professional status. Most of my clients at this site were African American adults and children involved with DCFS. Since this referral was an upper class White woman, an atypical client, it was difficult for me to believe that she would have been abusive to her baby. I explored my prejudices with my on-site supervisor, and he praised me for identifying them. As a result, I learned a great deal about my human vulnerability to prejudice. Instead of being discouraged, I became more motivated to critically examine my perceptions and those of my clients.

For my clinical research project, I chose to examine ethnic identity among second-generation Asian Indians. This project was fueled by my desire to better understand how ethnic identity might be impacted by family dynamics, the cultural history of Indians' immigration to the United States, and increasing global awareness in American society (Ruiz, 1990; Sue & Sue, 1990; Uba, 1994; Vaidhyanathan, 2000). I also sought a context within which to better understand myself. Berry (1980, 1983, 1990) proposed a model of acculturation in which individuals in ethnic minorities may be *integrated* (involved in both their own minority group and the majority group), *assimilated* (involved in the majority group but relinquish involvement in their minority group), *separated* (involved with their minority group but not with the majority group), or *marginalized* (not involved with either group). Much of my childhood was spent in a marginalized state, in which I felt excluded from both my Indian culture and American society. I sought assimilation by attempting to disown my Indian qualities and adopt those of mainstream America. As a graduate student, with greater self-awareness and a desire to reconnect with my Indian roots, I began to move toward a state of integration. My findings showed that most of my Indian subjects, who are at least one generation younger than I am, felt comfortable embracing both India, their country of origin, and America, their country of residence. The younger generation in my study approached having an integrated identity (Berry, 1980, 1983, 1990).

In any clinical setting, I believe it is important to work with colleagues and supervisors who consider diversity and countertransference issues. As clinicians, we are responsible for examining our feelings, attitudes, and behaviors throughout our professional and personal evolution. By challenging myself and examining my beliefs, I continue to grow and surprise myself. I no longer strive to blend in and be invisible. Instead, I now stand up and want people to see me for the multifaceted Asian Indian American woman that I am.

Reflections, Questions, and Exercises

The following questions may be helpful to students, educators, and clinicians in fostering discussions. Please feel free to choose the questions that best suit your audience and goals.

1. What are some reasons related to your identity that led you to choose a career in mental health? As you learn more about yourself and your relationships, what issues become salient for you regarding diversity?

2. What messages did you receive about different ethnic groups, including your own? Were these messages different for men and women? From where did these messages come (e.g., your family, American media, your peer group, etc.)? How do these messages influence your behaviors and attitudes toward members of diverse minority groups and members from the majority group (i.e., mainstream White Americans)?

3. Think back to the settings that comprise your past—whether you were a student, an employee, or a member of an organization. How might institutionalized racism have been a part of your life in these settings? Did you believe you were unfairly advantaged or disadvantaged? What role did you play? How might other minority groups or the majority group have been affected by the institutionalized racism?

4. Was there a time or incident in your life during which you experienced internalized racism or negative perceptions about your ethnic group? What were some of the beliefs and perceptions? How did you respond to them? How do you wish you had responded?

5. Do you believe it is important to address diversity issues with clients? Would you feel comfortable bringing these issues up with your clients? How would you determine when to address these issues? How would you discuss these issues with them?

References

Agarwal, P. (1991). *Passage From India: Post 1965 Indian immigrants and their children—Conflicts, concerns, and solutions.* Palos Verdes, CA: Yuvati.

Berry, J. W. (1980). Acculturation as varieties of adaptation. In A. M. Padilla (Ed.), *Acculturation: Theory, model, and some new findings* (pp. 9–25). Boulder, CO: Westview.

Berry, J. W. (1983). Acculturation: A comparative analysis of alternative forms. In R. J. Samuda & S. L. Woods (Eds.), *Perspectives in immigrant and minority education* (pp. 65–78). Lanham, MD: University Press of America.

Berry, J. W. (1990). Psychology of acculturation. In J. J. Berman (Ed.), *Cross-cultural perspectives* (pp. 201–234). Lincoln: University of Nebraska Press.

Jones, C. P. (2000). Levels of racism: A theoretic framework and a gardener's tale. *American Journal of Public Health, 90*(8), 1212–1215.

Pinderhughes, E. (1989). *Understanding race, ethnicity, and power: The key to efficacy in clinical practice.* New York: The Free Press.

Ruiz, A. S. (1990). Ethnic identity: Crisis and resolution. *Journal of Multicultural Counseling and Development, 18*(1), 29–40.

Sue, D. W., & Sue, D. (1990). *Counseling the culturally different: Theory and practice* (2nd ed.). New York: John Wiley.

Uba, L. (1994). *Asian Americans: Personality patterns, identity, and mental health.* New York: Guilford.

Vaidhyanathan, S. (2000). Inside a "model minority": The complicated identity of South Asians. *Chronicle of Higher Education, 46*(42), B4–B6.

3

Our Stories

Convergence of the Language, Professional, and Personal Identities of Three Latino Therapists

Luis Antonio Rivas,
Edward A. Delgado-Romero,
and Kelly Ramón Ozambela

During the academic year 1999–2000, the three of us, Ed, Kelly, and Luis, were brought together at the University of Florida (UF) Counseling Center. We are three bilingual[1] Latino therapists, each of us used to being "the only one" in our training history, and working with each other inspired us to take a look at what it means to be a Latino bilingual therapist. In this chapter, we first provide a brief overview of the bilingual counseling literature, follow it with personal narratives about our professional

Authors' Note: The authors wish to thank Dr. Amy Heesacker, Dr. Mary Fukuyama, and Dr. Cassie Hessler-Smith for their valuable comments on an earlier version of this chapter. Correspondence concerning this chapter should be addressed to Edward Delgado-Romero, Ph.D., 205 N. Rose Avenue, W.W. Wright Education Building, Room 4060, Bloomington, IN 47405; Email: edelgado@indiana.edu; Phone: (812) 339–8334, Fax: (812) 856–8333.

and personal development, and conclude by highlighting what we consider to be important themes reflected in our experiences. Readers will note that we raise many more questions than we answer, and that was part of our goal. We raise questions because we believe that psychology has not adequately addressed the training and professional development needs of therapists who are Latino and bilingual.

Being Bilingual

If you speak two languages you are bilingual. If you speak three languages you are trilingual. If you speak one language you are an American.

—Anonymous

Despite a historical monolingual bias favoring English, the United States of the 21st century is far from monolingual. Census 2000 officially identified a minimum of 55 different languages spoken in the United States (U.S. Census Bureau, 2003a), and other estimates have placed this figure as high as 300. Other than English, Spanish is the most common language spoken in the United States, where there are over 28 million Spanish-speaking people (U.S. Census Bureau, 2003b). Several forces impact the growing use of the Spanish language: globalization in the marketplace (e.g., the North American Free Trade Act—NAFTA—with Mexico), steady immigration from Spanish-speaking countries, and the growth in numbers and influence of the U.S. Latino population (although not all Latinos speak Spanish). Therefore, the likelihood that therapists will come in contact with individuals proficient in languages other than English, especially Spanish, continues to increase.

Psychotherapy has long been known as "the talking cure." However, until recently it has been assumed that the language used in counseling would be English. In the 1990s, the American Psychological Association (APA) and the American Counseling Association (ACA) began to address the issue of therapy with non-English-speaking clients. Specifically, APA *Guidelines for Providers of Psychological Services to Ethnic, Linguistic, and Culturally Diverse Populations* (APA, 1993) stated, "Psychologists interact in the language requested by the client and, if this is not feasible, make an appropriate referral" (p. 47). More recently, the *Guidelines on Multicultural Education, Training, Research, Practice, and Organizational Change for Psychologists* (APA, 2002), approved as APA policy by the APA Council of Representatives, further underscored the importance of language by considering a client's "fluency in *standard* English (and other languages or dialects)" (italics added; p. 46). The ACA, through the Association of Multicultural Counseling and Development (AMCD), proposed and adopted the Multicultural Counseling Competencies (Sue, Arredondo, & McDavis, 1992), which state that culturally skilled counselors value bilingualism and do not view a client's being most fluent in a language other than English as an impediment to counseling. APA has also recently (at the 2002 national conference) adopted the Multicultural Counseling Competencies.

Research reflects that language can be a barrier for the underutilization of mental health services by populations that are linguistically diverse (Guttfreund, 1990; Leong, Wagner, & Tata, 1995; Preciado & Henry, 1997), and that Latinos have unique language needs (Smart & Smart, 1995). Language has also been studied as a client variable (Altarriba & Bauer, 1998; Altarriba & Santiago-Rivera, 1994; Aragno & Schlachet, 1996; Javier, 1995; Marcos, 1994; Rozensky & Gómez, 1983; Santiago-Rivera, 1995) and as a therapist variable (Fuertes, 1999; Fuertes & Gelso, 2000; Lijtmaer, 1999; Malgady & Constantino, 1998; Ramos-Sánchez, Atkinson, & Fraga, 1999), but it has traditionally been neglected as a therapy variable in the professional literature (Ramos-Sánchez et al., 1999). Seay Clauss (1998) argued that research into the effects of bilingual interactions on the counseling process (and resultant training and supervision needs) is lacking. Finally, Atkinson and Lowe (1995) stated that "the failure of past research to take into account counselor language . . . is a serious limitation of multicultural research to date, and may reflect psychology's penchant for attributing therapeutic success to client characteristics while ignoring therapist characteristics" (p. 406).

The purpose of this chapter is to express through the use of personal narratives (Howard, 1996) our challenges and the issues we have confronted as three bilingual therapists. We chose to use this methodology for two reasons. First, the use of narratives is culturally consistent with the Hispanic value of *personalismo*—the preference for personal attention (Sue & Sue, 2003). Second, personal narratives provide in-depth, first-person accounts of individuals' experiences of being and becoming a bilingual counselor. While these narratives do not necessarily provide data that are generalizable, we are sharing our experiences in the hope that they will be useful, as have some of the narratives in the counseling literature recently (e.g., Robinson & Ginter, 1999; Seay Clauss, 1998), in helping to shape and inform research and practice.

We are therapists who met each other at a clinical training site where Kelly and Luis were predoctoral interns and Ed was a staff psychologist. The intense experience of working together with other bilingual Latino professionals (a first for all of us) provided the "critical mass" necessary for us to fully immerse ourselves in the issues of training and practice concerns in bilingual counseling. At the end of our time together at the clinical training site, we decided to develop personal narratives in an attempt to capitalize on this unique clinical opportunity and contribute to the emerging literature on bilingual counseling and Latino professional development. Each author reflected in writing, in an open and unrestricted manner, on the convergence of language and identity in both his professional and personal development. We then provided reactions to and feedback on each other's writings and summarized the common and unique themes we discovered.

Kelly Ramón Ozambela

I am the son of Cuban refugee parents. Most of my family came to the United States in 1962, fleeing political persecution. No one in my family spoke English when they arrived here, but they were all soon immersed in it as an essential part of their adjustment to this country. I was born in 1968 in Washington, D.C., and I am uncertain which language I learned first, Spanish or English. Spanish was the language we spoke at home, which was wherever we lived at the time. When I was a child my family moved back and forth between the United States and Spain, where I began to pick up a third language—*Gallego* (a Spanish-Portuguese dialect). After my family returned from Spain for the last time, we continued to move throughout the United States almost every year. These travels led me to acquire a varied and rich set of cultural experiences. They also resulted in my receiving a fragmented educational experience, as I attended at least 14 different schools before graduating from high school.

Not feeling like I fit in was always a theme in my life as a result of both my travels and being a bilingual first-generation Cuban American. I often felt like I was living in two worlds. When I was growing up I sometimes felt ashamed and embarrassed when my parents would speak Spanish to me in public. In one of the many high schools I attended, I was nicknamed "the Cuban," and I remember going home to tell this to my father, who reminded me (in his heavily accented English) that I was and always would be an American. It was very confusing, and I often struggled to clarify my identity.

This situation continued through my graduate training in counseling psychology, where I was the only Latino and bilingual student. No opportunities ever emerged within my training for me to engage in bilingual therapy, despite the fact that I was training in a very diverse urban environment. My ever-present question to myself was always "Will I be able to do therapy in Spanish some day, even though all my training has been in English?" Due to the prejudice I had experienced as a speaker of Spanish, as well as to my limited opportunities to speak Spanish, this question raised many fears and insecurities in me that kept me from being more intentional about seeking opportunities to be a bilingual therapist.

I finally found the courage to confront this question the year I applied for my internship. I was matched with the Counseling Center at the University of Florida, an institution with a large Pan-Latino bilingual student population. In addition, I found out that I would have the opportunity to work with a bilingual psychologist and a bilingual intern, and that gave me the strength to face my uncertainties. It turns out that they both played an essential role in my struggle to integrate my Cuban American and bilingual identities into my different tasks as a psychologist.

During my internship year, I became very intentional about presenting myself as a Latino bilingual psychologist. For example, I requested that my middle name, Ramón, be included on my business cards and the nameplate for my door. This was important to me because my first name, Kelly, does not necessarily communicate that I am Latino. In fact, I have found that my first name usually leads people who have never met me to assume that I am an Anglo woman.

Several questions have come up for me through my own developmental journey in embracing the role of a bilingual psychologist. For example, how does one decide to do bilingual therapy? What does it mean to become a bilingual psychologist? Does one do therapy the same way as a bilingual psychologist? What are the ethical considerations in bilingual psychotherapy? I hope that through sharing my experiences in exploring the answers to these questions I can contribute to others on this same path.

When I first began working with bilingual clients, I noticed a great variance in how they chose to communicate. While some switched between Spanish and English, some spoke exclusively in Spanish. Others chose to flow freely between the two languages in a creative language construction commonly referred to as *Spanglish*.

I have found that the use of language switching by clients creates a subtle process that usually informs some aspect of the therapeutic relationship. For example, I worked with a client who would begin each session by telling me the language he wanted to use for that day. A trend developed over time: He would use Spanish in sessions when he had powerful emotions to express and English in sessions when he was more cognitively focused. In sessions in which he was speaking Spanish and I prematurely attempted to deepen the affective process, he would guard himself by responding to me in English. Since working with this client, I have learned to attend to clients' language switching in session. Sometimes I will attempt to facilitate greater access to client emotions by reflecting affect in Spanish to bilingual clients speaking to me in English.

Becoming a bilingual psychologist is an ongoing process for me. I have become aware that my bilingual ability has helped me to further explore and experience aspects of my cultural and ethnic identity with both Latinos and non-Latinos. I have seen evidence of this in my clients and colleagues' various reactions to and assumptions about me. For example, because of my unaccented pronunciation and native fluency in both English and Spanish, I have occasionally not received referrals of clients who requested a bilingual therapist from staff. I became aware of this one day when comparing caseloads with a colleague. This made me question myself in many ways: Am I not Latino enough? As a Cuban American, am I culturally compatible with other Latinos? Do staff and clients make assumptions about my ethnicity because I speak English without a Spanish accent?

The process of learning to conduct bilingual therapy has opened new opportunities for me to connect with bilingual clients in a manner that feels different from my work with monolingual clients. I have experienced that some clients approach therapy with a sense of relief knowing that they can connect with another person who can speak their language and move between their worlds. This creates a dynamic that enables these clients to make choices about how to communicate, choices that are not always available to them as a minority living in a culture that values assimilation.

A less positive aspect of being a bilingual psychologist is the potential for being exploited that is inherent in this role. The colleague I mentioned above who was seeing mostly bilingual clients may have ended up with too many bilingual clients. As a trainee, he consequently may have missed opportunities to work with other types of clients or presenting issues. At the professional level, there is often no additional compensation or consideration for the extra demands made of bilingual psychologists, and it is simply assumed that we will just do whatever needs to be done because we can. There have been instances where I have been asked to cover emergencies outside of my shift because they required a Spanish-speaking psychologist. Examples of other tasks I have been asked to perform in similar settings include translating documents, writing correspondence, offering consultation, interpreting, and assessment. Considering that this is the reality for bilingual professionals, where is the line drawn between doing my job and being exploited? Is it acceptable to seek additional compensation when part of my professional reality is that I am the only one who can take on additional duties due to my second-language skills? Furthermore, what if as a student or trainee I am not in a position of power to assert these needs?

Supervision has been essential in my education and growth as a bilingual therapist. The opportunity to work with a bilingual Latino supervisor has allowed me to articulate my fears, questions, and accomplishments. It has also provided me with room to explore and embrace my cultural and professional identity as a bilingual psychologist. Supervision has expanded my awareness of process issues related to language switching by clients and therapists. Ed's modeling and self-disclosure of his own journey in reaching a comfort level with Spanish-language therapy and supervision has given me permission to make my own determinations.

In closing, my overall sense is that individuals feel better understood and validated when they are free to choose their own construction of their thoughts and emotions. As a bilingual psychologist I am in a wonderful position to positively impact a population whose needs are not fully being met. My efforts to establish myself as a bilingual psychologist have provided me with a deeper sense of connection to my own ethnic and cultural identity. Consequently, I feel that using my bilingual ability makes me a better therapist and allows me to more effectively contribute to my community.

Luis Antonio Rivas

I was born in Puerto Rico, where Spanish is the native, dominant language. In school I was taught both Spanish and English (the other official language of Puerto Rico). When I went to college in the United States, English became the primary language of my education. This was also the language of my graduate training as a psychotherapist. My foray into and continued immersion in the field of counseling psychology has brought me full circle with my work in Spanish and bilingual counseling.

I first realized that working with clients in another language was different when I found myself struggling to identify and label emotions for a Spanish-speaking client. I noticed that I was processing the content of the session in English (which provided grounding for me, as I was doing something I was trained for and knew how to do) and then translating it into Spanish.

After several experiences with bilingual clients, I began to feel comfortable working in Spanish. Throughout this time, I was training myself to think on my feet as a counselor in Spanish. I realized that what initially interfered with my ability to feel comfortable with clients were the small differences in the words we used and the intricacies of the language, as in different countries there may be different meanings for the same Spanish word or different words or colloquialisms for the same meaning. A good portion of the time these end up relating to sexual behaviors and organs or some form of cursing. For example, the word for an insect in Spain may be slang for a sexual organ in Puerto Rico. The word in Colombia for grabbing something may be the term in Mexico for having sex. In addition, in different countries there are different accents and pronunciation styles. My experiences with friends from other Latino countries made me aware of these language dynamics and prompted me to look for them in therapy, which made it harder for me to connect with clients. Not only did I have to think of what to say, but I also had to think about the words that I would use, their phrasing and pronunciation, and how each client would interpret them. I had to be careful not to unintentionally insult my clients.

There have been times when searching for the right words to use in Spanish allowed me to connect with clients more easily. I could use this stumbling to foster a collaborative relationship between myself and the client and create our own working language. Yet at other times this stumbling would cause clients to lose faith and trust in my ability to help them. This was particularly evident in situations when clients would repeatedly question my command of Spanish or would feel like they had to correct my use of the language. Power dynamics and within-group prejudice (e.g., a bilingual client who may not like Puerto Ricans) quickly become issues that need to be addressed in therapy.

Deciding on the language that was to be spoken in therapy also made for interesting dynamics. For some clients it was evident that therapy was going to be conducted in Spanish, as this was the only language they knew. Usually I was assigned as their counselor for that reason. For other clients who were bilingual the choice of language was not as obvious. How then do I approach this aspect of our work? Is it a negotiation, or do I follow the lead of the client? Do I initiate this process? Some of the clients I have worked with would talk to me in Spanish only during our walk to and from the office, others would only use Spanish to greet me and say goodbye, and yet others would only use Spanish during a crisis. I worked with a client who switched to talking in English as we processed the termination of our working relationship.

Training issues have always been at the forefront of my thinking about the practice of bilingual counseling, and I feel very fortunate to have finally had the opportunity to immerse myself in these concerns as part of my internship experience. As I increasingly have more confidence in my counseling skills and more experiences with bilingual clients, I am becoming interested in what constitutes effective bilingual counseling from a training and research standpoint. Psychologists are licensed according to their therapy skills and knowledge, but there are no such criteria established for the practice of bilingual counseling. What criteria define competence and language proficiency? How much language does a counselor need to know? How much training should be required? What are the therapeutic implications of the language that the counselor chooses to use? What is the interface between language and culture?

Closely tied to these concerns are the pragmatic aspects of this practice. For example, if a client demonstrates difficulty expressing herself or himself in English, do I attempt to accommodate these needs? Do I refer? Are there therapists in the community who can better serve this client? Does the agency have forms and intake paperwork translated into the language that is prominent in the community where the agency is located (or is the agency imposing English comprehension as a cultural value)? Is there a procedure established to handle these types of questions? Is it ethical to take a stab at doing this work when I have genuine doubts about my ability to do it? Is it acceptable for me to refer to a dictionary during a session?

The reader will have probably gathered by now that there is more to bilingual counseling than meets the eye (or ear!). I feel that my struggles in learning to conduct bilingual counseling have often mirrored my struggles to conduct monolingual counseling. Learning how to be a psychotherapist has been one of the most humbling experiences in my life, both professionally and personally. Similarly, learning about bilingual counseling has challenged my professional development as a therapist as well as my own personal development and growth as a human being.

Culture and ethnic identity have been very salient for me in this context. It is my belief that a bilingual client lives (or has lived for some amount of time) between two worlds and, ultimately, between two cultures. The same can be said of a bilingual therapist. This has certainly been true in my own personal experience. Being raised in Puerto Rico, one of the last remaining political colonies in the world, I bring with me a very distinct cultural identity and language. However, it is an identity that has been heavily influenced by a colonizing culture (the United States). Through my experiences in the United States I have gradually come to associate language with socioeconomic class, power, and representation status. For me, Spanish represents the cultural experience of an oppressed individual of minority status, whereas English represents the experience of individuals who are in the majority or dominant culture. Therefore, I feel a sense of shared cultural experience when I am able to interact with clients in my native language.

What does it mean for me as a therapist that I have the ability to identify with clients at a deeper, more personal level? How does this shape our relationship when what I construe as deep may not be perceived as such by my client? How does my bilingual ability impact or shape the way I relate to clients? Counseling my bilingual clients has at times challenged my cultural identity more than has counseling any of my other clients. Working with these bilingual clients has also forced me to confront my own comfort level with my status as part of the minority in the United States and part of the majority in Puerto Rico. The question of what it means to be a Latino professional was not one I often asked of myself before my experience with bilingual counseling.

Having these opportunities to connect with clients through our use of language and cultural background has also forced me to revisit the way in which I interact with those clients with whom I do not share these similarities (i.e., monolingual clients) While I originally thought that I had the ability to develop good working relationships with these clients, I now realize that I can take these relationships to an even deeper level. Working with bilingual clients has made me more conscious of my ability to establish therapeutic relationships, forcing me to find other ways to connect with my monolingual clients.

I conclude my narrative by echoing Kelly's concerns regarding the fine line between a therapist's being ethically bound to act in the client's best interest and being exploited. I previously worked in an agency where I was expected to take on most of the duties that related to Spanish-speaking clients because nobody else was available. These duties included everything from translating client rights and responsibilities, billing information, and DUI self-assessments to working with children and adolescents (without the proper training to do so). I believe this experience is frighteningly common among bilingual therapists. My understanding of what a "no-win" situation this is crystallized as my clients shared some of the ethically inappropriate and destructive interactions of their previous counseling experiences (e.g., first-generation children acting as interpreters during their parents' counseling, treatment recommendations based on invalid translations of culturally bound testing instruments, and inappropriate medication prescription and/or monitoring related to communication difficulties). The parallel process of client and therapist regarding feelings of disempowerment is striking. Therefore, I feel that developing training programs and increasing the visibility and prominence of this field will ultimately benefit the clients as well as the counselors who work with them—whether they are bilingual or monolingual.

Edward Delgado-Romero

In 1965 my parents immigrated to the United States from Colombia, and I was born one year later. The first language I learned to speak was Spanish. English was a language that I learned as a way to comprehend the world outside of my family's apartment. However, once I grew old enough to watch television and go to kindergarten, English became my dominant language.

Being able to speak and understand both Spanish and English was not a desirable ability as I grew up in the suburbs of Atlanta, Georgia. Being bilingual carried with it considerable stigma. My non-Latino peers would often ridicule my parent's strong accents and delight in mispronouncing my name. At the same time my Latino peers would often criticize and correct the way I spoke

Spanish. I felt like I was in a "no-win" situation. For many years, although I would comprehend Spanish without a problem, I spoke exclusively in English.

Like many bilingual individuals who learn a language orally, I learned to speak and comprehend Spanish, but I didn't learn its grammatical rules or how to write Spanish. It was not until college, when I took several years of Spanish, that I learned the basic rules of the language. An unforeseen benefit of my working knowledge of the language was that my college classmates turned to me for help with Spanish—from that point on, my confidence in my Spanish began to grow.

When I began graduate training in counseling psychology, my bilingualism was an interesting footnote about me but not something that I could use. I had no training in using Spanish in therapy and few opportunities to use it with clients. None of my professors or supervisors were Latinos. It was not until my third year of clinical training that I had my first bilingual counseling experience. The clients (a couple) were relieved to finally find someone who could understand them. My monolingual supervisor helped me the best he could with these clients, but he relied on my translation to understand what was going on. I remember wishing that I had a bilingual supervisor to help me not only with the language but also with the cultural aspects of this case. I later had the opportunity to supervise a master's level Latina therapist who worked with clients entirely in Spanish. I felt that I was of help to both the therapist and her clients, but I also felt the lack of a "safety net" that a bilingual supervisor could have provided me.

It wasn't until my internship year that I had my first bilingual supervisor, a Chicano social worker who helped me identify and accept the cultural contributions that being Latino brought to my clinical work. He was able to evaluate and supervise my work in Spanish, as well as conduct supervision in Spanish when needed. He was a model of the integration of professional and personal identity that I longed to have. One of the most powerful things he said to me was, "If you want to know me, you have to get to know my family." This statement helped me validate and normalize my strong connections and identification with my family, which some had labeled dependent. This normalization of my cultural values has been for me a strong source of connection with my Latino/a colleagues and clients.

Although my internship experience was powerful, there was still something missing from it. During graduate school and my internship, I primarily interacted with Mexican American peers and clients (although we all called ourselves Latinos). Chicano pride and activism was something I valued but felt excluded from. I personalized this feeling as my failure to be truly Latino. It wasn't until I became an advisor to a Colombian student group that I realized I needed to claim my ethnicity as a Colombian before I could truly call myself

Latino. In my interactions with the Colombian Student Association I began to learn about my own cultural heritage and was able to practice speaking Spanish in a familiar atmosphere. I realized that many of the differences I experience with other Latinos were merely differences between Colombian culture and other Latino cultures. Having established this cultural base, I found myself more readily able to connect with peers and colleagues from all over the Latino world—and especially with other first-generation Latino students and professionals. I was relieved to find that other Latino professionals shared many of my struggles with language and culture.

Clinically, I began to see an increasing number of Latino students in therapy and intake appointments. As I became a more skilled clinician in general, I was surprised to find the many ways in which I could use my bicultural and bilingual abilities in a subtle fashion. Initially I felt that I had to announce and inform clients about my ethnicity, but this seemed rather artificial and tended to put distance between my clients and myself. Latino clients in particular seemed perplexed by my need to say the obvious. As my clinical skills and identity as a Colombian Latino increased, I found myself more comfortable in just being myself.

I had conceptualized bilingual therapy as an all-or-nothing event. That is, one either spoke English or Spanish during the session. I had read enough of the literature to know that clients normally tend to use their first language under stress. However, I was surprised to find out that clients did not behave in such a rigid manner. I found that many of the clients I was seeing tended to flow between the two languages, often creating new words with remarkable skill. Rather than expecting me to be able to conduct the entire session in Spanish or English, many of my clients expected me to be able to follow them as they navigated both languages and cultures, as well as to understand that they were creating a dynamic new language and culture of their own.

Consequently, my clients looked for subtle signs that I understood them. I was surprised to find that often the correct pronunciation of a name or one Spanish phrase could open a connection with a client. For example, as I greeted a young woman I saw on intake at the front desk, I correctly pronounced her first name. When we got back to my office, I pronounced her last name and asked her "¿Así se dice?" ("Is that how you say it?"). Although that was the only Spanish spoken during our session, she quickly began to talk about cultural issues surrounding gender role expectations. My being able to say her name correctly and speaking Spanish signaled to her that I knew Spanish and, more important, that I had the potential to understand Latino culture (and her experience in it).

On internship matching day in 1999, I learned that two of the new interns were Latinos, and that they were both bilingual. Although I was excited about the potential of having Latino colleagues at the center, many of my old fears and feelings of inadequacy returned. I feared that I might not be able to connect with them and, even worse, that they would be searching out a Latino and bilingual role model and I would not be up to the task. I also worried that my colleagues might expect me to have a special connection with the Latino interns, and I bristled at that notion. So for me this was a time of both trepidation and excitement.

When Kelly and Luis arrived on internship, I found them to be very open to learning and interested in working with me. Rather than questioning my competence, they wanted to immerse themselves in their training and concentrate on working with bilingual Latino clients. I believe that I helped matters by taking the risk of sharing my ambivalence about my professional and personal role as a Latino and relying on my Latino professional network for support and encouragement. In addition, Kelly, Luis, and I share a dedication to Latino activism, and we actively participated in the Latino student community, which I believe provided a larger context to our clinical work. Kelly and Luis became my supervisees, and I found that their confidence grew as the internship progressed and as we worked through challenges with clients. As their supervisor, I found myself faced with new challenges as I tried to answer questions such as: What is the center's policy on having a letter to a client written in Spanish in the client file? What is the Spanish translation of the word *transference*? Is there a Spanish word for being gay that is not an obscenity? Do I have consent to speak to my client's *abuelita* on the phone? We were all covering new territory.

Initially I thought that having bilingual Latino therapists in a counseling center was a luxury, but I felt differently when there were no bilingual Latinos in the next internship class. Having lived through a year where bilingualism was an integral part of therapy with many clients, I now feel it is a necessity in places that serve bilingual clients. The university where we worked had 4,000 Latino/a students, and a good number of them were bilingual. It wasn't a luxury to provide service to bilingual Latinos; it was a need that had previously gone unrecognized.

Reflections, Questions, and Exercises

We have attempted to convey through our personal experiences that bilingual counseling is more than just counseling in different languages, as the language variable adds a layer of complexity to the practice and process of psychotherapy (Perez-Foster, 1998). Important themes that emerged through these narratives could be classified under three domains: (1) the impact that language has on therapy and the therapeutic relationship; (2) the professional challenges that bilingual counseling poses to the bilingual therapist; and (3) the personal challenges that bilingual counseling poses to the bilingual therapist.

The first domain includes issues such as the meaning behind clients' choice of language (e.g., which language they use, at which points in the session, and for how long), the implications of when a therapist chooses to address (or not to address) language use, the power dynamics involved with language, the effect that these factors have on the therapeutic relationship, and the extent to which language and related dynamics interfere with or deepen the therapy process. The second domain includes issues such as the inadequate training available for bilingual therapists, the lack of accreditation criteria, the lack of resources available to bilingual therapists (e.g., appropriately validated assess-ment tools and therapeutic instruments), agency policies regarding record keeping and other pragmatics of bilingual counseling, and the concerns regard-ing the exploitation of bilingual therapists. The third domain includes issues such as therapists' comfort level with their own culture, their comfort with their language proficiency (including reading, writing, speaking, comprehend-ing, and communicating), and their ethnic identity and acculturation status.

Important limitations in the personal narratives shared here must be noted. Our views are those of first-generation American males in our late 20s and early 30s whose primary clinical experience comes from working at univer-sity counseling centers. Furthermore, all three of us speak very fluent English (without much of an accent), and our experiences are therefore probably dif-ferent from the experiences of counselors who speak English with a heavy accent (Fuertes & Gelso, 2000). Most important, our experiences are all derived from an English-Spanish bilingual context. Therapists whose frame of reference for bilingual counseling is based on other languages may not neces-sarily identify with all the points raised in our narratives. Their experiences also deserve attention, as do the experiences of Latina bilingual therapists, but we do not feel qualified to do more than acknowledge their importance.

From Kelly's struggle to find a place where he fits, to Luis's struggle to find meaning for himself while being caught between two worlds, to Ed's struggle to learn what his culture is and what it means for him, the stories shared here have tried to respond to Atkinson and Lowe's (1995) and Seay Clauss's (1998) call for an increased focus on the therapist characteristics that invariably come into play in the therapeutic relationship. We hope that our stories have also provided some insight into the experiences of bilingual clients. What emerges from these narratives are the following practice and training implications that, in a country where so many languages are spoken, are important for both bilingual and monolingual counselors to give their serious consideration.

Practice

Consistent with the first domain identified in the three narratives, counselors and mental health practitioners can utilize insight gained through these stories as a starting place to work more holistically with bilingual clients. Research in the field of linguistics and neurology has consistently shown that individuals who speak more than one language encode and process information differently from those who speak one language, and that the brain structure of bilinguals is different from that of monolinguals (Heny, 1994; Kecskes & Papp, 2000; Lambert, 1972; Ojemann & Whitaker, 1978; Paradis, 1998). Santiago-Rivera and Altarriba (2002) addressed the differences in the feelings individuals associated with emotion words (e.g., *sad, anxious*) in their native language versus their second language. For example, the word *sad* may elicit more intense feelings in bilingual individuals when it is presented in their mother tongue as opposed to their acquired language. Marcos (1994) suggested that this phenomenon could help account for misdiagnoses of Spanish-dominant clients by English-speaking therapists. Therefore, whether a counselor is bilingual or monolingual, language concerns need to be explicitly addressed with clients who are bilingual, as such clients may not necessarily be communicating in precisely the same language used by their therapists. Moreover, ties between language and cultural concerns also need to be explored.

Training

Consistent with the second domain identified in the three narratives, counselors who are in a position of authority or power within their departments or agencies can utilize the insights in this chapter to be more mindful and more effectively address the needs of their bilingual trainees, as well as students who work with bilingual clients (Malgady & Constantino, 1998; Santiago-Rivera & Altarriba, 2002). Programmatic changes as well as changes in the delivery of individual supervision could be implemented, and the following questions could be used to assess what changes need to be made.

1. Are the training needs of bilingual trainees being met?

2. Do the training model and supervision validate and promote the professional development of bilingual trainees?

3. Are within-group differences valued by Hispanic and Latino bilingual trainees? Are these trainees being empowered to actively explore and embrace the ethnic and linguistic aspects of their developing professional identity?

4. Do supervisors know how to guide trainees to attend to language switching in session? Are there bilingual role models and mentors available and accessible?

5. Are the mental health needs (e.g., assessment, individual and group therapy) of bilingual clients being met by linguistically competent professionals?

Research

Consistent with the third domain identified in the three narratives, counselors can follow up on the many different points raised in our stories by developing research paradigms that address bilingual counseling concerns. In need of increased and continued attention are therapist characteristics, including the cultural and professional development of the therapist. The insight and self-reflection we have presented here can perhaps best be understood by using what Stone (1996) calls a "cultural affiliation perspective." He refers to the cultural affiliation conceptualization as encompassing constructs such as racial or ethnic identity theory, acculturation, and worldviews. Utilizing these perspectives may offer researchers a more comprehensive understanding of the complex therapist characteristics salient in the practice of bilingual counseling. Other examples of future work include the development of a standardized level of bilingual proficiency, scientific development of therapy protocols and training guidelines for bilingual counseling, analyses of therapist counseling styles across languages, gathering of therapeutic process and outcome data on the impact of language (such as when both therapist and client are monolingual and/or bilingual), and exploration of the effect of bilingualism in the therapeutic and supervisory relationship.

We would now like to call on other scientist-practitioners to follow our offering on this important topic. Bilingual counseling concerns should not be the exclusive interest of bilingual individuals, for the continuing diversification of the United States impacts monolingual and bilingual counselors alike. We must ensure that bilingual counselors, as well as bilingual clients, are given visibility and attention in the professional literature.

Epilogue

We wrote our narratives at the end of the internship year and have all moved on since then. Kelly spent a postinternship year at the UF Counseling Center, then relocated to Philadelphia, where he currently works at a community agency while completing his dissertation. Luis finished his dissertation and is now a staff psychologist at Seton Hall University in New Jersey, where he has continued to evolve bilingual counseling as one of his specialties. Ed worked at the UF Counseling Center for 2 more years before moving to Indiana University to accept a faculty position in counseling psychology. He is presently conducting research on Latino issues and is the treasurer of the National Latino/a Psychological Association. In each of these positions we continue to be advocates for bilingual therapists and the needs of bilingual clients.

Note

1. When we refer to people who are "bilingual," we mean those who speak Spanish and English, unless noted otherwise.

References

Altarriba, J., & Bauer, L. M. (1998). Counseling the Hispanic client: Cuban Americans, Mexican Americans, and Puerto Ricans. *Journal of Counseling and Development, 76,* 389–396.

Altarriba, J., & Santiago-Rivera, A. L. (1994). Current perspectives on using linguistic and cultural factors in counseling the Hispanic client. *Professional Psychology, Research & Practice, 25,* 388–397.

American Psychological Association. (1990). Ethical principles of psychologists. *American Psychologist, 45,* 390–395.

American Psychological Association. (1993). Guidelines for providers of psychological services to ethnic, linguistic, and culturally diverse populations. *American Psychologist, 48,* 45–48.

American Psychological Association. (2002). Guidelines on multicultural education, training, research, practice, and organizational change for psychologists. Washington, DC: Author.

Aragno, A., & Schlachet, P. (1996). Accessibility of early experience through the language of origin: A theoretical integration. *Psychoanalytic Psychology, 13,* 23–34.

Atkinson, D. R., & Lowe, S. M. (1995). The role of ethnicity, cultural knowledge, and conventional techniques in counseling and psychotherapy. In J. G. Ponterotto, J. M. Casas, L. A. Suzuki, & C. M. Alexander (Eds.), *Handbook of multicultural counseling* (pp. 387–414). Thousand Oaks, CA: Sage.

Fuertes, J. N. (1999). Asian Americans' and African Americans' initial perceptions of Hispanic counselors. *Journal of Multicultural Counseling and Development, 27,* 122–135.

Fuertes, J. N., & Gelso, C. G. (2000). Hispanic counselor's race and accent and Euro-Americans' universal-diverse orientations: A study of initial perceptions. *Cultural Diversity and Ethnic Minority Psychology, 6,* 211–219.

Guttfreund, D. G. (1990). Effects of language usage on the emotional experience of Spanish-English and English-Spanish bilinguals. *Journal of Consulting and Clinical Psychology, 58,* 604–607.

Heny, J. (1994). Brain and language. In V. P. Clark, P. A. Eschholz, & A. F. Rosa (Eds.), *Language: Introductory readings* (5th ed., pp. 201–225). New York: St. Martin's.

Howard, G. S. (1996). *Understanding human nature: An owner's manual.* Notre Dame, IN: Academic Publications.

Javier, R. A. (1995). Vicissitudes of autobiographical memories in a bilingual analysis. *Psychoanalytic Psychology, 12,* 429–438.

Kecskes, I., & Papp, T. (2000). *Foreign language and mother tongue.* Mahwah, NJ: Lawrence Erlbaum.

Lambert, W. (1972). *Language, psychology, and culture.* Stanford, CA: Stanford University Press.

Leong, F. T., Wagner, N. S., & Tata, S. P. (1995). Racial and ethnic variations in help-seeking attitudes. In J. G. Ponterotto, J. M. Casas, L. A. Suzuki, & C. M. Alexander (Eds.), *Handbook of multicultural counseling* (pp. 415–438). Thousand Oaks, CA: Sage.

Lijtmaer, R. M. (1999). Language shift and bilinguals: Transference and counter-transference implications. *Journal of the American Academy of Psychoanalysis, 27,* 611–623.

Malgady, R. G., & Constantino, G. (1998). Symptom severity in bilingual Hispanics as a function of clinician ethnicity and language of interview. *Psychological Assessment, 10,* 120–127.

Marcos, L. R. (1994). The psychiatric examination of Hispanics: Across the language barrier. In R. Malagdy & O. Rodriguez (Eds.), *Theoretical and conceptual issues in Hispanic mental health* (pp. 143–153). Malbar, FL: Krieger.

Ojemann, G. A., & Whitaker, H. A. (1978). The bilingual brain. *Archives in Neurology, 35,* 409–412.

Paradis, M. (1998). Aphasia in bilinguals: How atypical is it? In P. Coppens, Y. Lebrun, & A. Basso (Eds.), *Aphasia in atypical populations* (pp. 35–66). Mahwah, NJ: Lawrence Erlbaum.

Perez-Foster, R. (1998). *The power of language in the clinical process: Assessing and treating the bilingual person.* North Bergen, NJ: Jason Aronson.

Preciado, J., & Henry, M. (1997). Linguistic barriers in health education and services. In J. G. García & M. C. Zea (Eds.), *Psychological interventions and research with Latino populations* (pp. 235–254). Boston, MA: Allyn & Bacon.

Ramos-Sánchez, L., Atkinson, D. R., & Fraga, E. D. (1999). Mexican Americans' bilingual ability, counselor bilingualism cues, counselor ethnicity, and perceived counselor credibility. *Journal of Counseling Psychology, 46,* 125–131.

Robinson, T. L., & Ginter, E. J. (1999). Introduction to the *Journal of Counseling & Development*'s special issue on racism. *Journal of Counseling & Development, 77,* 3.

Rozensky, R. H., & Gómez, M. Y. (1983). Language switching in psychotherapy with bilinguals: Two problems, two models, and case examples. *Psychotherapy: Theory, Research, and Practice, 20,* 152–160.

Santiago-Rivera, A. L. (1995). Developing a culturally sensitive treatment modality for bilingual Spanish-speaking clients: Incorporating language and culture in counseling. *Journal of Counseling and Development, 74,* 12–17.

Santiago-Rivera, A. L., & Altarriba, J. (2002). The role of language in therapy with the Spanish-English bilingual client. *Professional Psychology: Research and Practice, 33,* 30–38.

Seay Clauss, C. (1998). Language: The unspoken variable in psychotherapy practice. *Psychotherapy, 35,* 188–196.

Smart, J. F., & Smart, D. W. (1995). Acculturative stress of Hispanics: Loss and challenge. *Journal of Counseling and Development, 73,* 390–396.

Stone, G. L. (1996). Multiculturalism as context for supervision: Perspectives, limitations, and implications. In D. B. Pope-Davis & H. L. K. Coleman (Eds.), *Multicultural counseling competencies: Assessment, education, training, and supervision* (pp. 263–289). Thousand Oaks, CA: Sage.

Sue, D. W., Arredondo, P., & McDavis, R. J. (1992). Multicultural counseling competencies and standards: A call to the profession. *Journal of Counseling and Development, 70,* 477–483.

Sue, D. W., & Sue, D. (2003). *Counseling the culturally different* (4th ed.). New York: John Wiley.

U.S. Census Bureau. (2003a). *Detailed list of languages spoken at home for the population 5 years and over by state: 2000.* Retrieved March 26, 2003, from http://www.census.gov/population/cen2000/phc-t20/tab05.xls

U.S. Census Bureau. (2003b). *Language use, English ability, and linguistic isolation for the population 5 years and over by state: 2000.* Retrieved March 26, 2003, from http://www.census.gov/population/cen2000/phc-t20/tab01.xls

4

When Turtle Met Rabbit

Native Family Systems

Janet M. Derrick

I am a Metis[1] woman of Mohawk ancestry. I live and work in western Canada. My family has married into the Secwepemc Nation in British Columbia. In the Native[2] world I am a mother, a grandmother, a teacher, and a learner. I walk beside those who ask for assistance and guidance, and I share with them what I have learned. In Aboriginal settings in Canada I am a clinician: I have a private practice serving individuals, couples, and families in a small urban setting surrounded by many rural First Nations. I work in residential Native trauma treatment programs, and I provide community-based training and workshops throughout Canada and the United States. This chapter focuses on my clinical work with my People in Native family systems.

In the mainstream world I am a registered family therapist, and I have worked in this capacity for 28 years. I am a Clinical Member and an Approved Supervisor of the American Association for Marriage and Family Therapy and the Canadian Family Therapy Registry, as well as a member of the Canadian Psychological Association. Most of my work has been as a practitioner in the field in both urban and rural settings. In the early 1980s, I began work in a small Native community under contract with Health Canada. This work led to one of the first live-in residential school court cases in Canada and to the documentation of the institutionalized, historical trauma of Aboriginal children in these schools.

As an adult I have devoted several years of my life to relearning how to live and to be in the circle system—the system in which my Native ancestors lived and upon which Native Nations in North America are founded. The circle system is a social system that is spiritually based and child focused, in which all living beings are equal in value and respectful relationships are believed to be essential for harmony and balance. I practice the traditional teachings of the circle as best I can, as does my family. As I begin writing these pages, I hold two images before me. One is the image of a woman Elder, Patricia Sterritt, Tsimshian, a powerful Teacher who spoke these words to me in 1991:

> Tell your Mother's People that they brought us many gifts which we accepted. And that in giving their gifts they took away ownership of what is ours. It is now time we regain our power and reclaim ownership of our Selves. It is time now for your Mother's People to use their gifts to see clearly who they are and what is true.

The second image is of the small circle of women I sat in a few days ago, in which each of us was preparing for something new in our lives. We gathered together in a sacred valley to bathe and cleanse in the glacial river water, to smudge and pray together, and to share our paths, our fears, our joys, and our laughter. Most of all, we gathered to support one another. With the women beside me in spirit and the guidance of my Elder, I write these pages.

Professional and Personal Background

I grew up in the "White" world, yet never really felt a fit. My maternal grandmother used to tell me about when I was born—that I was a "Red Indian hanging over the nurse's arm," that I was "a shame" to my family and "should never have been born." It has taken me years to heal from this message. It was the Native teachings of my ancestors that allowed me to shift beyond the trauma of that message, as well as the trauma of my childhood generally.

From the teachings I learned to walk with forgiveness of the spirit. I was provided with concrete tools, with perspectives of love and wholeness, and with support to be accountable and purposeful in my behavior and to honor the life force granted to me. These teachings took me far beyond any healing I found in mainstream psychotherapy or family therapy.

I spent years unravelling my personal history and my family's history in order to know how best to identify myself and stand in the world. As I unravelled the truth, I was struck with the intense terror of being Native within a society that condemns and attacks anyone who is different. My family appears to have survived by denying the heritage and keeping the ancestry a secret. This terror has been " paid forward" to my grandchildren: When my eldest grandson was 5 years old, he refused to allow his parents to attend his kindergarten class to tell traditional Native stories—he did not want anyone to know he was "Indian" (even though his facial features tell the world of his heritage).

I find this terror common throughout our families and communities. It is usually worn as a cloak over the soul and over the emotions and not spoken of publicly. I know of people who wear make-up to appear to have lighter skin. Some speak with fake accents and tell the world they are from France or Germany. Often people deny their heritage completely to become "White." Others move to the cities and blend in with mainstream society.

I feel blessed to have found Virginia Satir in my adulthood. I had attended a university and become a teacher. This profession did not completely fit me, as I found it too difficult to teach children who were hungry or beaten or abused in some other way. It seemed to fit me better to work directly on these difficult situations with the children and their families. I returned to the university and studied counseling psychology. It was in graduate school that I read Virginia Satir's work and had the opportunity to attend her workshops and intense weeklong trainings.

Virginia Satir provided the bridge for me between the systemic teachings of Native tradition and my training to become a professional family therapist. When she described her two systems of congruence and incongruence, I related to it. This world of two systems was my world. For me, the traditional teachings are always about congruence, balance, inner peace, and forgiveness. The mainstream world is about incongruence, masks, negativity, and aggression. The way I have been taught in the Native world is systemic. Specifically, I have been told: "We are all One. What we do to one we do to all. What we do to all we do to one" (traditional oral teaching).

Virginia Satir was one of the grandmothers for me. What she spoke was True, and she spoke it from a place of wisdom. The Ancestors guided her words and her work. I recall her saying to me that not all Native people achieve wholeness, nor did all Native communities achieve wholeness during precontact times. I have reflected upon these words over the years and arrived at the conclusion that as in all human endeavors, some of us—as individuals, as families, as communities, and as nations—achieve greater wholeness than others. Believing this has become important in how I work. When I travel to communities and First Nations, I remain open to discover where the people, families, and communities are in the circle of growth and wholeness. I want to hear from the Elders what their traditions and ceremonies are. I want to know how the women and children were traditionally treated by the families and contrast that with how they are treated now. I want to know the role of the men traditionally and what it is now. And I particularly want to understand the traditional view of the relationship between men and women and the current view of the relationship between men and women.

In the circle system, women and men traditionally had equal-in-value relationships. Most circle-based Native cultures were not only predominately female but also matrilineal. This has changed for many cultures since their contact with Europeans. Again I recall what Virginia Satir said during a weeklong training: "It is only in Native families that true equal-in-value relationships between women and men have been achieved."[3] I hold these words close to my heart, and I honor Virginia Satir for the work she did with Native people. It is one of my regrets that I did not have the opportunity to complete my Ph.D. with her, as we had agreed I would shortly before she died.

In addition to Virginia Satir's work, the work of two other mainstream professionals—Anne Wilson Schaef and Riane Eisler—validated my Native-based systemic views and the perspective of two systems. First, Anne Wilson Schaef in *When Society Becomes an Addict* (1987) described the Addictive System as synonymous with mainstream society. She further described the Living Process System, which is a paradigm shift away from the Addictive System. In my life, I translated this to mean that the White world lives the Addictive System, which is a paradigm shift from the traditional Native system of the circle of wholeness.

Second, Riane Eisler in *The Chalice and the Blade* (1988) described the androcracy system or dominator mind and contrasted this system with the gylany system or partnership mind. Again this replicates my experience in the non-Native and Native worlds. The androcracy system or dominator mind is the "White" or mainstream system, which is a paradigm shift from the gylany system or partnership mind of the Native world.

Riane Eisler's work reinforced for me the traditional emphasis on the female and the female energy in both women and men. I learned from the tradition that as a woman I am the creator of the relationship and my mate, who is equal in value with me, is my cocreator. This is a circular perspective. It is not linear as in the androcracy system or dominator mind.

Murray Bowen's (1978) systemic work strongly influenced me as a graduate student as well. It was his work that provided me with details of family systems: the descriptors, names, and tools that allowed me to follow the intricacies of family systems generally. In turn, this allowed me to begin to make sense of Native family systems in their current state and later to identify the traumatized Native family systems—the trauma as a result of genocide[4] in North America.

One of my strongest recollections in graduate school is sitting in my family systems seminar one long wintry afternoon. We were discussing healthy systems and debating whether such a thing as a "healthy system" or a "healthy family" actually exists or has ever existed. My gut was churning, but I did not yet have the inner strength to speak up in a training setting, especially a setting that was part of a system at odds with my worldview. The seminar discussion was a debate, and no conclusion was reached, but the question of whether a healthy system could exist remained in my mind.

The answer to this question came to me several years later while I was sitting in a healing circle in a Native community. A young man I did not know joined the circle. He had lived out of the community for some time and had come home to visit his grandfather. He described these teachings of his grandfather:

> We must walk together with love and support for each other, even those we do not like; our relationships and our family are the most important parts of our lives and we must do everything we can to honor and respect our relationships; what we do affects others and we must be aware of this before we act; we affect our relationships by everything we say, we feel, we do, we think.

He took 15 minutes to describe how our people had lived together in community before the coming of the White people—an experience still held by some Elders in the community at that time. I realized as I listened that what was being said was about systemic living, a systemic worldview, and it was being described beautifully, lovingly in 15 minutes. It had taken nearly 3 years in graduate school for me to hear the same thing said. And my experience in graduate school was not loving. In fact, it was often a very hard walk.

With this realization, I *knew* that my Native Ancestors had achieved a great sense of healthiness, of wholeness, and that this was far beyond what I presently knew in my own life. And it was worlds away from what my European Ancestors lived when they arrived in North America. What was most wondrous to me was that I could still touch the circle by sitting with the Elders. I could feel it in the families and in the community. The circle was still alive and I could learn from it. Yes, there are healthy systems, healthy families—they exist in the circle system.

It is many years now since I completed graduate school. My work currently focuses on rebalancing families in which the parents and/or grandparents were forced to attend a residential school. This work creates a powerful and potent interweaving of the Native family and community and the church and government that ran the residential school. It also triggers emotions in me as a member of the family therapy profession.

I attended a supervision course several years ago to become an Approved Supervisor with the American Association for Marriage and Family Therapy. On the first day, we were asked to define what the word *supervisor* means to us. I immediately found a huge lump in my throat and rage swelling throughout my body. I had images of the supervisor of many small boys who had sexually, physically, and psychologically harmed them for years in the residential school in the community. It was a challenge for me to separate the images and emotion associated with the word *supervisor* and apply it to myself as a member of my profession.

A current challenge to me professionally is the reaction to Native family systems work from non-Native professionals. I often find myself needing to breathe slowly and pray, and to forgive, forgive, and forgive, as is taught traditionally. I am learning over and over how to speak gently. I realize that what I am presenting often requires a paradigm shift for non-Native people. And what I am presenting can be traumatizing for the listener.

Usually there are several predictable reactions or responses: There is dismay at the death and trauma levels in Native family systems; people feel overwhelmed by the complexity of the system and tell me they wish me well and that they would not know where to begin as a therapist; I am told to stop being dramatic or political; the circularity of the system is not recognized, nor is my language of the circle understood; the focus moves away from Native family systems and back to a mainstream, European focus by the use of stories, by someone saying "It's time to move forward and forget the past," or by an "expert" stepping out and telling me what I should be doing differently; there is little awareness of Native history or the impact on it of European contact, or of the genocide that occurred, and people sit in stunned silence; and finally, the response I so greatly appreciate is when people say, "I didn't know this," "I want to learn more," and "How can we work together?"

Native professionals who fear speaking the truth sometimes challenge me. This usually occurs when I use the word *genocide*. Not everyone is in the same place in rebalancing the historical trauma of our people, nor does everyone agree on how to proceed. I accept this diversity of places and respect it as best I can.

Literature Review

FAITH

> my prayers are embedded
> in an old, cracked rosary strewn
> with black fibs chained
> to a tarnished crucifix
> I swore I could heal
> your tormented heart
> but my real words hide
> in the private places of my soul
> waiting to voyage to the outer limits of my skin
> when my eyes give birth
> to the Thunder Beings sleeping within
> it is then, they speak stories
> of the sun-bleached blade
> we found dormant above the wet earth
> after the rain exposed bone piles
> my soul is cool now
> like those isolated skeletons,
> waiting for a healing song
> to call us home.

This poem by Garry Gottfriedson, from his book *Glass Tepee* (2002), establishes the focus of this literature review. The review is based in the Native/Aboriginal perspective; it contains an understanding of the state of Native persons, families, communities, and Nations that includes historical trauma, genocide, two broader level metasystems, and the current focus on rebalancing and reclaiming wholeness in the circle. The authors of this literature more often than not are Native/Aboriginal.

In the Spirit of the Family (1989) is a publication of the National Native Association of Treatment Directors and was written by a team: Vera Manuel, Elaine Story, Mahara Allbrett, and Bea Shawanda. It described Native family systems using the current mainstream language of family systems, and it incorporated the understanding of grief, loss, and culture change in Aboriginal families.

Marlene Brant Castellano described Aboriginal perspectives on the family and focused on change in *Aboriginal Family Trends: Extended Families, Nuclear Families, Families of the Heart* (2002). She told of an Anishnabe Elder who said that to heal we must find sacred knowledge and heal our spirits first. She stated, "He spoke of sifting through the ashes to discover embers from the sacred fire which, when it is rekindled, brings the people back to their true purpose" (p. 19). She described the population explosion in Native communities in Canada between 1971 and 1996, when the population increased from 200,000 to 1,200,000. Marlene Brant Castellano further outlined the need to control the research processes conducted about Aboriginal People (i.e., by doing family research). This control is necessary for two reasons: (1) the research needs to be shaped so that it responds to information needs of the community itself, and (2) it must "reflect fundamental precepts of Aboriginal knowledge and understanding of the world" (Brant Castellano, 2002, p. 11).

Several authors meet Marlene Brant Castellano's requirements regarding research on Aboriginal People. Maria Yellow Horse Brave Heart has conducted significant research within the discipline of social work on issues related to trauma, such as historical and/or multigenerational trauma with families and communities. She has also described culturally appropriate clinical interventions. Some of Maria Yellow Horse Brave Heart's works are "Oyate Ptayela: Rebuilding the Lakota Nation Through Addressing Historical Trauma Among Lakota Parents" (1999), "The American Holocaust: Historical Unresolved Grief Among Native American Indians" (1998), and *Examining Two Facets of American Indian Identity: Exposure to Other Cultures and the Influence of Historical Trauma* (Weaver & Yellow Horse Brave Heart, 1999). Maria Yellow Horse Brave Heart joined two outstanding Native American researchers and authors, Bonnie Duran and Eduardo Duran, in contributing to the books *Studying Native America: Problems and Prospects of Native American Studies* (1998) and the *International Handbook of Multigenerational Legacies of Trauma* (1998). Bonnie Duran and Eduardo Duran also wrote *Native American Postcolonial Psychology* (1995), which focused on the Native worldview and addressed the impact on Native people of contact with Europeans.

The understanding of two worldviews, two metasystems, is described in my article "The Box and the Circle: Two Systems of Life—A Model for Understanding Native/Non-Native Issues" (Derrick, 1993). In this article, I detailed the two metasystems that met here in North America and described tools for rebuilding and creating positive change for Native people.

Joseph Stone has written the thorough paper *Current Issues in Tribal/ Native Behavioural Health: Cultural Disenfranchisement, Colonialism, Neo-Colonialism, and Post Traumatic Stress Disorder: Clinical and Scientific Implications for Native/Tribal Behavioural Health* (2003), in which he described the multiple impacts of trauma and loss on Native individuals and families.

The impact of the residential schools on Native families is being addressed across disciplines. I conducted research in 1985 for an unpublished thesis called *Cultural Foundations of Personal Meaning: Their Loss and Recovery.* This research used Peter Marris's model of social loss and change (from his 1975 book, *Loss and Change*) and identified the residential schools as the primary agent of cultural loss and change among Native Elders in British Columbia. Individuals are sharing their personal experiences in the schools, as in *Out of the Depths* (1994) by Isabelle Knockwood; Native Nations are hiring researchers to document the loss of children through adoption and fostering, as in *Stolen From Our Embrace* (1997) by Suzanne Fournier and Ernie Crey; students are conducting research by collating oral history and storytelling, as in *Resistence and Renewal; Surviving the Indian Residential School* (1988) by Celia Haig-Brown; Native academics are documenting statistics and the social ramifications of the schools, as in *The Circle Game* (1997) by Roland David Chrisjohn, Sherri Young, and Michael Maraun; playwrights are producing plays, as in *Two Plays About Residential School* (1998) by Oskiniko Larry Loyie and Vera Manuel. Non-Native authors are compiling information for the public, as in *The Dispossessed* (1989) by Geoff York and *A National Crime* (1999) by John Milloy. All these books contain vital information for family therapists working with Native people.

Clinical Applications: Traditional Application

In the Native circle whenever something strong needs to be shared, a story is told. This shares the message metaphorically, and the listeners can use the information for themselves as it best fits them. Here is a story of the meeting of two metasystems.[5]

WHEN TURTLE MET RABBIT

A time ago, Rabbit was a powerful warrior and a fearless leader. He became a great friend of Turtle's. The two would spend hours sharing, laughing, walking, or sitting together while reflecting on ideas and events on Mother Earth. Turtle would move slowly and carefully if they were walking. Because her body was so close to Mother Earth, she held ancient knowledge deep within her shell. Rabbit moved faster along the path, making large leaps or short hops and arriving at their destination much faster than Turtle. Because Rabbit moved quickly over Mother Earth, he often missed important details along his path.

One day the two were walking together and began climbing a mountain trail. They were deep in conversation and time passed quickly. Rabbit suddenly began to feel hungry and realized that he had forgotten to eat. He stopped his climb and said, "Turtle, I am hungry and I must stop and eat, but I see nothing here but rocks."

Turtle motioned to Rabbit to leave the trail and together they sat amidst the rocks. Turtle carefully studied the rocks around them, then reached over and touched several closest to her. Instantly the rocks became a variety of vegetables, and Turtle invited Rabbit to eat. Rabbit said nothing, but he looked at Turtle in a startled way. Then he accepted the food and ate hungrily.

The two then continued their walk up the mountain trail. They talked as they walked, but something had changed between them. Rabbit seemed quieter than before he had stopped to eat.

The day grew warmer and as they climbed, Rabbit now grew thirsty. He looked around him but could see no water to drink. Eventually he stopped walking and said to Turtle, "I am hot and thirsty and I can see no water to drink."

Turtle motioned to Rabbit to leave the trail and together they sat down on the earth. Turtle carefully studied the earth around her, then reached over and touched the ground closest to Rabbit. Instantly, water began oozing from the earth until a clear pool of water lay beside Rabbit. Rabbit was silent, but his eyes grew wide. He sat still for a long, long time. Finally, he bent to the water and drank eagerly.

Rabbit seemed uncomfortable after he completed his drink. He sat quietly again, not moving. Eventually he agreed with Turtle to continue along the mountain trail to the top, as they were nearly there. Once again they resumed their climb.

Conversation between them had now stopped, but Turtle enjoyed herself and the company of her friend. She loved Rabbit, and she let the silence sit between them.

The trail became steep and narrow and full of stones. Turtle moved slowly and easily, taking her time over the earth. Rabbit, however, was now tired as well as hot, and he lost his footing and slipped. He tumbled off the trail and could not regain his balance. He fell to the earth, and then slipped down the mountain, bouncing off rocks and shrubbery, scraping himself on logs and sharp tree branches until he finally came to rest in the valley below. Rabbit lay still, badly hurt.

Turtle moved as quickly as she could down the mountain to Rabbit, very concerned that he was still alive. When she reached him, Rabbit was breathing shallowly. Turtle looked at the plants surrounding where he lay. She gathered leaves, roots, flowers, and bark, carefully choosing what she needed. She applied these to Rabbit, bandaging and soothing him, singing to him as she worked.

Turtle stayed with Rabbit for several days, continuing to change the medicines as needed, until Rabbit made his recovery. Turtle was overjoyed to see her friend stand and walk after such a serious fall. However, Rabbit said nothing to her. He simply stared in her direction, then as quickly as he could, he hopped away.

Many, many Moons passed and Turtle did not see Rabbit at all. She called on him at his home and he did not answer her knock. She watched for him as she slowly moved along the path on her daily walks, but she saw no sign of him. She inquired about Rabbit's well-being with his relatives, but they walked silently away from her.

After much Time had passed, Turtle was walking by herself one day and looked up to see Rabbit moving toward her. Rabbit looked up too and saw Turtle, and he began to run. He appeared to be frightened. He ran erratically, in all directions, circling round and round, and going nowhere—doing his best, it seemed, to avoid Turtle.

Turtle called to Rabbit and asked what was happening. "What are you afraid of? What has kept you silent for so long? What has kept you from visiting with me as we used to?" she called.

Rabbit looked terrified and shouted, "I AM AFRAID OF YOU!! You make vegetables out of rocks and water come from the earth! You used plants to heal my wounds! Who are you?! Are you some kind of Magic?! I want nothing more to do with you!"

And with that, Rabbit ran down the path straight toward Turtle, pushing past her hard and hurtfully. He stepped on one side of Turtle's back and, purposefully it seemed to Turtle, flipped her over. Rabbit kept running, shouting loudly and cruelly until he disappeared in a whirlwind of dust.

Turtle lay on her back on Mother Earth. No one was around to assist her. She knew Rabbit would not return, and she knew Rabbit would probably not tell anyone of her predicament. Turtle also knew that without assistance, she would soon die. She lay on her back for a long, long time. She grew weaker and weaker.

Other animals came by and saw Turtle. They wondered what had led to Turtle lying on her back for so long. They studied her and could find no answers. Turtle did her best to tell them what had happened and ask for what she needed, but the animals could not seem to hear her. They pronounced her sick and dying.

Rabbit went to a nearby part of the earth and there he built a box of tree branches to hide in. He was now consumed with fear. It filled every part of him. When he heard a sound, he would freeze motionless in one position. His nose twitched constantly as he sat in his box, smelling the wind for the scent of other animals.

Whenever he caught sight of Hawk or Eagle or Owl flying overhead, he would jump out of his box and shout at them, "Go Away! Do not hurt me! Go Away!" And Hawk and Eagle and Owl would hear his shouts and swoop down to attack him.

Rabbit had become a Fear Caller. What he called came. He had lost his power and no longer walked as a fearless leader and powerful warrior.

Turtle lay on her back, preparing to die. She could hear Rabbit calling Fear, and she thought of the days she had spent with her friend, sharing and walking together. She felt incredibly sad and she grieved for what had become of Rabbit. She grieved for the life she could not live while lying on her back.

One day, Coyote, the Creator of the World came along the path. She looked over at just the right moment and saw Turtle lying on her back at the side of the path. Turtle was weak and barely alive. Coyote gently nudged Turtle with her nose, carefully rocking her back and forth on the top of her shell until she flipped over. Turtle was upright at last.

Turtle lived. She grew stronger. The earth had changed while she was lying on her back, but she was able to find enough of the plants and water she needed in order to heal herself.

Rabbit remained in his box shelter. He continued to call Fear for all to hear.

Turtle decided to go one day when she was ready and speak with Rabbit.

Clinical Applications:
Mainstream Application—Case Study

The following case study serves to illustrate some common dynamics in current Native family systems. The case is not any one particular family but contains a composite of the major family themes that I see regularly in my practice.

A 53-year-old grandmother, Jean, brought to therapy her three grandchildren, ages 10, 12, and 15. The two youngest children are the sons of her youngest daughter, and the oldest is the daughter of her eldest son. The mother of the boys is a regular user of alcohol and drugs and is in a physically abusive relationship. Whenever she is around Jean's home, the mother participates in the parenting of her two children. The 15-year-old lost both her parents when she was 8. They were killed in a car accident. Her grandmother has cared for her ever since her parents died. Jean is the legal guardian of all three children.

Jean is a residential school survivor. She was forcibly removed from her parents' home when she was 6 and returned to their home when she was 12. Her parents made a point of going to the school and bringing her home for most Christmas and summer holidays. However, they drank heavily during these times. She feared the chaos and abuse that accompanied the drinking, so when she was home from the school she would stay with an aunt or uncle instead of with her parents.

Jean was physically and sexually harmed in the school and has never spoken of this harm with anyone. "I put it behind me," she says.

She married young and had four children within 6 years. When the children were young, her husband drank on weekends while she stayed home. When he came home, he would beat her severely while the children hid in the woods nearby. Her husband was a survivor of residential school as well and was harshly treated there by the priests and the supervisors.

Eventually Jean decided to join her husband in drinking on weekends, and as a result the Welfare took her youngest daughter away for adoption. Jean felt she had no say in the adoption. The daughter is now an adult. Jean is aware of where her daughter is now living, and the daughter knows Jean is her biological mother. Jean is waiting for her daughter to make the contact. The daughter appears cold and distant if ever they are together at Ceremonies.

Jean's husband died of cancer at the age of 42, and she got together with another man shortly after her husband died. Her second husband is still with her, has been sober for 10 years, and assists her in the parenting of her grand-children. He has children and grandchildren from previous relationships, and his family joins with her family in family gatherings. The children and grand-children of both grandparents now treat each other as sisters and brothers.

In addition to raising her own children, Jean also raised her sister's daugh-ter. This was a cultural adoption. Her sister left for the nearby city at the age of 16 and came home whenever she was pregnant. Her first child, a daugh-ter, was left with Jean, who raised the girl as her own. The sister eventually died in the city and was brought home to be buried in the community grave-yard next to her parents.

Jean had a second son who is now deceased. He died of AIDS. He hid his illness from the family until he was dying, and he remained away from the community to die. The family visited him in hospital occasionally. When he passed over, his body was brought home to the community to be buried. The family told no one he died of AIDS. Jean grieves silently for her son and feels ashamed of how he died.

Jean drank until 17 years ago, and she has been sober ever since. She wants to see the grandchildren in her care grow to be strong adults and not experience the alcohol, drugs, and violence that her own children experienced. She wants to keep all the grandchildren in the care of the family and not lose any to adoption or fostering. She is afraid for her 15-year-old granddaughter, who has already begun drinking and skipping school.

Jean heard the cultural teachings and stories as a girl from her aunts, uncles, and grandparents. She shares these now with her grandchildren.

Common Native Family System Themes Illustrated in This Case

1. *Historical trauma.* This is the multigenerational harm created by family, community, and life systems being changed from balance to imbalance as a result of genocide. The symptoms can include the criteria for post-traumatic stress disorder and acute stress disorder, and they are transmitted across the generations. Underlying the symptoms is terror and the belief that death may occur without notice at any moment because it is wrong to be who we are.

2. *Two metasystems.* The metasystem that Native cultures are based on is the circle system—a spiritually centered, child-focused system with a holistic worldview of love and respect and forgiveness for all living things. This circular, systemic worldview was harshly supplanted by the other metasystem, the box system—a linear, patriarchal, dominating system, with a focus on survivorship and fear, that attacks what it believes to be wrong or different. The box system brought genocide, warfare, and the relocation of whole nations and communities; the dispossession of lands, culture, and language; residential, industrial, boarding schools and the forced removal of children to these schools; biological warfare; colonization of the people; overall mass death and loss.

3. *Lateral violence.* This refers to the organized, harmful behaviors between individuals within an oppressed group of people. It is internalized colonization and genocide. A form of safety has been found at the bottom of the patriarchy, and group members reinforce this violently with each other. This violence is acted out within the family, within Native organizations, within Native politics, within Native communities. One characteristic of lateral violence is that the harmful behaviors within the oppressed group tend to be harsher than the original behaviors from the oppressor.

4. *Compound loss and grief.* This is the result of the mass loss for Native people on all levels and throughout the generations since the genocidal

contact with Europeans. Until the last 40 years, Native people have simply not had time to grieve and see all that has been lost in these areas: culture, family relationships and family members, the traditional family system in the circle, many of the teachings and traditions of the circle, community, Nation, spirituality, personal power and self-esteem, identity, healthy sexuality, physical health, safety, language, parenting ability and parenting style, the ability to attach to children in a healthy way, governing systems, circle based law and justice systems. Suicide rates in most Native communities are higher than mainstream norms. Life expectancy rates are lower than mainstream norms.

5. *Shame.* There is a high degree of cultural, family, and personal shame carried by Native people. Shame-based messages abound—"It is wrong to be Native," "Natives are heathens," "Natives are savages," "The only good Indian is a dead Indian," "Indians are dirty," "Indians are bad," "Indian giver"—messages given by the genocide, the colonization, and the residential schools. At the opposite extreme are the pseudopositive messages from the colonizers, which further alienate Native people from themselves and can create greater shaming behavior—"the cigar store Indian," "the Medicine Man," "the noble savage," and "the savage warrior." Alcohol and drugs anaesthetize the shame for some, while creating more painful, harmful, and shaming behavior.

6. *Current microaggression.* This refers to the attitudes, beliefs, and linear perceptions of the mainstream that continue the original precepts of the box system and its genocidal behavior toward Native people. The box perpetuates the innate superiority of its members over Native people. As a result, Aboriginal people are targeted in small ways every day when others says things like, "You have freckles, you can't be Native," "Can I feel your hair?" "You Natives and your animal parts!" "I pay taxes"; when a store employee silently follows them around the store as they shop; when they are introduced to a non-Native person who speaks slowly and loudly to them; when a car pulls up beside a Native car, blocking it in a parking lot and the owner yells obscenities, laughs, and peels away; when Native children are teased and bullied constantly on the school ground.

7. *High levels of disease and alcohol and/or drug use.* Hepatitis A, B, C, HIV/AIDS, diabetes, and addictions are rampant in most Aboriginal communities. The incidence of heart disease and cancer is also high. People die young. This is understood to be symptomatic of the stress of the historical trauma.

8. *Shattered extended family system.* Family members are often unaware of who their relatives are. Family members have been fostered out and adopted

as far away as Europe and Australia. Children died in the residential schools. Family members cut themselves off from their community and became "White," hiding their Native roots from their children and grandchildren.

Healing and Rebalancing

Since the 1960s, there has been a movement to heal and rebalance the genocide and its effects within Native families and communities. The following are common Native perceptions of healing and beliefs about the current rebalancing within the Native community and family systems:

1. There is great resilience and strength of the People to survive and claim Life once again.

2. The power of the circle system lives on and can be reclaimed.

3. It is important for Native People to heal Native people.

4. There is power and a healing effect in Native humor.

5. It is necessary to place spirituality at the center of our lives again.

6. It is necessary to place the children as our focus again.

7. There is a need to once again have cocreative female-male relationships that are equal in value.

8. There is a need to heal the multiple harm, especially sexual abuse, and disrupted attachment created by the residential schools.

9. There is a need for an increased economic base and secure land base to ensure that people live in safety, can care for themselves and their families, and can build up their lives.

10. There is a desire to understand trauma and its effects upon our lives, families, and culture.

11. There is a desire to work holistically to rebalance by emulating the use of traditional forms of communication—language, art, music, drama, and storytelling.

12. There is a need to speak the truth and be accountable for our actions now.

13. There is a need to be sober and clean from drugs.

14. There is a need for continued microaggression to be named and for current and past harmful behaviors to be called into accountability.

15. There is a need for education in both systems; the circle and the box.

16. There is a desire to bring those who were fostered and adopted back into contact with their family and community.

17. There is a desire to learn the languages again, as they are based in the circle worldview, and to have access to the Elders who still hold the teachings.

18. It is important for non-Native people to understand the truth of the original contact and to now look at themselves.

19. It is important for non-Native professionals to learn from the People and not recolonize the People.

Please note that not all Native families, communities, and Nations agree with every statement above.

Conclusion

To summarize, there is some prominent research and documentation of Native family systems and Native healing from the Native perspective, but it is a small amount of research and virtually nonexistent in the family therapy literature; there is a need for family therapy to work with Native family systems; there is a need for family therapy to understand two metasystems are at work within Native communities; the genocidal contact with European peoples has created historical trauma within Native families and communities; there are strengths and abilities within the Native family and individual and circle system to heal and to rebalance the multiple generations of harm.

For non-Native professionals working with Native family systems, I pray that some of what I have shared is of assistance to you. From my experience, I believe it is essential that the Native perspective—the circle system—be respected and used when working with Native people. This will be a challenge—to undergo a shift in systemic paradigms, whether in whole or in part. It is also essential to be aware that non-Native professionals can be triggers of the genocide, can perpetuate innate superiority, and can continue the microaggression toward and colonization of Native families.

Reflections, Questions, and Exercises

I believe that family systems therapy can serve a vital role in the healing of Native people. It speaks the same language as the cultures, that is, the language of systems. It is essential, however, to become aware of which system is being used in therapy—the box of the mainstream or the circle system of Native people. Native families usually begin their therapy work in the box, but more and more they are seeking to find their way home to circular family systems. Consider how you might work with the major issues discussed here. These suggestions may be helpful:

1. Drop the role of expert and become a fellow human being.

2. Learn what is true.

3. Be ready to hear stories that hurt.

4. Listen with the heart first and then the head.

5. Know that most Native families live systemically and will be well ahead of you in this area.

Changes

You robbed me of my youth I never realized,
playground seemed so empty all the time,
you robbed me of my skin you took my pride,
they said it was our way or no way.
I say now, hey, hey, hey . . . they all said we would fall down . . .
Now it's time for some change
its time for changes.

—Wayne Lavallee, Metis, from his 2000 CD *Liv Again*
(Used with permission from the author)

Kwekstiem. Thank you for listening. *Homalth.* It is ended.

Notes

1. The Metis People are of mixed Native and European ancestry and have maintained an identity primarily with the Native ancestry. They have created a distinct Native culture. Currently, the Metis People are reclaiming their legal rights under the law and constitution to be entitled to full rights as people of Aboriginal ancestry.

2. I have used several terms interchangeably to denote *Native* in this chapter. I have not used *Native American* because this term refers to Native people in the United States rather than in North America. I live in Canada and therefore do not

see myself, nor do the people I work with generally see themselves, as Native American. The terms listed below may give the reader an idea of the current wide range of perception and changes within the Native families of North America. Some of these terms are more politically correct than others. When in doubt, it is best to ask the person or family what they call themselves and what is acceptable to them. These are the terms in common usage in Canada and the United States:

- *Aboriginal:* This is an all-inclusive term commonly used in Canada to describe all people of Native ancestry; First Nations, Native, status on-reserve, status off-reserve, non-status, Metis, and Inuit.
- *First Nations:* This term is used often in Canada and sometimes in the United States to describe people of Native ancestry who are members of a recognized Native Nation. *First Nations* generally replaces *Native* or *Indian* and is used now to name Nations and Tribal Councils, as in "Lytton First Nations" rather than "Lytton Indian Band."
- *Indian:* This is what Christopher Columbus called Native people when he got lost and thought he was in India (rather than North America).
- *Inuit:* This term refers to the people and cultures of the northern territories of the continent who were formerly called *Eskimo.*
- *Native:* This is an all-inclusive term to describe the cultures and the people and their descendants who had established territories in North America prior to European contact.
- *Native American:* This term is commonly used in the United States to describe all people of Native ancestry.
- *Non-status:* This term refers to Native people whose Native rights have been lost either through marriage (of women to non-Native men) or through their decision to give up Treaty or Indian Act rights and live in the mainstream.
- *Off-reserve:* This refers to Native people living in mainstream communities and cities, who do not have the rights and entitlements that would be available to them if they lived on reserve (e.g., nonpayment of taxes).
- *On-reserve:* This refers to Native people who, in living on reservations or reserves established by the government, are entitled to certain rights (e.g., land use).
- *Status/Tribal enrolled:* This refers to the Native person who is recognized as having enough blood quantum to be Native and receive Treaty or Indian Act rights.

3. I have this statement on a videotape of this training seminar, which took place in March 1988 in the Gulf Islands, British Columbia.

4. The term *genocide* is used in Native rebalancing according to its definition under International Law and the General Assembly of the United Nations Genocide Convention Resolution 96(1) dated December 11, 1946. It is defined as follows:

Article II: In the present Convention, genocide means any of the following acts committed with intent to destroy, in whole or in part, a national, ethical, racial or religious group, as such:

1. Killing members of the group;
2. Causing serious bodily or mental harm to members of the group;
3. Deliberately inflicting on the group conditions of life calculated to bring about its physical destruction in whole or in part;
4. Imposing measures intended to prevent births within the group;
5. Forcibly transferring children of the group to another group.

5. I have shared this story in other settings—first in 1996 at the Mokakit Education Conference in Calgary, Alberta, and then in 1998 at the Canadian Psychology Conference in Edmonton, Alberta.

References

Bowen, M. (1978). *Family therapy in clinical practice.* New York: Jason Aronson.

Brant Castellano, M. (2002). *Aboriginal family trends: Extended families, nuclear families, families of the heart.* Ottawa: The Vanier Institute of the Family.

Brave Heart, M. Y. H. (1999). Oyate Ptayela: Rebuilding the Lakota Nation through addressing historical trauma among Lakota parents. In H. Weaver (Ed.), *Voices of First Nations people: Considerations for human services.* New York: Haworth.

Brave Heart, M. Y. H., & De Bruyn, L. (1998). The American holocaust: Historical unresolved grief among Native American Indians. *National Center for American Indian and Alaska Native Mental Health Research Journal, 8*(2), 56–78.

Chrisjohn, R., Young, S., & Maraun, M. (1997). *The circle game: Shadows and substance in the Indian residential school experience in Canada.* Penticton, British Columbia: Theytus.

Derrick, J. (1993). The box and the circle: Two systems of life: A model for understanding Native/non-Native issues. *Mokakit Education Research Journal,* 161–198.

Derrick, J. (1998). When rabbit flipped turtle: Psychology and the Native perspective. *Canadian Psychological Abstracts, 39*(2a), 27.

Derrick More, J. (1985). *Cultural foundations of personal meaning: Their loss and recovery.* Unpublished master's thesis, University of British Columbia, Vancouver.

Duran, B., & Duran, E. (1995). *Native American postcolonial psychology.* Albany: State University of New York Press.

Duran, B., Duran, E., & Brave Heart, M. Y. H. (1998). Native Americans and the trauma of history. In *Studying Native America: Problems and prospects of*

Native American studies (pp. 60–76). New York: Social Science Research Council.

Duran, B., Duran, E., Brave Heart, M. Y. H., & Yellow Horse-Davis, S. (1998). Healing the American soul wound. In Y. Danieli (Ed.), *International handbook of multigenerational legacies of trauma.* New York: Plenum.

Eisler, R. (1988). *The chalice and the blade: Our history, our future.* Toronto: Harper & Row.

Fournier, S., & Crey, E. (1997). *Stolen from our embrace: The abduction of First Nations children and the restoration of Aboriginal communities.* Vancouver: Douglas & McIntyre.

Gottfriedson, G. (2002). *Glass tepee.* Saskatoon, Saskatchewan: Thistledown.

Haig-Brown, C. (1988). *Resistance and renewal: Surviving the Indian residential school experience.* Vancouver: Tillacum.

Knockwood, I. (1994). *Out of the depths: The experience of Mi'kmaw children at the Indian residential school at Shubenacadie, Nova Scotia.* Lockeport, Nova Scotia: Roseway.

Lavallee, W. (2000). Changes. *Liv again* [CD]. Vancouver: Gotham City Studios.

Loyie, O. L., & Manuel, V. (1998). *Two plays about residential school.* Vancouver: Living Traditions Writers Group.

Manuel, V., Story, E., Allbrett, M., & Shawanda, B. (1989). *In the spirit of the family.* Saskatoon, Saskatchewan: Apex.

Marris, P. (1975). *Loss and change.* New York: Doubleday.

Milloy, J. S. (1999). *A national crime: The Canadian government and the residential school system 1879 to 1986.* Winnipeg: University of Manitoba Press.

Satir, V. (1967). *Conjoint family therapy: A guide to theory and technique.* Palo Alto, CA: Science and Behavior.

Satir, V. (1972). *Peoplemaking.* Palo Alto, CA: Science and Behavior.

Schaef, A. Wilson (1987). *When society becomes an addict.* San Francisco: Harper & Row.

Stone, J. (2003, March). *Current issues in tribal/native behavioral health: Cultural disenfranchisement, colonialism, neo-colonialism, and post traumatic stress disorder—clinical and scientific implications for Native/tribal behavioral health.* Unpublished paper presented at the Tribal Conference in Portland, OR.

Weaver, H., & Brave Heart, M. Y. H. (1999). Examining two facets of American Indian identity: Exposure to other cultures and the influence of historical trauma. *Voices of First Nations people: Consideration for human services.* New York: Haworth.

York, G. (1989). *The dispossessed: Life and death in Native Canada.* Toronto: Lester & Orpen Dennys.

SECTION II

Ethnicity and Race
in the Therapy Room
and in the Classroom

5

African American Women in Client, Therapist, and Supervisory Relationships

The Parallel Processes of Race, Culture, and Family

Shalonda Kelly and Nancy Boyd-Franklin

Cross-racial and cross-cultural therapeutic and supervisory relationships in the mental health field have been studied (Boyd-Franklin, 2003; Helms & Cook, 1999); however, relational dynamics among clients, therapists, and supervisors of the same race have been relatively neglected. This chapter describes how racial, cultural, and familial factors become manifest for African American clients, therapists, and supervisors. We present these factors in our backgrounds and use a case example to demonstrate how they impact our treatment and supervisory relationships. We further describe the application of a combined family systems and cognitive behavioral approach to address racial and cultural factors. In particular, we pay attention to how the use of such factors can lead to a parallel process of empowerment across these three relationships.

Personal and Professional Backgrounds

In this chapter, we explore our contexts as therapist (Shalonda Kelly) and supervisor (Nancy Boyd-Franklin) and as African American women. Like many African Americans, we embody both continuity and diversity. Our African roots ensure that we value kin, friends, and community. We both have grandparents who left Southern states for urban coastal areas in other parts of the country that had similar family and community values. We were raised in egalitarian households where both parents worked outside the home. Our families stressed education, often citing how its lack had held them back in society. It was expected that we would obtain advanced degrees, and we are the most educated members of our families of origin.

We both are close to our families—we talk to family members regularly and involve them in our important decisions. This level of connection may be considered "enmeshed" by therapists from other cultural backgrounds. Our natural hairstyles and clothing with African accents are symbols of an ability to stay connected to our heritage and culture while engaging in our professional roles at the university. As much as we share in common, we also embody the diversity found among African Americans. Our individual statements illustrate this diversity.

Shalonda Kelly

I am a 33-year-old, single African American woman, and the younger of two sisters. I grew up in a married-family household in Long Beach, an urban area of Southern California. One of the most basic values imparted to me by my family was the necessity to show strength in the face of adversity. Every member of my family has manifested this value: my father, whose entrepreneurial and independent endeavors enabled him to be a major resource for my extended family during their hard times; my mother, who worked for the telephone company from her high school graduation on and fought a valiant struggle against the cancer that claimed her life in 1993; and my sister, who rose in the corporate world in an era of layoffs and regularly contributes to the family.

I consistently received the following messages from my family: (1) work hard, be a jack of all trades, and obtain the highest degree possible; (2) always be there for family; (3) discrimination and racism are alive and well in America; (4) a straightforward, charismatic manner is a valuable asset, and displaying weakness of any kind should be avoided. My extended family value maintaining ties with and assisting their members, and they express pride in the accomplishments of all family members. Unlike my parents, who broke from the church, most of my extended family are Baptist.

I received my master's and doctoral degrees in the child and family track of the clinical psychology-urban studies dual degree program at Michigan State University. I am an integrationist who uses both systems and cognitive-behavioral perspectives in conducting therapy. As a tenure-track assistant professor in the Graduate School of Applied and Professional Psychology (GSAPP) at Rutgers University, I have research interests in couple and family relationships and diversity. I teach and supervise students, such as in the Family Treatment of Childhood Disorders and Diversity and Racial Identity courses that I created. I also maintain a small private practice.

Nancy Boyd-Franklin

I am a 53-year-old African American woman. I was raised in a family with African American and Jamaican roots. My father's family are African American with Southern roots and moved to Harlem from North and South Carolina. My maternal grandparents emigrated from Jamaica in the West Indies. My parents were born in and met in Harlem.

My family transmitted many important cultural values to me. My early childhood experience of living with my extended family in Harlem high-lighted the value of extended family relationships. When I was 6 years old, my family moved to a low-income housing project in the Bronx, where I became the "parental child" who helped to care for my three younger siblings while my parents worked. This experience instilled in me the value of helping family. Education was strongly emphasized in my family, and the role of familial sacrifice as a pathway to educational attainment was continually stressed. It was expected that I would help other family members once I had obtained my own education. My family also emphasized spirituality and religion, and my mother played a large role in transmitting these values. Another influential message I received was that I must "give something back" by contributing to the African American community.

My involvement in my family and extended family is and has been important to me throughout my life and is balanced with my professional responsibilities. I am married to Dr. A. J. Franklin, with whom I share a deep personal and collaborative professional relationship. I am also a mother, stepmother, and grandmother.

Given my background, it is not surprising that I have specialized in family therapy, the treatment of African American families, and multicultural issues in therapy, which have also been my mechanism for making a contribution to the African American community. I received my doctorate in clinical psychology from Teachers College, Columbia University in 1977. I studied structural family therapy with Salvador Minuchin, among others, during my clinical internship at the Philadelphia Child Guidance Clinic. Throughout my career, structural and other family systems models have influenced my work with African American families at community mental health centers and hospitals. In 1992, I joined the faculty of GSAPP at Rutgers University, where I teach courses on family therapy and the treatment of ethnic minority clients and families.

Our Relationship

Our experiences, as well as our shared interests in family and diversity issues, brought us together in GSAPP's clinical Psy.D. program. It was very important to both of us that there was another African American woman in the department. Initially, our supervisory relationship was one-sided, as Nancy modeled how to balance academia and clinical practice, clarify and teach others about one's theoretical standpoint, and develop one's career. Yet, from the beginning, she emphasized a collaborative approach, in which we could share our ideas regarding interventions with each client. Given that Nancy is a family therapist and Shalonda incorporates both systems and cognitive behavioral orientations, Nancy encouraged Shalonda's use of other cognitive behavioral colleagues as supervisors. This was crucial in allowing Shalonda to develop her own clinical style and in helping both of us clarify the basis for our individual clinical decisions. The fact that we are both African American women quickly led us to develop a relationship in which we became each other's support system when other colleagues might not understand our cultural needs. We were also able to discuss our experiences of racism in the mental health field.

Commonalities in the African American Community

The common threads evident in our lives are also present in the lives of many African Americans. Some cultural strengths and values that we share with the African American community include role flexibility and egalitarianism, extended family structures, spirituality and religion, and preferences for expressiveness and experience (e.g., Boyd-Franklin, 2003; Kelly, 2003a). For the two of us, these common threads are most prominently manifest in our experiences of racism and discrimination, socioeconomic concerns, and general approach to addressing race and ethnicity.

Racism significantly affects most African Americans today, despite the claims of those who believe that affirmative action is no longer needed. For example, studies have shown negative, prejudicial responses of Whites to African Americans (Oliver, 1999; Oliver & Fonash, 2002); that African Americans report higher race-related stress as compared to other ethnic groups (Utsey & Ponterotto, 1996); and that African Americans' experiences with racism are associated with physical and psychological distress (Kelly, 2003b; Krieger & Sidney, 1996). We both have been touched by these experiences.

Largely because of racism, many African Americans experience harsher socioeconomic realities than do their White counterparts. Since 1959, African Americans have had substantially higher poverty rates than all other ethnic groups except Latinos/as, according to the U.S. Census Bureau (Dalaker, 2001). Since 1954, even in times of economic growth, African Americans' unemployment rates have been twice those of Whites (McLoyd, 1990). As is common with many other African Americans, beginning with our first experiences of breadwinning, we often have given to the "family pot" for those who are less fortunate.

African Americans' similarities in cultural strengths and values are balanced by differences in how they perceive and cope with racial and cultural issues. One major variation exists in African Americans' understanding of why they disproportionately experience adversity. This understanding includes views on whether the blame lies with the system or themselves (e.g., Jackson, McCullough, Gurin, & Broman, 1991; Niemann, O'Connor, & McClorie, 1998), as well as views on spirituality and religion (Taylor, Mattis, & Chatters, 1999), racial identity (Parham & Helms, 1981), and socialization of racial and cultural values (Boyd-Franklin, 2003; Stevenson, 1994). In the first year of our therapist-supervisor relationship, some of these differences became apparent. Because of Shalonda's family's emphasis on being strong, whenever difficulties arose in her therapy sessions, she attributed them to something that she "should have done." Nancy stressed the utility of a "both/and" systems perspective that enabled Shalonda to see that while it is necessary continually to improve one's skills, contextual and systemic factors contribute to difficulties in treatment, such as clients' reactions to her race, her age, and other factors. The supportive nature of this perspective helped to decrease Shalonda's stress and increase her ability to empower others.

Cultural Factors Relevant for Young
African American Undergraduate Women Clients

As shown in our own narratives, issues of race and culture frequently arise in the everyday professional and personal lives of African Americans. One common example, evident in the case described below, involves young African American undergraduate women who are connected to their heritage and face new developmental and racial stressors related to starting college at predominately White universities. Like most undergraduates of any ethnic group, this may be their first experience living away from their families, and they may take advantage of the increased freedom by engaging in too much socializing and too little schoolwork. For African Americans, this vulnerability can be compounded by feelings of racial and cultural alienation on campus (Joiner & Walker, 2002). They may compensate for this by joining Black student organizations, living off-campus with other African Americans, and making forays into local urban areas to develop friendships. The latter alternative may give rise to certain stressors—the student can feel torn between school friends and friends who "did not make it" into higher education, and their friends may feel a conflict between supporting the student's achievement and justifying their own situation by glorifying street life.

A second complicating issue is that many African American undergraduate women are first-generation college students. These women are often painfully aware that upon graduation, they will have surpassed their parents or entire family educationally. However much pride the family and student may feel in such attainment, it is not unusual to fear that it threatens cultural similarities, which each might believe will be lost as the student progresses in her education. The challenge of the newness of college is compounded by these women's feelings of anger at the system, which is caused by a range of factors. These include discrepancies between the level of preparation for college provided by inner city schools and the expectations of their professors, campus experiences with racism and discrimination, a curriculum that devalues or completely ignores the contributions of African Americans, few African American faculty, problems with financial aid, and other concerns involving ethnic disparities.

At predominately White universities, these women may be likely to seek treatment for depression and failing grades when they have significant stressors in their personal or family life in addition to the ones just described. This can be seen below in the case example of a depressed client, which fits the profile of issues that confront many young African American undergraduates (as described above), illustrates the types of racial and cultural issues they commonly encounter, and highlights useful therapeutic techniques. To protect the confidentiality of the client, all identifying information has been changed. In this case, the supervisor (Nancy), the therapist (Shalonda), and the client (called Lakeshia here) are all African American women.

Case Study

Lakeshia was a 21-year-old African American woman who was raised in Chicago and had been a good student in high school. She became very depressed within the first 6 months of college and her grades deteriorated progressively. She withdrew from school, returned home, and continued to experience severe difficulties in functioning until she was prescribed antidepressants and treated briefly by a psychotherapist. This enabled her to return to college for her second year; however, she then sought treatment at the university clinic for her continued depression and an inability to complete her schoolwork. Lakeshia attributed her problems to a belief that she was unwanted and that her educational aspirations were a burden to her family. Her low self-esteem and interpersonal problems included the beliefs that she was ugly and that her friends had left her behind as their lives blossomed.

Lakeshia's parents both worked—her father as a bus driver and her mother as a housekeeper. They paid for most of Lakeshia's college expenses out of their meager salaries. Consistent with the cultural notion of contributions to the "family pot," Lakeshia was torn between guilt over draining their resources and fears that upon finishing school she would be expected to support them because they were older and had health issues. Lakeshia reported that her elder brother, a high school graduate, worked at the bus company with her dad and did not contribute to the family. Lakeshia's mother had severe arthritis, and her father abused alcohol. Lakeshia was often put in an unhealthy triangle with her parents as her mother habitually called Lakeshia at college, crying about how Lakeshia's father had spent their spare resources on alcohol. Lakeshia did not feel comfortable discussing her own difficulties with her mother, feeling that her mother was already under enough stress. Being home and witnessing her father's drinking and verbal abuse of her mother furthered Lakeshia's depression. Her parents also were less committed to African Americans' advancement than she was, and when she began to get Fs, she reported that her father said, "Maybe you should just realize where you came from and get a job at the bus company." This hurt her deeply and exacerbated her fears of not succeeding. Throughout therapy she expressed fears of both failure and success that often increased her depression and left her immobilized.

Healthy and Unhealthy Ways in Which African Americans Cope With Racial and Cultural Factors

It is important to note that in healthy African American families, many aspects of Lakeshia's family situation exist, but they are dealt with more successfully. For example, reciprocity in family members' support of each other is more manageable outside of the context of substance abuse. Many African Americans may also draw upon extended family for financial and emotional support. In Lakeshia's case, she cut herself off from her brother, and her nuclear family was cut off from their relatives in the South, which greatly limited the amount of support upon which they could draw. Further, the cross-generational alliance formed between Lakeshia and her mother against her father, and her mother's own lack of support, were other patterns not common to healthy African American families. Finally, many African Americans typically need to discuss and develop ways of combating alienation and injustice within the larger society. For many, the family provides this forum. Yet Lakeshia took her father's way of coping, his passivity and acceptance of the situation, to mean that he did not believe in her, and she never discussed these concerns with him.

Many African Americans experience clashes between African American culture and the larger U.S. culture, which can adversely affect their adjustment when handled poorly. Unlike African Americans who cope well, Lakeshia was unable to deal with her justifiable feelings of anger over her alienation on campus appropriately, such as with friends and through extant channels for addressing grievances. African Americans have a cultural tendency to be expressive, but Lakeshia took this to an extreme. She believed that if she did not express to others how wrong they were and how angry they made her every time she saw them, then she would be phony. In fact, she held the irrational belief that this was how anger should be expressed with everyone.

On the positive side, Lakeshia possessed a great deal of charm and could be endearing. She cried for catharsis, and her crying brought her nurturance from others when she needed it. Like many of her African American peers, Lakeshia engaged in positive racial coping that included joining a number of Black student organizations, finding a "church home," and wearing African-accented jewelry. Coping behaviors like these have been associated with greater identification with African culture and increased psychological functioning (e.g., Baldwin, Brown, & Rackley, 1990; Blaine & Crocker, 1995). But she also engaged in negative racial coping, such as involving herself romantically with a local drug dealer she thought she could "save from the streets," and devaluing her African features, such as with her statement, "I'm too Black and ugly." Anti-Black beliefs such as this have been empirically associated with psychological distress (Kelly, 2003b).

The clashes African Americans experience between the larger U.S. culture and African American culture are partly the result of differences in the value systems of the two cultures. For example, because of the childhood lectures received from her father about the cultural value of working hard in an unjust world, Lakeshia would exercise very poor judgment in taking too many classes, failing them, and succumbing to depression. While many groups espouse a work ethic, for African Americans this can mean also being "hard" and invulnerable to negative situations (Majors & Billson, 1992). In healthy African American families, this external invulnerability may be balanced with family members' support of one another. For Lakeshia, however, her reported belief in the value of being invulnerable and not weak prevented her from seeking support by nurturing herself, sharing her difficulties with her parents, and attempting to structure her life so that her tasks were more manageable and less overwhelming.

The Integration of Family Systems and Cognitive Behavioral Approaches in the Treatment Process

Treatment with Lakeshia consisted of an interweaving of family systems and cognitive behavioral methods designed to decrease her depression, increase her self-esteem, and improve her interpersonal relationships and academic performance. The systems approach provided the overall framework of the treatment and was used to facilitate bonding with Lakeshia, increase her motivation to engage in positive self-supporting and interpersonally rewarding behaviors, and help her understand the role of family dynamics in her current life. The cognitive behavioral approach was used to teach Lakeshia behavioral principles and interpersonal and decision-making skills. The therapist modeled the skills, role-played them with Lakeshia, and provided feedback. Then the therapist assigned these skills as homework and encouraged Lakeshia to use positive self-talk when using them, wherein Lakeshia coached herself in a supportive fashion.

We integrated these two approaches because we deem them to be compatible and complimentary. For example, both focus upon client strengths and the development of a productive working relationship, both can involve feedback and coaching by the therapist, and both seek to change the inappropriate ways in which the client views the world. Moreover, the use of each can serve to facilitate the use of the other, as when cognitive behavioral techniques build the skills to enable clients to act upon systems directives and when systems reframes increase the client's motivation to learn the skills that cognitive behavioral techniques seek to teach.

A number of well-known family systems and cognitive behavioral techniques were used with Lakeshia. The most useful systems interventions used by the therapist involved joining (Minuchin & Fishman, 1981) while using a culturally appropriate style (Boyd-Franklin, 2003), using "family therapy with one person" techniques (Carter & McGoldrick-Orfanidis, 1994), employing solution-focused methods of countering Lakeshia's frequent homeostasis (Walter & Peller, 1992), and selective use of self-disclosure (Hill & Knox, 2002). The most fruitful cognitive behavioral techniques used with Lakeshia included cognitive restructuring, which involves challenging irrational, negative beliefs with objective evidence (Beck, Rush, Shaw, & Emery, 1987), and psychoeducation, in which the client learns about normal thoughts, feelings, and behaviors. In addition, standard cognitive-behavioral interventions of communication, problem solving and decision-making training, and emphasis on antecedents and consequences of client behavior were also used (Sanderson & McGinn, 1999). A description of how the therapist's integrated use of these techniques addressed the racial, cultural, and familial aspects of Lakeshia's presenting problems is discussed below.

Culturally Relevant Joining: The Older Girlfriend Technique

The structural family systems concept of joining with clients typically involves the therapist's accessing aspects of the self that are congruent with the client, such as using similar language patterns, conveying a sense of understanding, and showing clients that she or he is working with and for them, all from a leadership position (Minuchin & Fishman, 1981). To be effective, the therapist also has to be able to simultaneously join and challenge the client when necessary (Minuchin & Fishman, 1981). In this case, given the marked similarities in cultural experiences, combined with the 10 year difference in age, it was comfortable for both that Shalonda joined with Lakeshia in a "close position" (Minuchin & Fishman, 1981, p. 33), in a role similar to an older girlfriend or cousin. This "older girlfriend technique" invited Lakeshia to fully express her thoughts and feelings without concern about being judged—and without experiencing an extension of the alienation that she already felt, sometimes even with other African Americans whose adjustment to college was better than hers. Thus, Lakeshia and Shalonda both used Black dialect and other behaviors common among African Americans, and Shalonda used culturally appropriate humor and irony in connecting with Lakeshia.

Shalonda and Nancy also monitored and maintained the boundaries of this close position. For example, Lakeshia's in-session behaviors were sometimes atypical, in that she would take off her shoes or sit on the floor, yell loudly when excited or angry, fall to her knees in a regressive manner, and put her head on Shalonda's knee when she cried. These behaviors were addressed as a part of the process because Lakeshia still did therapeutic work during these times, the strong emotional expressions seemed cathartic, and it allowed Shalonda to show that this older "girlfriend" could handle and understand the emotions that apparently put off many others in Lakeshia's life. In order to maintain boundaries, however, Shalonda often used her "doctor" title, kept firm control of the direction and content of each session, and challenged Lakeshia's negative behaviors. It is important to note that this stance was also consistent with their culture. In the African American community, it is common to address older individuals by titles such as "Miss" or "Mister," even in a close relationship, as a sign of respect. There is also a cultural value related to "being real," "speaking the truth," and challenging negative behaviors of others in close relationships.

Lakeshia's overwhelming expression of anger is one example of a negative behavior for which Shalonda's "older girlfriend technique" was useful for joining with Lakeshia in both a supportive and challenging manner. At first, Shalonda was validating and supportive, such that Lakeshia proudly proclaimed their sessions as the one place where she could "let it out." Next, Shalonda used the cognitive behavioral technique of identifying the negative consequences of her behavior. To do this, she began to point out the hurt behind Lakeshia's anger. Next, she pointed out that although it felt good in the moment to vent her anger, it harmed her by keeping others away, which prevented her from righting perceived wrongs and forming solid relationships. For example, although Shalonda validated Lakeshia's justifiable anger at racism, she helped her to see that constantly yelling at her White peers for racial insensitivities resulted in further alienation and a dismissal of her claims, which prevented her from getting true grievances redressed.

Shalonda also used humor regarding her own experiences of Lakeshia's anger in session to encourage Lakeshia's empathy for the recipients of her anger. After successfully reframing Lakeshia's way of expressing anger as problematic, Shalonda then began to challenge it by interrupting its buildup, praising Lakeshia for containing it, and using the "older girlfriend technique" to humorously challenge the notion that Lakeshia was as angry as her outbursts implied. When Shalonda's queries and homework assignments revealed that Lakeshia had no idea how people successfully worked on their interpersonal problems, Shalonda referred to the relationship between herself and Lakeshia, emphasizing how they successfully talked through disagreements in their perspectives. Finally, Shalonda used cognitive-behavioral skill-building techniques to de-escalate Lakeshia's anger and teach her assertiveness skills. In each of these interventions, the "older girlfriend technique" of joining fit with the cultural style of both; it seemed most comfortable for Lakeshia to vent with and receive help from an older mentor and friend, and Shalonda truly could understand Lakeshia's developmental and cultural concerns.

Family Therapy With One Person

One systems approach that is often useful with individual African American clients is called "family therapy with one person" (Carter & McGoldrick-Orfanidis, 1994). This approach is derived from Bowen's theory that change in one client can reverberate throughout the family system to change the client's family members (Bowen, 1976, 1978). In conducting family therapy with one person, the therapist coaches the individual client in the session to implicitly or explicitly work with his or her family on their problems outside of the session. This approach has been successful with African American women because many report that they are overwhelmed by their family's needs and demands (Boyd-Franklin, 2003). They commonly express ambivalence regarding these needs and demands because they are raised both to be independent and to help other family members in need (Boyd-Franklin, 2003).

It is important for therapists to assess whether the family therapy with one person approach is appropriate for an individual client. The first indication that this approach would be useful for Lakeshia was that she attributed many of her problems to her family concerns. Also, consistent with Boyd-Franklin's (2003) clinical observations, Lakeshia's ambivalence regarding receiving and giving emotional and financial support demonstrated that she was torn between the mainstream American value of individualism and the African American value of familial interdependence. The therapist noticed that those and other family issues often led to the self-defeating behaviors in school that furthered Lakeshia's depression.

Therapists may find that they have to counteract an automatic tendency to think in individual terms when seeing clients in individual treatment. Although Lakeshia's family lived too far away to participate in her treatment sessions, the family therapy with one person approach allowed her to address family issues. Because of geographical distance, anger, and the ambivalent and conflictual manner in which a value of interdependence may manifest, some therapists may mistakenly assume that African Americans only want to separate from their families, missing the other side of the client's internal struggle of independence versus interdependence. The family-oriented approach allowed Shalonda to explore both sides of this ambivalence in Lakeshia's treatment.

Shalonda gradually introduced family therapy with one person with Lakeshia, starting with normalizing reframes and cognitive interventions rather than requests for Lakeshia to take explicit actions toward her family. First, Shalonda framed the problem as Lakeshia's tendency to forget about her "life classes" when focused on academic work, so that Lakeshia would feel encouraged to put her family life on par with her depression and academic problems. After finding out more about Lakeshia's family relationships through the use of a genogram (Guerin & Pendagast, 1994), Shalonda introduced a ritual of "boxing" up her family problems so that each could be either pulled out and discussed or left on the shelf until a time when Lakeshia felt that she was strong enough to deal with it.

When discussing family issues, Shalonda began to normalize Lakeshia's feelings by providing alternate perspectives on her family's behavior. This included Shalonda's highlighting parents' common fears and hopes with regard to their child in college and characterizing Lakeshia's parents as a unit, which weakened Lakeshia's coalition with her mother and interrupted her pattern of demonizing her father. In addition, noting that Lakeshia tended to see herself as the reason that her mother stayed with her father, Shalonda reframed the situation as both parents' recognition of Lakeshia's worth and their desire to see her happy. And in an effort to engender Lakeshia's acceptance of both independence and interdependence, Shalonda encouraged Lakeshia to see that her parents made their own choices and that she could not help them emotionally or financially until she helped herself by developing the skills to stand on her own two feet. Cognitive behavioral methods of challenging her automatic negative interpretations of her father's behavior and feelings based upon objective evidence were also used.

The family therapy with one person approach often involves explicit coaching by the therapist on how to talk with key family members about important issues (Carter & McGoldrick-Orfanidis, 1994). Thus, Lakeshia's regular calls home increasingly included conversations with her father in addition to her mother. Still, Lakeshia continued to express strong anger at her father, despite frequent attempts at cognitive restructuring, and she also reported fears of talking directly with him about her negative feelings. Consequently, Shalonda used the "empty chair dialogue" gestalt technique (Greenberg, Rice, & Elliot, 1993; Peris, Hefferline, & Goodman, 1951) to counteract Lakeshia's homeostasis. Pretending that her father sat in the empty chair, she emotionally discussed her feelings that he did not fully support her, and that their relationship could "never be the same" because of it. Shalonda then emphasized that most people, including her parents, were not all good or all bad, and that maybe what she saw as her father's lack of support for her goals was related to his doubts regarding his own abilities. Prompted by Shalonda's requests for evidence to prove the veracity of Lakeshia's assumptions, Lakeshia began to provide ample evidence—of her father's caring, such as his keeping her picture on his nightstand and financially supporting higher education for her and not her sibling.

The systems concept of intergenerational transmission (Bowen, 1976) was then introduced to Lakeshia with the information that negative self-perceptions can be passed down and can prevent parents from seeing to their children's needs. Finally, Shalonda encouraged Lakeshia to imagine herself as a child in the chair and to give herself the nurturing that she missed from her father. Afterwards, Lakeshia said that she felt "lighter and better." About a year later, Lakeshia reported that her graduation goal had become a family goal, which had increased the closeness between Lakeshia and both of her parents.

Solution-Focused Methods of Highlighting Client Strengths

The solution-focused approach grew out of the strategic branch of systems theory, which holds that problems are based on family members' conceptual framework and there is no one reality. The solution-focused approach is unique in that it explicitly uses client strengths to engender change (Clark-Stager, 1999; De Shazer & Berg, 1993; Nichols & Schwartz, 1998) and emphasizes the construction of solutions as opposed to the solving of problems (Gingerich & Eisengart, 2000). According to the strategic branch of systems theory, clients' methods of dealing with their problems are logical and consistent according to how they view them (e.g., Haley, 1987). For clients who report "I can't change" or "I don't know how to change," a problem-centered focus may inhibit change (Miller, 1992). A solution-focused approach can help such clients to experience the problem differently by finding "exceptions" to a perceived lack of ability to change (Miller, 1992; Walter & Peller, 1992), and then building on these perceptions to engender a new, more positive perspective that can facilitate engagement in constructive behaviors (Friedman & Lipchik, 1999).

A solution-focused style of highlighting client strengths can also be helpful for therapists. For example, sessions dealing with Lakeshia's low self-esteem sometimes revealed that in some respects, Lakeshia and Shalonda had vastly different cultural values and methods of coping. Lakeshia's frequent denigration of her appearance led Shalonda to tell Nancy how she sometimes felt both sad for Lakeshia and angry with her, because Lakeshia's attitude went counter to Shalonda's racial pride. Lakeshia's lack of confidence in her academic abilities also frustrated Shalonda. Although everyone experiences self-doubt at times, Lakeshia's response of immobilization was the opposite of Shalonda's cultural value of responding through working harder. Beyond supporting Shalonda while she expressed her concerns, Nancy also discussed with Shalonda in supervision the theoretical benefits of refocusing clients on their own strengths, and she introduced an example of how they both use students' strengths in the teaching process. They noted that the use of strengths is compatible with both the solution-focused systems approach and the cognitive behavioral approach.

Shalonda's approach to her next sessions with Lakeshia was to identify and highlight positive "exceptions," particularly gains Lakeshia had made toward her goals. Once the frame of strengths was activated for Shalonda, she realized that there were many ways in which Lakeshia had improved in their sessions together. For example, Lakeshia had decided not to get pregnant by her drug-dealing boyfriend and then to end their relationship. Lakeshia's ability to set limits with her friends and also receive support from them had improved. She also continued to work toward her degree despite her depression. Moreover, Shalonda noticed, the pattern of highlighting Lakeshia's gains and teaching her to use the cognitive behavioral technique of positive self-talk brightened Lakeshia's affect and sparked further gains, particularly in academics.

Shalonda then introduced a technique to Lakeshia that was consistent with solution-focused premises. The technique involved comparing her current status on an area of concern to how she had coped with it in the last 6 months, which typically revealed many small accomplishments. This began to replace her former tendency to compare her current status to her fantasized status, which typically led to a focus on her overall life deficits and made her more depressed. Regarding Lakeshia's appearance, Shalonda had Lakeshia compare herself with other African American women. Lakeshia admitted that weight concerns did not prevent other African American women from having loving male partners. Her issues about weight were thus reframed more as health related concerns than as internal signs of inadequacy. Shalonda also spent part of a session looking in the mirror with Lakeshia, discussing signs of beauty, which led Lakeshia to acknowledge her nice features and conclude that "I don't look that bad." In addition, these interventions helped Shalonda to feel more connected to Lakeshia and more empowered to help her.

Selective Use of Self-Disclosure

Therapists' selective self-disclosure can be an extremely useful and powerful therapeutic tool. Care must be taken, however, to ensure that this disclosure of personal information to a client is done only under specific conditions. First, self-disclosure must be used selectively, and it should never be done for any reason other than for the benefit of the client. Second, the therapist must have had an experience or problem related to the client's issues that the therapist has already effectively coped with or solved. Thus, it is best not to use recent or emotion-laden experiences. Third, the therapist must feel confident that subsequent to the disclosure, she or he can still maintain her or his therapeutic relationship with the client, such that the client maintains respect and a belief in the therapist's credibility. Finally, it is very important that therapists not assume that their feelings mirror those of the client or that the client will see the similarity in their experiences. For this reason, statements such as "I know how you feel because . . ." or "I had a similar experience" should be avoided.

The shared racial and often cultural heritage of African American therapists and clients can often lead to a unique therapeutic alliance between them. In this situation, however, therapists must be careful to avoid inappropriate self-disclosures in the form of venting due to overidentification with these clients, which can be monitored in supervision. Clearly, there were many commonalities among the client, therapist, and supervisor in our case. We were all in an academic setting and were the most educated members of our families; we shared resources with our families; we valued both independence from and interdependence with our families; we shared our cultural heritage and the expression of emotion; and we had each experienced racism and discrimination in our personal and academic lives. This made self-disclosure an appropriate technique for Shalonda to use with Lakeshia.

If the client's knowledge of the therapist's personal experience will not bring an added benefit, however, self-disclosure may also be accomplished through a therapist's embedding of her or his personal experience in an anonymous educative statement. For example, Shalonda conveyed her positive experience with parental educational support by telling Lakeshia that it is common for parents who have not gone to college to want that opportunity for their children and to struggle with how to best help them in this new venture.

Based on their review of the literature, Hill and Knox (2002) concluded that therapist self-disclosures should be used to normalize, validate reality, model, strengthen the therapeutic relationship, and offer alternative behaviors to the client. They also note that multicultural theories advocate using self-disclosure as a means to show the client that the therapist is worthy of his or her trust (Hill & Knox, 2002). In addition to its use in facilitating the joining process by showing the client that the therapist can relate to his or her concerns, we also believe that when a client who otherwise respects the therapist still rejects problem-solving assistance, selective self-disclosure can help to reinforce the credibility of the solutions.

Over the course of treatment, Shalonda successfully used selective self-disclosure with Lakeshia in the areas of friendships, African American women's standards of beauty, and academics. When Lakeshia was unable to turn in academic work, despite her weekly resolutions, because her fear of submitting "shoddy" work led to neverending rewrites, Shalonda stressed the necessity of corrective feedback as a way of developing writing skills. When Lakeshia seemed skeptical, Shalonda disclosed the feedback she received regularly in her academic career that enabled her to hone her skills as a writer, such as in incorporating references into college papers, and currently, as a published author, in the peer review process.

Lakeshia was prone to discontinue friendships because of fears of rejection, and when she felt she was giving far more than she was getting in return. Cognitive behavioral efforts to challenge her negative assumptions with evidence and to build her relationship skills did not result in Lakeshia changing her habit of refusing to speak to friends once problems arose between them. Shalonda therefore disclosed how she came to realize the difficulty in expecting to have all her needs met by one person, and then began to accept what each of her friends had to offer. This intervention led Lakeshia to continue her friendship with someone she believed had let her down.

Shalonda's selective self-disclosure with Lakeshia regarding beauty involved a complex issue. The issue of skin color overlaid Lakeshia's feelings of low self-esteem related to her looks, as it does for many African American women. Lakeshia is dark skinned, with traditional African-derived features, and often identified herself as "ugly." Since slavery, American racism has valued light skin over dark skin and European features over African features. Sadly, these biases have resulted in the internalized racism of light skin color preferences in the Black community. Such biases have also resulted in the tendency for light-skinned individuals to receive more opportunities for educational and occupational advancement and higher socioeconomic status in American society than do dark-skinned individuals (Boyd-Franklin, 2003). We were aware that these realities presented a potential complicating factor in the treatment process because both Shalonda and Nancy are light skinned.

Shalonda decided to use selective self-disclosure, combined with psychoeducation, subsequent to several episodes in which Lakeshia denigrated her own appearance. Shalonda acknowledged that racism has often created a separation between dark-skinned and light-skinned African American women, and it has led many dark-skinned women to feel inferior because their type of beauty is undervalued in America. Shalonda explored Lakeshia's feelings of anger about this. To combat the feeling of alienation that this experience might engender in Lakeshia, and to take herself off the pedestal Lakeshia might have placed her on, Shalonda revealed that she and many women of differing hues sometimes have negative feelings about their appearance. When Lakeshia responded with surprise, Shalonda described her medical condition of rosacea, a facial skin condition that results in episodic red spots. It is important to note that while Shalonda normalized Lakeshia's concerns about her looks as a factor common to many women of any color, she did not minimize the trials that may be specific to dark-skinned women in this society. Shalona's combination of a normalizing reframe and respect for Lakeshia's experiences was repeated often in treatment. Because of Lakeshia's feelings of despair about her relationships, Shalonda also highlighted the men in Lakeshia's life who found her desirable. Given that Lakeshia's estimate of her own attractiveness increased over time, it is likely that this set of interventions helped.

The Supervisory Process and Relationship

The evolution of our supervisory relationship presented many challenges and excellent learning opportunities for both of us. The first of these challenges was the multiplicity of our roles. Similar to many professional women of color, our small number often forced on us the dilemma of balancing the boundaries of such complex personal and professional relationships as providing mentoring, supervision, and mutual support; being colleagues; sharing bonds as African American women; and developing our friendship. For example, there were times when an important event in both of our professional and personal lives required discussion and problem solving before case supervision began. In the beginning, we discussed these challenges openly, and then set clear boundaries around our clinical supervision. This set a tone for our evolving supervisory relationship. Ironically, the interconnections of our multiple roles and the support and meaningful challenges that they generated became an antidote to burnout for both of us (Boyd-Franklin, 2003).

The second important challenge for us related to differences in our theoretical orientations and training. Nancy was trained in a number of family systems models, such as Bowenian (Bowen, 1978), family therapy with one person (Carter & McGoldrick-Orfanidis, 1994), multisystemic, strategic, solution-focused, and narrative approaches, but she felt most comfortable with the structural, Bowenian, and multisystemic approaches. Shalonda's systems training was more general, and she integrated this approach with her cognitive behavioral orientation. At first, Nancy assumed more of a shared conceptual framework and would recommend a series of interventions, resulting in Shalonda's becoming "flooded" and alarmed at the differences in our styles and orientation. After we recognized the process, we clarified our different perspectives. Nancy learned to slow down and not assume commonality; Shalonda learned to speak up and assert her own theoretical perspective.

Through this process, an important supervisory goal emerged of helping Shalonda to find her own voice and clarify her unique treatment approach. As two strong African American women from a culture that values that strength, we learned to negotiate our points of view within the supervisory relationship (Aponte, 1994). This process, together with Shalonda's task of teaching theory and intervention in her classes, empowered Shalonda to fully articulate and own her theoretical orientation and interventions. It forced Nancy to examine the imbalanced power and authority dynamics inherent in most supervisory relationships and to struggle with her desire to make supervision an egalitarian, give-and-take process. This has produced innumerable insights and considerable growth for both of us.

Parallel Processes in Supervision and Treatment

Often, supervisor-therapist dynamics mirror therapist-client dynamics, as in this case, where supervisor, therapist, and client are all African American women. Our similarities facilitated joining and self-disclosure in both relationships. For example, the older girlfriend technique, phrases in Black dialect, and culturally related humor fit with all of our styles and backgrounds.

While there were many similarities between us, we were also reminded often of our different points of view. For example, while spirituality plays a role in each of our lives, as it does in the lives of many African American women, our individual experiences of spirituality are very different. Whereas Nancy expresses her spirituality privately and through her church family, Shalonda expresses it in daily prayer and is not religious. Moreover, we were both surprised to find that although Lakeshia attends church, she did not respond to interventions designed to apply her spirituality to her life problems. This emphasized a potential pitfall of assuming commonalities when supervisors, therapists, and clients are from the same racial or cultural group.

Another parallel process related to differences in our ages and stages in life. At the time, Nancy was 53, Shalonda was 33, and Lakeshia was 21. Because of Nancy's professional accomplishments, experience, and grounding in African American culture, Shalonda saw Nancy as a mentor and role model, while Lakeshia saw Shalonda as a role model for becoming a professional with a doctorate and for maintaining positive relationships. As a result of this process, Shalonda and Lakeshia both began to recognize their own power and strengths and gain the freedom to define their own identities. In family systems terms, each increased her *differentiation of self* in these relationships (Bowen, 1978).

Conclusion

This chapter provided a unique description of the parallel processes that can result when the supervisor, the therapist, and the client are African American women. We described complex and multilayered aspects of race, culture, and family backgrounds in treatment and in supervision. The most salient feature of the supervisory and treatment processes described is the necessity of a constant emphasis on strengths at both levels. It was this emphasis that allowed us to transcend our theoretical differences, because both family systems and cognitive behavioral approaches are strength based. It was also the focus on strength that ultimately resulted in empowerment and personal growth for the client, therapist, and supervisor alike.

Reflections, Questions, and Exercises

1. Consider your racial and ethnic background, your family influences and values, and your training as a therapist and/or supervisor. Which factors are most important in your own life?

2. Have you ever worked with a client of a similar background? How were the above variables similar and different for you and your client? How did these similarities and differences impact the treatment process? Did you find yourself using culturally related techniques or adapting your treatment to fit with values and factors that you consider to be characteristic of your own culture? If so, what adaptations did you make and why?

   a. Did the above similarities and differences between you and your client impact your ability to distinguish between healthy and unhealthy culturally related functioning? Did it raise questions or concerns about this issue in your mind?

3. Consider your clinical supervisory experiences. Have you ever supervised or been supervised by someone of a similar racial, ethnic, and/or family background? What were your similarities and differences? How did they influence the supervisory relationship?

   a. Were there differences in your theoretical orientation to treatment? What issues did these differences create in your relationship, and how did you negotiate them?

   b. How were both members of the supervisory dyad similar to and different from your racial and ethnic community as a whole?

4. Have you ever had an experience in which the client, therapist, and supervisor were all of a similar background? What were the dynamics that ensued from this set of relationships?

   a. What were the strengths apparent in the client, therapist, and supervisor in this experience? Were these strengths utilized in both the supervisory and treatment processes?

   b. Even with the similarities in your backgrounds, were there areas of difference in terms of how the three of you applied your values?

   c. Were there any parallel processes of the type discussed in this chapter?

5. What are the pros and cons of having similar racial and ethnic dyads in the therapeutic and supervisory relationship?

References

Aponte, H. (1994). *Bread and spirit: Therapy with the new poor.* New York: Norton.

Baldwin, J. A., Brown, R., & Rackley, R. (1990). Some socio-behavioral correlates of African self-consciousness in African American college students. *Journal of Black Psychology, 17,* 1–17.

Beck, A. T., Rush, A. J., Shaw, B., & Emery, G. (1987). *Cognitive therapy of depression.* New York: Guilford.

Blaine, B., & Crocker, J. (1995). Religiousness, race, and psychological well-being: Exploring social psychological mediators. *Personality and Social Psychology Bulletin, 21*, 1031–1041.

Bowen, M. (1976). Theory in the practice of psychotherapy. In P. J. Guerin (Ed.), *Family therapy: Theory and practice*. New York: Gardner.

Bowen, M. (1978). *Family therapy in clinical practice*. New York: Jason Aronson.

Boyd-Franklin, N. (2003). *Black families in therapy: Understanding the African American experience*. New York: Guilford.

Carter, E., & McGoldrick-Orfanidis (1994). Family therapy with one person and the family therapist's own family. In P. Guerin (Ed.), *Family therapy: Theory and practice*. New York: Gardner.

Clark-Stager, W. (1999). Using solution-focused therapy within an integrative behavioral couple therapy framework: An integrative model. *Journal of Family Psychotherapy, 10*(3), 27–47.

Dalaker, J. (2001). *Poverty in the United States: 2000*. Washington, DC: U.S. Census Bureau.

De Shazer, S., & Berg, I. K. (1993). Constructing solutions. *Family Therapy Networker, 12*, 42–43.

Friedman, S., & Lipchik, E. (1999). A time-effective, solution-focused approach to couple therapy. In J. M. Donovan (Ed.), *Short-term couple therapy* (pp. 325–359). New York: Guilford.

Gingerich, W. J., & Eisengart, S. (2000). Solution-focused brief therapy: A review of the outcome research. *Family Therapy, 39*(4), 477–498.

Greenberg, L. S., Rice, L., & Elliot, R. (1993). *Facilitating emotional change: The moment by moment process*. New York: Guilford.

Guerin, P. J., & Pendagast, E. G. (1994). Evaluation of the family system and genogram. In P. J. Guerin (Ed.), *Family therapy: Theory and practice*. New York: Gardner.

Haley, J. (1987). *Problem-solving therapy* (2nd ed.). San Francisco: Jossey-Bass.

Helms, J. E., & Cook, D. A. (1999). *Using race and culture in counseling and psychotherapy: Theory and process*. Boston: Allyn & Bacon.

Hill, C. E., & Knox, S. (2002). Self-disclosure. In J. C. Norcross (Ed.), *Psychotherapy relationships that work: Therapist contributions and responsiveness to patients*. New York: Oxford University Press.

Jackson, J. S., McCullough, W. R., Gurin, G., & Broman, C. L. (1991). Race identity. In J. S. Jackson (Ed.), *Life in Black America* (pp. 238–253). Newbury Park, CA: Sage.

Joiner, T. E., & Walker, R. L. (2002). Construct validity of a measure of acculturative stress in African Americans. *Psychological Assessment, 14*, 462–466.

Kelly, S. (2003a). African American couples: Their importance to the stability of African American families, and their mental health issues. In J. S. Mio & G. Y. Iwamasa (Eds.), *Culturally diverse mental health: The challenge of research and resistance* (pp. 141–157). New York: Brunner-Routledge.

Kelly, S. (2003b). *Underlying components of scores assessing African Americans' racial perspectives*. Manuscript submitted for publication.

Krieger, N., & Sidney, S. (1996). Racial discrimination and blood pressure: The CARDIA study of young Black and White adults. *American Journal of Public Health, 86,* 1370–1378.

Majors, R., & Billson, J. M. (1992). *Cool pose: The dilemmas of Black manhood in America.* New York: Simon & Schuster.

McLoyd, V. C. (1990). The impact of economic hardship on Black families and children: Psychological distress, parenting, and socioemotional development. *Child Development, 61,* 311–346.

Miller, S. D. (1992). The symptoms of solution. *Journal of Strategic and Systemic Therapies, 11*(1), 1–11.

Minuchin, S., & Fishman, H. C. (1981). *Family therapy techniques.* Cambridge, MA: Harvard University Press.

Nichols, M., & Schwartz, R. (1998). From strategic to solution focused: The evolution of brief therapy. In M. Nichols & R. Schwartz, *Family therapy: Concepts and methods* (pp. 355–396). Boston: Allyn & Bacon.

Niemann, Y. F., O'Connor, E., & McClorie, R. (1998). Intergroup stereotypes of working class Blacks and Whites: Implications for stereotype threat. *Western Journal of Black Studies, 22*(2), 103–108.

Oliver, M. B. (1999). Caucasian viewers' memory of Black and White criminal suspects in the news. *Journal of Communication, 49,* 46–60.

Oliver, M. B., & Fonash, D. (2002). Race and crime in the news: Whites' identification and misidentification of violent and nonviolent criminal suspects. *Media Psychology, 4,* 137–156.

Parham, T. A., & Helms, J. E. (1981). The influence of Black students' racial identity attitudes on preference for counselor's race. *Journal of Counseling Psychology, 28,* 250–257.

Peris, F., Hefferline, R., & Goodman, P. (1951). *Gestalt therapy.* New York: Delta.

Sanderson, W. C., & McGinn, L. K. (1999). Cognitive behavioral treatment of depression. In M. Weissman (Ed.), *Treatment of depression in the new millennium.* Washington, DC: American Psychiatric Association Press.

Stevenson, H. C. (1994). Validation of the scale of racial socialization for African American adolescents: Steps toward multidimensionality. *Journal of Black Psychology, 20,* 445–468.

Taylor, R. J., Mattis, J., & Chatters, L. M. (1999). Subjective religiosity among African Americans: a synthesis of findings from five national samples. *Journal of Black Psychology, 25,* 524–543.

Utsey, S. O., & Ponterotto, J. G. (1996). Development and validation of the Index of Race-Related Stress (IRRS). *Journal of Counseling Psychology, 43,* 490–502.

Walter, J. L., & Peller, J. E. (1992). *Becoming solution-focused in brief therapy.* New York: Garland.

6

Taking Off the Mask

Breaking the Silence—The Art of Naming Racism in the Therapy Room

Larry Jin (Kwok Hung) Lee

I'd rather not see an Asian doctor. My experience with them is that they are cold and unfeeling. You never know what they're thinking. But you, you're okay.

—A client

In my almost 20 years of clinical practice and supervision of trainees, I have heard countless comments, such as the above example, that have evoked what I think of as an internal wince. Most of these comments have gone unanswered primarily because I could not pull up any templates from my training that prepared me to respond to these upsetting encounters. On most of these occasions, I have been caught off guard and felt paralyzed. As a therapist, I had been indoctrinated to bypass issues of oppression and race as presenting problems. I had learned to perceive such issues as completely discrete from my role as a psychotherapist. Social workers and therapists are instructed to focus on individuals and their presenting problems and symptoms, not to change societal phenomena such as racism and intolerance. Consequently, I unconsciously held the belief that there was no room to engage in these conversations therapeutically. However, I discovered that absorbing these disturbing and hurtful statements and accepting them in passive silence began to take their toll on my use of self and authenticity with clients. These off-handed, mindless statements had a cumulative, caustic effect. I struggled to be fully present with clients and colleagues who implicitly or explicitly expressed racist attitudes. I felt I was losing trust in my intuition, which I relied on to feel effective and connected to myself and my clients. I began to wonder if my predicament was unique or whether there were other clinicians of color who experienced the weight of carrying this pain. My silent collusion with these racially tinged innuendos aroused in me a growing sense of shame that I was somehow betraying myself and what I believed was sound ethical and socially just practice.

Racist comments—both inadvertent and blatant—fueled an urgency within me to find constructive ways to cope with the frustration I experienced. This was the genesis of my search for models that demonstrated how to harness the energy of this pain. I therefore invited practitioners of color, and others who were willing to engage with me around this unspoken frustration, to think these quandaries through with me. I also began to scour the professional literature hoping to find that I was not alone in my struggle. Much to my dismay, I discovered there was a dearth of practical, balanced, real-life based models written on how to engage in treatment narratives around oppression. There was even less on therapists' effective use of self and on their internal process vis-à-vis their experience of racism in the therapy encounter. I hope that through this chapter I can invite many of you to think out loud with me, to take off the masks that have covered our authenticity around the powerful unspoken dialogues about oppression and racism. With our clients and with each other, let us begin to break the silence.

Personal Background

I am a native-born San Franciscan. My grandparents and parents were born in Canton, China. My great-grandfather came to the United States in the late 1800s, as many men did, to find some way to survive and to send aid home to his family, who were suffering as a result of famine, oppression, and war. I grew up in an extended family with my grandparents and my uncle and his family. Living with my grandparents as such strong figures in my life provided ample opportunity for me to retain much of my Chinese heritage and culture.

Very early in my life, I played the role of the translator and mediator of the English-speaking world for my parents and grandparents, helping the elders negotiate the demands of bill collectors, mail, forms, and phone calls. I struggled with the role and resisted it at times, but in retrospect, I believe this responsibility shaped my sensitivity to the situation of being the other and on the outside. Ironically, I also experienced being the other within the culture of my parents.

A pivotal aspect of my childhood was that my grandparents, my parents, and other adults of their generation would frequently use a pejorative Cantonese term for American-born Chinese—*jooksing,* which is translated literally as "empty bamboo," all form with no substance. And I often heard my father refer to me as *mo know* ("brainless"). It has been a common experience in my life to feel caught in the empty space between the American and Chinese cultures. My awareness of this emptiness became even more acute in 1989 after my son's birth, when I realized that if I did not change this situation, I would be passing the emptiness on to him.

The experience I am about to describe was significant in my search for my bicultural identity and equilibrium. A few years ago, my family and I took a vacation in a predominantly White area where we received the looks and stares that communicate "You don't belong." This was the type of place where I would be asked where I learned to speak English so well, as the people there found it cognitively dissonant for a Chinese person to speak perfect English. On our way home from the airport, we went to a Chinese restaurant, where I found myself in an argument with the Cantonese-speaking waiter; he had brought food I didn't order, even though I had ordered in Cantonese. I had to argue in English, because when I get angry, it's in English. I had to endure hearing the staff in the restaurant call me names in Cantonese: the brainless, stupid American-born Chinese. At home afterward, I found myself enveloped by a profound despair. It was almost visceral: I felt like I was suffocating. What I felt in being a *jooksing* was culturally and psychologically homeless. The depth of my emptiness was profound, and I knew at that moment that I had to be vigilant in my search for substance to fill that emptiness. I had to do this for the sake of my son and, subsequently, my daughter, who was born in 1998. I felt fragmented and disintegrated, but I needed to learn how to equip my children with the tools to be whole. Learning how to do this has been an ongoing process. Not coincidentally, there has been a parallel process occurring in my professional development as I have searched for more effective models for working across difference. Surprisingly, I have come to learn to embrace the space itself, because space is what makes the bamboo useful and resilient.

Professional Background

I began my career in a community mental health clinic in San Francisco, where I specialized in working with adolescents and families. The next phase of my journey brought me to Kaiser HMO, first in the department of psychiatry and most recently in behavioral medicine in the department of medicine. In addition to my clinical work, I have held academic positions in graduate psychology and social work programs and provided training and workshops as a diversity consultant. Throughout the past 20 years, I have found a common thread in my experience that I can best describe as a nagging restlessness about a collusion of silence around oppression and racism in clinical work.

Racism continues to be this country's dirty little secret. Similar to secrets in a familial context, not naming its existence fuels its power. It also involves magical thinking—that if we don't see it, then it doesn't exist. It is anathema to allude to racism as a viable reality on our professional radar screens. I struggled with the irrationality of trying to extract the dynamics of racism, privilege, and oppression from the therapeutic experience while immersed in the historical and societal context of racism. We are continually informed by the unique multiple contexts that define our daily realities and our position in the world. Many of the contexts we carry unconsciously involve the trauma of racism and oppression, dominance and subjugation. It is essential to understand the power of these contexts in working with clients of color. These can be points of connection or contention, contingent upon our denial or awareness of the impact of these schemas within the therapeutic milieu.

The Power of Context: Cultural Templates

Everything we do is embedded within multiple contexts of collective and individual historical events that culminate in present day encounters. Unfortunately, the historical impact of racism still reverberates in our lives today. For example, a young African American man who was experiencing recurrent anxiety was referred to me by his primary care physician. As specified by initial evaluation procedure, I inquired about his past and current substance use. He disclosed that he had been smoking marijuana daily since the age of 16. At the end of our session, I suggested that he be evaluated by our chemical dependency services and made an appointment for him.

Initially, it appeared that he agreed to the treatment proposal. Then he had second thoughts:"Wait, I don't want this appointment. I told you that

I wanted to deal with my anxiety, not my 'addiction' problem. I mean, would you refer a White man, if he told you that he drank two or three martinis every night, for substance abuse treatment?" Stunned and off balance, I was caught between thinking, "Have I been stereotyping, driven by an unconscious racist ideological script?" and "Is this the manipulation and wiles of an addict in denial?" The answer is most likely that both truths were viable. What could possibly have been the cultural schema that was activated by this interaction with this African American man? Would it have made a difference if these issues had been made explicit? What I was reminded of by this interchange was that racial and cultural templates have tremendous salience in what may appear to be simple routine encounters.

It is a powerful realization that such a brief exchange can tap into the energy of multiple historical legacies and stories of our collective struggles with the issues of racial oppression, learned roles, and stereotypes. If I had been a White clinician, I believe the contextual tension would have been even more apparent. Also, such interactions can be as evocative with a therapist of color and a White client.

I saw a White man and his family in a session. He owned his own tech company and had many Asians working for him. At one point, he vehemently disagreed with his wife. In an attempt to slow things down, I interjected with a process comment and was met with "Don't you interrupt me when I'm speaking. I don't need your help. I can handle this very well without your interference. You know, I really don't know if you are really qualified to help us. I work with a lot of Asians and see that we're different."

What cultural templates were operative here? What are the relevant power issues that were activated, and what impact do they have on the Chinese American therapist and the White client? It is not uncommon for me to find myself in the dissonant and at times awkward position of being a Chinese American psychotherapist with White clients. Where I am stereotypically seen as quiet, unassuming, and accommodating, imbued with little institutional power within the context of society, in a therapeutic milieu with White clients, I am in a position of comparatively more power. This is probably the only environment where I can consistently experience power in relation to White men. I believe that this unfamiliar power dynamic can induce anxiety in White male clients. The unspoken question is, "Can these exchanges be opportunities for mutual growth and learning?"

The frustrating reality of these potentially powerful moments where racial and therapeutic dynamics intersect is that few choose to openly acknowledge the importance of this dimension of clinical practice. At best, these narratives are relegated to closed-door discussions between clinicians of color hoping to receive validation. At worse, these flash point encounters get internalized and absorbed by therapists of color and stored in hidden containers of frustration and shame. Therapists in such situations are left second-guessing about what they *should* have said, and they walk away with the feeling that they silently colluded in their own oppression. There is a tremendous price to pay in perpetuating the silence around racism.

There continues to be an investment in not naming racism. The diagnostic manuals (e.g., *DSM-IV*) that guide our treatment planning and interventions do not name racism as a pathology or an illness. Early diagnostic nomenclature such as *drapetomania* characterized behaviors such as acting out against slavery as pathological, absolving the oppressor of responsibility.

This historical bias within our profession and in the larger context of this country reinforces our collective denial and unconsciousness around racial legacies of pain. There is no precedent for the dominant group taking responsibility for their oppressive actions. A side effect of this silent collusion is that we and our clients meet at racial fault lines where cultural templates collide and people of color are made to hold onto their anger and helplessness, without a clue as to how to describe what is happening. I believe the answer to this problem lies in our profession's willingness to question some basic tenets of practice—in particular, therapeutic neutrality and the notion that the therapeutic encounter is immune to racism.

The Context of Power and Privilege

An important part of the solution to racism in clinical practice is that White clinicians need to examine the contexts of power and privilege that pervade every encounter with a client or colleague of color. To deny the impact and existence of these contexts is irresponsible practice. To illustrate the notion of taking responsibility for White contexts of power, I will use a particularly difficult exchange that I had at a conference on racism and clinical practice.

At this conference, the participants had been divided into groups of four to five people. There were two groups in which there was only one woman in a group of White men. These two women happened to be women of color. When we were checking in about what had occurred in our respective groups, both women disclosed that they had felt invisible and did not get a chance to speak. One male participant interjected that this might have been a result of sexism. The facilitator noted that these two individuals were not only women but also women of color, implying that there may have been a racial context to this scenario. At this point, one White male denied that it was sexism or racism; rather, it was just plain old rude behavior on his part. This elicited a laugh in the room, but many people of color did not find it funny.

At that moment I felt I had to make a point about the power of context, and one's intent versus one's impact. I expressed that I, as a male therapist, have to be conscious of what I embody purely based on the context of my gender when sitting in a therapy room with a woman who has been sexually or physically abused or both. Most White clinicians have absolutely no problem accepting this as ethical and responsible practice. However, when I make this very same point in the context of working with a person of color who has experienced repeated trauma by White people, or who had been a victim of a hate crime, White clinicians defensively respond that they are not racist or responsible for this client's victimization. Many of the White people, particularly the white men, in the room vehemently disassociated themselves from being White. One White man claimed his sexual orientation rather than his Whiteness as his identity. Another person exclaimed, "You don't know anything about me. You're assuming that I'm White!" I wondered, "What would your clients see?" This person looked White. I felt both incensed and confused. It is the epitome of White privilege to have the benefits of being White and yet be able to exercise the choice of identifying as White or denying it and claiming another identification. It may be convenient for therapists to invoke this right and believe they are thus absolved of the responsibility for the privilege conferred by their Whiteness and its unspoken power over oppressed individuals, but it does not serve their clients.

I thought to myself, "Why would caring, compassionate healers embrace empathy in one situation of trauma but absolve themselves of professional responsibility in a similar scenario?" Frankly, I find their response frightening because I would not want to be treated by a clinician who would deny or was unconscious of the power he or she has to potentially replicate the very trauma that brought me into therapy. Just as I would not deny that I, as a male, represent the perpetrator to an abused woman, it is incumbent upon a White therapist not to deny that she or he could represent the oppressor to a person of color. I believe that a key developmental step in becoming a culturally competent therapist is developing the ability to be fully aware of and to tolerate what you represent, while at the same time being present with the reality that you are not the perpetrator. In other words, there is enough room for two truths to exist:

1. You are not the perpetrator and the fear and anger is not about you specifically.

2. You carry some racist ideology. You represent the threat of a potential perpetrator based on your context of being, for example, White and male, which possesses a power unto itself.

I would add that this attitude of not acknowledging privilege categorically silences and invalidates the reality of people of color. Therefore, a cornerstone of culturally literate practice is practitioners' willingness to commit to full awareness of the use of their contexts of dominance and power. Clinicians are the "brokers of permission" and dictate what can or cannot be expressed in the therapy room (Hardy, 1998).

I have heard disclaimers from therapists that they cannot take responsibility for this type of displaced anger or emotion. There are claims that therapeutic neutrality is the best guiding principle in these clinical scenarios. These are ineffective positions at best, and they are clinically irresponsible in some situations. I have also heard therapists explain that the key to dealing with such a situation is to redirect a client's racial anger back to a symptom focus, a safe therapeutic default. Imagine being a client who has struggled to get in touch with her or his anger over racial trauma or violence and is being redirected to manage anxiety symptoms. Clearly therapists need to ask themselves, Is therapy practice supposed to preserve the comfort of the clinician? Or should it be focused on the best interests of the client?

One defining quality of a seasoned mental health professional is that person's ability to be fully present in the face of an angry client who sees him or her as the oppressor. How can the therapist hold and provide space for this pain and emotion? How can this anger be used to heal and empower the client? How might the therapist overtly or inadvertently shut this down? What implications are there for re-injury and/or invalidation, for silencing the victim once again?

The Double Bind

Therapists are placed in a double bind whether they choose to speak up or remain silent about racism. Why is there so much investment in preserving the silence around racism in clinical practice? While some of the explanations may be obvious, others may not be as readily apparent. I have heard White clinicians frequently express fears that they may say the wrong thing and come off sounding racist themselves. They describe the predicament of naming race in treatment and inadvertently offending a client of color (e.g., the client who says, "Why are you bringing up racism? Just because I'm Latino?") versus not naming race—even when it is begging for attention—and then being blamed for being insensitive and unaware. As one of my colleagues expressed in frustration,

It's just not worth taking the risk. I realize that I don't have much experience talking about racism to others outside of the therapy context and even less so within the practice context. I don't like feeling out of control or vulnerable. So it is easier for me just to not bring up the issue. I'd rather be accused of being unaware than be called a racist.

In the situation of a White therapist with a White client who expresses racist attitudes, the therapist who does not confront the racism is understood as colluding with the client's racist beliefs. On the one hand, a silent therapist appears to be aligning with the oppressor; on the other hand, a confronting therapist may be accused of being judgmental, invalidating, and evoking guilt.

For clinicians of color, the dilemmas are even more acute. In the instance of the therapist of color with a White client who espouses racial intolerance, there is a parallel double bind because if the therapist takes a therapeutically neutral position, he or she is left holding a reactivated anger and injury—in essence, colluding with his or her own victimization; however, if the therapist actively speaks up and confronts the racism, he or she risks having the client deny the racism or accuse the therapist of misinterpreting what was said. Clients may also claim that they are not responsible for the therapist's racial issues or express how hurt they are for being accused of a racial act. The therapist is then in the position of soothing and taking care of the client. The examples from therapy included in this chapter are reconstructed from memory based on actual exchanges I have had with my clients; the ellipses in this material represent pauses. The example that follows illustrates the slippery slope of addressing racism in therapy:

Client: You know, you have to watch them Mexicans. They'll steal the rug out from under you if you let them.

Therapist: What do you mean by that?

Client: (Immediately getting defensive) Hey, don't get me wrong, I'm not a racist or anything like that. I work with a lot of them. I have just had some negative experiences with them that make me suspicious.

Therapist: Do you think that all Mexicans steal and can't be trusted?

Client: (Defensive and hurt) Hey, man, are you saying I'm a racist for what I said? You're a therapist and you're making me feel like a bad person.

It can be overwhelming to consider the range of situations you can encounter with clients and colleagues. However, retreating from these situations potentially places our profession in the position of being another system of oppression. It is important for us to revise some of our attitudes to address the *whole* person—to make room for the daily lived realities of people of color within our practices. It is increasingly obvious that we need to develop the art rather than just the skills of culturally literate practice. In the remaining part of this chapter, I will present an approach to working with oppressed individuals.

Creating the Container: A Safe Place

I approach this part of the chapter with some reluctance because there are no formulas to propose. To develop effectiveness across differences requires a deep and patient commitment to "not knowing," to the humility of a beginner's mind. I was not encouraged to embrace this virtue during my training because much of my professional identity, in particular being a clinician of color, was premised on being as competent as possible, without room for struggle or mistakes. The measure of my success or failure was based on outcome, not process. Upon reflection, I wish that I had understood how doing nothing—watching while embracing the discomfort of not knowing—could be the best learning strategy. My greatest learning has come from situations in which I was willing to take risks, feel uncomfortable, and let go of safe, familiar, unquestioned beliefs. I invite you to be willing to do likewise as you join me in exploring a different, possibly better use of self and context to meet people of color in a more equitable place.

Test Shots: Assessing for
Safety, Looking for Permission

One of the most powerful and poignant moments I have experienced was during a workshop where an African American woman disclosed, "My whole life is about *never* feeling safe." What was moving about this statement was the way she expressed it from her soul. I could feel the ache of her spirit and the longing for the safety that we call home. I found myself connecting with her despair. It was a pivotal moment in my struggle to understand racism and the role of our healing profession with regard to it. I wondered, Is therapy a safe place for disclosing racial injury and the pervasive sense of devaluation and despair one experiences living as the other?

What really happens in therapy when a person of color brings up such painful feelings? How would a person of color feel a sense of safety with a therapist? What cues would she or he be attuned to?

In therapy, the potential for harm is high, but so is the opportunity for a corrective experience. Most clients do not come into treatment presenting their oppression or devaluation experience as a primary complaint. Similarly, we wouldn't expect a sexually abused woman to initiate a discussion about sexuality without trepidation. Such experiences usually come out couched in the context of some life situation or event. I wish to provide some case examples from my practice to illustrate how clients put out "test shots" to assess the level of safety in and permission for bringing up racial issues. I have also provided some questions for you to ponder before I present how I, in my context as a 45-year-old Chinese American therapist, helped the client. While reading these vignettes, consider whether you have had clients who expressed similar feelings in your sessions with them. Most important, I invite you to closely examine how you, in your unique contexts, could use your *self* to connect with each client.

Case 1

Case Vignette

A 53-year-old African American woman was referred by her primary care physician for uncontrolled hypertension, irritable bowel symptoms, and fatigue. She complains about having been responsible for others all of her life, first for her siblings and then as a single parent for three sons. She is especially concerned about her 23-year-old son, who is in college but quite irresponsible with his money. She then says in exasperation, "Do you have any idea what it is like to have to raise three Black sons in this country? You would worry too."

Questions

- How would you respond to or answer her question?
- From your contextual position, how would you validate and affirm her daily lived experience?
- How would you connect with her struggle and accomplishment without sounding patronizing?
- How would you frame the racial context in connection with her medical issues?

Therapeutic Process

Therapist: First of all, I'd like to ask your permission to comment on your question. Would that be okay, because I'm not sure if you wanted me to answer it.

Client: Certainly. I appreciate your asking me.

Therapist: I'd like to say that I am honored that you were willing to tell me a bit about your life story, having to be responsible and caretaker at such a young age and for so much of your life. (Checking in, watching for nonverbal cues) Feel free to tell me if I'm not hearing you correctly. The part that I feel the strongest emotion about [in] what you said was that your experience of raising three African American sons in this country was and is a very difficult and stressful process, and your worry hasn't stopped even though they are grown. Am I missing anything so far? (Client leaning in, listening closely) But there's one thing that I know you didn't say, but if you don't mind, I need to say now. Please feel free not to agree with it . . . I don't want to put words in your mouth. (Preparing to bring race into the room and name it, providing permission and space for this part of her story) When I imagine having to raise African American male sons, I think about the struggles with race and discrimination—how it is a constant battle and struggle. Am I in the ballpark with this?

Client: Thank you (body cues communicate relief). I don't talk about this to very many people, especially non-Black people. I never want anyone to think I am making excuses or looking for pity. I was always taught to keep your business to yourself and to never let on about what you really feel, because it could come back at you. My heart breaks when my eldest son tells me how even though he is a manager at work that people still ask him for I.D. when he is walking to his car when he works late. There's nothing I can do to help him. (Continuing to share about her sons' experiences and then about her own growing up in Louisiana, her body seems to release tension as she talks, even though she is tearful)

Therapist: I want to let you know that I deeply appreciate your strength. I believe you and everything you have told me about you and your sons. I also acknowledge that I, as a Chinese man, do not have the same experience and in some ways have privileges that your sons don't. I especially want to acknowledge and respect (a very important word to use authentically and at the right time) how you have carried the pain, worry, and anger of your family and children for so many years. That is the love you have provided for your children (client sobbing). It is my hope to assist you to address now how it has affected your health and how you can help yourself. Would that be okay?

Client: Yeah, thank you. I think I'd better.

Case 2

I include this example to illustrate how race can come up in therapy with a White client.

Case Vignette

A 46-year-old White woman was referred for stress symptoms secondary to her work environment. She feels that her coworkers are uncooperative and do not carry their share of the work. In her second session, she is more specific about her problems at work. She says with contempt, "I don't get it with these people. The ones who do speak English have an attitude and a chip on their shoulder, and the ones who don't speak English—well, who knows what they're thinking, chattering away in their separate corner."

Questions

- What is the racial subtext of this client's comments? What groups is she implicating?
- How does a therapist balance the need to "name the problem" and address the unspoken racism with the need to validate and support the client?
- If you were the therapist, what would hold you back from directly addressing the racial issues?
- What would be different for a clinician of color versus a White therapist in this situation?

Therapeutic Process

Therapist: (Struggling to stay connected in the face of the racial subtext) I believe that you do work hard or you wouldn't be experiencing the symptoms of stress that you have. May I ask you to describe the people you work with a bit more specifically; for instance, what ethnic or racial groups are you referring to?

Client: In my department, there are mostly African Americans, Filipinos, and a few Mexicans. There's only one other White person in my department, but I don't work directly with her. Most of them are in management. I don't get to see them much.

Therapist: Would you be so kind as to tell me again what you have the most difficulty with at your workplace?

Client: (Hesitant, thoughtful) Well, the workload is unreasonable, the people I work with . . . we don't work together. They seem to do their own thing . . . separately. Everyone is with their own group.

Therapist: Do you feel alone or excluded? (Trying to stay focused on the client's issue, not my own experience of exclusion and the implication of reverse discrimination)

Client: Sometimes, but I do my work fine. Don't get me wrong. I mean . . . I'm not prejudiced or anything like that. I just can't get them to cooperate.

(Most of the staff and management are White and male. Her department is on the lower end of the organizational hierarchy.)

Therapist: Well let's look at this. I do believe that we all carry around certain preconceptions about each other. Perhaps you even had a take on me as a Chinese therapist when you saw me for the first time. I call these preconceptions cultural templates. They are passed on to us by our parents, and they can be powerful influences on how we have learned to relate to or not to relate to others who are different from us. First of all, I want to acknowledge and respect that you want to find a better way to collaborate with your coworkers and to function more effectively as a unit. I'm just wondering, Why do you suppose these groups of people would want to stay separate or in their small groups?

Client: Well, uhh . . . I guess based on what you're saying, everyone likes to hang around with people like them.

Therapist: Exactly, and you're telling me that you feel alone and excluded where you work. Is that a new experience for you?

Client: I think in this way, yes.

Therapist: It is not a good experience to have with any regularity (client nodding). I want to say that I realize this is hard, to talk about races and differences. So please feel free to tell me if you are not okay with continuing.

Client: I'm okay with it.

Therapist: So you describe a company that has people of color in service positions and not really included in any decision making. Do your coworkers in your department ever tell you about how they feel their needs are addressed by the organization?

Client: Yeah, they complain about feeling like they're second class citizens and not taken seriously.

Therapist: Do you feel this way, too—kind of powerless?

Client: I absolutely do! (Dramatic body language)

Therapist: Well, can I be perfectly honest with you about my reaction to what you were telling me earlier about your reactions to your coworkers? (Taking a risk in an attempt to balance authentically naming race and continuing to provide space and safety) The first time you made your statement about the attitudes of your coworkers and your feelings about people speaking in languages other than English, I had a reaction. It felt as though you did not like these types of people. I imagine your coworkers feel just as powerless as you do about the work and the work environment. Do you think they may be keeping their distance from you because they sense that you don't accept them? Perhaps even that they are distrustful of you because you are White? (Client looking a bit irritated) Let me check in with you about what you're feeling about what I'm saying.

Client: I'm not sure if I understand what you're saying. I have tried to be nice.

Therapist: I believe you. The templates that I mentioned are very strong, and because of them everyone loses. I don't condone anyone being excluded. I see that the bigger problem is with the organization of a workplace in which people feel this sense of distrust, of being invisible and discounted. I wonder if you have more in common with your coworkers than you think. As in society, prejudice and racism affects everyone. None of us is to blame for how this came to be, but we need to find ways not to perpetuate it.

Client: So . . . you're not calling me a racist, right?

Therapist: I think we have all been inundated by stereotypes that have given us misinformation about each other. This is how we are all affected by racism. (Feeling a bit impatient with having to take care of a White person and her unconscious racism and yet empathizing with her experience) Again, I want to acknowledge that it is a very difficult environment you work in and that you do work hard.

Case 3

I have included this hypothetical example as an exercise—a case for you to think about.

Case Vignette

A 38-year-old Mexican American man was referred by his physician for symptoms of somatization. He had had many medical tests and the results were unremarkable. His primary care physician is frustrated at his persistent complaints and visits, stating, "I can't satisfy this guy. He won't take no for an answer. It's all in his head!" The client is in management and reports that he has had to "fight and struggle" for everything in his life. He sees his actions with health care and his doctor as being proactive and assertive. In the third session, he indignantly states, "I think Dr. Smith (a White doctor) is not taking me seriously. He thinks I'm crazy! He even told me to leave his office one time. I have experienced this over and over again in my life."

Questions

- What is the subtext of the statement "I have experienced this over and over again in my life"? (the test shot) If you were the therapist, what theme in this client's life would you say he wants you to validate?
- What message (subtext) was conveyed by the doctor to this client that has upset him? How might you replicate this message to the client?

- What might you say that would encourage further disclosure of his struggle and racial oppression? What might you say that may "blame the victim"?

These case vignettes and process accounts illustrate just one approach to promoting a safe space for therapeutic dialogue about race. I wanted to present a cross-section of how clients present the masked faces of racial issues in the treatment interface. As you may have noticed, some clients present the desire to disclose their racial predicament in more obvious terms, while others were more veiled about their intention. In the case of the White client, there was probably no intention of initiating a racially focused dialogue. This case specifically illustrates the clinician of color's necessary response in naming the unspoken racial context. As I mentioned previously, some therapists will refuse to acknowledge racism even when it is explicitly expressed. It is worth thinking about what the consequences are of not recognizing these test shots.

I also wish to make one final point about the cases that I selected to include in this chapter. The faces of our clients go beyond just Black and White. Including additional ethnic cases would be beyond the scope of this chapter. However, I wish to emphasize that there is tremendous depth and variety in the way these issues can present themselves (e.g., a client's shame around her or his accent or ability to speak English, a collectivist versus individualist orientation and its impact on the therapeutic interaction).

Disconnection: Dual Consciousness, False Selves

There is a learned coping response that people of color have developed as a consequence of having to endure the repeated experience of being dismissed, invalidated, and made invisible. This response serves to create distance and disconnection, thus providing protection against further acts of shame and invalidation. I call this the flight into a false self or activation of a dual consciousness. Once the client senses a lack of permission or safety, this mask or coping tool manifests itself in the client's deference to authority figures or making a White person or therapist feel comfortable. This can take on the form of the client's being overly ingratiating, saying what the therapist wants to hear, or discounting what he or she has expressed that may have caused discomfort. A client may manifest this by an excessive use of "thank you" or meticulous attention to addressing the therapist as "doctor" repeatedly or, at worst, by minimizing his or her own needs in order to help the clinician feel more competent. The mask of accommodation thus becomes predominant in the treatment, and the energy of treatment shifts away from the client in the direction of the therapist. Neither the client nor the therapist is well served by this situation.

Furthermore, it is frustrating to hear therapists, in service of protecting their own competency, describe clients as being psychologically unsophisticated or concrete. This amounts to blaming the victim or pathologizing the client's behavior. Practitioners can actually believe that they have been effective in their interventions and are left dumbfounded when clients do not return for a follow-up session. I have also heard clinicians express confusion and frustration when they discover that their client has not complied with a treatment suggestion, stating, "I don't get it. I remember the client smiling and nodding his head in agreement when I was making this suggestion. I really thought we were on the same page." Many people of color are so attuned to shame issues that it doesn't take much to derail the flow of therapeutic energy away from the client toward the therapist.

Even in my own life, I have always known that I floated from one persona to another, almost imperceptibly, accommodating to one set of rules and expected behaviors at home and another set of rules outside of my home. DuBois (1906/1994) described this survival mechanism many decades ago in reference to African American slaves who had to develop a dual consciousness in order to survive through the horror of slavery. Many of us have had to learn the rules of a dominant power group in order to function and be successful. Women have had to stifle certain dimensions of their personalities to avoid threatening men or bringing unwanted, negative attention onto themselves. In *Reviving Ophelia*, Pipher (1995) referred to the false self that develops as a result of persistent messages from the dominant group with regard to their expectations and prohibitions. Pipher described how one must be *better than* the norm just to be provisionally accepted into the fold. In the same way, clinicians of color must also wear this mask of accommodation to function with colleagues and clients who make inflammatory statements and to maintain their professionalism and be provisionally accepted.

The mask of accommodation is a powerful coping tool to protect the self from harm ("You can't hurt me if I keep my true self hidden"), as well as a way for a person to get what she or he wants in spite of racism. Hardy (1993) captured this behavior powerfully in what follows:

> To avoid being seen by Whites as troublemakers, we suppress the part of ourselves that feels hurt and outraged by the racism around us, instead developing an "institutional self"—an accommodating façade of calm professionalism calculated to be non-threatening to Whites. To survive in the White world, African Americans learn to become "good, effective, mainstream minorities" or what I call a GEMM. I have found that when I am in my GEMM-mode, Whites approve of me and wonder, "Why can't all black people be like Ken?" (p. 52)

I, myself, worked hard to put on the mask of ultra competency. I honed my ability to be impeccably articulate in order to gain entry into the White world. As an example of how well I presented this false self, I recall being thanked by clients for not having an accent; in my unconscious days, I actually thanked them for the compliment.

As clinicians we need to be attuned to the brief moments where we can connect and engage in these healing conversations. We must respect the energy it takes for the client to hold these stories for long periods of time before there is the safe space to disclose them. The consequences of silencing these voices can be profound for clients of color. How do we create the container of safety to promote these disclosures? How do we create the safe space? I wish to take the opportunity to present a framework within which this can be facilitated.

Therapist as Authentic, Compassionate Witness: The Art of Being Fully Present

> *Please call me by my true names, so that I can wake up and so the door of my heart can be left open, the door of compassion.*
>
> —Hanh (1987, p. 64)

I have found it useful to draw from trauma and abuse theory to define guidelines for healing the hidden wounds of racism. I will borrow relevant applications from Herman's (1997) treatise in *Trauma and Recovery,* as well as from Ina's (2001) Compassionate Witness model, which she developed in her work with survivors of the Japanese concentration camp experience. Both authors propose a triad model that can facilitate a deeper conceptual understanding of what plays out in situ during a therapeutic exchange.

In working with a client of color who has experienced racial trauma, as with all trauma, there exist symbolic representations of three entities that were present in the original perpetration of the injury or crime: the victim, the perpetrator, and the witness.

Trauma Triad

Victim
(Client, Therapist, Colleague)

Witness   Perpetrator
(Client, Therapist, Colleague)   (Client, Therapist, Colleague)

When a client revisits or a therapist recreates the "scene of the crime," that person essentially invokes the symbolic presence and power of the victim, perpetrator, and witness in the therapy room. At any time, the therapist or client can fall into any one of these roles.

Therapist as Perpetrator

The therapist can easily be the perpetrator when a client is making herself or himself vulnerable in retelling a narrative about her or his racial experience. In the case with the 38-year-old Mexican American man, an example of a therapist-perpetrator response would be,

> Perhaps we should examine why you don't get taken seriously so often in your life. Did you wonder whether perhaps you are taking the wrong approach in getting your needs met and that is why you keep getting the same frustrating result? You may need to look at your attitude. I don't believe that Dr. Smith is treating you any differently than he treats any other patient. I think you may have misunderstood him.

Even if a therapist doesn't express this verbally to the client, the highly sensitized client can potentially read the nonverbal cues of the therapist. These cues often take the form of a fluctuation in attention, a poorly timed sigh, a disinterested expression, or other body language that conveys disconnection or negative judgment. In this response to the client, the clinician blames and invalidates the victim and unfairly places the responsibility of change onto the client. At the moment of disclosure, the already injured client is fearful of re-injury, shame, minimization, invalidation, and devaluation. Clients have expressed to me how they experience more acute fear in retelling their stories than they did when the victimization occurred, especially given their heightened vulnerability. Therefore, any action or inaction that silences a client's attempt to disclose his or her racial narrative aligns the therapist with the perpetrator.

Therapist as perpetrator can also manifest itself as the clinician "taking too much space." As in the case with the African American mother, a therapist-perpetrator can respond,

> I have heard many of my African American clients mention to me how difficult it is for them, especially for Black men. I certainly have read the statistics about "driving while Black." It brings to my mind women's struggles with sexual harassment, marginalization, and objectification. I remember that was the reason I participated in the civil rights marches in the 60s.

This is an obvious example not only of taking too much space but also of making the issue about the therapist. The client may then respond in a compliant, accommodating manner but experience feeling invisible. Often the client will disconnect from the process. I realize that when I hear about my clients' gut-wrenching and painful experiences with racism, I quickly want to ease their pain and make it all right again. I also wish to alleviate my own anxiety and distress about racism and to preserve my efficacy as a good therapist and person. This is almost impossible. There are no easy answers to the racial problems experienced by our clients. Ironically, what most clients need is a container of safety and space to tell their truth and have it validated as just that. The "answer" may not be what is most important.

I wish to reiterate that the flight into a false self is always looming nearby as a possible response to the therapist-perpetrator. There is high potential for the client to default to this kind of coping.

Therapist as Victim

The cardinal emotional indicators of the role of therapist-victim are guilt, fear, helplessness, anger, and hurt. I will present two different perspectives of the victim role of the therapist. The first involves the clinician of color's encounter with racism in the therapeutic exchange. A clinician of color can be easily made to feel incompetent and helpless in this type of encounter. In Case 2, the case with the 46-year-old White female client, the therapist of color can be paralyzed by anger and hurt: "I don't know how to respond to what you're saying. You have a right to express your opinions, but I'm not comfortable with what you've expressed." The therapist is caught up in an internal process, unable to harness the energy of the anger and hurt that she or he is experiencing.

The second situation is one in which the client directs the full force of her anger onto the therapist. This can reduce the therapist to the same sense of helplessness and shame that the client is experiencing. A White therapist can be on the receiving end of a client of color's anger at his or her oppressor because the White therapist resembles the oppressor based on racial context. The White therapist in turn can defend against this by shifting into the perpetrator role, regaining the power: "I will not tolerate your anger or abuse in this office." The therapist can be overwhelmed by guilt and shame: "I am not the type of White person you are talking about. I did not do this to you. I am not a racist in any way." It requires quite a commitment to hold the emotion of the moment and not to rush to put the client in her or his place with the power imbued to us as therapists.

Rather, the healing power of a therapist lies in the role of the authentic, compassionate witness.

Therapist as Authentic, Compassionate Witness

The healing potential of an authentic, compassionate witness cannot be understated. However, the true challenge is in developing a vision of what this would look like in practice. Revisiting the analogy of the scene of the crime, the witnesses have a pivotal role in the traumatic impact of the crime. Many victims describe a profound betrayal and secondary injury by witnesses who stand by silently without intervening in the injustice. Therein lies the danger of therapeutic neutrality. In what follows, Ina (2001) clearly described the benefits of taking an involved stance:

> The familiar stance of "therapeutic neutrality" is challenged as a failure to assist the client in actively searching out and accurately labeling the experience of racism . . . Active empathy-driven involvement by the therapist is essential to strengthen the victim's sense of self. By challenging the silence of neutrality, the therapist also differentiates him/herself from the perpetrator. The powerful witness offers dignity to the distress and offers safety and containment for the work. Only then will the client be able to retrieve memories, discharge suppressed emotions, integrate racism trauma, and ultimately transform the victimization experience into one of self-empowerment. (p. 42)

The primary pitfall of the therapist-witness position is overidentification. When a client expresses feelings of hopelessness, it is tempting to take on the role of rescuer. This can imply to the client that he or she is not capable of acting for himself or herself, thus reinforcing the disempowerment of the original injury. Particularly in the case with the Mexican American client, the clinician may react with anger toward the physician, getting righteously indignant for the client. In essence, the therapist preempts the client's anger with his or her own anger.

Many of my interns and colleagues have without realizing it shared with me instances when they filtered experiences of people of color through their own lenses, making the experiences theirs rather than those of their clients. It is of utmost importance that the therapist permits the client's experience, albeit raw and gut-wrenching, to be in the therapy room without interference from the therapist. It is the therapist's responsibility to become the safe container for and witness to this process. It is my deepest hope that these case vignettes will enable you to extract some useful clues about how to define your authentic, compassionate witness style.

What follows are what I believe to be the core components of being an authentic, compassionate witness to clients of color:

1. Validate the client's experience at face value; three of the most powerful words are "I believe you."

2. Get out of the way. Don't interrupt. It is not about you—don't make it about you.

3. Take time to frame the question. In the context of a client's culture, the client will react not just to the content but also to the framework of a question and the pacing. In other words, don't rush in with a direct, linear question.

4. Don't make the client of color take care of you or defer to you as a White person. This is a learned role that comes automatically to some clients; it leads to resentment and premature termination.

5. Practice mindfully observing your reactions rather than rushing in to fix the client's problem.

6. Don't make the client responsible for a problem that the client can't change and that he or she didn't create—namely, racism.

7. Respect your power as a therapist; recognize the client's power to effect change in her or his life.

8. Practice and embrace not knowing. This will create more space for the client's experience to be visible.

9. When in doubt, ask permission. Don't assume trust exists.

10. Accept the expression of appropriate anger as a possible precondition to the client regaining his or her voice and dignity. Don't shut it down because it makes you uncomfortable.

11. Seek support from your colleagues and like-minded therapists, because the work is harsh and painful. Be kind to and compassionate with yourself. The more space you have, the more generous you will be with your clients.

12. Explore and become aware of the masks you have had to wear to function in the world.

The Conclusion and the Challenge

Thirty spokes converge upon a single hub;
It is on the hole in the center that the use of the cart hinges.
We make a vessel from a lump of clay;
It is the empty space within the vessel that makes it useful.
We make doors and windows for a room;

But it is these empty spaces that make the room livable.
Thus, while the tangible has advantages.
It is the intangible that makes it useful.

—Lao tzu (1972, p. 11)

Even as I write this, I find myself frustrated as I continue to struggle with how best to respond to colleagues and clients when they make racially unconscious comments. I even find myself guilty of making such mindless statements as the smog of racism pervades my neurons. There is no quick fix for the ongoing disease of racism and oppression. However, I am passionate about pressing on in the process of not knowing and asking the questions. I need to acknowledge the struggle and gains of my forebears and the path that they have cleared for me. I believe the heart and soul of this wonderful profession we have chosen is to create a more equitable and socially just society for our clients and children. I can think of no greater challenge than for us to begin the conversations we have often thought but seldom had.

In conclusion, I wish to make one last point. There have been a growing number of cases of a condition named Hmong sudden unexpected nocturnal death syndrome. Its victims are male Hmong refugees who have discontinued their traditional customs in order to assimilate to life in the United States and be accepted. It appears that they experience sudden cardiac arrest in their sleep. I leave you with this question: Can assimilation and accommodation kill? If I had to exist betraying everything of meaning to me, to wear a mask and suffer this daily experience in silence, I would be as good as dead. Let us create space for people to be whole individuals. We can begin by taking off our masks and breaking the silence.

Reflections, Questions, and Exercises

I would be remiss if I did not urge you to take the case material presented in this chapter a step further. I invite and encourage you to enter a process of developing a vision for what being a compassionate witness would look like within your contexts.

1. I have already invited you to personally respond to Case 3. I encourage you to review each case vignette again, this time without reading the questions or therapeutic process accounts provided.

2. Check in with your initial thoughts or reactions. Be mindful of any strong emotional responses or subtle racial templates or scripts that may be evoked. (You may want to write these down.)

3. Carefully examine the concepts and impacts of the multiple contexts that are most salient in each vignette for both the therapist and the client. Consider the dynamics of privilege and power. (It may be useful to ask yourself: How would it be different if the client were White?)

4. Identify the test shot in each case and what the client wants to seek permission to talk about. If you were the therapist in this situation, what could you say or do to create and communicate safety to the client?

5. How would you go about naming the racial issue in the session and when?

6. Identify how you as the therapist could be the perpetrator, victim, and compassionate witness in each respective case.

7. Take time to develop your vision as a compassionate witness for each client. It would be helpful to write your own script in order to connect with your own authentic, compassionate witness voice.

8. Finally, seek out a clinician or supervisor you feel safe with, someone with whom you can discuss your answers. Preferably, this should be someone who would not be afraid to challenge your views.

References

Du Bois, W. E. B. (1994). *The souls of Black folks.* New York: Dover. (Original work published 1906)

Hanh, T. N. (1987). *Being peace.* Berkeley, CA: Parallax.

Hardy, K. V. (1993). War of the worlds. *Networker,* July/August, 50–54.

Hardy, K. V. (1998, October). *Treating the invisible wounds of oppression.* Keynote at the Multiethnic Task Force Conference of Kaiser Northern California, Oakland.

Herman, J. (1997). *Trauma and recovery.* New York: Basic Books.

Ina, S. (2001). *Children of the camps: The documentary, teacher's guide.* Sacramento, CA: Children of the Camps Documentary and Educational Project.

Lao tzu (1972). *Tao te ching* (G. Feng & J. English, Trans.). New York: Random House.

Pipher, M. (1995). *Reviving Ophelia.* New York: Ballantine.

7

When Racism Is Reversed

Therapists of Color Speak About Their Experiences With Racism From Clients, Supervisees, and Supervisors

Saba Rasheed Ali, Jonathan R. Flojo,
Krista M. Chronister, Diane Hayashino,
Quincy R. Smiling, Danielle Torres,
and Ellen Hawley McWhirter

Within the last two decades, mental health practitioners have paid increasing attention to multiculturalism. A great deal of the mental health practice and research literature has focused on training student therapists to conduct therapy with individuals from diverse ethnic and racial backgrounds (Pedersen, 1988; Sue & Sue, 2002). This literature has emphasized multicultural competencies, which include three major components: knowledge, awareness, and skills. This emphasis has increased student therapists' attention to and awareness of racial and ethnic differences and potential issues among clients. It has also increased attention within training programs to issues of therapists' awareness of how their own cultural background and worldview influence the ways in which they conduct therapy. This literature seems to converge around the theme of training of White, European American therapists to understand their own racial identity and the ways in which their values may influence the therapy process (e.g., Kiselica, 1998). While the focus has been on these important strides in multicultural training, very little attention has been paid to the training of therapists of color and their experiences in conducting therapy. In particular, there is no research or practice literature that attends to the racism experienced by therapists of color from their clients or supervisors. While more research on this subject is important, it is also important to hear the stories firsthand from student therapists of color who have experienced racism. The accounts detailed in this chapter give voice to experiences of racism directed at student therapists of color from clients, supervisors, and supervisees and provide information about the ways in which these trainees handled these situations.

Impetus for This Chapter

This chapter originated in a symposium that we presented at the American Psychological Association (APA) Convention held in Washington, D.C. in August 2000. The impetus for the symposium was a discussion that occurred among us in a seminar class about the issue of racism directed at us by supervisors and clients and how to handle it. We noted that while there seemed to be an abundance of literature and training experiences related to becoming a multiculturally competent therapist, there was not much training on how to deal with clients' and supervisors' insensitivity to the issues of racism and culture. One of the major points that arose from this discussion was the difficulty of "calling" supervisors and clients on their racism, especially when one is in training. We decided to present at the APA convention in order to share these experiences with students and faculty in other training programs. We hoped that these experiences would spark a more in-depth discussion of the issue of reversed racism, namely, racism that is directed at one from a supervisor, client, or supervisee.

Student Therapists in Their Own Voice

During the time that the narratives for this chapter were written, all except one of us were students. Since then, all but one of those who were students are now employed in the professional arena in a variety of occupational positions, including as faculty members and practicing therapists. This diverse group of students developed a connection with each other because of shared values and experiences related to multiculturalism. As Diane Hayashino noted,

It was not too long into our program that we realized our shared values and began an ongoing process of discussions and validation that issues related to racism deserve more attention. We talked openly about our struggles with our own racist attitudes, and how we react when racism is directed towards us as the therapist, supervisor, and supervisee. Although we had a difficult time finding models to assist us in dealing with the issues we were experiencing in our counselor training, we found support from one another that we were not alone.

Our intent is to begin this chapter by giving voice to some very real, concrete, and difficult experiences with racism in the context of counseling and supervision.

Danielle M. Torres: Racism in Child and Family Therapy—The Perspective of a Therapist in Training

Working with children and families in therapy involves a variety of complex skills. Indeed, such work requires specialized training in terms of coursework, theory, and field practice. The same can be said of multicultural issues in therapy. Gaining descriptive knowledge about particular groups of people and building self-awareness are critical and often times difficult components of multicultural training. Both fields of training are demanding and complicated in their own right; striving for adequacy in either field, much less both fields, can be overwhelming to a student.

I believe that graduate students of color have unique experiences when it comes to training in these areas. For example, the traditional child and family therapy training is often complemented by our firsthand experiences of our own diverse upbringings in terms of family roles, child-rearing practices, and parent-child communication. Multicultural skills training is also experienced uniquely by students of color. Material presented in a multicultural course or a class discussion regarding multicultural issues in therapy hits students of color in a personal way. Their reaction (either internal or overt) may be sympathy, confirmation, or defensiveness, but regardless of the particular reaction, the issues are usually more personally and emotionally relevant for the student of color than they are for the White, European American student.

Thus, considering that experiences during training within these two distinct fields (i.e., child and family therapy, multicultural issues in therapy) are unique for students of color, it is logical to expect that experiences of multicultural issues within the child and family therapy setting would also be unique for this group of students. These are the experiences that are the premise for my perspective.

Racism in a child or family therapy context usually manifests as a discriminatory comment by a parent about a particular ethnic group or as a child's report of a parent's prejudiced belief. In my personal experience, I have heard comments such as "My mom and I were talking about how Mexican men are so loud and drunk all the time, not all of them, but most of them," "As a parent, I believe that interracial dating is wrong—and what about their kids?" and "This guy at work is a tightwad; he's Jewish, you know how they are." During such interactions, I am aware of feeling alone, unprepared, and yet highly responsible.

When a situation like this occurs, it always takes me by surprise. As a therapist of color, it knocks me off my professional balance by stirring up emotions often provoked in contexts outside of a therapy room. I find myself looking inward, wondering, "They know that I'm not White, they know I am a person of color, why do they think that they can say something like that and not offend me?" I become vulnerable and confused and ponder whether my educational status gives the impression that I am less a person of color because of my academic success. Then I begin struggling for an explanation for clients' behavior—maybe they meant to offend me, or maybe they have no exposure to my group of people of color, or maybe they had a negative experience once with a person of my ethnic group. It is also difficult not to feel outnumbered in a figurative and literal sense: This is a situation in which several family members feel a particular way and one therapist disagrees. Then I realize that right then and there, the explanation, the self-doubt, the solitude, none of it matters. The clients believe in what they just said, and I am left to respond. Only I am not sure how and what it means to me. This is difficult to deal with in the session and even after the session has ended.

Krista M. Chronister:
Experiences From a Biracial Supervisee

Do others see me as White or Brown? Do they even notice the color of my skin? Or, does it make others uncomfortable that I am neither White nor Brown, but that I am both? How do I see myself? I identify as biracial, half Filipino and half European American. Yesterday, I felt a little more White. Today, I feel more Brown. And tomorrow—well, I'll have to wait for tomorrow.

Biracial individuals often experience their ethnic identity differently in different contexts. It is important for supervisors working with biracial supervisees to understand biracial ethnic identity development and to ask themselves, as well as their supervisees, questions about their beliefs and perceptions of biracial identity. When done with respect, this questioning fosters a strong supervisory alliance built on acknowledgement, learning, and understanding. A trusting supervisory relationship can empower supervisees to explore their own ethnic identity and its influence on their clinical work, resulting ultimately in clients' empowerment. Not much has been written about the racism experienced by biracial students in clinical training. Although the experiences of biracial individuals may be similar to those of many ethnic minorities who are not biracial, there are also differences that deserve attention.

The purpose of this narrative is to share one of my supervision experiences in order to highlight the interrelationships among biracial ethnic identity, racism, and the supervisory relationship, as well as to outline the possible consequences of racism on trainees' development, clinical training, and relationships with clients. That is, not all supervisory relationships are trusting and respectful. Students may experience racist comments and actions from their supervisors. These comments and actions may be directed toward the supervisee, the client, or both. The imbalance of power in supervisory relationships makes it especially difficult for trainees to confront racist behaviors and to cope with the feelings of anger, confusion, and helplessness caused by these behaviors. For biracial trainees, experiences of racism may come from supervisors of one or both of the ethnic groups with which they identify, often leaving biracial trainees feeling confused and guilty about their ethnic identity and racial loyalties.

A case in point involves the story of John. John was a 20-year-old, White male who presented with signs of depression and reported difficulties keeping his "anger under control." John and I had been working together for only a few weeks, and the theme of our work was his frustration with how unfair life had been for him. He complained about many things, including people, politics, and economics. One day John became very angry in session and stated, "I'm so sick of minorities and women getting all of the breaks. They get all the handouts while the rest of us have to work for what we get."

Different thoughts and feelings overwhelmed me: Why did he just say that? What does John know about my race? Do I represent for him all that he hates? I'm so angry! Can I hide behind my Whiteness so that I don't feel this pain so deeply? If I express my anger will he say, "Why are you angry? You're not really a minority." Does he see White or Brown when he looks at me? I'm afraid and confused. Maybe I'll address his anger with women first because I am *definitely* a woman.

I shared my experience in supervision. Unfortunately, my supervisor was not aware of issues related to biracial identity or my life experiences with racism, different cultures, and identity development. Neither was I. I tried to convey to my supervisor that I felt conflicted about which of my identities to attend to—being female, Filipino, or European American. I expressed feeling angry with John and at the same time feeling afraid of him. I was also fearful of my despicable thoughts of John as a racist White man and of my own racist thoughts that seemed to support what he expressed.

My supervisor attempted to validate my feelings by reassuring me of my "ownership" of ethnic minority status: "When I look at you, I don't even see anything but Filipino." While my supervisor's intent was to offer me legitimacy and give importance to this part of my identity, I felt conflicted. I felt invisible because a significant part of me was not acknowledged, and at the same time I felt proud, accepted, and empowered as a woman of color. I also felt like an imposter, however, because some have told me that I'm not an ethnic minority. I felt guilty for being half White. My supervisor's statement resembled those more commonly heard: "I don't really think about the color of your skin when I look at you. I see you as a whole person. I don't really see color."

It is important for supervisors and supervisees to discuss ethnic identity. My supervisor made assumptions about how I identify ethnically and seemed to convey an acceptance or approval for only half of who I am. Consequently, I felt that I had to choose one ethnic group, and it was clear which ethnic group my supervisor acknowledged most. I also felt afraid to choose only one ethnic group because of the expectations that might go with choosing either group. I didn't want to be a fraud. My supervisor also was unaware of my life experiences of racism. Many biracial individuals experience racism or rejection from one or both of the ethnic groups with which they identify, and acceptance by only one ethnic group did not necessarily offer me a complete sense of belonging and legitimacy.

If I could go back and talk to my supervisor, I might say the following: Ask me what it means to me to be biracial and about my experiences of Filipino and American cultures. Listen for experiences of racism that I may not acknowledge. Assure me that I don't have to choose only one ethnic group to make you feel more comfortable and our supervision seemingly less complicated. Understand that my gender, age, or sexuality may be most salient for me and that it is okay—I am not denying my ethnic cultural background. Know that my feelings about being biracial may be different with each client, and that what I feel today may not be the same as what I felt yesterday or will feel tomorrow.

I've grown since the time when I worked with John. I continue to make mistakes, and I am sometimes still afraid of clients' anger and racism. But I also feel more confident and competent to utilize my fears and to process clients' racist and sexist comments. It has taken time for me to appreciate both sides that make up who I am. And I still ask myself every day, "Do you see White, Brown, or a little of both?"

Diane Hayashino: Experiences With a Supervisee

I want to share a little bit of who I am and where I am speaking from in my own development. I am entering my fourth year in a counseling psychology doctoral program on a predominantly White university campus. As a third-generation Japanese American whose parents, grandparents, and extended family members were imprisoned in internment camps during World War II, I was taught to avoid focusing on my ethnicity because it would only bring anger and disappointment. I grew up believing in many of the positive and negative stereotypes of Asian Americans. I am aware of my struggles with power and my tendency to blame myself when I do not succeed. This is my example of the insidious nature of internalized racism. At times in my training I have worried that this process of "higher" learning and pursuit of an "advanced" degree was resulting in the oppression of others and that I was actually buying into the institutional racism and prejudice that exist on so many of our university campuses. By sharing this, I am trying to say that I can only speak from the place of my own experiences and awareness of who I am today, and that I will most likely be in a different place tomorrow. I also want to be wary of making the assumption that all students of color share feelings and experiences similar to mine.

As a counselor in training, I am learning how to negotiate a variety of roles: supervisor, supervisee, child and family counselor, graduate teaching assistant, researcher, and so on. The supervisory relationship is complicated by the unique qualities (e.g., gender, sexual orientation, and social class) that supervisor and supervisee bring to the relationship. In addition, ethnic heritage contributes to the power differential between a supervisor and a supervisee. I grew up believing that collectivism and power were at opposite ends of a continuum. It was not until I was in graduate school, and through role models such as my advisor, that I realized that power and collectivism can coexist. I am learning to embrace the power afforded me as a supervisor without sacrificing other values, such as collaboration. My experience with racism has occurred within my role as a beginning level supervisor, and this is the perspective I want to share with you. I have had various opportunities in the past to engage in supervision, with co-workers, students, or peers, but few models to guide my development as a supervisor of color. As I develop these skills, I realize that my potential for personal and professional growth is influenced by my ability to confront defenses, take risks, and be committed to multicultural competence.

Sharing my experiences with racism as a supervisor of color begins by acknowledging the existence of racism. My primary concern is how to most effectively work with a supervisee who fails to see the impact of racism on his or her life. It is likely that the supervisee will feel unsupported, blamed, and even defensive, while the supervisor feels disempowered and frustrated. A White supervisee once told me that she knew that I had a difficult time giving feedback and she wanted to give me permission to be open with her. My initial reaction was to take responsibility for my lack of skill in providing feedback. I sought supervision for myself and focused on improving my skills and expanding my style of providing feedback. However, these adjustments did not address the issues between us. The learning between us stopped when I internalized this interaction and began feeling ineffective and invalidated as a supervisor. Rather than processing what was going on, I took on all the responsibility of what was occurring between us. As an Asian American woman, feelings of inadequacy and pressure to conform were familiar. Not knowing how to address White privilege, or if it was even appropriate for me to do so, left me feeling unprepared as a supervisor.

The lack of awareness of the supervisee to issues related to persons of color can also lead to their clients feeling distrustful and misunderstood. I feel responsible as a supervisor to protect the client from harm, yet at times I have hesitated to confront others on issues that have been harmful to me. I am learning that racism is also bidirectional. It is not only what the supervisee is doing to me but also what I am doing to the supervisee. My feeling of being stuck with regard to confronting racism is partly due to the difficulty many of us have in talking about race. The comment by the supervisee about my ability to provide feedback initially resulted in my making adjustments in my style of supervising. Our supervision sessions became more structured as I found myself tiptoeing around issues of race. I became more concerned with respecting her boundaries and lacked the confidence in my use of power to confront and take risks. It was awkward and uncomfortable as I struggled with being on this multicultural platform. *However, by processing my feelings and struggles in my own supervision, a greater appreciation for and validation of my values occurred.* I began to feel more confident about engaging in a dialogue addressing race and privilege with the supervisee. By doing so, we were able to learn from one another and respect our differences.

Another concern of mine is the potential for inexperienced supervisees to categorize my values as those of all Japanese Americans or even all Asian Americans. At times I have felt that others assumed I am multiculturally competent simply because I am Asian American. A few years ago, I was assigned to supervise three Southeast Asian caseworkers (first-generation

Hmong, Vietnamese, and Laotian) because my supervisor thought I would be able to establish rapport more easily since we were all from the "Asian culture." It quickly became clear that we had strong assumptions about each other, and we spent hours discussing our within-group differences and learning to see each other as individuals as well as members of our respective groups. As we began to listen to each other's stories of family, community, religion, and class, we were able to understand that as members of different groups we were afforded different levels of privilege and opportunity. In the end, this experience served as a valuable learning opportunity and example of the power of true multicultural training. Multicultural training embraces differences and does not shy away from the potential conflict that exists as a result of these differences.

Jonathan R. Flojo: Therapists of Color and Racism in Individual Counseling and Therapy

From a multicultural perspective (Atkinson, Morten, & Sue, 1998) and an ecological framework (Moen, Elder, & Lüscher, 1995), individual therapy and counseling occur embedded within a broader context of social forces. The boundary between the therapy session and the outside world is artificial and transparent. In many respects, the therapy session is a reflection of the social conditions existing outside in the "real world." Oppressive conditions of racism that exist in the world will insinuate themselves into the therapy room. Consequently, therapists of color are challenged to navigate not only through their own racial attitudes and racism but also those of their clients.

To negotiate the attitudes and biases that surround racism is not without cost. Often, the examination of a client's racism will trigger an intimate and personal examination of the therapist's own identity and racial attitudes. To clarify the confusion, therapists in training often seek answers from their trainers. From a trainee of color's perspective, the majority of the curriculum and training materials are geared toward White, European American trainees and their specific needs in a multicultural counseling environment. The specific needs and experiences of people of color who have experienced racism in and out of the therapy room have rarely been addressed.

Thompson and Neville (1999) wrote that "putting an end to pathology that surrounds racism entails a struggle . . . the struggle requires the individual to examine the aspect of identity that relates to one's socialization as a racial being and to daringly confront how one has succumbed to the malignancy of racism" (p. 200). My experiences with racism are some of my most unpleasant memories. I struggle with sharing the extent of my hurt, my insecurity, and my shame when I have witnessed racism.

It was my second day of interviewing and working with Vietnam veterans at a clinic. I am an Asian American and I was working with White, European American veterans. As the therapist in the counseling relationship, do I bring up the racial differences between my clients and myself? My conviction to not explore the differences comes from my fear. What will the Vietnam veterans see in me? Instead of the eager healer, will they see the "enemy," the "foreigner," or the "person who will never be an American no matter how hard he tries"?

After 30 minutes of speaking about Vietnam—the humidity, the confusion, the foot fungus—the veteran and I begin to talk about his life now that he's back in the United States. The adjustment has been hard for him. He says that in the town he'd been living in, he'd had no friends and multiple arrests by police: "The town was full of Vietnamese. Yeah, the sheriff made me leave town because I would see one of them and hit 'im across the back of the head . . . just like that. I couldn't help myself. Every time I would hit 'im."

He nonchalantly shares that he committed acts of violence on people that I resemble. How am I supposed to take this? Has my training covered this? What is appropriate professional behavior? Anger and fear rise up in my throat. My confidence in my skill is precarious. Surely a more competent therapist would be able to manage these feelings in session even in the face of this abuse. While I dwell in the misguided belief of my incompetence, I think about blending in with the American White majority. I want to hide, blend in, and be invisible to defend myself from my client's racism. Being confronted by his racism led me to examine my own identity and racial fears. Racism reminds me of how despite my higher education, and my middle-class values and aspirations, I reside inches from marginalization and what seems like miles from my client.

For several minutes, we speak about baseball, the new baseball stadium, salary caps, the sound a bat makes when the ball hits the bat in just the right spot. "Before I was drafted, I was one helluva pitcher. I always wonder how far I could have gone," he confessed. He fears not having a relationship with his children. He watches them grow up and grow apart from him. He fears seeing his wife tire of trying to live in the same house. He secretly dreads when she'll stop trying.

What an odd combination—the violence and racism of my client coupled with his vulnerability and regret. I am scared and repulsed by him and also feel close to him. It would be easier to just hate and despise him or to just feel compassion for him. Feeling and holding both disgust and compassion is a confusing place. Months later I am still left with confusion. My client is much more complex than I thought he would be. And for me, my repulsion and connection to him is complex. Am I inches or miles apart from my client?

The specific needs and experiences of trainees of color who have experienced racism in and out of therapy have rarely been addressed in my training. As an Asian American, the examination of my client's racism has compelled me to examine the intersection of my professional and personal identities. I am both scared by the veteran's racism and connected to him by his vulnerability. In confronting the racism in the therapeutic room and holding both fear and compassion for my clients, I have been able to navigate my own racial attitudes and racism. My identity has been challenged, throttled, and deconstructed. The therapeutic relationship has challenged me to turn an uncomfortable gaze toward my identity. Navigating the racial attitudes of my clients and my self-doubt, I have begun to integrate my own identity as a professional and as a person of color.

Quincy R. Smiling: Racism, Supervision, and African American Teaching Assistants

African American teaching assistants (TAs) study more, read more, work harder to prove to everyone that they deserve to be where they are. But performing well is extremely hard when the expectations for success are so low, when race plays a huge factor in how TAs are received and respected. In many cases, if you are a White TA, the perception of the students is that you are competent and capable of performing your duties well; however, if you are an African American TA, your competence is often questioned or challenged.

Over the years, racism has played a significant role in African American lives. Many African Americans believe that racism serves as a catalyst for their success, motivation, and high aspirations. Performing teaching duties requires a lot of motivation and dedication, especially if you are an African American TA. Students from the majority culture may have second thoughts about being taught by someone outside of their ethnic background. Those thoughts cause conflict for minority students; they may experience rejection, isolation, and negative perceptions from their peers. These controversies may hinder minority students' academic performance and behavior in the classroom.

My personal experiences have forced me to deal with rejection from society and accept the negativity that racism brings to higher education. One specific example comes to mind from my own experience as a TA for a practicum class for school counselors. The professor of the course gave a class assignment for the students to complete a case conceptualization. Along with the class assignment, the professor gave a handout to illustrate how the case conceptualization should be completed. The assignment was due 3 weeks later. On the day it was due, one student did not turn in her assignment and asked for an extension. The professor and I granted the extension. Then, the student indicated to the professor that I misled her on the assignment. She asked for another extension and it too was granted. The student finally turned in the case conceptualization 2 weeks late. She was then asked, "Do you feel that you should receive full points although you turned in your assignment 2 weeks late?" She thought she should receive full points, but the professor and I had had an individual supervision meeting and concluded that points should be detracted from the student's grade for turning the case conceptualization in late. When I revealed the outcome of the meeting to the student, she accused me of incompetence and inability to perform the duties required of a teaching assistant. The student decided to fill out a grievance form with the chair of the department. She stated that I, the TA, was incompetent, and she also raised the issue of whether African American TAs with Southern accents should be allowed to teach or lecture master's level students. Also, the student indicated that I showed favoritism to certain students and that consequently I should not be allowed to teach master's level courses.

Finally, the dilemma ended when the chair met with the student and discovered that she was supplying false information. Also, the chair reviewed a paper that the professor and I presented, which indicated that we had followed the ethical guidelines for due process in this situation. For me, this situation reinforced the idea that it is extremely important for predominantly White institutions of higher education to promote diversity among graduate students, teachers, and research assistants. Institutions should strive to promote an atmosphere of respect for and appreciation of diversity. In addition, it is equally important to support ethnically diverse students who serve as teaching assistants, especially when they encounter such overt racism. It is opportunities like this one that can provide training environments and students with "teachable moments" regarding how to deal with racism that is directed at supervisors and TAs of color. It is in the way that these types of situations are handled that true learning occurs.

Ellen Hawley McWhirter: Racism and Its Effects on Therapists of Color—A Reaction

I am a White counseling psychology faculty member and have been involved in training master's and doctoral level counselors and psychologists for about 11 years. I would like to share my thoughts on the preceding reflections in this chapter. These young professionals have conveyed very personal and powerful training experiences. They have reached inside of themselves and engaged in a difficult and even painful struggle to put into words experiences that so often go unnoticed, are unrecognized—are ignored. Yet these experiences are common to graduate students of color in clinical training and may be among the most influential.

Why is it that today, when the call to increase the number of ethnic minority psychologists is so familiar, when most training programs are admitting a greater proportion of students of color than in the past, and when terms such as *multicultural counseling* and *diversity* and *sensitivity* are common and unremarkable in academic counseling psychology circles—why is it that these experiences are not described in journal articles or books on training? Why aren't these experiences addressed as a routine part of the content of practicum, externship, and internship training? Maybe the answer is embedded within the stories that you have just read.

Danielle Torres shared with us her feelings of vulnerability, confusion, and aloneness when children or parents make racist remarks in a family counseling session. Jonathan Flojo experienced hurt and shame when his Vietnam veteran client spoke of smacking Vietnamese American people on the head. Krista Chronister spoke of feelings such as anger and confusion in relation to a client's comments about women and minorities. Diane Hayashino noted that she felt ineffective and invalidated when her White supervisee assumed that Diane, as an Asian American woman, had difficulty delivering feedback. And Quincy Smiling shared the blatant racism directed at him by a student colleague, a graduate student in training. So maybe the reason that White supervisors and White teachers—like me—do not prepare our students of color to deal with racism in their clinical training is because *we ourselves* do not want to experience those same feelings. We do not want to experience anger, vulnerability, confusion, and aloneness. Maybe we do not want to let go of the collective power of our White, European American identities long enough to critique the basis of that collective power and the oppression carried out in the name of that power. Perhaps we dread asking our students questions about how racism manifests in their counseling and supervision sessions because it is uncomfortable, and we are afraid of not having any answers—or—we are afraid that we *do* know the answers and they involve confronting ourselves and our colleagues.

Maybe we do not want to feel ineffective and invalidated when our supervisees and students of color tell us that we are minimizing their experiences. Or maybe it is an issue of basic narcissism. Maybe we are so wrapped up in our own experiences that it does not occur to us that our privilege has directly influenced what we are and are not confronted with in our own clinical work. Maybe we think that sharing standard training content, and sprinkling in what we ourselves experienced in training, is enough.

I do not like any of these possibilities. They all suggest a general lack of some combination of courage, insight, empathy, and responsibility. We could probably spend years debating the proportions—for example, fighting over whether it's 10% or 25% lack of courage and 30% or 50% lack of taking responsibility—but instead, I propose that White supervisors and trainers and counseling psychology faculty do not waste time with such details, and that we start addressing the problem. In order to accompany our students of color in facing racism within their clinical training, we must ask risky questions of our students, of their supervisors, and of our colleagues. Harder than that, we have to listen to the answers and take action. We have to be prepared to advocate, confront, empathize, and problem solve (McWhirter, 1997). We also have to actively foster departmental and program environments in which the pain, the anger, the embarrassment, and the shame that racism provokes can be named, shared, and processed. We can't do this if we have big feet, or if maintaining our professional identity of being the "good guy" is a higher priority than supporting the clinical training of students of color. We most certainly can't do this if we think that racism is not a problem, or that it is not a problem "on *my* turf." Danielle, Jonathan, Krista, Diane, and Quincy have given us some data. If it makes us uncomfortable because there are no total scores or tests of significant differences, then let's go out and collect some *more* data—but by all means, let's not ignore the data in front of us here. I am proud, hopeful, and inspired by the courage of these students who were willing to deeply examine their difficult and painful experiences of racism so that they could share them with us. They are my teachers and now they have also become your teachers. We are so very fortunate, because they are the future of counseling psychology.

Implications for Multicultural Clinical Training Programs

The five experiences presented in this chapter have served to enhance the multicultural literature through a description of the affective and personal nature of racism and how it is experienced when one is in a helping role. All of the five student therapists who presented their experiences have emphasized the need for more training and safe places to discuss these issues. Ellen McWhirter has outlined ways in which faculty mentors may be able to better address these issues within training programs.

Further recommendations can be made regarding how to assist faculty in mental health training programs in addressing the needs of their ethnic and racial minority trainees. One of the predominant themes of the five narratives was that racist experiences led trainees to feel low self-confidence and confusion about places where they may discuss these issues. All five of the trainees mentioned lack of safe places to discuss their experiences with racism from supervisors, supervisees, or clients. They also expressed feelings of doubt about their capabilities as therapists or supervisors in these situations. It seems that one of the most important places to begin to address this situation in training programs is by providing room for acknowledgement and discussion of these issues. Recently, in one of the first author's advanced practicum courses, a White male student facilitated a discussion about a client's racist comments that led him to feel extremely uncomfortable. His openness about his own struggle in dealing with this situation led other students (both White and of color) to share their experiences and feelings about the subject. As the instructor of this course, I asked these students what would be most helpful to them in their training to deal with such experiences. Overwhelmingly, the students answered that explicit discussions were most helpful. An important part of the process of dealing with these experiences, both for the students in my course and for the students who shared their experiences in this chapter, is support from others who may have experienced similar incidents. Part of the insidious nature of racism is that it can lead to silence and inaction. Without open and safe places for students to discuss their experiences, students may internalize racism, which may undermine their confidence in their abilities as therapists, students, and supervisors.

Reflections, Questions, and Exercises

Graduate training programs can assist therapists of color during these difficulties. Danielle Torres has made specific suggestions based on the experiences she described previously. These suggestions are as follows:

1. Therapists of color need a decision-making framework in these situations. In a moment when personal emotion is likely running high, such a framework would be helpful in guiding appropriate professional behavior that does not compromise the therapist's emotional experience. It is important to consider how certain decisions affect the client-therapist or supervisor-supervisee relationship, the family relationships, and the client's progress and behavior change. It is impossible to know what the long-term implications are in these terms, but having a framework could help therapists organize their considerations of how particular responses achieve or hinder client and therapist goals.

2. Therapists of color need an opportunity to explore what types of clients or supervisees are more or less challenging in these situations: Is it more

comfortable to address racism with graduate students, young children, adolescents, mothers, or fathers? How does the age, ethnicity, sexual orientation, disability, or family role of the client influence the perception of racism in the therapist or supervisor of color? What cultural issues of respect, authority, and power are involved for the therapist of color? How can therapists or supervisors of color empower themselves to be assertive in situations that involve racism?

3. Therapists and supervisors of color need support in examining their role and responsibility in addressing diversity issues with clients and supervisors. How does the child and family therapist's responsibility interface with parental responsibility with regard to educating children about multicultural issues? How do these responsibilities differ for a therapist of color and a European American therapist? How might the responsibilities reflect the personal attitude of the therapist of color, and what are appropriate and comfortable avenues of expression of such attitudes in therapy with children and families?

4. Therapists of color need support from supervisors and faculty in exploring the issue of racism in therapy during practicum experiences. All involved should address the trainee's responsibility to the placement site in which he or she is working. In addition, are placement supervisors and administrators prepared to articulate their perspective in a situation if a parent is dissatisfied or upset with the therapist's response to racism? It is important that training programs convey the importance of discussing these situations with on-site supervisors and administrators during students' practicum placements.

5. Training programs also need to provide opportunities for student therapists of color to address issues related to racism that might be perpetrated by an individual who is in a position of power over a student, such as a faculty member or supervisor. It is important that advocacy for a beginning level therapist, supervisor, or supervisee be in place in the event that a student experiences such a situation. At the very least, more explicit discussions about how to handle these situations need to be conducted.

6. Finally, more research needs to be conducted on student therapists of color's experiences with racism in the context of training environments. It is assumed that the racist incidents presented in this chapter by five student therapists are a small sample of a widespread phenomenon. Considering that one of the goals of most mental health training programs is to increase enrollment of students from diverse ethnic and racial backgrounds, it is equally important that those who are doing the training increase their understanding of the possible barriers that students of color may face in successfully completing such programs. As the students have described in this chapter, racism can undermine student therapists' confidence and lead them to feel isolated and incompetent, which may eventually lead them to leave the profession. Research on

these experiences may lead to a better understanding of how mental health training programs can better prepare students to deal with such incidents so that they do not internalize their negative experiences.

In conclusion, it cannot be assumed that all counselors of color experience difficulty in such situations. Yet for those who do struggle, the opportunity to explore reactions, decisions, and attitudes as a component of graduate training programs would be invaluable to the personal and professional development of student therapists of color. It is through these discussions that student therapists of color may come to feel more comfortable with addressing these issues with supervisors, supervisees, and possibly clients.

References

Atkinson, D. R., Morten, G., & Sue, D. W. (1998). *Counseling American minorities: A cross-cultural perspective* (5th ed.). Boston: McGraw-Hill.

Kiselica, M. S. (1998). Preparing Anglos for the challenges and joys of multiculturalism. *Counseling Psychologist, 26,* 5–21.

McWhirter, E. H. (1997). Empowerment, social activism, and counseling. *Counseling and Human Development, 29,* 1–14.

Moen, P., Elder, G. H., Jr., & Lüscher, K. (Eds.). (1995). *Examining lives in context: Perspectives on the ecology of human development.* Washington, DC: American Psychological Association.

Pedersen, P. (1988). *A handbook for developing multicultural awareness.* Alexandria, VA: American Association for Counseling and Development.

Sue, D. W., & Sue, D. (2002). *Counseling the culturally diverse* (4th ed.). New York: John Wiley.

Thompson, C. E., & Neville, H. A. (1999). Racism, mental health, and mental health practice. *Counseling Psychologist, 27,* 155–223.

8

Toward a Liberation Pedagogy

Creating a Safe Environment for Diversity Conversations in the Classroom

Debra A. Nixon

When I began work as a faculty member in family therapy, I was thrilled. At last, I was fulfilling one of my childhood dreams. But as a child I did not give any thought to how my color would affect my dream, because in my dream I envisioned myself teaching people who looked like me. Everyone was Black, so color was not a concern. When I received the MFT teaching appointment, I thought hard about what my being a woman of color meant for the university, which was predominantly White, and my department, which was exclusively White. I also had thoughts about having to prove myself because I am Black. In my experience, the majority system had made it very clear that the rules were different for Black people and White people (Culotta, Holden, & Gibbons, 1993; McGowan, 2000; Zamboanga & Bingman, 2001). Honestly, I wondered how much of my being Black contributed to my getting the job, as I know there is pressure in the academic community to diversify (Culotta et al., 1993; Zamboanga & Bingman, 2001). However, I am not the type to focus on things that I cannot control. My concern then was how I was going to make a difference now that I was a faculty member. How was my voice going to shape a system that seemed cemented in a tradition that was predominately a White male regime (Churchill, 2000)?

Accordingly, my contribution to this book centers on my experiences as a woman of color in a predominantly White institution. In the first section of this chapter, I share some of my experiences as a minority student in majority universities, focusing on my struggles to engage faculty and colleagues in conversations about racism. In the second section, I highlight my pedagogical style and offer it as one possible solution to what seems like an agreed-upon code of silence regarding race talk. I discovered while doing the research for this section that my teaching style is germane to African American women, who are known for creating learning environments that invite open engagement (Boutte, 1999; Bower, Auletta, & Jones, 1993; hooks, 1994; Hyde & Ruth, 2002; McCarthy & Willis, 1995; Van Soest, 1996). Furthermore, I see similarities in this pedagogy and the therapeutic relationship that therapists desire to create with clients. Therefore, within this discussion I will challenge MFT instructors and supervisors to bring the relational nuances that they seek to create with clients to their teaching and training endeavors. In both sections I provide personal anecdotes and related academic publications to support my assertions.

Talking About Race

> *The problem of the twentieth century is the problem of the color line—the relation of the darker to the lighter races of men in Asia and Africa, in America and in the islands of the sea.*
>
> —W.E.B. Du Bois (1903)
> (cited in Back & Solomos, 2000, p. 3)

Definitions

Since the impetus for this discussion is race and diversity issues, I offer the following designations of terms for people, as well as definitions of *race*, *racism*, and *diversity*. According to the *Oxford American Dictionary* (1980), *race* is one of the great divisions of humankind by certain inherited physical characteristics (such as color of skin and hair, shape of eyes and nose). *Racism* has been described as a system of advantages based on race (Wellman, 1997). Tatum (1997) suggested that racism is so pervasive that African Americans and Europeans Americans are unaware of how it influences their lives.

The terms *African American, Black,* and *people of color* are used interchangeably throughout this chapter; however, *people of color* may also refer to persons who are Asian, Latin, Pacific Islander, and Native American. The terms *European, Eurocentric, majority culture,* and *White* are also used interchangeably. The term *diversity* applies to all minorities or persons belonging to a variety of ethnicities, gender identifications, and cultures.

Race Talk, Teaching, and Therapy

The United States has always been a multicultural society, but what we will see in the next few years with the increase in people of color is an increase in the physical evidence of that diversity. Some have projected that by the year 2007, minorities will comprise over 50% of the workforce (Mindell, 1998). Accordingly, as the face of the United States changes, the faces and cultures of our clients will also change (Constantine, Juby, & Laing, 2001; Nelson et al., 2001). Therefore, MFT training programs must find ways to prepare trainees to respond to the needs of a diverse population (Constantine et al., 2001). This preparation must be intentional and permeate entire MFT programs. Moreover, it must be reflected in a teaching style that models the hallmark qualities of effective therapists: open, collaborative, respectful, and curious. McGowan (2000) and hooks (1994), two African American college instructors, have suggested that a pedagogical style is most effective when it reflects these effective therapeutic qualities.

I believe that the qualities of a good therapist are similar to the qualities of good teachers. For me, an effective therapist creates an atmosphere that allows for freedom of expression and comfort. My suggestion, then, is that as MFT instructors and supervisors we can use our therapeutic skills in class. By being therapeutic in our teaching efforts, we can make learning difficult lessons a good experience for our students (hooks, 1994). This is especially important with lessons like those on racism, which are difficult to teach as well as to learn.

In my experience, racism is one of the most difficult topics to discuss in any environment. However, the changing "peoplescape" in our country makes discussions about race of extreme importance, especially in academia. The literature, although scant, suggests that White academics struggle with talking about the "r" word (Boutte, 1999; Bower, 1993; Chan & Treacy, 1996; Hamilton, 2002; Tatum, 1997). However, to talk about race in academia, it is important that one's approach to learning be open (to listening to students' perspectives) and the dialogue interactive (Gay & Fox, 1995; Hyde & Ruth, 2002). I propose that pedagogical styles that are nurturing and collaborative create teaching and learning atmospheres that are ideal for discussing sensitive topics such as race (Bower, 1993; Van Soest, 1996).

As an African American woman who employs this style of teaching, I know that it works. Therefore, this chapter offers my understanding of (1) how I as a Black student in White academia struggled to engage a learning style reflective of my emerging pedagogy, and (2) how I as a college professor connect students in conversations about race in a way that allows them to feel free in that dialogue. This material may be helpful to other faculty who either struggle with dialogues about race or avoid the topic all together (Boutte, 1999; Bower et al., 1993; Hyde & Ruth, 2002). The focus here is on bringing effective, even therapeutic, diversity conversations into the classroom.

Intentionality

Bringing effective diversity conversation into the college classroom requires intentionality. Someone must initiate the talk on purpose and with a purpose. Unfortunately, the initial response to such conversations—from my former classmates and instructor and, now, *my* students—appears to be fear, silence, and anger. My motivation in this section is to suggest to readers that we must face the fear, banish the silence, and embrace the anger that accompanies these conversations so that we can begin the task of healing ourselves and building community (Benjamin, 1996; Van Soest, 1996). I strongly suggest that the *healing begin with the healers* (i.e., MFT faculty and clinical supervisors, administration, and professional organizations).

My hope is that those responsible for training new therapists will decide (by whatever means they choose) to be intentional about diversity topics such as race (Benjamin, 1996). Intentionality is displayed in one's pedagogical practices. In short, one's teaching style can lend itself to the kind of conversations that avoid topics such as race, religion, gender, and class. Or it can be one that fosters a learning environment that promotes open and uncensored, honest communication about these topics (Bower, 1993; Boutte, 1999; Hamilton, 2002; Hyde & Ruth, 2002; McCarthy & Willis, 1995). If we, as MFT instructors, create an open platform of learning, we challenge our students to engage in conversations that (in my opinion) resemble conversations of the respectful, genuine, empathic scholars and practitioners we purport to be. We then participate in a discursive process similar to ones created in therapeutic practice where the therapist-client relationship is a collaborative engagement in which neither voice is allowed to dominate (McNamee, 1996). The instructor and student take on this kind of dynamic with a mutual sharing of knowledge (Freire, 1970; Jacobson, 2000; Neville & Cha-jua, 1998). I hope that this offering will arouse a desire for pedagogical practices that create an atmosphere of mutual learning so that all voices in the classroom will be heard, especially those that speak of issues of diversity.

Professional and Personal Background

I began my teaching career as an assistant professor 8 months ago, when I was hired by a private, predominately White university. While I had taught as an adjunct professor for over 12 months prior to my full-time appointment, I am new to the teaching profession, that's if you don't count my more than 20 years of church school teaching experience. I always wanted to teach college-level students rather than younger students. I wanted to engage the motivated students at a university, and I wanted to share in the rigors of their learning experience.

Cultural Background

I was born in Dallas, Texas, and for the first 11 years of my life lived in an urban housing project, but it was not until I was about 10 years old that I began to hear rumblings of the so-called devastation of living in a governmental housing community. I loved my community and the families that lived in our cul-de-sac.

I had many wonderful, enriching experiences in the West Dallas Project (which was also called The Jets). In the projects, I learned that family were more than blood relatives. I saw a kind of sharing and caring that I wanted to see recreated in other educational settings. In our community was a Christian woman, Mrs. Gipson, who baked cookies to coax us kids into Wednesday Bible Class. Under Mrs. Gipson's guidance, I learned the 23rd Psalm and recited the verses at her church. So, fused with our seeming poverty was a rich sense of family and a spiritual heritage that has kept me conscious of the importance of strong, nurturing Black women.

The sense of community and the strength of my spiritual heritage were vital to my survival as a person of color in a hostile society. In our African heritage, which seems to possess an invisible collective consciousness about God and community, there was this blending of the sacred and the secular. So I never at any point in my life or educational endeavors felt that I had to neglect or abandon either my sense of community—my Blackness—or my faith for acceptance into the larger majority community (Henderson, 1994). Closer to the truth was that these cultural experiences supplied me with the courage and will to strive for excellence in everything and, most especially, in my educational pursuits.

Educational Background: A Community

My formal education began in Dallas, where I graduated from one of the largest predominantly Black high schools in the city. I had several teacher-mentors that helped to prepare me for my postsecondary education. While there were teachers of other cultural backgrounds at the school, the Black teachers seemed to take a personal interest in me and provided me with a sense of confidence. The pedagogical style of African American teachers was legendary (Beauboeuf-Lafontant, 2002; hooks, 1994). With their guidance, I was able to move from the safety of my nearly all Black high school to an overwhelming university system where the majority student population outnumbered the Black student population by more than 39,000 students. Historically, the university had been known for its blatant discrimination against Blacks. For example, one of my classmates, a premed student from Houston, shared with a group of us that his White biology professor told him that our people were inferior to Whites and that he should change his major. The racist construct about Black intellect and scholarship still pervades the thinking of Americans, Black and White (McGowan, 2000).

When this kind of story began to circulate among the incoming freshmen, we knew that we *needed a community* of our own. So I stayed rather isolated in my undergraduate program, in that I made a partly conscious, partly unconscious decision not to engage what seemed like a huge, White, unfriendly system. I had almost no personal contact with my instructors, who were mostly White males. Of course, in an institution of its size that contact may have been next to impossible anyway. However, I had decided that I would keep to what was familiar—a clique of about 12 Black students who joined me there from high school. Consequently, I have no war stories from my undergraduate experience. However, for those who struggled for acceptance, there was a loving grandmotherly matriarch known as "Mother" who worked in the Student Affairs office. Mother provided many students with the much-needed community: It seemed that we all were sojourners in a foreign and hostile land.

While reflecting on my academic career, I realized that every institution of higher learning that I had ever attended had been foreign to me. They were foreign in the sense that I was an ethnic minority in each of them, which meant that I had to learn how to fit in with the larger culture. While I believe that I had found a higher education institution that worked for me, I have often wondered what I missed by not attending a Black college. From the outside, the Black college experience seemed much like the community I had experienced growing up in the projects. Honestly, what I experienced in majority schools was much more hostile than anything I had experienced while living in the projects (Alfred, 2001). The hostility that I experienced in majority schools was the kind of subtle violence that suggested to you that your ideas, your intellect, or your scholarship either did not count or was a fluke (Alfred, 2001; Culotta, 1993; McGowan, 2000, Zamboanga & Bingman, 2001). Worse yet, was the collective violence that suggested that I was not there, but invisible.

Perhaps the most explicit struggle I had was being visible. My invisibility was never more evident than when I worked in groups. Group work was a significant part of graduate studies, and most of the time I was the only person of color (Black or otherwise) in the group. I found that the White participants tended to address other White students when they talked, rarely giving me any eye contact. I also noticed that my ideas were often slighted. I'd make what I thought was a brilliant assessment or comment, and it was almost as if I had not said anything or as if the group did not accept my comment—until someone else (always a White person) said the same thing and *then* it was a brilliant idea. I was accustomed to this happening, and many of my Black friends have shared similar experiences—it's no big deal, we said matter-of-factly, White people think they're smarter than we are.

I guess I was so accustomed to this response from White people that I stopped noticing it. No, I never stopped noticing it; I just excused it as the way things were. Besides, I had learned from other experiences that this was the status quo in White America. I suppose that was how some Whites in this country continue to believe that there was no race problem—it was so much a part of how things were that it was invisible.

Graduate School Experiences

Visibility and credibility are issues that I have had to deal with through all of my graduate studies. A few of my graduate school experiences stand out in this regard because they suggested either that I was not there or (when my presence could not be denied) that I did not have much to offer. In one of my classes, a White student waited for the instructor to validate my intelligence before she would consider joining me in a study group outside class. An instructor in another class directed what she was saying to me while she scolded the class—as if I were the sole culprit. Another instructor looked at me with amazement while I spoke, as if he could not believe that I could think. But the one defining experience for me was when I initiated a conversation about race in a theory class and most of my fellow classmates chided me for bringing it up. I mentioned the struggles of Black people in this country—racism. The students in the class almost unanimously agreed that the classroom was not the place to have that conversation. Some of them were clearly offended and accused me of being the only one with the problem—in fact, one student said that she had "already dealt with this," so this was my stuff.

What was perhaps the most disturbing part to my experience was that once we began our conversation, no one entered the discussion to validate my reality, not even the instructor or the teaching assistant (TA). They were postmodern, trained family therapists, and yet it appeared that none of them could see the value in validating my reality as they would validate the reality of a client telling her story. I expected more, but then I realized that they were not accustomed to having this conversation. So the vocal students found ways to marginalize me, the silent ones sat petrified at the thought of having to talk about race, and the instructor was invisible.

Our instructor used the nondirective approach—I think—and did not intervene in the process. This approach, if you value building a community and fostering mutual respect for all voices, was not very useful. We needed the guidance of a community builder. We could have used the benefit of her negotiation skills, or even her therapeutic skills—her skillful command of language. Unfortunately, her pedagogical approach did not lend itself to what some call the teachable moment (Rice, 2001). Clearly, this was an opportunity to talk about this very difficult issue and to engage us in a much-needed scholarly conversation about racism. It was a rare chance and a moment not seized. I concluded that either she did not know what to do or she was just as afraid, angry, hurt, and/or confused as the rest of us.

Declaration of Intentionality

After that experience, I made some unconscious decisions. I decided that if I ever got the opportunity to teach, I would make what I did as a therapist isomorphic to what I did as an instructor or trainer. In other words, I would practice respect for students' voices, show curiosity about their stories, and display openness to their realities; that is, I would do for my students just what I did for my clients. In her book *Teaching to Transgress* (1994), hooks made a similar declaration as she compared the sterile teaching styles of her undergraduate professors to the approaches of her elementary school teachers, who created a nurturing environment that invited students to participate in their own learning.

Creating a Therapeutic Community in the Classroom

As a family therapist instructor and clinical supervisor, it is clear to me that several seminal traits characterize the effective therapist: empathy, curiosity, and respect (Patterson, Williams, Grauf-Grounds, & Chamow, 1998; Walter & Peller, 2000). These finer therapeutic traits can be used in therapy and in the classroom. My focus here is on bringing these hallmark attributes to the graduate training environment. In the following discussion, I present how I have made my unconscious determination a conscious, intentional effort in graduate training. In other words, my goal is to bring the same kind of community that I experienced as a young girl growing up in the projects to an MFT training setting. I have discovered that mine is a pedagogical style that is part a collective consciousness of African American female teachers (Beauboeuf-Lafontant, 2002; hooks, 1994). So I now know that when I enter the classroom, I enter with the collective mind of legendary African American women scholars and teachers.

I was the first African American on the MFT faculty, so the Black students in the master's program were elated. Black instructors in other predominantly White institutions have reported having similar experiences (Hamilton, 2002; McGowan, 2000). One female professor noted, "Some days it seems that every marginalized student on campus ends up camping outside my door" (Culotta et al., 1993, p. 1092). The Black doctoral students, a much smaller group, expressed their excitement about my hire as well. I understand and share their excitement, especially because when I went through the program, there were only two Black doctoral students in my cohort and, of course, no Black faculty. The other Black student, a male, had to drop out for personal reasons. Therefore, I went through the program with no Black faculty or cohort, with no one I related to or identified with. The literature confirms what I sensed—that identification and community are important to academics of color (Culotta et al., 1993; Henderson, 1994; McGowan, 2000). Many African Americans (especially before desegregation) were nurtured in a cocoonlike environment by female teachers who in many cases were like mothers (Beauboeuf-Lafontant, 2002; hooks, 1994; Stanford, 1998). Our communities were designed so that every child was everyone's responsibility, as expressed in the African proverb, "It takes a village to rear a child."

My effort to create a village is clearly paying off. After my recent presentation "Race and Postmodernism," one African American student commented that she's glad I'm here, that she's much more relaxed in the program and more vocal in class because I'm here. Several students nodded in agreement. It was clear that they were in search of that community I discussed earlier. Furthermore, I realized that I had found what I had been looking for since I left high school—a Black collegiate experience.

Searching for My Own Community

So strong was my need for a Black academic experience that during my final year of graduate school, as I worked on my dissertation, I enrolled in the

Interdenominational Theological Center (ITC), a Black theological graduate institution, to complete my seminary training. I could have done correspondence coursework from the White seminary where I had received the bulk of my religious training, but I longed for the Black academic exchange. I wanted to engage in deep theoretical discussions with people who looked like me. I wanted to experience the brilliant minds of men and women of color and be in awe of their brilliance for a change. My weekly flights from Fort Lauderdale to ITC in Atlanta were well rewarded, as I established experientially the reality and beauty of the Black scholarship.

I now had mentors who looked like me and who, without condescension, valued me as a thinking person. During class discussions, the men and women at ITC looked at me expectantly (rather than with surprise, which is what my participation in class discussions had elicited from my teachers elsewhere). They knew that I was a good student and they challenged me to be a better one. Therefore, I identified most emphatically with the students who signed up for my classes. They were looking, as I had, for a place to feel safe, at home, and affirmed (Chan & Treacy, 1996; Henderson, 1994; hooks, 1994; Hyde & Ruth, 2002; Jacobson, 2000).

However, not all students have felt at home in my classes. This past semester, I taught the Diversity class and spoke candidly and provocatively about racism in this country. Afterward, a White American student reported that she and several other students felt that I would not be able to grade them fairly because of my views on White America. Her fear grew out of a discussion about stereotypes. Although at least two other White female students reported verbally in class and via email that the discussion had been helpful to them, my comments disturbed her and reportedly disturbed others as well. So, I invited her into a conversation about it in class.

Exploring What Divides Us: The Stereotypes Exercise

I invited the class to list all the stereotypes of Black women, Black men, White women, and White men. After we listed those stereotypes on the easel board, we talked about where they originated and how they are perpetuated. We talked about the possibility of there being "truth" in some of them and about the wisdom behind such truth. After we listed the stereotypes of White men, I asked the question, "Of all the stereotypes listed, who has the most positive stereotypes?" The class agreed unanimously that White men have the most favorable stereotypes. Then I asked why they supposed that was the case. A White male responded, "Because they make the rules." All agreed. I said, "Honestly, I have never sympathized with White men before, but looking at this list, I can imagine the pressure of trying to live up to the things in this list." It was this comment that caused the student concern.

However, what I did in the exercise was what we try to train therapists to do in therapy—understand the other's reality and the wisdom in the other's behavior given her or his contexts. But in therapy, the other is the client. We train therapists to be curious about clients' stories and to allow clients to tell them. By being curious, we learn what it is like for clients to negotiate their lives in a fashion that makes sense to them. Listening curiously helps us to genuinely validate clients' experiences (Freedman & Combs, 1996). So as a result of our discussion, I was able to see White men (generally) in a different light, and I voiced my discovery.

Inviting Open Dialogue

The week after the class did the stereotypes exercise, the aforementioned student, at the urging of one of the Black female students, came to see me to discuss her fears about her grade. She shared with me that her fear generally had to do with remarks I had made about White men. I invited her to bring the topic up in class so that we could all talk about it.

During the lecture the following week, I mentioned my conversation with this student and invited the class to speak openly about the issue. We discussed my comment and her fear. During the discussion, I asked the class to think about the larger story, discourse, and predominant belief system that exist in our country that create a context within which a White student would question the integrity of a Black instructor on the basis of race. Acknowledging this context served to make us all more aware of the need to talk openly about the diversity issues that influence our thinking and behavior toward others. Furthermore, it helped to open up an avenue for creating a safe place (hooks, 1994; Hyde & Ruth, 2002). Although there were some students in the class who still seemed to resist joining the efforts to create this space, many students welcomed the community and joined me in cocreating a safe place.

Opening Issues for Discussion

On another occasion, a student of Arab ancestry asked the hypothetical question, "What if someone said that Black people ought to get over it and stop dwelling on the past?" Then I asked the class, "If clients come into your office and insist on retelling the same story and dwelling on past events, when do you think they will stop feeling the need to tell the story?" A couple of students said in unison, "When they feel that you have heard them."

We then talked about how Black people may need to talk about the atrocities and residuals of slavery because they don't feel heard. An Israeli woman in the class wrote in her journal that when her husband asked her why Black people don't forget the past, she responded, "How can they, when the past is so much a part of the present?"

This type of openness and honesty is what I believe effects change in therapy and introduces change in discussions about controversial topics such as racism and religion. However, not all students relax and receive the invitation to be a part of the community. Their reluctance is understandable, because if they voiced an unpopular opinion, especially when traditional pedagogical practice avoids certain topics, they might suffer both academically and socially. One White female student shared that she was socially ostracized for mentioning the ill effects of the American slave trade on Blacks in this country.

My pedagogical style is to invite students to be themselves and speak their minds about difficult topics such as race and religion—and I do the same. For example, when I introduce myself, I tell students that I am a minister, so that opens the door to discussion of God talks. I make my feminist views known, so students are not surprised when I express my ideas about patriarchy. My intention is to create a therapeutic atmosphere in the classroom so that the relationship between the students and the teacher is collaborative. I try as much as possible to eliminate that traditional hierarchal distance that interferes with genuine learning and community.

Building Community

Community begins with a community developer, and in my classes I am the primary community developer. I try to create and establish an atmosphere of openness and receptivity. It appears to work for some students, and it may be thought unacademic by other students (Henderson, 1994). Nevertheless, I believe that for a student to approach me with a concern that is potentially explosive, such as the student I mentioned earlier who came to me with a fear about her grades, the student must feel some sense of safety. Some of my Black colleagues may argue that this is an example of White arrogance and/or entitlement and that the student was simply challenging my credibility (Hamilton, 2002; McGowan, 2000). I want to believe she trusted me, or at least wanted to.

This incident notwithstanding, I have been able to create a safe environment with some of my other classes. For example, in my Introduction to Marriage and Family class, which consisted of a diverse group of students, one African American student was amazed that students talked openly about things that she considered very personal. Two other students immediately suggested that it was possible because of the warm and caring atmosphere generated in the class. I agree with these students—they were acknowledging the fulfillment of my hidden agenda to create a therapeutic atmosphere in my classes.

The nature of my method is such that I may not be taken as seriously as those instructors who work hard to create a hierarchy that separates them from their students. However, my not being taken seriously is a minor loss if my students feel a sense of community that will allow them to grow as clinicians, scholars, and people. This is sometimes a difficult task because most students hold the image of the all-knowing professor and seem to struggle with my style (Henderson, 1994; hooks, 1994).

In the example above, the student who questioned my integrity did not get the mark that she wanted. However, she also failed to rise to the challenge in her assignments. I honestly felt that she took me and the coursework for granted. We talked about her grade, and she did not file a formal complaint. Freire (1970) maintains that this is liberation pedagogy, where learners share in their learning and refuse to be deposit boxes as in the banking system of traditional learning.

In my approach to the teaching and learning endeavor, students use the designated text and other selected readings as guides for class discussion, but my goal is that we spend class time finding our own voices or developing our own ideas about what others in the field of MFT are saying. Therein lies the difference between a pedagogy that centers on the relationship of instructor, text, and students to each other and a pedagogy where the instructor is the center, period. The former pedagogical emphasis has been useful for me in engaging students in conversations about race and other issues of difference; it has been life changing for us all.

African American Pedagogy

While the available research highlighting the teaching styles of African American scholars is slight, McGowan (2000), Hamilton (2002), Neville and Cha-jua (1998), and hooks (1994) have offered provocative and innovative ways of engaging students in the collegiate learning endeavor. In the following discussion, I will focus on some of the ideals of African American pedagogy, as I believe that in them is a formula for effective academic engagement, especially in the discussion of race and other volatile topics. Although, Freire (1970, 1998), perhaps the father of liberation pedagogy, popularized this nontraditional teaching and learning epistemology, it has been the worldview and practice of African teachers or *griot*—storytellers— since before our arrival on American shores. In African American culture, knowledge and wisdom are transmitted through storytelling. From my perspective, this art of teaching and learning remains an integral part of the African American collective consciousness and therefore of Black pedagogy, and it provides a foundation for the following discussion.

Kufundisha, a Kiswahili word meaning "to teach," articulates the educational epistemology and strategies for classroom praxis that characterize (in part) the work of many distinguished Africentric thinkers (Neville & Cha-jua, 1998). Although Kufundisha was designed specifically for teaching Black studies courses, and it places special attention on the learning styles of African American students (Neville & Cha-jua, 1998), I believe that some of its elements are reflective of the pedagogical emphasis of many Black professors, including myself.

Thus bell hooks (1994) has written about establishing community in the classroom. She reports that she has made an effort to recreate in her classes the community that she enjoyed growing up. Tatum (1997), an African American dean and clinical psychologist at Mount Holyoke College, and others (Zamboanga & Bingman, 2001) suggest that creating a community is an essential goal for multicultural learning. hooks (1994) noted,

> We want to build community. Any school leader will talk about building the school community and creating a positive learning environment, where people are connected to one another and feel concerned about each other. You want to bring people together. (p. 42)

Another outstanding element of African American teaching is that of teachers' engaging students in challenging, thought-provoking discussions. This collaborative style of learning constructs and facilitates a classroom environment that encourages free discussion and interaction, which increases students' investment in the course and leads to deep learning (Freire, 1970; Neville & Cha-jua, 1998). It also creates the type of environment that hooks (1994) has insisted the classroom should be, that is, "an exciting place, never boring" (p. 7). I have often preached that I want to have fun in class and that if I wasn't having fun, then more than likely the students weren't either. After my first trimester of teaching, I told one of my colleagues that I believed I had had "way too much fun." Another professor reported that on the first day of class, he has to inform his students that laughing and joking does not mean that they should not take his class seriously (Hamilton, 2002). His opening speech resonates a struggle of nontraditional pedagogy, especially for African

American women (Henderson, 1994), with reaching students who hold traditional views of academic exchange and have difficulty adjusting to the new pedagogy (Gay & Fox, 1995; hooks, 1994; McGowan, 2000). According to hooks (1994), such students

> continue to cling to the belief that an all-knowing professor should stand before the class and deposit valuable bits of information into their heads and not ask them to get involved in the negotiation of meaning and the production of knowledge. (p. 7)

She informs her students at the beginning of each semester that they are required to participate in class discussion. Similarly, class participation is usually a substantial component of students' grades in most of my classes. Like hooks (1994) and Freire (1970), I find this communicative process places students at the center of the learning endeavor in class and not at its margins. As hooks (1994) put it, it is important that every student's voice be heard. She further asserted that an inclusive classroom environment is one where each student's voice is acknowledged and affirmed. The privileging of marginalized voices is precisely what we as MFT supervisors stress when training students to respect clients' realities. The pedagogical strategy I am proposing reinforces other ideals of MFT training, which makes it easy for me to incorporate it in the classroom or in training students in a clinical environment.

For me, then, there is a natural fit between the climate that makes for good therapy and the atmosphere one must create for effective teaching and learning experiences. I believe that this teaching style works especially well for students of African descent because it resembles something familiar—it feels like home. Moreover, this Africentric pedagogy has enabled me to create the same "at home" relationship with White students and international students so that we have been able to talk about difficult issues in ways that promote community and not disunity (McGowan, 2000; Zamboanga & Bingman, 2001). My task now is to create even more "at home" experiences for students, so that through our dialogue we continue to cocreate and perpetuate an academic community that is not afraid to talk about hard topics such as race and that welcomes and even invites such topics, with the collective understanding that our discussion can only serve our good will.

Filling the Research Gap

I join McGowan (2000) and Neville & Cha-jua (1998) in their lament over the sore lack of serious inquiry about the pedagogical experiences of

African American academicians. I encountered the same problem of a lack of material when I looked for what had been written about Black scholarship and found little beyond issues of affirmative action (Boutte, 1999; Culotta et al., 1993; Hamilton, 2002; Neville & Cha-jua, 1998; Williams, 1995; Wilson, 2002; Zamboanga & Bingman, 2001). However, the literature is clear that there is a problem with hiring and retaining Black professors, as Black scholars continue to be marginalized when hired by predominantly White institutions (Alfred, 2001; Hamilton, 2002; Henderson, 1994; McGowan, 2000; Nast & Pulido, 2000).

My contribution to the shortfall in the literature is this analysis of my experience in these two areas: the promotion of academic discussions about diversity issues (especially race) and the pedagogical experiences specific to Black scholarship. I have also explored how the specialized pedagogical practices of African Americans help to create and facilitate an atmosphere conducive to open dialogue on difficult topics. Therefore, this may be considered an efficacy study of how the specified teaching practices are used to encourage students to talk about difficult sociological issues that they may not otherwise have been open to discussing. This chapter then adds to the limited body of literature about the efficacy of African American pedagogy in promoting classroom discussions about matters of diversity.

Conclusion

Du Bois was right in his assertion that the problem of the 20th century would be the color line. I wonder if he had considered whether we would have the same problem in the 21st century. My goal in writing this chapter is to suggest that part of the reason we are still faced with this problem is that in institutions of higher learning we are either afraid to talk about race and color or we don't know how to talk about these issues in productive ways. Thus, we perpetuate the color problem in America.

If we are to eliminate the color problem in this century, we must begin now by talking about it to each other, not just among ourselves. For instructors interested in participating in this revolution, I have the following generic suggestion: "Be honest with yourself and the students about your own bias." This approach will probably get you into trouble at first, but eventually all may benefit. Then invite students to join you by sharing their open, honest thoughts. I have found this approach to be effective in establishing a collaborative teaching and learning atmosphere, which then translates to a different, more effective way of talking about race and responding to others who are of a different culture.

Reflections, Questions, and Exercises

Consider the following questions as you seek to incorporate the above ideas into your work.

1. What racial, gender, and/or religious biases or convictions might I have?

2. Of the above biases or convictions, which do I believe to be absolutely true?

3. How many times have I experienced these "truths" personally?

4. How does holding onto my biases serve me? How does it serve others?

5. What would happen if I shared my bias (about anything) with my students?

My Teaching and Learning Environment

1. What kind of learning environment have I created in my classes?

2. How am I taking responsibility for the learning that takes place in my classes? How do I engage the students in critical thinking?

3. When I look into the eyes of the students in my class, what do I see?
   a. Do I care about what I see in their eyes?
   b. What would I like to see there?

4. Do I teach the students or do I teach the material? I would describe my relationship with my students as _____.

5. Think of your favorite or your best teacher or professor. What made her or him your favorite or best?

References

Alfred, M. (2001, Spring). Reconceptualizing marginality from the margins: Perspectives of African American tenured female faculty at a White research university. *Western Journal of Black Studies, 24*(1), 1–11.

Back, L., & Solomos, J. (Eds.). (2000). Theories of race and racism: A reader. New York: Routledge.

Beauboeuf-Lafontant, T. (2002, March). A womanist experience of caring: Understanding the pedagogy of exemplary Black women teachers. *Urban Review, 34*(1), 71–86.

Benjamin, M. (1996). *Cultural diversity, educational equity and the transformation of higher education: Group profiles as guide to policy and programming.* Westport, CT: Praeger.

Boutte, G. (1999). *Multicultural education: Raising consciousness*. Albany, NY: Wadsworth.

Bower, B., Auletta, G., & Jones, T. (1993). *Confronting diversity issues on campus*. London: Sage.

Chan, C., & Treacy, M. (1996). Resistance in multicultural courses: Student, faculty, and classroom dynamics. *American Behavioral Scientist, 40*(2), 212–222.

Churchill, W. (2000). White studies: The intellectual imperialism of the U. W. higher education. In S. Jackson & J. Solis (Eds.), *Beyond comfort zones in multiculturalism: Confronting the politics of privilege* (pp. 17–35). Westport, CT: Bergin & Garvey.

Constantine, M. G., Juby, H. L., & Laing, J. C. (2001). Examining multicultural counseling competence and race-related attitudes among white marital and family therapists. *Journal of Marital and Family Therapy, 27*(3), 327–340.

Culotta, E., Holden, C., & Gibbons, A. (1993). Finding and keeping minority professors. *Science, 262*(5136), 1091–1094.

Freedman, J., & Combs, G. (1996). *Narrative therapy: The social construction of preferred realities*. New York: Norton.

Freire, P. (1970). *Pedagogy of the oppressed*. New York: Continuum.

Freire, P. (1998). *Pedagogy of freedom: Ethics, democracy, and civic courage*. Lanham, MD: Rowman & Littlefield.

Gay, G., & Fox, W. (1995). The cultural ethos of the academy: potential and perils of multicultural education reform. In S. Jackson & J. Solis (Eds.), *Beyond comfort zones in multiculturalism: Confronting the politics of privilege* (pp. 239–247). Westport, CT: Bergin & Garvey.

Hamilton, K. (2002). Dual dilemma. *Black Issues in Higher Education, 19*(18), 40–42.

Henderson, M. (1994, Spring). What it means to teach other when the other is the self. *Callaloo, 17*(2), 432–439.

hooks, b. (1994). Teaching to transgress: Education as the practice of freedom. New York: Routledge.

Hyde, C., & Ruth, B. (2002). Multicultural content and class participation: Do students set censor? *Journal of Social Work Education, 38*(2), 241.

Jacobson, L. O. (2000, Summer). Editor's choice: Valuing diversity—student-teacher relationships that enhance achievement. *Community College Review, 28*(1), 49.

McCarthy, C. & Willis, A. I. (1995). The politics of culture: Multicultural education after the content debate. In S. Jackson & J. Solis (Eds.), *Beyond comfort zones in multiculturalism: Confronting the politics of privilege* (pp. 67–88). Westport, CT: Bergin & Garvey.

McGowan, J. (2000). Multicultural teaching: African American faculty classroom teaching experiences in predominantly white colleges and universities. *Education, 8*(2), 19–25.

McNamee, S. (1996). Psychotherapy as a social construction. In H. Rosen & K. Kuehlwein (Eds.), *Constructing realities: Meaning making perspective for psychotherapists*. San Francisco: Jossey-Bass.

Mindell, A. (1998, September 7). Executives learn how to mentor minorities. *Crain's Detroit Business*, p. 15.

Nast, H., & Pulido, L. (2000). Resisting corporate multiculturalism: Mapping faculty initiatives and institutional-student harassment in the classroom. *Professional Geographer, 52*(4), 722–737.

Neville, H., & Cha Jua, S. (1998, March). Kufundisha: Toward a pedagogy for Black studies. *Journal of Black Studies, 28*(4), 447–471.

Nelson, K. W., Johnston, M. B., Mize, L. K., Lad, K., Hancock, C. C., & Pinjala, A. (2001). Therapist perceptions of ethnicity issues in family therapy: A qualitative inquiry. *Journal of Marital and Family Therapy, 27*(3), 363–373.

Oxford American dictionary. (1980). New York: Oxford University Press.

Patterson, J., Williams, L., Grauf-Grounds, C., & Chamow, L. (1998). *Essential skills in family therapy: From the first interview to termination*. New York: Guilford.

Rice, C. M. (2001). *The Ellison Model: Building inclusive communities through mentoring*. North Miami, FL: I.C B Productions.

Stanford, G. (1998, September). African American teachers' knowledge of teaching: Understanding the influence of their remembered teachers. *Urban Review, 30*(3), 229–243.

Tatum, D. B. (1997). *Why are all the Black kids sitting together in the cafeteria? And other conversations about race*. New York: Basic Books.

Van Soest, D. (1996). Impact of social work education on student attitudes and behavior concerning oppression. *Journal of Social Work Education, 32*, 202.

Walter, J., & Peller, J. (2000). *Recreating brief therapy: References and possibilities*. New York: Norton.

Wellman, David T. (1977). *Portraits of white racism*. New York: Cambridge University Press.

Williams, J. D. (1995). Recruitment & retention (non-White faculty and school administrators). *Black Issues in Higher Education, 12*(20), 35.

Wilson, R. (2002). Stacking the deck for minority candidates. *Chronicle of Higher Education, 48*(44), A10–A13.

Zamboanga, B., & Bingman, L. (2001). The diversity challenge: Recruiting prospective faculty of color. *Black Issues in Higher Education, 18*(11), 124.

9

Post 9/11: Combating Racism in the Sanctity of Healing

A Clinical Vignette Utilizing a Cultural Process Dialogue

Azmaira H. Maker

Zeitgeist: Post 9/11

The current climate of fear, anger, and paranoia as the United States is in a perpetual state of war with terrorists and the "Axes of Evil" has perhaps done irreparable damage to ordinary professional immigrants from South Asia and the Middle East. The media have succeeded in creating powerful images of a "violent and primitive" people based on the "oppressive" religion and culture of Islam. Heightened negative stereotypes in the aftermath of the trauma of 9/11 have given rise to stark moments of discrimination, even in the hallowed hallways of academia and clinical centers. This resurgence of targeted racism may be similar to the experiences endured by Chinese, Korean, Vietnamese, and Japanese professionals after the wars of their respective countries with the United States. Tung (1981) highlighted

Author's Note: I would like to deeply thank the faculty at the University Center for the Child and Family, University of Michigan, Ann Arbor, for their exceptional clinical training and their wisdom and insight, which perpetually guide me.

her clinical experiences as she was branded a "Chink" and a "Jap" and clients disclosed wanting to "kill Chinks." As a Muslim psychologist faced with related experiences in the current hostile sociopolitical climate, I can no longer rely only on my previous theoretical knowledge and clinical expertise to successfully navigate as a healer and a teacher during moments of intolerance. The existing literature certainly does not provide any resources or insights for responding to post-9/11 reactions to Muslim Arabs and South Asians in professional contexts. In fact, a review of the literature conducted by Iwamasa (1996) clearly pointed to the lack of adequate training in multicultural issues in general, particularly for therapists of color. Thus, I find that I must discover novel tools and a distinctive language to communicate and connect beyond stereotypes, fear, hostility, and rejection, while maintaining my professional stance as a therapist and supervisor. In this chapter, I hope to highlight some of my own encounters and interventions since 9/11 as a Muslim, Pakistani, female psychologist. I hope that the following clinical vignette and suggestions provide kernels for others to use in formulating their own strategies in similarly difficult moments. I strongly believe that our using overt and proactive "combat" tactics in sessions and with supervisees can serve as an antidote to racism toward therapists of color and have a profound impact on our clients and supervisees, thus facilitating therapy in a more productive and effective way. This chapter focuses on three primary themes:

1. how cemented stereotypes of Muslim women (i.e., specific negative gender roles, values, and cultural norms) emerge in the family therapy session;

2. the assumptions of differences between therapist and client based on race, religion, nationality, and culture;

3. the therapist's use of the self and the cultural process dialogue with clients to confront racism and discuss race and ethnicity, culture, religious beliefs, and values.

Personal Background

I am a first-generation South Asian, Muslim, immigrant woman from Pakistan residing in the U.S. Midwest. Before I delve further, I would like to address the image some may have conjured of me given the recent media spotlight on my country. No, I do not resemble the now prevailing picture of a burkah-clad woman that is splattered frequently on CNN or in *Time* magazine. Like many Americans, I look Westernized and come from a diverse background. My mother, who is from East Africa, and my father, who is from India, have very different religious backgrounds and now reside as permanent South Asian immigrants in Pakistan. As a legacy of colonialism, my parents studied in England, I went to a British school, and my family sways comfortably in the suspended realm of East meets West, with our core rooted in a tricultural identity of East African, English, and South Asian (Akhtar, 1999). This is particularly evident in our use of language, as family discussions frequently integrate English, Urdu, Gujrati, Katchi, and Swahili, all in the same conversation. My immigration to the United States added yet another dimension to my worldview, especially as feminism and psychology entered my schooling. In this chapter, I intend to reveal some of the potent conflicts I faced and systemic interventions I shaped as a clinical psychologist when compartmentalized by my clients in simplistic and often highly negative terms as *Middle Eastern* and a *Muslim woman*. The negative connotations are particularly potent since 9/11, as the nation is flooded with unidimensional information on the Middle East and South Asia.

Professional Training and Background

Having received my bachelor's degree from Vassar College in psychology, I entered the realm of standardized admission tests for doctoral programs in clinical psychology. One particularly challenging test for an immigrant that is required by some excellent schools is the Miller's Analogies Test, which specifically assesses "integration and knowledge of American culture, history, politics, and values." Despite my overt protests at the implicit and not so implicit ramifications of screening via a clearly culturally biased test, I was admitted to the University of Michigan, Ann Arbor. However, the biased hoops I had to jump through did not end there. In order to fund my education via teaching assistantships, I had to undergo further oral and written testing in English, despite my educational record at Cambridge, Oxford, and Vassar. Fortunately, the chair and faculty of the clinical department were very supportive of my dissension and have since then worked hard to abolish both of these discriminating practices.

My education at the University of Michigan was stellar, as I trained under the Boulder-Colorado model. Much of my training and clinical experience is from a systems orientation, working extensively with children and adolescents in inpatient, outpatient, community, and school settings. I have also been trained from a psychodynamic perspective and have worked at length with outpatients in long-term psychotherapy. When I returned to Pakistan for some time, I practiced and taught in hospital, outpatient, and educational settings and struggled to transfer my Western techniques to an enormously different psyche and community. Unfortunately, the focus of this chapter prevents me from elaborating on these experiences here; however, I must stress that those experiences led me to conclude that it is essential to question the notion that Western models of psychopathology and psychotherapy can be effectively transported to vastly different cultures, and that higher educational institutions and researchers should be encouraged to carefully gauge the application of these models.

Literature Review

After conducting an extensive literature review, I identified research focusing on the impact of race, ethnicity, and other cultural factors on the therapeutic relationship. However, I was able to locate only a few articles on racism directed toward therapists of color. Beutler, Machado, and Neufeldt (1994) conducted a literature review on the impact of therapist ethnicity on therapy outcome and concluded that most of the literature focused on client-therapist similarity, client preference for therapist ethnicity, and client drop-out rates. They determined this research to be equivocal, at best, and they found no direct measurement of racism toward therapists of color in the literature. Perhaps the predominant research and theoretical focus on the White therapist working with a minority client is a reflection of the field being dominated by White therapists, and hence the attention on the predominant group working with clients of different racial and ethnic origins. However, given the rapidly expanding population of African American, Hispanic, and Asian therapists in training (Sue, Bingham, Porche-Burke, & Vasquez, 1999), it is imperative to conduct extensive research on therapists of color working with similar and different racial and ethnic groups.

The few studies that focus on therapists of color strongly point in the direction of racism and discrimination that significantly interfere with the essence of healing. Tinsley-Jones's (2001) qualitative study with a small sample of psychologists of color showed that the race and ethnicity of the therapist are profoundly important, clarified that a negative appraisal of the therapist predominates the professional relationship, and contained the psychologists' descriptions of covert acts of racism directed toward them as therapists. In particular, the therapists surveyed felt that their individuality was disregarded, that they were viewed as representatives of their race or ethnicity, and that others perceived them as possessing stereotyped characteristics. Tinsley-Jones (2001) pointed out the critical need to develop alternate psychological constructs that address racism toward therapists of color, t   o

build theories from the perspective of psychologists of color, and to facilitate the fuller inclusion of such ethnic and racial models of therapy in the field of psychology.

Similarly, Iwamasa (1996) noted the unique experiences of therapists of color with both ethnically different and ethnically similar clients, about which little training and guidance are provided. He suggested that although "multicultural" treatment frequently has been addressed as a special issue in the field, therapists of color engage in addressing issues of diversity regularly. Moreover, these issues usually have a negative tone, as indicated by his research. For example, a survey Iwamasa (1996) conducted revealed a bias against therapists of color in assumptions of their incompetence and the belief that therapists of color are only able to effectively work with ethnic minority clients. The survey also identified how the therapists' ethnicity affected their clinical work in positive and negative ways. The therapists identified the positive aspects as being able to empathize more effectively with similar clients, being sought after by clients of color, and having some level of expertise in working with diversity. The negative aspects the therapists reported included clients' stereotypes of the therapist and feelings of prejudice and mistrust that interfered with the therapeutic alliance and effective treatment. Some therapists had also experienced clients' direct refusal to see a therapist of color simply based on the therapist's race or ethnic minority name. A smaller study of White, African American, and Native American counselors also indicated higher incidents of racism in treatment of a similar nature (Davis & Gelsomino, 1994).

Based on his research, Iwamasa (1996) suggested the urgent need to address issues of racism toward therapists of color—in training, in academic settings, and with clients—by adopting an "idiosocial" approach. That is, we must approach racism at an individual (idio) level and at a larger social level in groups, programs, institutions, and mental health settings. Iwamasa suggests that this model must incorporate *all* therapists' understanding of their own race, ethnicity, and culture, as well as how these factors impact their work. To simply focus on the race and ethnicity of the client, and assume that therapists do not have a racial and ethnic identity that can powerfully influence treatment, is to only partially grasp the complexity of the therapist-client dyad. Further research on the therapist of color specific to various ethnic groups, as well as research on the shared experiences of therapists of color, is also necessary to better understand the multifaceted dynamics of racism in therapy. The development of theoretical models and appropriate interventions that depict the influence of therapist ethnicity on treatment is also critical to furthering the disarming of racism in the sanctity of the healing profession.

Thus, there is clearly a strong need for the field to acknowledge racism toward therapists of color and for us to take the critical step in challenging all subtle acts of racism in the clinical, academic, and research realms of the field. As Tinsley-Jones (2001) eloquently stated, "As psychologists, we have the privilege of helping our clients transform their lives; we also have the opportunity and responsibility to transform our own profession—to be courageous and take on the obvious" (p. 579).

Unfortunately, the literature remains extraordinarily sparse regarding the experience of therapists of color in general and of South Asian therapists in particular. Moreover, few high profile South Asian role models are available in training, in clinical practice, or in administration to promote a voice for this rather marginalized group. It is critically important that we shift our attention to systematically and scientifically investigating the experiences of therapists of color, especially given their increasing number in training. The data on these experiences and the response of the field to such data are particularly vital for South Asian and Arab therapists in the wake of 9/11.

Although I cannot provide hard data at this point regarding racism toward South Asian therapists, in the following section I outline one systemic case that delineates the primary theme of racism toward the therapist. For this case, I provide the context, the presenting problems, the conflict with the therapist, the interventions, and the resolution. Woven within the case I present the importance of and suggestions for a process-oriented approach to create a dialogue and a space to confront racism, and I discuss the issues of race and ethnicity, culture, religious beliefs, and values between therapist and client.

Case Study: Stereotypes of a Muslim Woman

Nicole is a White, Christian, middle-class woman with a bachelor's degree in education, and she is a licensed day care provider. She was divorcing her African American husband, with whom she had two biracial daughters, ages 4 and 9. Nicole and the two girls were struggling with the recent loss of their husband and father and with the very different parenting styles in their home and that of the girls' father. Nicole was also concerned about her oldest daughter's ambivalence around her racial identity and emerging gender role. The father was presented as a relatively unreliable and unavailable man who refused to participate in the treatment. I saw the mother and her oldest daughter in family sessions and separately in individual sessions for a year. The younger daughter would only sporadically join the family sessions, as there were some developmental delays in her cognitive development.

Nicole was a high functioning, insightful, and well-informed mother who was acutely aware of her daughters' anger, confusion, and helplessness regarding the divorce. The initial family sessions focused on discussing the loss, repeated disappointments with the girls' father, and confusion regarding parenting styles, roles, and rules in the two parental homes. Over time, and with much reluctance, Nicole began to share her concerns about her children's abrupt rupture from her ex-husband's African American community and her reluctance to integrate her children's White and African American female identities. The mother was also recently "banished" from the ex-husband's community, and she defensively rejected and stereotyped African Americans, perhaps stemming from her recent anger at her ex-husband. Underlying these racial and ethnic tensions was the struggle of the oldest daughter's gender role development. Being 9, the oldest daughter was at a stage in which she strongly identified with her mother, and Nicole was adamant that her children's role in the family incorporate characteristics of independence, self-sufficiency, and assertiveness, as befit "liberated girls." Nicole's own struggle with her emerging "feminist" identity as a single mother was clearly being blended with her oldest daughter's identity development, as boundaries blurred between the two.

The rupture in the homeostasis of Nicole's own identity development in conjunction with her oldest daughter's racial and gender role development was not easy to access. Although I had felt a strong initial alliance with the family and had been able to successfully work on facilitating the daughter's ability to negotiate appropriate boundaries between her parents, and loosen the strong coalition between mother and daughter against the father, I felt blocked when approaching the racial and gender issues. Even though Nicole sporadically touched on her concerns, every time I attempted to explore these concerns a little further or obtain details, she would shift or become evasive. Instead, some momentary crisis would emerge that needed immediate attention. After several sessions of this nature, I began to feel frustrated, as I could not put my finger on the slippery pulse of this family and could not fathom the mother's elusiveness. Nicole too must have felt stifled, as she began to occasionally skip sessions.

It was about the 15th session when Nicole shifted directions and began to bring up distal themes of racism and stereotypes by complaining about the community she lived in. She was on SSI benefits and lived in low-income housing. She described at length how her neighbors were mostly immigrants who seemed to have family lifestyles and values that were very different from hers and that she did not approve of. In particular, there were several Middle-Eastern families who were "loud, lazy, aggressive with their children, and dirty."

In addition, "the women were oppressed, wore veils, and didn't value education or empowerment for their daughters." Over the next few sessions, Nicole elaborated on her stereotypes and condemnation of her Arab neighbors.

Being in denial about Nicole's perceptions of me as a South Asian woman, I simply responded with empathy and some mild psychoeducational commentary. It was not until a few sessions later when I experienced Nicole as being "stuck" on this theme, and felt my own sense of indignation and anger surfacing, that I realized what Nicole was communicating: She was talking about me! It was only when I allowed myself to explore and identify my own affective reactions to Nicole's biases that I was able to grasp the underlying racist messages in what she said. Had I not allowed myself to genuinely connect with my anger and not used my sense of resentment to inform me, perhaps I would not have come to this important realization. Of course, it would have been more comfortable to deny the racial tension between us and to continue to be the "placated, helpful, and understanding therapist"; however, that clearly would not have facilitated my understanding of Nicole's racial and cultural concerns and biases about me.

Nicole's ripe intrapsychic and intrafamilial conflict regarding racial and gender identity development—given the recent disruption in her family system and the disparagement of Muslims in the current sociopolitical milieu—served as a perfect catalyst for Nicole to be potently confused and suspicious about working with a South Asian female psychologist. My error in failing to proactively address the racial, cultural, religious, and associated ethnic and gender role differences between us cost us many sessions and almost splintered the relationship.

Once I recognized Nicole's underlying message of negative assumptions about and stereotypes of me as a Muslim woman, I knew I had to address it in a direct but delicate manner. Because of norms of deference to the professional, and most people's inexperience in creating a space and dialogue about race, I felt it would be more effective for me to directly question Nicole about her attitudes and preferences than to wait for her opinions to emerge or ask in more indirect ways. An exploratory but direct line of questioning perhaps gives the client permission to share her or his thoughts without offending the therapist and thus places the client in an empowered role. Via this role, I felt Nicole might be willing to express her ambivalence, doubt, anxiety, and unfamiliarity with a therapist of color, without shaming me in the process. Thus, I asked a simple question—"Nicole, what is it like to work with me? A woman who looks and sounds so different from you and your children?"—which served as an effective opening for us to use in exploring her assumptions and concerns about me.

At first Nicole was hesitant to respond, but as I assured her that it was safe to share her feelings and perceptions about me, she ventured forth. Without much self-disclosure, I adopted an exploratory role to further inquire, Where did she think I was from? What did she think my values were about women and family? What did she believe my religious beliefs were? Did she think I could understand and relate to her? More important, did she feel "culturally" understood and validated in her concerns and goals so that I could actually help her?

My direct line of questioning was enormously helpful in mobilizing Nicole and the treatment process. Nicole revealed that she assumed I was a Muslim woman from the Middle East and that, therefore, I must be "conservative" and "traditional." When I asked her to elaborate on what she meant, Nicole described how she felt that I would not understand why she divorced her husband. Worse, I was probably judging her to be a "bad woman" and a "failure" for leaving her husband. She assumed that because I am Muslim, I would be hostile to her beliefs in independence and self-sufficiency. Moreover, given my cultural and religious background, that I would not endorse her wish to inculcate these values in her daughters. My being from the Middle East also alienated Nicole from discussing racial concerns and conflicts about her daughters being biracial. Her stereotypes of Arabs being "aggressive and lazy" in many ways coincided with her negative stereotypes of African Americans, which were linked with her anger at her African American ex-husband. How could she discuss these matters with me when I perhaps identified with characteristics similar to those she assigned to Arabs and African Americans?

I understood Nicole's perceptions as a kaleidoscopic product of her own intrapsychic issues (anger at and loss of her husband), systemic disruptions (mother vs. father roles), and an intense psychosocial conflict revolving around race and gender, which was fueled by personal and sociopolitical interracial tensions. Perhaps the latter conflict came to fruition more quickly in our relationship because I am a South Asian woman, and because the media are currently ripe with negative stereotypes of Arab and South Asians, both of which tapped directly into Nicole's presenting psychological struggles and quickly gave rise to her "stuckness" in our therapeutic relationship.

Nicole's disclosure of her stereotypes about me, based on my questioning, brought to the forefront the importance of discussing race and ethnicity as a critical factor that needs to be addressed early in the treatment. To not speak to differences and similarities between therapist and client would be like ignoring the elephant in the middle of the room. Racial, ethnic, religious, and language differences can hugely impede the alliance between therapist and client, particularly if the client feels the therapist is ignorant, judgmental, or misinformed about the client's sociocultural system. Therapists are likely to gain much trust and confidence if they openly ask their clients about what it is like to work with a therapist who is so different from them, acknowledge their limited understanding of their clients' cultural and religious beliefs (if appropriate), and state that they are open to learning from their clients. Creating a space and a language to bridge differences can greatly facilitate the alliance and the therapist's understanding of the client. This is equally true if the therapist is from the same racial, ethnic, religious, or regional background as the client. For such a therapist to assume parallels in beliefs would be a grave error, as there are many variations in acculturation, identity, immigration history, and education levels within racial groups. All these factors could contribute to determining unique attitudes and preferences, and for the therapist to simply assume that "we are the same" could be a setup for a disruption later in therapy as unspoken differences hinder the treatment. (For further reading, see Maki's 1990 essay, which uses a case study to elaborate on how overidentification with a client based on assumed shared values and cultural beliefs can impede therapeutic work with clients.)

Although, based on the above theoretical considerations, I felt I had a substantial intellectual grasp of Nicole's racism and the impediment it was creating in our relationship, I experienced her words with much anguish. Despite what I considered my adaptive integration into and presentation in Western society, my skin color and accent gave rise to an image of me endorsed by the media that highly contradicted my sense of self. I knew that I would have to pay close attention to my inner voice in order to guide the treatment and not allow self-indignation and righteousness to supersede my interventions. I continued my stance of limited self-disclosure, but I felt that once I had explored Nicole's concerns about me and stereotypes of me in some depth, I had to reassure her that on some levels we did exist on the same cultural plane. I felt that if I did not do so, she would be unable to maintain an alliance with me. Moreover, I believe that clients have the right to question their therapist's value system to assess if the therapist is an appropriate match for them (e.g., a lesbian couple working with a therapist who maintains strong beliefs against homosexuality, based on religious beliefs, have the right to know the therapist's position).

Thus, I adopted a direct stance in informing Nicole that I believe in women's rights, divorce, and education for girls, and that I hold other similar values. Although this self-disclosure constituted a significant departure from my training, similar disclosures about race and ethnicity have been considered crucial by some (Thompson & Jenal, 1994). When I made my disclosure, it was an important moment for Nicole—what I said created enormous relief for her and she visibly relaxed (even though I had made no mention of my specific background or religion). Thus, over the next few sessions, I was able to challenge Nicole's stereotypes about my gender role beliefs by asking her if she felt any contradiction in my presentation as a working woman with a doctorate in clinical psychology and her perception of me as an oppressed traditional Muslim female. My probing of her stereotypes enabled her to work through some of the stereotypes she had that were based on her singular experiences with her African American ex-husband and her recent exposure to one-dimensional reports in the mass media. I also adopted a psychoeducational stance in questioning some of her rigid thinking regarding racial and religious groups within her own cultural context. I asked her questions such as, Do all Christians have the same level of faith and practice? Are all White women feminists? Are all African Americans "aggressive and lazy"? As she reflected on such questions, Nicole's assumptions about me loosened and she was able to make the connection that just because I look Arab and probably am Muslim does not mean that I do not endorse her value system.

The latter step was crucial to opening up our dialogue around her daughters' biracial identity. Just as she was thinking rigidly in terms of my being a Muslim woman, she was experiencing her daughters as split between their African American and White identities. Nicole struggled with experiencing contradictions and blends in terms of her daughters' identity development prior to our conversations about racism and her stereotypes about me. By way of our direct dialogue, she came to realize that her oldest daughter was beginning to associate being "unreliable, bad, a loser, and a failure" with being African American, based on her mother's and her own experience with her father. Instead, the daughter wanted to be "White" and "independent" like her mother, a split that Nicole perhaps reinforced. Having explored the mother's racism and gender stereotypes about me, we could now address the deeper issue of how Nicole could appropriately respond to her daughter's biracial and gender identity development in a constructive manner, given the context of her own rage and disappointment with her ex-husband.

We could now turn to more intense mother-daughter sessions in which we explored the meaning of race and womanhood. What did it mean to be African American? White? Biracial? How could a girl have multiple identities? What did it mean for the oldest daughter to be an independent, self-sufficient biracial girl and still love and depend on her mother and father, who look very different from each other? Could a girl choose and develop unique characteristics of her racial and gender identity independent of certain negative images and stereotypes? Whom did this girl *choose* to be? These explorations were intensely powerful—for all of us. We were all venturing into new territory, as few of us are taught to talk about race and gender in such a direct manner. My own multilayered ethnic and gender identity clearly informed and guided my probing and was critical in that I used of my sense of self to facilitate the treatment. I clearly recognize and embrace my multicultural feminist Muslim identity, and working with Nicole and her daughter allowed me to better reflect on and utilize my multidimensional and perhaps contradictory sense of self as a means to endorse new developmental pathways for this family. Also, in retrospect, I know that had I not taken the challenge to feel my anger toward Nicole's stereotypes of South Asians and Arabs, had I not taken directly explored and confronted her racist views of me, perhaps the outcome would have been disastrously different. Nicole would have probably terminated treatment with a confirmed perception of me as an oppressed and traditional Muslim woman with whom she could not work, and I would have festered with anger and injured pride in enabling the racism with my silence. Instead, through my relatively nontraditional interventions and use of myself as a female therapist of color and an immigrant, we were able to gradually but successfully resolve Nicole's and her daughter's conflicts around biracial female identity development in an adaptive and effective manner.

Reflections, Questions, and Exercises

By way of the case presentation, I hope to have highlighted how therapists can create and implement cultural process dialogues between themselves and their clients. Clearly, such culturally oriented processes can critically influence the unspoken impact of race and ethnicity on the therapist-client relationship when one or more of the parties involved are people of color. This cultural dialogue involves the therapist's profound and reflective use of the self as a therapist, awareness of self in the relationship, and development of the self to conduct effective psychotherapy. Surprisingly, many schools of thought do not create a space for the emergence of the therapist's self around issues of culture, racial and ethnic identity, religious beliefs, and values in the treatment. Nor do any theoretical guidelines exist that delineate the process of generating cultural process dialogues between therapist and client around issues of race and ethnicity and their associated characteristics.

The racism, biases, and stereotypes documented in this chapter clearly exist in the field and toward therapists of color, which can significantly interfere with the therapeutic process. It is imperative that therapists of color in practice and in training learn how to address and integrate these issues with their clients in the therapeutic relationship. Doing so will be extraordinarily challenging for three reasons: (1) there is little written about racism and the cultural dialogue process between therapists of color and clients from different racial backgrounds; (2) graduate institutions are still unsure about the most effective process of training therapists of color; and (3) the more experienced supervisors are ambivalent about and perhaps inexperienced in engaging in such conversations with their supervisees, perhaps because of their own largely White backgrounds and/or their own historical lack of training in cultural processes. Nevertheless, it remains imperative that administrators, faculty, researchers, and practitioners commit themselves to the task of understanding and combating racism toward therapists of color, particularly in the post 9/11 era of targeted intolerance.

References

Akhtar, S. (1999). *Immigration and identity: Turmoil, treatment, and transformation.* Northvale, NJ: Jason Aronson.

Beutler, L. E., Machado, P. P., & Neufeldt, S. A. (1994). Therapist variables. In A. E. Bergin & S. L. Garfield (Eds.), *Handbook of psychotherapy and behavior change* (4th ed., pp. 229–269). New York: John Wiley.

Davis, L. E., & Gelsomino, J. (1994). An assessment of practitioner cross-racial treatment experiences. *Social Work, 39,* 116–123.

Iwamasa, G. Y. (1996). On being an ethnic minority cognitive behavioral therapist. *Cognitive and Behavioral Practice, 3*(2), 235–254.

Maki, M. T. (1990). Countertranference with adolescent clients of the same ethnicity. *Child and Adolescent Social Work, 7,* 135–145.

Sue, D. W., Bingham, R. P., Porche-Burke, L., & Vasquez, M. (1999). The diversification of psychology: A multicultural revolution. *American Psychologist, 54,* 1061–1069.

Thompson, C. E., & Jenal, S. T. (1994). Interracial and intraracial quasicounseling interactions when counselors avoid discussing race. *Journal of Counseling Psychology, 41,* 484–491.

Tinsley-Jones, H.A. (2001). Listening to psychologists of color. *Professional Psychology: Research and Practice, 32*(6), 573–580.

Tung, M. (1981). On being seen as a "Chinese Therapist" by a Caucasian Child. *American Journal of Orthopsychiatry, 51,* 654–661.

10

Stories From Urban and Rural Landscapes

The Development of a Cultural Identity

Laurie L. Charlés

PROLOGUE

I went to accounts payable to locate the reimbursement check for my moving expenses. They didn't have it. I said I didn't know which dept. the check was coming from, but I knew it was a moving check. Someone said, "We don't give reimbursements for moving." I thought maybe I shouldn't be so vocal about it. They suggested I check at payroll. I walked back down the hall and knocked on one of the three doors in a small corner of offices. I was told to see Sandy. Someone was in Sandy's office; I waited outside. When I walked in and sat

Author's Note: This chapter was written while I was living and working as a university professor in a rural area of the American South. I currently live in Tampa, Florida, where I am an assistant professor of family therapy at the University of South Florida. The experiences I describe in this chapter, and the voice in which I speak about them, are situated within the period during which I lived in the South. While the chapter describes experiences I have had throughout my life, it revolves around occurrences that took place during my tenure in that part of the country.

down, I explained that I was looking for a moving check. Sandy didn't know if their office received moving checks; she'd have to check. Another woman walks in, leans on the door, and listens to my story, now told for the third time. The woman asks, "Well, when did he submit it? Did he submit it recently?"

I realize she thinks I am not here for myself. I tell her, the check is for me; it's my check. She makes a face, a little bit embarrassed face, and adjusts herself. "Oh, well, when did you submit it?" We go on with the discourse a couple of minutes—I'm not upset or surprised. Until I get home and have a chance to think about the encounter. She did not think the check was for me. She did not see a professor when she saw me. Who did she see? A wife, looking for her husband's check? Did she see my Hispanic-ness? My female-ness? Youth? A secretary? Or a student? I don't think she mistook me for a student. I was dressed professionally, in slacks, blouse, and trench coat. But apparently it is unusual for profs to go searching for their own checks. That's what graduate assistants are for. And wives, too, perhaps?

Several weeks later, another incident happened. This one could not be blamed on the South, or on my "look," whatever that is. I was ordering an exam copy of a book from AltaMira Press. I explained that I wanted to review the book first. I gave the ISBN, etc . . . and the agent asked me, "Does he want this for a class this semester? Or next semester?" I said, somewhat pointedly, that the book was for me. I emphasized the word "me." Silence. The conversation continued; I ordered the book. (Charlés, 2003, p. 1)

I am from San Antonio, Texas, and currently live in a small town in a rural state in the Southern United States. I took an academic position here 2 years ago as an assistant professor of family therapy. The experience described above took place about 2 months after I arrived. It is one of the most vivid experiences I have had that captured the stark differences between my assumptions of the world and the assumptions of those I work with every day. Though I mention just two examples, I have had many other similar experiences. However, it is one experience in particular that spurred the writing of this chapter; that event was a pivotal moment in my development as an MFT supervisor. I will return to it in a moment.

In this chapter, I discuss the evolution of my perspective on my cultural identity, outline the training and professional experiences that have shaped it, and illustrate some of the implications of it on my work as an MFT. When I discuss culture, I am including gender (Falicov, 1988). I have found my femaleness, the fact that I am a woman, to be something of a cultural marker for others, almost to the point of being a culture in itself. Thus, it cannot be overlooked.

I talk throughout this chapter about how my cultural identity has changed over time, across contexts, and in varied geographical areas. For it is the urban and rural landscapes where I have lived that have dictated the moments of epiphany, growth, and discomfort I have experienced in the development of my cultural voice.

This chapter is a discussion of my observations on and reflections about my experience as an MFT supervisor. In it, I share ideas about how my personal and professional experiences in both rural and urban landscapes have shaped my work, culminating in a supervisory experience with a student that marked a transformative cultural awakening, one I was not prepared for as a supervisor. I begin with the story of that experience, then delve into the development of my cultural landscape.

Case Study

As a teacher in an MFT program, I am responsible for the regular supervision of both master's and doctoral level students. Recently, I had a notable experience with a student in one of my practicum groups, at the time comprised equally of males and females. While the students were all good clinicians, I had trouble supervising one of them. I will call him George.

George came to our program from another state in the South. In his first sessions I supervised, George made a lot of beginner's mistakes. He did not listen well to his clients; he gave unsolicited advice; he failed to appreciate his clients' dilemmas before attempting to introduce change. These errors surprised me, as George was not a beginner; he had had previous experience as an MFT.

George seemed to be aware of the things he was not doing well; after his sessions, he'd make comments such as, "I got on my soapbox there for a minute." Though he would do better immediately after hearing my feedback, after each session that followed, he would repeat his mistakes. Thinking George was undisciplined or not receptive to supervision, I was frustrated. Although our supervision meetings outside of practicum seemed productive, George's behavior in the room remained unchanged. He listened respectfully to me, then ignored my suggestions. Compared to my other students, he seemed careless, even flippant. I did not know why my supervision with him seemed so difficult.

George earned a satisfactory grade in the practicum. When he came to me to discuss this, he expressed surprise at my comments on his evaluation (see Flemons, Green, & Rambo, 1996). I reminded George that he had received a similar midterm evaluation; hadn't he used it to guide him? It did not seem so. I told him of his right to contest his grade if he disagreed with it. He knew this, but he said he grew up learning to respect authority, adding that he did not want to make me an "enemy."

Several months later, in an unrelated class discussion, the topic turned to gender issues. A student who had been in the practicum with George remarked, "You know, we had gender issues in our practicum. George said to me the other day, 'I am everything Dr. Charlés hates: Big, White, and male.'" This remark completely caught me off guard—I was momentarily stunned. "I told him that you did not feel that way," the student offered, "but he didn't believe me."

Trying not to show any reaction that conveyed the reigniting of my frustration with George, I laughed off the comment. I said, "Oh, I guess I only like small, dark men, right?" The students chuckled. Later, however, I thought long and hard about the remark. Did George really think I hated him? The two other men in the practicum were like George in several ways; they were all White males from the South. I had had no problems with them.

While these thoughts slightly reassured me, I was taken aback that George saw me as a supervisor who had judged him on his race and gender. George's remark was doubly offensive in that by choosing those words, he had also labeled me as a minority female supervisor. I felt angry that he had chosen this way to explain to himself (and others) why he had not done well in my practicum. The remark also inspired curiosity: What was happening in my practica that I was now a particular type of supervisor? Specifically, an "ethnic" and "gendered" one? Previously, my most oft-used supervisory labels were "AAMFT-Approved" and "licensed." Nobody had ever focused so blatantly on my race or gender as a supervisor.

As you can see, I asked myself many questions. Prior to this incident, I had never thought to identify myself in professional MFT contexts as a woman of color. This supervisory experience (the end of which I will address later) was a defining moment in my life as an MFT supervisor. I believe it was the moment my professional "gendered" identity as a "woman of color" was born.

Cultural Context of the Case Study

As a female academic who is of Mexican Spanish *mestiza* descent, I am privy to lots of interesting cultural scenarios where I live, some humorous, some absurd, and some unpleasant. The part of the country where I live is in the Bible belt. It is also the home of self-identified rednecks and Southern belles. Confederate flags are mounted on front doors in the wealthiest neighborhoods. You still hear people use the word *colored* to describe African Americans. The Ku Klux Klan marches yearly in a nearby town.

The typical citizen in my town is Baptist and married with children. I am Catholic, and like the writer Sandra Cisneros, "nobody's mother and nobody's wife" (Cisneros, 1991). My counterpart here—that is, a minority female in her 30s—typically has had several children, has less than a high school education, and is unemployed. I am unmarried, with no children, and have three college degrees. My boyfriend is an African American physician. In addition to these factors, my postmodern views of therapy and supervision conflict with many of the values inherent in my students' religious beliefs (Wieling et al., 2001). I am an outsider here in nearly every way imaginable.

I am new to this unique part of the country. My past experiences were typically in larger cities. While I have lived in small towns, I have never lived in a small town in the American South. Further, I have never had the experience as an MFT of a place where my race and gender spoke so much more loudly than my credentials and qualifications. I expected supervisees to question me because of my theoretical orientation; I had not expected them to question me because of my race or gender. The experience with George forced me to become explicit about the cultural assumptions that were brought forth by his pronouncement. The graphic nature of his remark at first offended me. However, eventually its weight encouraged me to reflect on my supervisory process and examine the cultural beliefs and values I proffer in my role as an MFT educator. I would find a way to deal with George's comment later.

Professional and Personal Background

I am an assistant professor at an MFT graduate program in the South. I am also a visiting professor of family therapy at De La Salle University in Manila, Philippines. I am a licensed MFT in two states, and I am an AAMFT Clinical Member and Approved Supervisor. I have been teaching in academia for 2 years. Prior to my years as an academic, I was a Peace Corps volunteer, and prior to that, I was a graduate student. I began my graduate MFT career in 1989. I hold a master's degree in counseling psychology, with a specialization in MFT, from Our Lady of the Lake University in San Antonio, Texas. I have a doctoral degree in family therapy from Nova Southeastern University, in Ft. Lauderdale, Florida.

I identify myself primarily as a systemic MFT clinician and supervisor, as well as a qualitative researcher. These identities have evolved over my 10 years in the field. My MFT supervisors in my master's program were trained in an MRI (mental research institute) approach (Watzlawick, Weakland, & Fisch, 1974), but their teacher had been Harry Goolishian (Anderson & Goolishian, 1988), so their therapy process and supervisory models were simple and clear, with a postmodern appreciation of the linguistic nuances of the therapeutic conversation.

In my doctoral program, I trained with professors who had been students of my teachers in my master's program. They had morphed their MRI and Goolishian and Anderson influences into yet something else. There, I grew to appreciate Erickson's (Haley, 1986) influence on MFT theories, and I developed a keen interest in qualitative and ethnographic approaches to unpacking the complexity of the therapy discourse process (Gale, 1996; Morris & Chenail, 1995). In my doctoral program, I grew into a more postmodern and social constructionist thinker (Gergen, 1991; McNamee & Gergen, 1992). In this setting, I found that my ideas about good naturalistic qualitative research became synonymous with my ideas about good systemic family therapy.

In both MFT programs, my professors had been male and female, as well as from various racial groups. I was accustomed to seeing this diversity in academia. The (sometimes heated) differences I observed among faculty seemed to be strictly theoretical. I did not notice any discrimination toward me or others. I was respected, and I never felt marginalized as a female or a racial minority.[1]

I am accomplished, seasoned, and confident in my professional identity. While I pay great attention to the nuances of the therapeutic process, as a supervisor and a clinician, my experience with George made me realize that there was an interesting gap in what I was exploring. I had never given much thought to how my own culture—my race and gender—might shape the responses I would get from supervisees during practica. Although I had experienced epiphanies when my clients reacted to my race and gender, and had learned how to skillfully manage their cultural assumptions about me, I had not prepared to deal with this issue as an MFT supervisor. The possibility that a trainee might leave my supervision with feelings of enmity toward me, much less that those feelings would have their genesis in racial and gender bias, had never occurred to me. As a supervisor, I had no frame of reference for this. I did not know how to handle it.

Relevant Literature

There is a great deal on the issues of ethnicity and race in the MFT literature. Attempting to provide a comprehensive picture of what *culture* actually comprises, Falicov (1988) defined it as *those sets of shared world views and adaptive behaviors derived from simultaneous membership in a variety of contexts,* such as ecological setting (rural, urban, suburban), religious background, nationality and ethnicity, social, class, gender-related experiences, minority status, occupation, political leanings, migratory patterns and stage of acculturation, or values derived from belonging to the same generation. (p. 336)

Thus, culture can be defined in a number of different ways. It has to do with connection, and the idea that people can be affiliated in ways that may be obvious as well as in ways that are not immediately apparent.

Current literature on managing issues of race and ethnicity in the MFT therapy room assume a proactive stance on the part of the clinician. According to COAMFTE (Commission on Accreditation for Marriage and Family Therapy Education) Standard 300.01, MFT programs are expected to "infuse their curriculum with content that addresses issues related to power and privilege as they relate to age, culture, environment, ethnicity, gender, health/ability, nationality, race, religion, sexual orientation, spirituality, and socioeconomic status" (American Association for Marriage and Family Therapy, 1991).

The importance attributed to dialogue on race and gender in MFT training contexts is a tenet of the profession. However, as Long and Serovich (2003) pointed out, it is dangerous to assume there are not MFT faculty and supervisors who only pay lip service to this standard. Support for such a view has been documented by Constantine, Juby, and Liang (2001), who stated that "the goal of recognizing the importance of cultural issues, particularly racial and ethnic issues, has yet to be seriously undertaken in many MFT training settings" (p. 353). These same authors noted the need for investigation of "MFTs perceived levels of cultural competence, *particularly with regard to various race-related attitudes*" (p. 353; italics added).

Using such literature as a guide, it is possible to expand MFTs developmental process with regard to exploring cultural frameworks and to make recommendations for training in that area. According to Sue, Arredondo, and McDavis (1992), competence in the area of cultural sensitivity includes at least three important areas: therapists' awareness of their own culture; therapists' knowledge of the cultural worldview of their clients; and the culturally sensitive action therapists take toward clients. It is exploration of this first area of competence that is particularly underrepresented in the MFT literature.

One of the ways to address this gap in the research is to provide a forum for the voices of minority MFT supervisors and educators. First-person discussion of the supervisory dilemmas that involve the complexities of race and gender provide a further contribution to the field. Storm, Todd, Sprenkle, and Morgan (2001) commented on the lack of research relevant to the actual practice of supervision. As clinicians, we talk often about how our clients feel labeled and misrepresented. However, there has been little discussion about what it is like when MFT supervisors are labeled because of some external characteristic or cultural affiliation.

In this spirit of such a discussion, I would like to share with you some stories from my cultural landscape. In doing so, I hope to address my own ethnocentrism, thus avoiding the inadvertent minimization of the significance of cultural differences (Falicov, 1988). Culture, as defined by Falicov (1988), is inclusive of gender; gender and race in combination can be a powerful indicator of identity. As Myers-Avis (1996) noted, "a family therapist who has not developed her or his own gender consciousness is at high risk for having stereotypical expectations of men and women" (p. 226). Thus, a discussion about the growth of my gender awareness is in order as well.

Stories From the Urban and Rural Landscapes of Ethnicity and Gender: Developing My Cultural Identity

Stage One: Experiencing a Culture of Sameness in South Texas

While I appreciate that several authors (Falicov, 1995; Hardy & Laszloffy, 1992) warned about the dangers of assuming homogeneity among similar cultural groups, I would still characterize my childhood years in Texas as an experience of life in a culture of "sameness": I felt that most people were like me and my family. My father was a banker; my mother a stylish housewife. Despite the fact that my parents sometimes entertained my father's mostly White co-workers, I thought that most people in the world were Hispanic and assumed that the few Anglo[2] folks who came over to dinner were really a minority. I rarely saw or met African Americans in my world. I remember once my brothers and sister and I welcomed a new African American boy to our neighborhood; I was so curious about his hair, I asked him if could touch it (he agreed).

I am a Texan of multiethnic origin: Spanish, Mexican, and Indian. I grew up in South and Central Texas, having spent my formative years in San Antonio, where most of my family still lives. I have lived mostly in two states my entire life—Texas and Florida. However, also significant to my cultural landscape are my travels as an adult. I have traveled extensively over four continents. I started traveling at 19, when I spent a year on the road with a singing group, visiting 90 cities throughout Europe and the United States. Recently, I lived in Togo, West Africa as a Peace Corps volunteer.

When I am visiting other countries, I tend to identify myself as a Texan rather than an American. I identify strongly with Texas because it is a place where there are many people *like me*—minorities sandwiched between the Mexican and American cultures. We are a little of both, not enough of either. For me, Texas represents that netherworld of "not American/not Mexican" citizenry—the group my sister calls "coconuts."

I am a U.S. citizen, but I do not feel American enough to claim America (despite the fact that my family has been here for four generations). Conversely, while I embrace my unique cultural heritage, I do not feel Mexican enough to claim Mexico (I don't speak Spanish and have never traveled into the interior of Mexico).[3] I am somewhere between two worlds of identity called Mexican and American. I am both, and I am neither.

While I am of Hispanic origin, I am not an immigrant, nor a child of immigrants. My relatives are of Mexican descent; however, their ancestors were Indians, Spaniards, and French. This background is atypical for the majority of Hispanics in the United States; however, in Texas it is not atypical at all. Regardless of these important distinctions, I am what most Americans would identify as *Mexican* or *Hispanic*. I find these terms unsettling. They fit me like slacks I need to hem and a jacket that doesn't appreciate my broad shoulders. I do not identify with them.

In my travels, I have been mistaken for many different ethnicities. In Israel, people thought I was Jewish (interestingly, in the Arab towns I visited, I was told I looked Persian). In Africa, I was mistaken often for German, sometimes for French. In Texas, my ethnicity is always accepted without question—I am Hispanic. However, in other states, people have wondered if I am Italian, or "Spanish, perhaps?" My looks reflect my varied ancestry: I have light brown (but distinctly brown) skin. I have brown eyes and black hair. I have a broad face. I stand 5'4". I am tall for a Mexican American but short by American standards. Growing up, I was not aware of my features because I looked like everybody else. I felt completely accepted for who I was and what I looked like. I grew up confident in and clear about my cultural identity in a place of sameness.

Stage Two: Developing a Metacultural Awareness in South Florida

While I grew up in Texas and went to high school, college, and graduate school in San Antonio, I moved to Ft. Lauderdale, Florida to earn my doctorate. I lived in South Florida for 6 years. This was a formative experience in that it was the first time I began to distinguish myself as a Hispanic who was different from other Hispanics. In South Florida, Latin American people were everywhere—on TV, in the newspaper, in political office, even more so than in Texas. Here, Latinos/as were truly the majority. Many cultural groups from different parts of Latin America were well represented in South Florida.

The Latinos/as I encountered in Florida were different from the Hispanics I was used to; I did not identify with these Hispanics. The Cubans, Haitians, Peruvians, and Colombians I encountered were strange to me, with their faster Spanish, their confusing accents, and their foreign food. Not surprisingly, I did not relate to them as I had related to my fellow Tex-Mex cohorts in San Antonio. I confronted my myth of homogeneity full force, just as Hardy and Laszloffy (1992) warned.

This was a new experience for me—to identify and distinguish myself from others who had a related cultural background. Living in South Florida brought to me a metacultural awareness. It broadened my scope and made me a more sensitive therapist. It also humbled me. I became more appreciative of cultural differences in general (and among Hispanics in particular), and I see this period of my life as a beginning in exploring my cultural background further.

At around this time, I began to conduct ethnographic interviews with my maternal grandmother about her experiences growing up in rural South Texas. My grandmother, Guadalupe Charlés Lopez, was born in Palito Blanco, Texas. She did not speak English, had little formal education, and was one of the more gentle souls I have ever known. I loved spending time with her, which I did as often as I could—even though I needed a translator to talk to her.[4] I was trying desperately to learn Spanish in a night class while I conducted these informal interviews, but then my grandmother became ill and I had to stop the interviews.

After my grandmother died, I changed my name to her maiden name, Charlés. I had been thinking about changing my name for several years. It made sense to change my name to connect with the side of the family that I felt close to, with those who knew me, with those I honored. That my grandmother happened to be such a special person helped make this decision very easy. Although I thought about doing this often, I vacillated for nearly 10 years. When my grandmother died, the decision seemed simple. I changed my name within weeks of her death.

Changing my name was an important shift in my identity in that it opened up a window into a new cultural and ethnic awareness for me. For the first time, I felt Latin. Each time people said my new name, I experienced an interesting feeling—like a small jolt of electricity in my body. When I heard people say "Charlés," I could feel my grandmother's presence, her background and her history.

Charlés is an interesting Hispanic name, because without the accent it doesn't sound Hispanic. Only the accent on the *e* indicates its Spanish origin: It is pronounced char-LES. My previous name, Hernandez, was the opposite in that way. When people see it, they know that it is a Hispanic name, accent or no accent. However, when spoken, the name was nearly always pronounced by me and others in an anglicized way: HER-NAN-DEZ, not ERR-NON-DEZ.

Stage Three: Changing Skin
Color in a Tiny Village in Togo

The next phase in my cultural development, both personal and professional, was in West Africa. Shortly after I completed my dissertation, in September 1999, I had an opportunity to become a Peace Corps Volunteer (PCV), something I had wanted to do for years. Having steeped myself in flexing the mental muscles needed to write a qualitative dissertation project, I looked forward to flexing my physical being in a cultural setting that was extremely different from my own. I also looked forward to living and working in another language, in a place I had never been, and within a cultural group I knew nothing about.

My Peace Corps service took me to French-speaking West Africa. I lived in the country of Togo, in a small village nestled in the coffee and cocoa mountains near the Ghanaian border. The intensity of living in Africa provided an entirely new platform for my cultural growth. Boyd's (1990) description of Africa's "rabid energy and bustle, its brutal frustrations and remorseless physicality" (p. 12) was accurate for me.

My home in Togo had no electricity or running water; there was no telephone in my entire village; I had to learn bits of the local language, Akebou, through French, which I had only learned upon arriving in Togo. I had a simple life but a complex existence. I took bucket showers outside under the stars; rose at 6 in the morning and went to bed by 8 each night, and took a siesta every day from 12 to 3. I used handwritten letters as a primary form of communication; I mountain biked about 40 miles a week to get my work done.[5]

In Togo, my cultural development took me down many new paths. The most unusual of these was that in Africa, I became a White woman. Even though I am a Hispanic American (or Texan, as I said before), in Africa I was seen as a White European. It was as if my cultural life was on a continuum for the Africans I encountered. The fact that I was an American from

Texas was not significant to them. More significant was the fact that I was not African and my skin was not Black. Thus, I could only be European.

The Africans were right. Essentially, with the exception of the Indian roots of my maternal grandfather, my ancestors are European. They came to Mexico from Europe—not Africa. To the Togolese, this seemed an obvious fact. Here in the states, even as I write it, it seems anything but obvious. I do not consider myself European. However, it was hard to argue with the logic of the Africans I met. In the long history of their immense continent, it is hundreds and thousands of centuries that frame history, not decades or a few hundred centuries. Thus, my being "Texan" or "Hispanic" was something of an aside, culturally speaking, in Togo.

In Togo, I was constantly approached by Africans because of my outsider status. My skin color gave me away—I was a *yovo*, or White person, foreigner. Usually, people who stopped me only wanted to chat. However, many times people wanted something material from me. I learned to field constant requests for money and my personal belongings—the shoes I was wearing, my watch ("You can buy another!"), my backpack ("You must give it to me when you go!").

The Togolese were never embarrassed to make these demands; they assumed I could afford to give things away because I was not African and expected me to willingly oblige. I corrected these assumptions fairly easily; I explained that I needed my shoes and backpack, that my watch was the only one I owned. I told people I had recently been a student and was now in their country as a volunteer. I did not have the riches that they assumed I had.[6]

Assumptions about my personal wealth were easily corrected; I had more trouble with Togolese cultural assumptions related to my gender. As an unmarried woman living alone in a foreign country, I was considered approachable by men interested in propositioning me for sex. Though I was vulnerable at anytime, anywhere, I was particularly at risk when alone in public; this was something of an open invitation for men to ask if they could "visit my house"—a euphemism for having intercourse with me. Some Togolese female friends taught me how to defuse such requests so that I was inoffensive but clear: Don't smile when you say "No"; Don't let people into your home—instead, buy some benches to sit on outside when people come to greet you.

As an outsider to African culture, I was always deflecting unwanted interest of some kind, and this attention unfailingly centered on my race and gender. Africans I met were transparent vis-à-vis their assumptions about me, which were always clearly related to their openly held views of others, of those unlike them. To many Africans in my village, people who aren't Black Africans can only be White Europeans; those who are White Europeans are all rich because they are not Black Africans, who are all poor. So transparent were these assumptions that I could deal with them clearly and openly; it was a routine part of my life.

That Togo opened up my eyes further to ideas about race and gender is an understatement. But Togo did do that for me. I thought that I was fairly well versed in such ideas; I had traveled, I had a doctorate, I considered myself worldly and cultivated. However, the cultural lessons I learned in Togo showed me how narrow my experience had been. I knew this even as it was happening, and I wrote profusely to capture the essence of those moments of cultural epiphany. The journals, essays, and poems I wrote serve as vivid records of my memories. The implications of these experiences with regard to my cultural awareness remain prescient in my life. In particular, they became highly relevant to me during the time of my experience with George.

In Africa, my cultural landscape shifted in a way I never expected. Before, I had been an educated, middle-class *mestiza* from Texas; in Africa, I became a wealthy White woman. I changed colors, ethnicities, and even social class, not because of *who* I was necessarily, but because of *where* I was. These potentially charged labels were gifts to me; they gave me a chance to talk about who I was, to learn from the Togolese who they were, and together to explore our different cultural landscapes.

From Rural Togo to the Rural American South

I moved to the South 3 months after I finished my Peace Corps service. When I arrived back in the states, I was mostly aware of my identity as a Returned Peace Corps Volunteer (RPCV) who had served in Africa. I had not attributed much to the fact that I was also a woman of color about to enter academia; this was not my primary identity. I thought of myself as an RPCV who happened to be an MFT. My race and gender did not cloak these identities.

I accepted being "othered" in Africa, where everything I represented was new for the people in my village, because there my experiences of being othered were an invitation to explore, discover, and exchange ideas. I could accept that Africans would treat me differently—they had never met a woman with a Ph.D. How could they *not* have inaccurate assumptions about what they'd never encountered? Our disparate backgrounds were literally on the surface, right where we could see them; this invited, rather than suppressed, generative dialogue. Back home in the United States, however, I found that others' attitudes about my race and gender were more likely to be hidden, ignored, or dismissed.

Case Study Follow-Up

Inclined to believe that inaccurate assumptions about race and gender are best tackled by transparent, generative dialogue, I knew the time would come for me to talk to George about the remark he was alleged to have made. After much reflection about how best to do it (and some procrastination), I decided on a plan: I would ask about the remark, find out if it was true that George had said it, then explore whether George felt he'd been treated unfairly because of his race and/or gender. I ran this by a colleague, who agreed it sounded like a good plan and offered to be there when I talked to George. I was grateful for this suggestion. I knew George liked and trusted my colleague; it would be good for both of us to have this presence.

When George and I met, I said what I'd planned to say, and then gave him the floor. He was surprised by the reason for the meeting and denied making any such comment about me. While he denied feeling that he was treated differently because he was a male, he said he once did talk openly about being treated differently in my practicum. In that conversation, which was in front of other students, George said that he was treated differently because, "You know, she[Dr. Charlés]'s a feminist and all that."

George's comment surprised me. How had George decided that I was a feminist? I had never identified myself that way. This prompted an interesting conversation. George had made assumptions about me based on the fact that I was the only female faculty member in the program. By virtue of my sex, I became the resident feminist in his eyes, despite anything I might have said about the issue. I thought to myself (and wish I'd told George) that some of the most assertive feminists I know are men.[7]

George asked me if I had ever had a supervisor I had not gotten along with. Of course I had, and I told him so. He was surprised; he did not expect me to say yes. The fact that we had common ground seemed to open him up. My colleague asked George if it was possible that the reason he had had a problem in my practicum was that he'd never been supervised by a woman before. To his credit, George said that it was a possibility he was willing to look at. Although I do not know if George examined his ideas further after our meeting, I was encouraged by this admission. I like to think our dialogue invited it to happen.

Most compelling in the conversation was a remark George made about something I had said during a brief talk I had once given in which I outlined some of my research interests. I had said that as an MFT, I appreciated differences. I mentioned cultural differences, among others. I remembered this remark; I had deemed it systemic in nature rather than cultural. In that moment, however, George heard only the cultural part. He said that in that moment he thought to himself that he had nothing to offer me, that he was "the opposite of all that." It was as if he saw himself as culturally bankrupt. I corrected George, saying he was someone very culturally unique. He expressed surprise, smiling. "Thank you," he said.

Discussion and Limitations

While I felt comfortable with how I handled my meeting with George, I can now see gaps in my process that were not visible to me earlier. In particular, I can think of things I would like to have done differently as a supervisor. I can imagine how if had I been more prepared for a student like George, I may have been able to find ways to make his assumptions transparent as well as productive in supervision. His comment was a great opportunity for discourse. Yet, I was unprepared to have this discourse, as I had no referent for it and found it personally offensive. Such circumstances made it especially difficult to do what I was striving to do, which was to create a generative supervisory context following the example of those who have done it (see Green, Shilts, & Bacigalupe, 2001).

I still have some questions about the situation with George. I have wondered, if I had been more experienced as a supervisor, how would I have dealt with George's comment differently? I try to be immediate and transparent in my supervision—but George's comments and manner with me precluded my typical praxis. I have wondered whether I would have reacted differently to George if I had lived in the South longer. Perhaps I would have had a stock way to deal with such a scenario. If I had, then, perhaps I also would have considered including his voice in this chapter in a more transparent manner than I have done so. In fact, this ideal is consistent with my postmodern views of supervision.

While such questions linger, this story is essentially about my experience with George (not his experience with me) and, as such, the story is necessarily told in a way that excludes his voice in favor of mine. I agree that George's comments on our experience would be useful and productive to share. However, I do not see this chapter as a venue for sharing them. That missing voice, however important, is destined for another chapter, in a different book. Perhaps someday I will even be in a position to coauthor it. At this moment, however, it is my own journey that is reflected on in this work.

Supervisory Considerations

According to Bean, Perry, and Bedell (2001), supervisors are responsible for helping therapists develop awareness of their own cultural background and knowledge about the client's worldview and experience. I have found it useful and interesting to inquire into students' assumptions about their clients, as well as my own assumptions about my students. Indeed, such practice has found its place in my work (Charlés et al., 2003), and I believe it will continue to do so. Investigation of one's bias, that sensitive, tacit knowledge, is natural to systemic work. As a supervisor, I want to construct possibilities that such knowledge can be made explicit, and thus open to challenge.

In this chapter, I have discussed the evolution of my cultural awakening as an MFT supervisor of color. My journey has taken me across rural and urban landscapes, over several continents, and is ongoing. As a supervisor, this experience has demanded I find ways to invite students to share their unique cultural stories, as well as their views on race and gender and how those views developed over time. In supervisory contexts, two of my most important goals are to encourage transparency and to challenge assumptions. I think it is required of us—indeed it is our charge as MFT supervisors— to develop methods that speak specifically to unpacking trainees' racial and gender bias, as well as our own. Cultural "landscaping," in the sense that I have begun to do, is one step in that direction; generative discussion on the questions I leave at the end of the chapter, another.

In writing this chapter, I hope to encourage others—MFT supervisors and students—to consider the story of my landscape, then, bravely explore their own. Such self-investigation may seem an indulgent, even self-absorbed, act. It is. Yet, its practice increases the possibility that therapy and supervision will be sound, comprehensive, and generative. In addition, such a self-reflexive process is the best way I currently know to further students' cultural awareness. It is an example they can follow; it paves the way for the next steps in developing their cultural competency.

Final Thoughts

There is a standard in cultural competency literature (Falicov, 1995; Hardy & Laszloffy, 1992) that in order for MFTs to learn more about increasing cultural competency, they must do so from an inside perspective rather than an outside one. The traditional view has been to examine others first, make oneself aware of the general life and views of those others, and then go out and do good work. An alternative direction is to reconsider who the target of that good work should be. Exploration of one's cultural landscape—the self-study of how one's cultural views have developed—is an ideal way to increase cultural competency. It also allows us to take what Harry Goolishian called "agency" in one's learning and personal and professional growth.

Americans are multicultural by birth. We are all people of color, in one way or another. It is long past time that we talk about it.

Reflections, Questions, and Exercises

1. What did you think of George's comment? Have you ever felt discriminated against by a supervisor because of your gender or race?

2. What has it been like for you to be in the presence of people who are distinctly culturally different from you?

3. Do you remember the first time you encountered someone distinctly different from you? What was it like?

4. What names or labels did your family give to cultural groups different from yours? Are you comfortable with those terms today?

5. What did you think of how I handled George's comment? How do you evaluate the reflections I made? Of what use were they?

6. What did you think of my experience of how I changed colors while in Africa? Did you think my allowing the Africans to categorize me was fair and just?

7. How did you make sense of George's concern that he might be "culturally bankrupt" because of his race or gender? Have you ever felt this way?

8. How do you treat people from countries other than your own?

9. If you have traveled outside your home country, what was it like to be a foreigner in a foreign land?

10. Do you think discussions on gender, femininity, and masculinity are passé? Of what use are such discussions in today's world?

Notes

1. I published several papers and did many projects with both my male and female faculty. In fact, my dissertation chair was (and remains) a very tall Canadian man.

2. As a child, *Anglo* was the word I heard used to describe those who were not Hispanic or African American.

3. In July 2003, I traveled for the first time to Latin America, where I took a Spanish immersion course in Costa Rica.

4. I did not hear Spanish spoken often in my home. Though my parents were fluent in Spanish, their first language was English and they were discouraged from speaking Spanish to me and my siblings. At the time, school districts in Texas were against bilingual education. Thinking that hearing Spanish would hurt our chances to learn, they never used it with us. As a result, none of us learned Spanish. This is common among my Texas-raised Hispanic peers. However, those who are just a few years older or a few years younger than we are grew up fluent in Spanish. The politics were different then.

5. My Peace Corps assignment was in the GEE (girls' education and empowerment) program. I taught a women's studies course to junior and high school girls, and I worked with Togolese nationals on improving the state of girls' education in the country.

6. I thank my fellow PCV Kathryn Bacon for telling me the saying, "People join the Peace Corps to learn what it is like to be poor, but what they really learn is what it is like to be rich."

7. Several months earlier, a female graduate of our program told me that at her exit interview (at which I had not been present), she recommended that the program focus more on issues of feminism in MFT. In response, she was told, "Well, Dr. Charlés is here."

References

American Association for Marriage and Family Therapy. (1991). *Commission on Accreditation for Marriage and Family Therapy Education manual on accreditation.* Washington, DC: Author.

Anderson, H., & Goolishian, H. (1988). Human systems as linguistic systems: Evolving ideas about the implications for theory and practice. *Family Process, 27,* 371–393.

Bean, R. A., Perry, B. J., & Bedell, T. M. (2001). Developing culturally competent marriage and family therapists: Guidelines for working with Hispanic families. *JMFT, 27*(1), 43–54.

Boyd, W. (1990). *Brazzaville beach.* New York: Avon.

Charlés, L. L. (2003, January). *"Villages are the same everywhere": Reflections on life in an African village and a Louisiana town.* Paper presented at the 16th Annual QUIG Conference, Athens, GA.

Charlés, L. L., Suranski, E., Barber-Stephens, B., Allen, L., Ticheli, M., & Tonore, G. (2003). "Speaking the language of the client": Bridging gaps in understanding. *Journal of Systemic Therapies, 22*(3), 55–67.

Cisneros, S. (1991). *Woman hollering creek and other stories.* New York: Random House.

Constantine, M. G., Juby, H. L., Liang, J. J-C. (2001). Examining multicultural counseling competence and race-related attitudes among White marital and family therapists. *Journal of Marital and Family Therapy, 27*(3), 353–362.

Falicov, C. J. (1988). Learning to think culturally. In H. Liddle, D. Breunlin, & R. Schwartz (Eds.), *Handbook of family therapy training and supervision* (pp. 335–357). New York: Guilford.

Falicov, C. J. (1995). Training to think culturally: A multidimensional comparative framework. *Family Process, 34,* 373–388.

Flemons, D. G., Green, S. K., & Rambo, A. H. (1996). Evaluating therapists' practices in a postmodern world: A discussion and a scheme. *Family Process, 35,* 43–46.

Gale, J. (1996). Conversation analysis: Studying the construction of therapeutic realities. In D. Sprenkle & S. Moon (Eds.), *Research methods in family therapy* (pp. 107–124). New York: Guilford.

Gergen, K. J. (1991). *The saturated self: Dilemmas of identity in contemporary life.* New York: Basic Books.

Green, S., Shilts, L., & Bacigalupe, G. (2001). When approved is not enough: Development of a supervision consultation model. *Journal of Marital & Family Therapy, 27*(4), 515–525.

Haley, J. (1986). *Uncommon therapy: The psychiatric techniques of Milton H. Erickson, M.D.* New York: Norton.

Hardy, K. V., & Laszloffy, T. A. (1992). Training racially sensitive family therapists: Context, content, and contact. *Families in Society, 73,* 364–370.

Long, J. K., & Serovich, J. M. (2003) Incorporating sexual orientation into MFT training programs: Infusion and inclusion. *JMFT, 29*(1), 59–67.

McNamee, S., & Gergen, K. J. (1992). (Eds.). *Therapy as social construction.* London: Sage.

Morris, G. H., & Chenail, R. J. (1995). *The talk of the clinic: Explorations in the analysis of medical and therapeutic discourse.* Hillsdale, NJ: Lawrence Erlbaum.

Myers-Avis, J. (1996). Deconstructing gender in family therapy. In F. P. Piercy, D. H. Sprenkle, & J. L. Wetchler and associates (Eds.), *Family therapy sourcebook* (2nd ed.). New York: Guilford.

Storm, C., Todd, T., Sprenkle, D. H., & Morgan, M. (2001). Gaps between MFT supervision assumptions and common practice: Suggested best practices. *JMFT, 27*(1), 227–239.

Sue, D. W., Arredondo, P., & McDavis, R. J. (1992). Multicultural counseling competencies and standards: A call to the profession. *Journal of Multicultural Counseling and Development, 20,* 64–88.

Watzlawick, P., Weakland, J., & Fisch, R. (1974). *Change: Principles of problem formation and problem resolution.* New York: Norton.

Wieling, L., Negretti, M., Stokes, S., Kimball, T., Christensen, F., & Bryan, L. (2001). Postmodernism in marriage and family therapy training: Doctoral students' understanding and experiences. *JMFT, 27*(4), 527–533.

11

The Process of Integrating Language, Context, and Meaning

The Voices of Bilingual and Bicultural Therapists

Carmen Aguirre, J. Maria Bermúdez,
J. Ruben Parra Cardona,
Jorge Antonio Zamora, and
Nenetzin Angelica Reyes

Many mental health professionals are currently faced with the challenge of translating the knowledge and training they receive into something that is useful and applicable when working with people from diverse cultures. The primary goal of this chapter is to illuminate some of the struggles we have had in trying to explore how our clinical training has influenced our cultural and professional identities. In addition, we address how we perceive our level of competence in doing therapy in our less dominant language (Spanish or English) and the ways in which we attempt to integrate our training into a culture and/or language other than the one in which we received training. We also examine how bilingual and/or bicultural therapists conceptualize the use of language, context, and meaning in the therapeutic context, as well as provide suggestions for future applications of these findings to supervision and research.

We are graduate students and faculty in a marriage and family therapy doctoral program at a university in the U.S. Southwest. This chapter contains our reflections on the contents of narratives we each wrote on our cultural identity and its relationship to our training and clinical practice in the mental health field. The sharing of these personal narratives led to numerous conversations about identifying our personal and professional cultural selves. In a broader context, the five of us saw this collaboration as an opportunity to give voice to the personal and professional struggles faced by bilingual and bicultural therapists. All too often, supervisors and faculty are not aware of the difficulty therapists in training have when trying to translate their clinical training into another language or culture. Often the process of translation has negative consequences and results in significant misunderstandings and in critical information being lost. This can undermine the client's faith in the competence of the bilingual therapist, as well as jeopardize the clinical goals for the client. Our hope is that the information shared in this chapter stimulates critical thinking on the part of faculty, administrators, supervisors, and majority and minority students in clinical training programs and other clinical settings, so that they will be more apt to accept the responsibility for understanding, supporting, and promoting the integration of cultural and professional identity issues related to international and ethnic minority therapists.

Language and the Mental Health Profession

Mental health professionals' interest in the bilingual and/or bicultural population has risen within the last 60 years. Although the available literature at this time continues to be limited, some literature suggests that mental health clinicians and researchers are seeking to understand some of the specific characteristics and needs of bilingual and/or bicultural populations. Several authors have delineated suggestions for better attending to the specific concerns of bilingual clients and communities from diverse ethnic populations.

First, there is a call for matching bilingual clients with bilingual therapists (Guttfreund, 1990; Marcos, 1976; Pitta, Marcos, & Alpert, 1978). This may seem obvious since language proficiency can add to the therapeutic relationship and therapy outcome, as well as lessen the chance of meaning being lost in the exchange between client and therapist (Marcos, 1976). This matching is even more essential given that by using their dominant language, bilingual individuals are able to access a deeper level of emotion—a level of emotion that is hard or impossible for them to access using the language spoken by the population majority (Guttfreund, 1990; Marcos, 1976; Pitta et al., 1978;

Rozensky & Gomez, 1983). Furthermore, Guttfreund, in his study "Effects of Language Usage on the Emotional Experience of Spanish-English and English-Spanish Bilinguals" (1990), proposed that Spanish, a Latin romance language, allows for a deeper expression of feelings regardless of the order of language acquisition.

As a result of these observations, there has been a shift toward accepting the use of language switching as a positive and powerful tool in therapy. Although language shifting is often shunned by Latin Americans who do not have the need to language shift, it is clearly common and accepted among Hispanics and Latinos/as who are from the United States. It has also been documented that language switching can be a useful tool in performing three techniques to enhance therapy. The first technique calls for the use of the dominant language as a way of bringing the client to a deeper emotional level, as well as unlocking some part of the client that may be language specific and only accessible in that particular language (Marcos, 1976, Rozensky & Gomez, 1983). The second technique, as used by Pitta and colleagues, is to access that deep emotional level or situation, and then switch to the majority language (the client's less dominant language) to allow the client to separate from his or her emotions and be able to talk with out being overwhelmed by the emotion. However, Pitta and colleagues stated that a problem can occur in using this technique when the client, who is given the power to decide when to switch, begins to use it as an avoidance technique. Similarly, Rozensky and Gomez (1983) found that their clients would use language switching as a form of resistance to engaging in the therapeutic process. The third technique calls for the use of *dichos* (Zuniga, 1991). *Dichos* is the Spanish word for "sayings." These sayings are used strategically to promote motivation and change in the client who speaks Spanish and English. Because of their familiarity, *dichos* seem to be persuasive for the bilingual client. Familiar sayings from languages besides Spanish may have the same effect on clients who speak those languages.

Awareness and exploration of the needs of bilingual and multilingual clients is visible in the literature, but the awareness and exploration of the needs of bilingual and/or bicultural therapists does not appear to have been mentioned in the literature until it was proposed as a need by Altarriba and Santiago-Rivera (Altarriba, in press; Altarriba & Santiago-Rivera, 1994; Santiago-Rivera & Altarriba, 2002). They offered a unique and innovative way to respond to the needs of both bilingual clients and therapists. A related effort was made by the University of the District of Columbia, which instituted a change in the curriculum that allowed students to specialize in bilingualism (Wright-Harp & Muniz, 2000). Programs like this could enhance the work of practitioners, especially in areas of the country where bilingual families commonly reside. We recognize this need and see this recognition as a start for such change.

To understand further the importance of culture, language, and the issues salient to Hispanic and Latino/a counselors, Manoleas, Organista, Negron-Velasquez, and McCormick (2000) conducted a study of Latino/a mental health professionals to examine their personal roles, goals, and motivations in their work with Latino/a clients. The study results showed that when it came to personal roles, the Latino/a clinicians consider their roles related to family functioning, such as parent, spouse, and child, as being the most important to them. These were followed by their professional roles of therapist, advocate, and counselor. When asked to rate factors of importance in their professional work, the Latino/a professionals rated "to work with other Latino/a staff, to help clients identify and utilize cultural strengths, and to contribute to 'el bienestar de mi gente' [the well being of my people]" (p. 387) as most important. Of particular interest was the order of the goals these Latino/a professionals had for their Latino/a clients. The number one goal was empowerment, while biculturation and acculturation were at the bottom of the list.

As Latina scholar, professor, and therapist, I (Maria) can certainly relate to this finding, since most of my interactions with students, clients, colleagues, and research participants center around the issue of empowerment, especially when the interactions are with Hispanics or Latinos/as or pertain to a minority group.

In "The Personal and Professional Development of the Counselor: The Relationship Between Personal Philosophy and Theoretical Orientation," Fear and Woolfe (1999) talked about the necessity of a counselor's having a matching personal philosophy (i.e., a vision of reality that is portrayed through personal narratives) and theoretical orientation (i.e., what the counselor professes his or her clinical theory to be). This approach enables counselors not only to develop professionally but also to ensure that their development reaches its full capacity. Fear and Woolfe (1999) went on to mention that a lack of matching or dissonance in these two areas can be the cause of burn out and drop out among clinicians. Because a narrative is based on the experiences and ideas of the narrator, there is a need to focus on allowing the individual (in the case of this chapter, the Latino/a bicultural and bilingual therapist) to tell his or her story and discuss it with others. In addition, Miehls and Smith (2001) talked about the importance of discovering our differences, specifically those of race, which are part of the complex working identity of the clinician. Miehls and Smith pointed out that the doors of knowledge regarding a person's identity are open when people of different races interact and a dialogue is formed. Thus, people's realization of our differences and of how they may have been undermining or overreacting to those differences means that they can learn more about themselves and grow personally and professionally.

It is our hope that this chapter, and our exploration of our process in writing it, will shed some light on the challenges of addressing the integrating issues of diversity in various clinical and training settings. As the mental health profession continues to focus more on these issues, there are various areas that deserve attention. The next section highlights some of the following major points that surfaced in our review of our individual narratives and in the conversations we had in our meetings to develop this chapter:

- Language, context, and meaning vary within a culture.
- Assumptions about the "sameness" of those who are viewed as being of a particular culture should be challenged (Hardy & Laszloffy, 1998).
- Experiences of racism, discrimination, oppression, and marginalization cannot be assumed to have been the same for all those in a particular ethnic group, a particular era, or a geographic region or according to a pattern of assimilation (see Parra Cardona, Wampler, & Busby in Chapter 19 of this volume).
- Students must receive acknowledgement of and respect for their struggle as they try to assimilate and balance the values and beliefs of their culture with the professional training they receive.
- There must be acknowledgement in the profession that experiences and beliefs about gender, power, privilege, and hierarchy can affect the work of ethnic minority students with families, peers, professors, and supervisors.

Our Voices, Our Selves

Sharing our struggles to write our personal narratives regarding our life experiences and what our roads to becoming MFTs have been like, it became evident that language, context, and meaning are common threads for all of us, and that our personal and our professional identities are intricately interwoven with each other. One of us made an observation about how others see us (all five are Latinos/as) as being the same, and yet, our narratives clearly paint very diverse and unique experiences. This manner of grouping together all Latinos/as and Hispanics despite our differences, which is usually well intentioned and done for pragmatic reasons, is evident in much of the social science and MFT literature regarding race and ethnicity (Flores & Carey, 2000; Garcia-Preto, 1996; Ho, 1987; Rodriguez & Cordero-Guzman, 1992). While we share many things in common, we also experience many differences in our groups based on the reasons, the manner, and the time we have been in the United States. In some instances, there is even conflict between our particular groups (i.e., countries of origin or ancestry) because our ancestors have either been oppressed by or the oppressors of the groups that the U.S. Census Bureau chooses to consolidate as "Hispanics" (Garcia-Preto, 1996). This situation has been confirmed by the social sciences, which have clearly stated that there are more within-group differences than between-group differences.

Quienes Somos Nosotros (Who We Are)

The diversity among Latinos/as is evident even among ourselves. Our ages range from 24 to 45, and we are from Mexico, Honduras, and Texas. Our ancestors' blood includes Mestizos, Spaniard, Mexican, Honduran, Irish, Austrian-Hungarian, Mayan, and English, and at least one of us identifies as being "transcultural and transracial." The range in the color of our skin is as varied as our experiences with racism, discrimination, and privilege, as also evidenced in research studies related to skin color and discrimination (Massey & Bitterman, 1985; Massey & Fischer, 2000; Ondrich, Stricker, & Yinger, 1998). Whether in our experiences with our own families or with the families we work with, we have all at times been painfully aware of the dynamics related to oppression and powerlessness, as well the guilt associated with having privilege. These thoughts led us to come together to work on this chapter. For us, our group process is what primarily informed our work together.

Trabajadno Juntos (Our Group Process)

The process we experienced as we collaborated in preparing this chapter was rich and powerful for all of us. Our group process was complex, mainly because many of the issues we were struggling with had not been articulated before. When we would get together to work, we were never able to start a meeting by "getting down to business" immediately. This struggle was not related to a lack of discipline but, rather, to an overwhelming experience that we had so many things to say and never enough time to express them. We were also aware of the clinical dynamics of Latinos/as and Hispanics—we need time to socialize before we work. It's the process of connection that enables us to work efficiently. Although we wanted to be outcome focused (not typically a Latino/a value), we understood that it was unequivocally important to make time to voice our experiences. We shared our painful memories, our current struggles, and our hopes of how we could make a difference as bilingual and bicultural mental health professionals.

We experienced many emotions and new insights while working on this project. We felt pain whenever someone shared a story of discrimination, and we also experienced joy and connectedness whenever we reaffirmed the beauty of our culture. We strongly believe that the richness of this chapter for all of us owes much to our commitment to creating weekly meetings that strengthened our sense of community and solidarity with each other. We learned that we did not all grow up with the same messages about being Latino/a, and that we live in a society that does not support the values that our families tried to teach us. Although each of us thinks family cohesion is a positive cultural value, some of us have experienced at some point in our lives a sense of shame about our origins and/or a desire to forget our roots, our language, and our ancestors. This forced assimilation was an attempt to gain acceptance in the dominant culture. For some of us, this internalized racism began during our childhood or adolescence, and yet for others it was something that hit us in the face in early adulthood. For another, being a bilingual Latina was always perceived as a source of pride, as well as a social advantage and resource. For most of us, however, it has been through the process of gaining maturity and advanced degrees that we have felt empowered and safe enough to explore our roots again and learn that we could be proud to have a personal identity that was our own and not imposed by society. We all remember our families' advice about being proud of who we are and of being bilingual and bicultural. As we have grown in our training as therapists, all of us have had an opportunity to explore our own family background and discuss with colleagues and faculty what our experience has been like. It has been these experiences that have helped us to grow in realizing that there must be a way to balance and integrate our personal identity with our professional identity. To continue the practice of cultural shifting only further degrades our efforts to feel whole.

Nosotros Como Profesionales (Our Professional Identities)

During our clinical training, we have become more aware of how we integrate the valuable lessons we have learned from our culture and families into our roles as therapists. For example, Ruben stated that getting in touch with his ancestry and race has been instrumental in helping him help clients find the freedom to express their feelings at a richer and deeper level. Carmen discussed how she brings the importance of respect for others to her work with clients. The ability to always be conscious of the importance of helping clients feel respected and heard has been something that supervisors have commented on and that is at the core of her work with families.

Nenetzin said that what her parents taught her—not to partition herself as a half-Mexican and half-Anglo American but, rather, to identify herself as 100% Hispanic and 100% Anglo American—helps her feel 100% present for her clients, regardless of the language being spoken. Jorge talked about the lessons his father taught him about respect and forgiveness as being the most influential for him in doing therapy. As for Maria, she told us that she will never forget the lessons her mother taught her about treating everyone the same, regardless of their race, social status, or way of life. By her actions, Maria's mother empowered Maria to be strong and independent, as well as open and accepting of people from different walks of life. These values clearly laid the foundation for Maria's feminist-informed approach to family therapy.

We also shared conversations about important factors such as power, privilege, gender, and hierarchy. Our relationships to these factors, the way they have been culturally ingrained in us, has had a tremendous impact on our personal growth, as well as on our desire to achieve advanced degrees in psychotherapy. As we have conversed about these issues, the topic of our professional identity has continuously arisen. We have all been very candid about our struggles with keeping our professional identity when we enter the therapy room and find ourselves struggling to find the correct therapeutic words and phrases. For those of us whose dominant language is English, we have become painfully aware that our ability to converse in Spanish and our ability to do therapy in Spanish are at two separate ends of the spectrum. As we think about our experiences of Hispanic and Latino families expecting to be seen by an expert who offers a prescriptive remedy to a problem (such as when they go see a medical doctor), we feel our doubt regarding our professional identity hit us full force in the stomach. When some of us have worked in Spanish (our less dominant language) with clients who need or want to perceive us as experts who have all the answers, then we have often been concerned about how our struggle with the language influences the clients perception of us as professionals. We are often left wondering about clients' views of us, doubting our abilities and professionalism, and frustrated with ourselves. Jorge mentioned that he has always thought of himself as being fluent in Spanish, has spoken Spanish his entire life, and was very excited about being able to offer therapy to Spanish speakers. However, after his first therapy session in Spanish, which was much more difficult than he had anticipated due to his struggle with therapeutic Spanish, he secretly wished that he would not get any more clients who needed therapy in Spanish. It was frustrating for him to realize that the Spanish he learned at home, although valuable, was not sufficient for him to feel strong in offering therapy in Spanish. Furthermore, this frustration intersected with the feelings of inadequacy he was experiencing, which are common to most beginning therapists. Since then, he has had the opportunity to do more therapy in Spanish and has become more comfortable with it and with himself as a bilingual therapist.

Maria added that she deals with the issue of hierarchy by keeping an open, not-knowing stance with her clients (unless they are in crisis), which feels more congruent with her bicultural identity: I am able to see advantages to working through a language struggle. I think struggling a little bit in session helps me maintain a more collaborative approach, in which I can attempt to flatten the therapeutic hierarchy and take a not-knowing stance (Anderson, 1997). I humble myself by clarifying what words and experiences mean instead of making assumptions and focusing on my expert stance and judgments. This way of working is my preferred way in English, but it is much easier to make assumptions when you and your clients think you are generating the same meanings. Most often, these assumptions go unchecked by everyone involved in the conversation. This is rarely the case when I have to struggle to do therapy in Spanish.

In regard to how respect can intersect with age, culture, and gender, we have shared the difficulty of challenging, interrupting, and being truthful with clients when clients are older than we are, of a different culture, or of a different gender. This struggle originated for us with the ways in which important cultural values and beliefs, such as family unity, personal warmth, respect for elders, and respect for others' dignity (Garcia-Preto, 1996), as well as values related to hierarchy, male dominance, and male privilege were transmitted in our experiences in and observations of our families of origin. We all agree that many of the values and beliefs transmitted by our families and culture are not a bad thing, but that the presence of those values and beliefs in the therapy room may, at times, hinder the progress of therapy within our own culture. We have all found ourselves at times questioning, reflecting on, and trying to make sense of how these issues may interfere with our work in therapy. We have also had experiences of supervisors and colleagues (who had previously observed our sessions in English) acting puzzled or surprised by how we had changed as a result of doing therapy in Spanish. Doing therapy in Spanish influenced us as therapists, regardless of whether Spanish was our dominant or less dominant language.

Courage is an important part of the process of becoming a mental health professional. Ruben spoke to this most eloquently in concluding his narrative, and what he wrote is very fitting for the conclusion of this portion of this chapter: I think that throughout this process of growth, courage from minority and international students is required; accountability and solidarity from

American faculty and students are also necessary in order to complete the equation. The final product is a beautiful painting and that piece of work cannot be beautiful unless all colors are incorporated. Are we aware of the beauty of our own unique color and do we honor the other colors? In the end, being a therapist is more than techniques and mastering a language. A core issue in being a therapist relates to feeling passion for the color we are and having the courage to paint, realizing that a mixture of colors is needed in order to create beauty. This can only come from the depth of our hearts and souls.

It is evident that acknowledgement of the aforementioned topics and issues needs to begin at the level of the training programs where the number of ethnic minority and international students is increasing. Next, we address areas related to clinical implications, such as therapists' sense of competence, the therapeutic alliance, and language as a primary process.

Clinical Implications for Bilingual and Bicultural Therapists

Attending to Language as a Primary Process

It is critical for therapists to attend to the language that informs the therapy process, especially when the client and therapist have different dominant languages. As mentioned earlier, all too often meanings go unchecked and the client's perspective may not be interpreted correctly. When therapists are doing therapy in their less dominant language, they may say something that the client understands to mean something different from what the therapist intended. Checking in with the client's understanding is critical and should be an ongoing process that is openly discussed as part of the therapy. Therapists should always be tentative in their assumptions and beliefs about what a client is saying and experiencing.

Keeping an Open, Not-Knowing Stance

Maria shared that taking a not-knowing stance (Anderson, 1997; Anderson & Goolishian, 1992) has been an important part of her work with clients: I think taking a not-knowing stance is especially important when therapists are working in their less dominant language. Even when therapists may be perfectly bilingual or multilingual, there are many nuances in language that lead to misunderstandings and confusion. The dilemma many therapists deal with, especially beginning therapists, is the contradictory feeling of developing a professional identity, a sense of competence and professionalism, while taking a one-down stance. Experience has taught me to feel more comfortable in this not-knowing stance and that by taking this approach, many Latino/a clients in particular have expressed a sense of empowerment. The key element is to remain in an open dialogue and continuously discuss the process occurring in relation to language.

Keeping the Therapeutic Alliance

We know that the therapeutic alliance is one of the most critical factors related to effective therapy outcome. We think that this is particularly true when therapists work in their less dominant language and when the language used is not the one in which therapists received their clinical training. Even if the therapist struggles with language difficulties, therapy can still progress toward achieving the client's goals if the therapist stays emotionally connected. Although no one likes to stumble when searching for the right words to say, by demonstrating empathy, connectedness, compassion, and a sense of commitment to the client's goals, therapists can make it evident that they value and respect the client more than they value their own need to feel secure and competent.

Maintaining a Sense of Competence

When therapists work in their less dominant language, it is natural that they may feel less competent. As part of our discussions in writing this chapter, we often commented on how some of us have struggled to do therapy in Spanish (our less dominant language) because our vocabulary in English far exceeds our vocabulary in Spanish. All too often we have felt frustrated when doing therapy in Spanish that feels as if it is at a grade-school level compared with our vocabulary in English, which is that of a graduate student and professor. In addition, our dilemma is further complicated when we try to articulate what we are doing in therapy in Spanish. All of our professional language has been formed in English, and it is difficult to think about therapy process in another language. This dilemma has made us more sensitive to what our international colleagues from Korea, Japan, China, India, and Mexico must feel when they learn how to do therapy in English, and then have to relearn how to do therapy and supervision in their primary language. Only by trying to discuss our therapy in Spanish did we realize how difficult it was to come up with the words. There was a certain dissonance that we experienced that we could not have articulated before we attempted supervision in our less dominant language. We were also able to empathize more with how international students must feel when trying to articulate what they are doing in therapy in their less dominant language. It is very challenging for them, and supervisors often misinterpret this difficulty in language to be a difficulty in ability or clinical competence.

For bilingual therapists in training, a challenging process takes place when the nuances of language impact in a direct way a therapist's sense of competence. For example, at the most basic level, it is common for these therapists to experience anxiety as a result of engaging in self-dialogue focused on their language limitations. It is not uncommon for bilingual therapists to think, "What do they think about my accent?" "What would happen if I made a mistake when speaking to clients in their primary language?" and "How are they going to react to my language limitations?" If therapists focus exclusively on this train of thought, there is a danger of their losing track of the process that is taking place with the clients in the therapy room. Therefore, it is important for therapists and supervisors to speak about the unspoken fears that bilingual therapists might be experiencing. Such dialogues might create the opportunity for the therapist to discover a professional identity based on embracing limitations and converting them into strengths. This experience has the potential of becoming an isomorphic process with clinical work. For example, if bilingual therapists realize that they are struggling to manage a language that is not their primary language, this awareness could enable them to have humility and be vulnerable in talking about this issue. At the same time, they might be able to turn their apparent weakness or lack of language skills into a powerful strength. Many of us have even gotten to the point where in session we laugh with our clients about our mistakes in mispronouncing words, and such vulnerability promotes an opportunity for intimacy with our clients by showing them that we also struggle with many things in life, including language. At the same time, we have learned to use such limitations to motivate us. In the end, much therapeutic work has the same principle; acknowledging areas of struggle, having the courage to face them, developing the skills to overcome them, and learning to convert struggles into strengths.

In sum, our "apparent limitations" in language proficiency as bilingual therapists might be a wonderful way to remind us that if we are going to invite our clients to engage in processes of vulnerability and humility, then we need to start by the example of our own lives, including those moments when we have to be humble and recognize that we are far from being "perfect professionals." This is an expression of our commitment to grow despite our "limitations." Such passion is what shapes our identity as bilingual therapists.

Bilingual and Bicultural Therapist Training and Supervision

Supervisors and Programs

How can supervisors help bilingual and bicultural trainees learn to feel comfortable in doing therapy in a language that is not their dominant language? This is a difficult issue, especially if the trainee is an international student, the supervisor does not speak the therapist's dominant language, or the trainee's level of language competency is significantly weaker than that of the clients. First, the supervisor should work toward becoming aware of the trainee's culture, values, and struggles. A culturally sensitive supervisor will be better able to detect when language is a therapeutic or self-of-the-therapist issue instead of something else, like a developmental issue. A supervisor should ask questions that would help the supervisee explore language as a clinical issue (for sample questions, see General Questions for Therapists on p. 206–207 in this volume). Second, the supervisor should encourage the trainee to openly discuss these issues and thus validate the trainee's struggle, which often goes unnoticed. Maria told the group that a supervisor never asked her about how doing therapy in Spanish might complicate her work as a therapist. While focusing on the therapeutic problem or clinical concern is usually an appropriate focus for a supervisor, it is possible that the supervisor is at risk for making false assumptions about the trainee's skills as a therapist when the struggle may lie in a language barrier. Third, supervisors need to find a way to observe sessions in languages other than their own. Currently, many supervisors don't even consider such observations, or if they do, then they may experience a sense of impotence or incompetence with regard to observing a trainee's session without understanding what is being said. It may be difficult for some supervisors to rely on the trainee or student observers for a translation. A way to ameliorate this dilemma could be to use a creative approach to supervision. For example, if no one in the observation team speaks the language being spoken in the observed session, then the supervisor could ask the observation team to watch carefully for body language and to make assessments based on physical and nonverbal cues. The supervisor could ask certain questions that may generate different clinical questions for everyone involved (for examples of a supervisor's questions in this context, see Questions for an Observation

Team That Does Not Speak the Language Spoken in Observed Session on p. 207 in this volume).

Recruiting Ethnic Minority and International Students

It has become evident in our work with families in the southwest region of Texas that the availability of services in clients' own languages, Spanish in particular, is a growing need. We have found that once the barriers of language are overcome, the barrier of negative attitude toward therapy among Latino/a families begins to disintegrate, thereby leading to more Latino/a families accessing therapeutic services. In our own experiences in our training program, we have seen a steady stream of referrals for clients who need Spanish-speaking therapists. As we went through our clinical training, there were times when we each found that the majority of our client load were families whose primary language was Spanish. Each of us has also experienced being the only available therapist for Spanish-speaking clients. We have each noticed as we attend the annual AAMFT conferences that ethnic minority representation is extremely low. For whatever reasons, many aspiring Latino/a graduate students choose to enter other fields. It is time for universities and MFT training programs to strive to inform more Latino/a students about the field of MFT and actively recruit at universities where there are substantial numbers of Latino/a undergraduates. We offer the following suggestions that may help universities recruit more Hispanic and Latino/a students into MFT and other mental health-related programs: (1) Be sure to model an appreciation for diversity by having a diverse faculty in terms of race, ethnicity, religion, sexual preference/orientation, ability, and so on; (2) Promote a diverse range of faculty research interests that deal with minority issues; (3) Look beyond GRE scores—there is ample evidence that shows that the GRE is not a good predictor of the academic success of minority students in graduate school; (4) Provide funding from the department, college, or university for minority students to come to the interview. If you value a diverse population, this a good way to recruit strong minority students for your program; and (5) Remind your faculty that minority students need continued mentoring and encouragement. Minority students often report feeling unsupported, and many of the contextual issues they deal with are often overlooked by more mainstream faculty.

We will all benefit by creating a positive and encouraging climate for minority and international students. Their clinical and scholarly contributions will be especially critical in societies like ours that are increasingly becoming more diverse.

Future Research

There are several areas of research that could enhance our understanding of the needs of multilingual and multicultural therapists and clients. Some of these areas of interest have been mentioned in previous literature in psychology and social work; however, it seems that several years later, these issues have still not been addressed by adequate research either in those fields or in the field of family therapy.

We encourage researchers and trainers to better understand the professional identity development of bilingual and bicultural therapists. We believe it is important that faculty and supervisors working with bilingual and bicultural trainees be sensitive to these trainees' cultural identity processes as well as their own agenda regarding cultural identity. Currently, Ruben and his colleagues have begun to examine the danger of professionals who are not aware of an unchallenged "acculturation" agenda present in the mental health professions. Trainers might not realize that the cost involved with their holding such an agenda, the cost of "acculturating" trainees, is to diminish trainees' cultural identity with their original culture. Phrases such as "he is struggling to acculturate" and "she is acculturating" are expressions of an acculturation agenda. And although many trainers espouse the ideal of creating an experience of social justice for all students, a lack of awareness of their own beliefs regarding cultural identity might prevent them from becoming aware of the different aspects of a cultural identity formation experience. Therefore, we consider it extremely important for supervisors and educators to be aware of their own beliefs regarding acculturation and cultural identity. Such awareness will greatly impact the way in which students embrace or avoid the challenges embedded in the journey of finding their own cultural identity. We truly believe that the degree of cultural development achieved by students will determine how effective they will be as bicultural therapists—especially in connecting with clients experiencing similar cultural challenges.

In addition to process research, we also encourage educators and clinicians to think more rigorously about how models of therapy need to be adapted to be more culturally sensitive and clinically effective for various ethnic groups. The models therapists use and the research that informs therapists' work are clearly biased. Currently, a lot of attention is moving in the direction of conducting outcome and process research. However, if these data do not account for the multiple experiences and contexts of diverse samples, then therapists continue to risk that the data will not be very helpful in guiding therapy with various groups of people.

Finalmente

We hope that our ideas and experiences shed some light on the issues that we, as Latino/a, bicultural, and bilingual professionals, believe are important for the advancement of our field. We continue to feel hopeful whenever we see examples of solidarity and commitment to social justice in the faculty we entrust to mentor and guide us in launching our careers as family therapists. It is only by all of us joining together that we will continue to learn how to better embrace our differences as well as see more of the similarities we share.

What seem to us the essential considerations with regard to the experiences of bicultural and bilingual students in clinical programs—acknowledging within-group diversity, understanding language limitations, and attending to process in supervision—are discussed below.

Acknowledging Within-Group Diversity

There is a permanent need to avoid thinking about bicultural and bilingual students as individuals sharing the same backgrounds and experiences. Assuming that Latino/a students can speak Spanish, or that if they identify with the Hispanic culture that they share the same cultural identity, can be misleading. It is important to keep in mind Hardy's (1990) definition of the Theoretical Myth of Sameness (TMOS) and avoid embracing a way of thinking that suggests that because a group of people share the same ethnic ancestry, they must be the same. For example, even though we all consider ourselves Hispanic, our experiences of cultural identity formation are dramatically different. Some of us have suffered racism in a crude form, and the result has been that those injustices have pushed us to find our cultural identity faster. Others have not faced injustice to the same extent, but they have experienced a difficult struggle in trying to reconcile the fact that they must navigate between two different worlds. We consider being aware of such intragroup differences one of the strongest qualities that faculty can offer to their students. Being sensitive to the fact that each student might experience different cultural identity struggles and have different needs will help trainers realized that bicultural students cannot be treated under the assumption that "they all are the same."

Understanding Language Limitations

Limitations such as not having the ability to speak English fluently should become opportunities not for pathologizing but, rather, for creating a sense of community. Although we agree that students whose primary language is not English should acquire a level of conversation and grammar comprehension according to graduate requirements, it is important to acknowledge that such students will face the challenge of continuing to master the English language in addition to struggling with the possible incongruence between two or more different cultures. Special processes should be explored with these students and supervisees in order to become aware of the process of adaptation that they are going through. For instance, taking the example of a student from Asia, it might be possible to make the wrong assumption by believing that because the student is obviously thinking while listening to others speak English, it means that she or he is struggling with the language and that this is evidence of a limitation. It might be that what appears to be a limitation is just an indication that such a student is trying to make sense of two very different worldviews, in that the Western way of thinking will in some ways conflict with her or his Eastern way of thinking. Another way in which a supervisor could misinterpret this student's silence is by viewing the student as passive or not knowing how to proceed in therapy. It is possible that for this student, such introspection is not a limitation but an active process of trying to make sense of the way in which one event can be perceived in very different ways. As the United States becomes a more diverse society, what we perceive to be others' limitations should ultimately make us more humble as we discover what those "limitations" have to teach us, that is, how much we have to learn from other cultures. We hope that we will continue to show solidarity to those who come to our culture in an effort to create bridges of understanding.

Attending to Process in Supervision

Supervisors should not stop offering live or video supervision just because they do not understand the language spoken in a session. Limiting supervision in these cases to "notes supervision" is evidence of the supervisor's (a) lack of humility in being unwilling to acknowledge his or her limitation as a supervisor and (b) lack of solidarity in not pushing himself or herself to face such a limitation. We have experienced beautiful supervisory experiences where supervisors made their best effort to focus on the process, even though they did not understand the language. That was a sign of supervisors' solidarity, justice, and clear understanding of the power to find ways to be with students who are different from themselves. Such supervisors use creative ways to track the therapy process and thus provide themselves with a powerful tool that can also compensate for their language limitation. On the other hand, we have struggled with some supervisors who just would not offer live or video supervision because they could not understand the language. We believe such an attitude impedes the advancement of trainees as therapists, as well as the advancement of our field, because it reflects a way of thinking that shows that differences *are just not worth the time*. If we mean to espouse ideals of solidarity in our field and support our ideals show-ing an active commitment to diversity, it is important for all of us to start being humble about our limitations (e.g., lacking the ability to understand a foreign language), accept them, and take responsibility for such limitations, instead of trying to make them *invisible* and overlook such challenges.

On a more personal level, through the experience of writing this chapter, we each have experienced a greater awareness of our growth (at times painful and at times enriching) and of how our culture affects our training and our work. It is our hope that our experiences and insights also challenge other students, professionals, supervisors, and people working in training programs to become more conscious of and promote discussions about how the struggle of integrating identity, culture, and language can make training, education, and the experience of doing and entering therapy either more meaningful and rich or disappointing and empty for all those who are affected either directly or indirectly by our profession.

We take pride in our chosen profession, and we have chosen this field because of our love for and concern for families, couples, and children. If we, ethnic minority and international students and faculty, truly believe in the value of systems work in therapy, should we not then also make it our duty to raise awareness and explore (or even acknowledge) our own struggles stemming from our values and beliefs, as well as engage in open and honest conversations on these issues with our colleagues? It's time that mental health professionals begin with a system like ours so as to promote second-order change related to these emerging issues. It is only by addressing these concerns in our own field that we can hope to address them with clients and society in general.

Reflections, Questions, and Exercises

General Questions for Therapists

1. Are you experiencing any challenges due to a language barrier? If so, which ones?

2. How do these challenges make you feel? Do you have any worries or anxieties?

3. How would the therapy be different if you were working in your dominant language?

4. What feelings are you experiencing when working with clients whose dominant language differs from yours?

5. How do you think the clients feel doing therapy in their dominant language? How do you think they experience you?

6. Although your supervisor does not speak your language, how might he or she be able to help you?

7. Are you experiencing a culture clash with the clinical model or approach you are using? Which parts fit and which ones do not?

8. How can the model or theory you are using be modified to be more culturally sensitive?

Questions for an Observation Team That Does Not Speak the Language Spoken in Observed Session

1. What do you think they (client and therapist) are saying?

2. How do you think they (client and therapist) feel? How do you think their bodies reflect their feelings?

3. How do you perceive the therapeutic alliance?

4. Who has the most power in the room? How can you tell?

5. What biases do you have that inform your observations?

6. What is it like for you to observe a session in which you do not understand the language?

7. How does this experience help you better empathize with clients you work with who have not mastered your language?

References

Altarriba, J. (in press). Does cariño equal liking? A theoretical approach to conceptual nonequivalence between languages. *International Journal of Bilingualism.*

Altarriba, J., & Santiago-Rivera, A. L. (1994). Current perspectives on using linguistic and cultural factors in counseling the Hispanic client. *Professional Psychology: Research and Practice, 25,* 388–397.

Anderson, H. (1997). *Conversation, language, and possibilities: A postmodern approach to therapy.* New York: Basic Books.

Anderson, H., & Goolishian, H. (1992). The client is the expert: A not-knowing approach to therapy. In S. McNamee & K. J. Gergen (Eds.), *Therapy as social construction* (pp. 25–39). Newbury Park, CA: Sage.

Fear, R., & Woolfe, R. (1999). The personal and professional development of the counselor: The relationship between personal philosophy and theoretical orientation. *Counseling Psychology Quarterly, 12,* 253–263.

Flores, M. T., & Carey, G. (2000). *Family therapy with Hispanics: Toward appreciating diversity.* Needham Heights, MA: Allyn & Bacon.

Garcia-Preto, N. (1996). Latino families: An overview. In M. McGoldrick, J. Giordano, & J. K. Pearce (Eds.), *Ethnicity and family therapy.* New York: Guilford.

Guttfreund, D. G. (1990). Effects of language usage on the emotional experience of Spanish-English and English-Spanish bilinguals. *Journal of Consulting & Clinical Psychology, 58,* 604–607.

Hardy, K. (1990). The theoretical myth of sameness: A critical issue in family therapy training and treatment. In G. W. Saba, B. M. Karrer, & K. V. Hardy (Eds.), *Minorities and family therapy* (pp.17–30). New York: Haworth.

Hardy, K. V., & Laszloffy, T. A. (1998). The dynamics of pro-racist ideology: Implications for family therapists. In M. McGoldrick (Ed.), *Re-visioning family therapy. Race, culture and gender in clinical practice* (pp. 118–128). New York: Guilford.

Ho, M. K. (1987). *Family therapy with ethnic minoritites.* Newbury Park, CA: Sage.

Manoleas, P., Organista, K., Negron-Velasquez, G., & McCormick, K. (2000). Characteristics of Latino mental health clinicians: a preliminary examination. *Community Mental Health Journal, 36,* 383–394.

Marcos, L. R. (1976). Linguistic dimensions in the bilingual patient. *American Journal of Psychoanalysis, 36,* 347–354.

Marcos, L. R., & Alpert, M. (1976). Strategies and risks in psychotherapy with bilingual patients: The phenomenon of language independence. *American Journal of Psychiatry, 133,* 1275–1278.

Marcos, L. R., & Urcoyo, L. (1979). Dynamic psychotherapy with the bilingual patient. *American Journal of Psychotherapy, 33,* 331–338.

Massey, D. S., & Bitterman, B. (1985). Explaining the paradox of Puerto Rican segregation. *Social Forces, 64*(2), 306–330.

Massey, D. S., & Fischer, M. J. (2000). How segregation concentrates poverty. *Ethnic and Racial Studies, 23*(4), 670–691.

McGoldrick, M., & Giordano, J. (1996). Overview: Ethnicity and family therapy. In M. McGoldrick, J. Giordano, & J. K. Pearce (Eds.), *Ethnicity and family therapy.* New York: Guilford.

Miehls, D., & Smith, C. (2001). The interface of racial identity development with identity complexity in clinical social work student practitioners. *Clinical Social Work Journal, 29,* 229–244.

Ondrich, J., Stricker, A., & Yinger, J. (1998). Do real estate brokers choose to discriminate? Evidence from the 1989 housing discrimination study. *Southern Journal, 64*(4), 880–901.

Pitta, P., Marcos, L. R., & Alpert, M. (1978). Language switching as a treatment strategy with bilingual patients. *American Journal of Psychoanalysis, 38,* 255–258.

Rodriguez, C. E., & Cordero-Guzman, H. (1992). Placing race in context. *Ethnic and Racial Studies, 15*(4), 523–542.

Rozensky, R. H., & Gomez, M. Y. (1983). Language switching in psychotherapy with bilinguals: Two problems, two models, and case examples. *Psychotherapy: Theory, Research & Practice, 20,* 152–160.

Santiago-Rivera, A. L., & Altarriba, J. (2002). The role of language in therapy with the Spanish-English bilingual client. *Professional Psychology: Research & Practice, 33,* 30–38.

Watts, R. J. (1987). Development of professional identity in black clinical psychology students. *Professional Psychology: Research & Practice, 18,* 28–35.

Wright-Harp, W., & Muniz, E. (2000). Preparing bilingual speech-language pathologists: The development of an innovative master's degree program. *Teacher Education and Special Education, 23,* 290–302.

Zuniga, M. E. (1991). "Dichos" as metaphorical tools for resistant Latino clients. *Psychotherapy: Theory, Research & Practice, 28,* 480–483.

12

International Academic Sojourners in the United States of America*

Color in the Ivory Tower

Mudita Rastogi and Carole Woolford-Hunt

G oing outside of one's culture of origin requires a flexibility of thought and spirit and often results in a whole new perspective on life and self. In 1998, over 60,000 (or 5.6%) of the faculty teaching in the United States at postsecondary institutions had international or noncitizen status (National Center for Education Statistics, 2001). These persons include permanent residents (i.e., "green card holders"), nonresident aliens, and other visiting scholars. The statistics cited above do not include the vast numbers of faculty who were born, raised, and educated elsewhere but have now become naturalized citizens. International faculty in the United States is growing in large numbers, as can be seen from the following: The number of nonresident alien faculty increased throughout the years from a mere 635 in 1954 to 1955 to 11,000 in 1993 (Almanac 1997–98; Smith, Byrd, Nelson, Barrett, & Constantides, 1992.) These individuals form a significant proportion of all

---

*The authors contributed equally to this chapter.

academics in this country. Their experiences, views, and work have a large impact on the entire system of higher education. These experiences are, at times, different from the experiences of faculty who were raised in the United States. In addition, the experiences of international faculty overlap with *and* differ from those of other ethnic minority faculty in the United States. This chapter focuses on our experiences in academia in the United States. Our narratives emphasize our experiences of the unique rewards and challenges of teaching at the graduate level in the mental health field, and thus may be different from the experiences of nonacademics or international faculty in other disciplines. Join us while we tell our stories and review the themes that emerge. We hope that this chapter will increase readers' awareness of the special issues facing international faculty, especially in the mental health field. We will conclude with recommendations to international faculty and to the academic systems that are their hosts.

Personal Backgrounds

Mudita Rastogi (M.R.)

I was born in Calcutta, India. By the time I was 5 years old, I spoke the local language, Bengali, and my native language, Hindi, fluently. When I entered first grade (known as "First Standard" in India), I was introduced to the English language through a textbook that had a character called Pat. In the first chapter, Pat's mother sings a song for him. Then he sings for his mother. Early on, characters like Pat brought me face to face with a world that was different from my own. I saw pictures of a White, blond-haired, English boy sitting with his mother. As most of my education beyond first grade continued in English, Pat was not the stranger supplanted in my life. I was the outsider in his world.

I come from an upper middle-class Indian family. My parents are highly educated, liberal, and socially well networked. My father's job took him to many different cities, and I have lived in seven cities in three countries. In many ways, I was raised with a good deal of privilege. But I had a "minority experience" in two significant ways. First, I am female. My education and upbringing could never compensate for my experience of sexism in society, in religious institutions, in school systems, and with extended family members. Second, I was raised in postcolonial India. Even though I was not a racial minority in India, I was impacted by my country's colonial history.

One of the many ways in which 174 years of colonial rule left its mark on postindependence India was in the form of Pat and his mother, singing to each other. They were standard fixtures in our classrooms and in our minds, although they were unrepresentative of the people in our lives. Most "good" schools at the time used English as the primary medium of education, even though the vast majority of students did not speak the language at home. Similarly, the culture at my private school idealized standards of behavior, lifestyle, and appearance that were borrowed from a foreign system and were remnants of the "British Raj." My early textbooks did not have pictures of brown-skinned girls with black hair. I internalized the message that I ought to learn about and fit into a world that was alien to me. To some degree, I believe that these experiences led me to my current interests in gender and cross-cultural issues.

To put this chapter in context, I should add that I have now lived in the United States for over 13 years. I hold Indian citizenship and have U.S. Permanent Resident status. I came to this country as a doctoral student and have resided in both large and small cities, some more ethnically diverse than others. For the sake of maintaining confidentiality, I have deliberately omitted from my narrative the names of some institutions and individuals. However, all the events are described as accurately as I can remember them. They are biased to the extent that they are reported from my sole perspective.

The Ivory Tower: First Impressions

Nine years ago, I conducted a national job search as I approached the completion of my Ph.D. in marriage and family therapy. A certain university set up a phone interview with me. The interviewers consisted of both faculty and graduate students. At one point in the interview, they talked about how much their institution valued diversity and asked how I might contribute to this area. I discussed my theory of therapy, my research, and my clinical work in both India and the United States, all of which were relevant to their question. The next questions took me by surprise. They asked me if I was married, whether I had an arranged marriage, how I met my husband, and what my religious orientation was. I felt I had no choice but to answer. However, I remember feeling deeply uncomfortable during and immediately after the conversation, since this was not light chitchat at a cocktail party. I have learned since that it is downright illegal to ask these questions. And I wish I could say that this was the only interview in which I was asked personal questions of this nature.

It is clear to me that my "otherness" sparked these questions. A White applicant in my place might not arouse the same degree of curiosity about the circumstances under which she met her husband. The interviewers' interactions with me were defined by their stereotypical image of an Indian woman.

It was not just that they asked me personal questions, but also the type of personal questions they asked. To me, their questioning revealed their need to view me as part of a stereotype and put me in prearranged slots. My clinical and research interests and my theoretical orientation were not enough to define me. Those dimensions did not complete their picture of "the average Indian woman." Their need to "complete the picture" took precedence over their common sense, as well as over their ethical and legal obligations in a job interview.

Entering the Ivory Tower: Defining Myself

Once I started teaching in an academic setting, I realized that I was expected to define myself as "either/or." The categories were "Person of Color" or "White," as there were no "Other" categories. In the U.S. cultural context, the unspoken expectation is that you must assert your racial identity as primary, and all other identities are secondary. It is my experience that others see me first as a person of color, and any other label they apply to me is a distant second. At a faculty meeting early on in the academic year, people were invited to join small groups to discuss various issues of diversity. As I walked across the room to join a particular group, I realized that people were laughing with embarrassment. It took me a while to realize that my colleagues were both shocked and uncomfortable that I sat with the Gender Committee and not the Ethnic Minority Committee. As I recall, there was some joking around my choice. It never occurred to me that I had committed a major faux pas. By joining the Gender Committee, I seemed to have sent a message that my gender identity was more salient than my ethnic identity. The truth of the matter was that at that point in my development, I still saw myself as an international person, and not necessarily as a person of color. (As an aside, I now embrace both of these identities, although it took me several years to get to this point.) It did not occur to my colleagues that I might *not want* to choose between the Gender Committee and the Ethnic Minority Committee. I got the same reactions from both my colleagues who identified as people of color and my White colleagues. Significantly, there was no group or diversity committee to consider the issues of international faculty and students.

Living in the Ivory Tower: Learning the Terrain

A few weeks into the term, it became clear to me that the faculty and administration expected me to contribute to and give an opinion on any and every issue related to minority concerns. At that particular time in the history of that institution, the relations between the administration and minority students and faculty had seen a decline. At the same time, the administration was urging all faculty to revise their syllabi to include "issues of diversity," including ethnicity. I was recruited to be on numerous ad hoc committees to discuss these issues knowledgeably and to help implement new ideas. The irony was that the ink on my doctoral diploma had not quite dried yet. I had a lot to learn as the sudden and inexperienced new champion of ethnic minority affairs. Although I had been interested in ethnicity as a doctoral student, I had retained my sense of being an international student. Here, the new identity was thrust upon me and I had no choice but to accept it.

Most clinical programs offer focused courses on diversity. At this institution, it was intriguing to note that faculty that considered themselves minorities, in the area of either ethnicity or sexual orientation, taught the majority of the diversity courses. I explained that I was reluctant to teach the courses on two grounds: (1) Having lived in the United States for only a few years, I did not have the knowledge and experiential base to address some of these issues in depth, and (2) I strongly believe that faculty belonging to the majority community ought to teach these courses too. One of the reasons that diversity issues become marginalized or compartmentalized is that they are frequently associated with minority faculty. It is then a short leap of logic that these issues concern only those particular "different" faculty or students, and not all of us. My arguments raised some eyebrows, but I was not pressured to teach the diversity courses.

My identity as an "other" led to an incident that still fills me with anguish. A young international student died suddenly. Her family rushed to the United States, and when they visited the university, the administration asked me to assist them in any way that I could. The administration assumed that since the student's family and I both came from Asia, we would get along well. However, that family and I did not speak a common language, so I communicated with them using the translation skills of another international student. The student's parents were naturally interested in learning about her interests and performance at the school. Not having known her, I was unable to answer most of their questions. Privately, I questioned why the school did not ask the student's advisor or direct teachers to assume the role they'd given me with the family. I felt very constrained in my ability to give them what they wanted, and I was angry that the administration did not think about the family's needs fully. I suspected that my identity as an international and an Asian person was the sole basis for the decision to connect me with the family. It appeared to be a case of skin color and nationality taking precedence over other important factors.

There was a barely functioning student-led organization at the school that focused on the issues of international students. Another faculty member and

I worked hard to revive it. Weekly meetings, social gatherings, and discussions led to an increased awareness of the issues facing international students. The majority of the brown-bag discussions focused on the major issues that seemed to dominate the lives of international students and faculty. By far the first and foremost issue had to do with dealings with the much-feared Immigration and Naturalization Service (INS). One had to be "in-status" with the INS or risk being deported. As it happened, the local INS office was a few blocks away from the school. Student Services staff sent international students there on a regular basis. The group's lunch discussions were filled with horror stories of the "war weary." Lines outside that INS office snaked around the block, and at times international faculty and students had to go and stand there at 5 a.m. to be at the head of the line. It was not uncommon for them to spend 4 hours in line, then to get to the window only to be told that something was missing from their paperwork and that they had to do this all over again. It took a great deal of lobbying by the students and faculty to get the school personnel to provide greater help to international students in their dealings with the INS. Other discussions in the international student group centered on cross-cultural communication issues and dealing with being homesick, as well as finding resources to cope with these challenges. I heard international students say over and over again that their concerns were different from those of ethnic minorities who were "American," and that unfortunately, staff, administration and other students did not often recognize this.

September 11, 2001 brought new challenges for international faculty and students. On the following day, in one of my classes, students began discussing ways to prevent acts of terrorism in the future. One doctoral student (White, third-generation British American, female, and about 26 years old) suggested that "those foreigners walking around" were a problem. I braced myself for the next part, because I instinctively knew what was coming. She then went on to say that all "foreigners" in the United States ought to carry ID cards at all times and should have to present them to enter all public areas. Apart from the complete impracticality of this idea, I was struck by the assumptions made by this woman. While a couple of students disagreed on the grounds that it would target the innocent, most seemed to at least consider this idea as a possibility. The general feeling was that the rights of "Americans" were more important than those of immigrants. Later, I shared with them that I was not a U.S. citizen and my feelings about being seen as "less than" a citizen, at best, or as a "suspect," at worst. This led to a larger discussion about civil rights, immigration, and what it means to be "American." I have often wondered how immigrants and international students across the United States fared when faced with hostile comments from peers.

As I write this, the U.S-led coalition has invaded Iraq. There are heated debates about the ethics and utility of war among some of my students. Yesterday, two students came up to me (separately) and said that they really appreciated my making space in the class discussions to talk about the war. They were disappointed that their other teachers did not mention the war at all. One student said that silence about the war was like behaving as if "there is no world outside of the classroom."

Finally, I want to address two questions that people ask me all the time. These questions are significant because they also reflect the questioners' views:

(a)   How come you have *not* applied for U.S. citizenship?

(b)   What do you like (or have) in the U.S. that you did not like (or have) in India?

To answer the first: I am simply not willing to give up my Indian citizenship. This has to do with my sense of identity and emotional connection with the country in which I was born and raised. However, the longer I live in the United States, the closer I come to considering dual citizenship as an option. The second question is far more complex, and I know that my answers will change with time. It is true that I felt explicitly oppressed as a girl and as a woman in India. In the United States, at times I experience more subtle oppression related to ethnicity and gender. While I personally have had access to educational, professional, and growth opportunities here, I have seen many of my international friends struggle with the corporate glass ceiling and with being denied their civil rights. It is possible that I have made huge trade-offs with different opportunities that I might have had in India. In addition, I think about the weakening extended family ties as I raise two young Indian American children. In the end, I think that my response to the second question remains bittersweet and inconclusive.

Carole Woolford-Hunt (C.W.-H.)

I was born and raised in London. I am the older of two girls of Protestant parents who are both graduate educators and administrators. My parents were born in the West Indian Island of Trinidad (a former British colony) and went to England in their late teens to attend university. They subsequently remained in England, married, and had a family. Like many in Trinidad, my parents are racially mixed—my father's heritage is Black and Spanish and my mother is biracial, with a Black mother and an Indian father. As a result of this inheritance, I can say that I am culturally English, I racially identify as Black, and I enjoy a mixed ethnic heritage from the Caribbean and India.

I remember as a small child sitting at the dining room table for breakfast and eating toast with Robertson's jam. As I nibbled the toast and savored the sweet jam, I often played with the Robertson's jam bottle with it's colorful Golliwog mascot prominently displayed on the label. The Golliwog is the British and European equivalent of the American Sambo. It is a jet Black doll with white-rimmed eyes, red lips, and fuzzy, twisted hair. It is a cruel reminder of an era when the White racial majority saw the Black racial minority as hideous and grotesque. After years of protest from racial minorities in Britain, the company finally discontinued using the Golliwog image in 2001. The Golliwog was depicted as dishonest, foolish, and a rogue villain in many popular children's storybooks during my childhood. Needless to say, the impact of this on the developing psyche of minority children in Britain is immeasurable. Despite the presence of such harsh cultural realities, I was fortunate to have gifted and determined parents who, because of their educational achievements and social standing, were able to provide me with opportunities that were not often available to minorities in Britain at the time. A major contributing factor to their ability to achieve this middle-class status in England despite being Black was their experience as part of the majority culture in Trinidad during their childhoods. They were not shackled by the challenges that often restrain members of the minority culture. Thus they were able to provide for their children a relatively privileged minority experience through avenues such as private school education, church, and travel. However, growing up Black in England I was still part of a minority culture riddled with Golliwog images that misrepresented racial minorities and idealized White majority people and culture. This contributed greatly to my development as a psychologist, my interest in cross-cultural issues, and my desire to work with racially diverse populations. My experience as a child also prepared me for some of the challenges I would face as an international minority person in the United States.

I have now lived in the United States for 18 years. I continue to hold British citizenship, but I also have Permanent Residency status here. Of the 18 years I've been in this country, I have spent 14 years as a student and 4 years as a faculty member. During this time I completed my undergraduate, master's, and doctoral degrees at universities in three different states. The narrative that follows is my recollection of events as I experienced them, but it was written so that it protects the anonymity of the institutions and individuals involved.

Sojourner Stories in a Strange Land: First Professional Experiences

When I graduated with my Ph.D. from a large Midwestern university, I started looking for that first "perfect job." I wondered if I should indicate on my application, in some way, that I am a person of color. My name and experiences gave no hints of my racial heritage, even over the phone my British accent did not reveal my race. I chose to make no specific mention of it because it should not matter. Without exception, when I showed up to interviews, there would be a brief pause. I would witness a momentary flash of confusion; regrouping and embarrassment would cross their faces as the interviewers extended their hands toward me saying "Oh!" (Pause) "Dr. Woolford-Hunt, it's so nice to meet you."

Since coming to this country, I have found myself in a unique situation. American majority culture historically, and to some extent presently, has a diminished view about people of African decent specifically and people of color in general. This has led to the harshest treatment and negative stereotypes of this group of people. However, the American majority has traditionally had a collective love affair with all that is British. This has led to the projection of positive stereotypes onto the British. The stereotypes of the British include their being intellectually gifted, articulate, highly cultured, and polite, whereas the stereotypes of those of African descent include their being intellectually inferior, speaking Ebonics, and being uncultured and violent. As a result of this, when I stand before many Americans they are confronted with diametrically opposed stereotypes and thus have little idea of how to categorize me (and therefore how to think about me, what to expect from me, and how to treat me).

Throughout my job search, I applied to university counseling centers and academic positions in departments of psychology. I found that despite the variation (location, size, status) in institutions, all of the schools I visited openly struggled with their ability to address issues of diversity within their community and curricula. This was dramatically evidenced when on completion of the initial stages of these interviews, three of the interviewers at three different schools openly projected the role of diversity "expert" and "savior" onto me, despite the fact that I had just received my degree. In the most extreme case, a senior interviewer spent 2 hours relating a long history of the struggle at that institution to address these issues and to retain faculty of color. Early in this review of his personal struggle with the system to diversify the counseling center, it began to feel less like an interview and more like I was conducting therapy. My sense that the situation had shifted from a formal interview to me providing psychotherapy was confirmed when the interviewer began to weep openly! On the surface, this experience might seem humorous; however, it was sad on many levels. I truly felt sympathy for this interviewer and the struggles he had had in trying to actively address the issue of diversity without adequate institutional support. However, it is highly unlikely that my American classmates from the majority culture had similar interview experiences, with such tremendous pressure put on them to "save" (i.e., resolve the issues of diversity in) systems as soon as they graduated. These interviews fatigued me physically, drained me emotionally, and partially robbed me of my "new graduate optimism and idealism."

Sojourner's "Truth": First Impressions

When I ultimately accepted an offer, I approached the task of learning my new setting, role, and context energetically. The environment supported me as a new, developing faculty member. I was initially flattered by the demand for my membership on multiple faculty committees, but as time went on, I was overwhelmed by it. Each request for my participation came with compliments about the unique insights I would bring and pressure to do my part by joining the committee. This was, however, a two-sided issue—I wanted to contribute, but I also came to the system with the underdeveloped skill of saying no and setting limits. My new faculty status and my inability to say no to any of these opportunities to serve resulted in my having an overloaded schedule. By the end of my first year at that institution, I was dubbed the "Faculty Committee Queen," as I had membership on several committees. Feeling overwhelmed and burnt out, I discussed the situation with another faculty member, who said to me, "You know why you are in this position, don't you? It's because you're a threefer." I did not know what a "threefer" was, so I asked and was told that I was "three for the price of one." By my inclusion, a committee would attain the equivalent of three minority memberships and would therefore be diversified in three ways. I am Black (a racial minority), British (international), and female, and all these group memberships made me a "valuable commodity." Once again my internal drive to rescue and the external system's pressuring me to be an expert on issues of race, ethnicity, cross-cultural relations, and women's issues had gotten the better of me. In addition to my multiple group memberships, there was another powerful stereotype at work here that must not be overlooked—the stereotype that all people of color are the same, regardless of their country of origin, which is limiting and dismissive of the natural diversity that occurs within any group. Americans of European descent are given the privilege of being seen as being very different from each other, based on their country of origin (for example, French, German, Italian, etc.); however, people of African, Asian, and Hispanic decent are generally all grouped together as American ethnic minorities, with little acknowledgement of the diversity that exists among these various groups. This has in large part contributed to the pressure on international minority faculty to become experts on their country of origin as well as on all U.S. minorities. With this expectation also comes the allied role of being the voice for all the aforementioned groups, which often results in the corresponding work overload that I experienced. This and some of my other early experiences in academia had a tremendous impact on my developing professional focus. There was an implicit expectation within the system that I would be interested in and motivated to champion issues of racial and ethnic diversity, not only administratively but also as my teaching focus. It's hard to know which came first—was it my interest in these areas that the system responded to, or was I responding to the system's stereotyped belief that racial diversity issues are only the concern of racially diverse people?

I am currently at the point where I am passionately committed to my professional focus on diversity. However, I made a decision to also actively try to broaden my teaching base for two reasons. First, I have several other areas of professional interest that I have neglected while focusing on diversity. Second, the current situation in academia necessitates that I teach courses other than those on diversity. There is a certain academic snobbery that exists within graduate psychology with respect to course content. Courses that fall under the diversity umbrella are often seen as not as rigorous or not as central or fundamental to the curriculum as other courses. This assumption is of course grossly incorrect, but academic systems are often a microcosm of the larger society and as such reflect the same biases. An academic ghetto effect has occurred, with corresponding White flight. As a result, the "market value" of those left teaching diversity courses has declined. This unfair reality translates into the indirect imperative for us to broaden our focus to maintain collegial esteem and status within the academic community.

Inhabiting the Hallowed Halls of American Academia

As I matured in my faculty and administrative roles, I became aware of the additional expectations that were placed on me and on other faculty members who held similar multiple minority group memberships. All ethnic minority and international student issues became our responsibility. Faculty of color and international faculty were expected to be faculty mentors and mediators for all people within the school community who were of color or international. We also became advocates for minority staff, students, and newer faculty. When faculty had difficulty dealing with an international student in class, they consulted me for possible solutions and mediation. I welcomed these brainstorming sessions about the possible cultural factors that might be influencing an international student's academic performance, as they were simultaneously challenging and stimulating to me; however, they were quite often time intensive. When international students had problems with faculty or administration, they consulted me and other international faculty about ways to get their needs met. Most recently, several international students came to my office to express their feelings about current world events. They were concerned that there was no official institution statement about these international events and no safe forum to discuss the issue. The metacommunication, as one student stated it, is that "if it happens outside of America, it doesn't matter." When minority staff felt unfairly treated, they often confided in faculty of color and sought support. This took the form of faculty of color providing a safe place for them to talk about their experiences of perceived bias in their work environment and helping them to explore their options. When some minority faculty felt oppressed by this tremendous responsibility, other minor faculty engaged in reciprocal provision of support. Despite initial efforts, there was no sustained institutional commitment to this type of formal support for this population, and so this work continued unacknowledged.

This additional responsibility, however, has had multiple ramifications. While I was intellectually stimulated and felt a great deal of satisfaction about the contributions I was able to make to my academic community, I was left constantly tired. With little time to develop other aspects of my professional life, I was not able to take advantage of opportunities to do private practice, do consultations, and publish. The multiple role expectations of faculty who already have the personal challenges of multiple minority group memberships is ultimately a double-edged sword. While personal and professional passion for issues of diversity drives me, I must also carefully protect myself from being consumed by a situation in which there are overwhelming needs and limited resources being devoted to addressing them.

On reflection, I can say that despite the challenges of being an international academic sojourner in the United States, the benefits, personal growth, and insight into self that I have gained have been invaluable. My experiences of challenge due to my racial group membership in my country of origin, Britain, and in this country have been equal in their intensity while being different in their expression. I found that although the verbal and nonverbal language of bias transmission differs in each culture, the intent of bias remains the same. Consequently, I felt no new internal struggle to accept the dissonance that often comes when attaching to an "object" that provides wonderful opportunities while simultaneously often inflicting pain. Bias was part of my reality in my much-loved country of origin and continues to be part of my reality in my new, deeply appreciated place of residence, the United States.

I have embraced the relatively unique opportunity I have to view my culture of origin from a different perspective, to be immersed in U.S. culture, and to work with students and faculty from around the world. These experiences have served to widen and deepen my understanding of diversity, self, and other. The struggle to become sensitive to all issues of diversity is a constant individual and collective endeavor, and I can only hope to continue to travel and sojourn.

Examining the Narratives: Emerging Themes

As we read our own and each other's stories, we are struck by our similarities, even though there are important differences between us. We traveled separate paths for the majority of our lives, lived in different countries and cultures, had unique formative experiences; yet many of our struggles have been similar. The themes that emerge from our narratives reflect the salient considerations for international students and faculty residing in the United States and for the institutions that host and support them. The themes, which are discussed below, are as follows: international is a separate category, international is a very diverse category, internationals often find it necessary to develop a new identity, others may lack knowledge of an international's country and its people, new international faculty are susceptible to role overload, international faculty may be isolated and lack role models, international faculty may find their course content selected for them, international faculty may be expected to support students from all world cultures, and institutions need to make formal changes to support diverse students.

International Is a Separate Category

Both of us have found through our experiences and those of our students that international issues cannot be integrated into existing U.S. minority group issues. However, because of the unique level of overlap of international and U.S. minority groups, educational administration often treats these two distinct groups as one. This might result in increased tension between international minorities and national minorities as both groups struggle for the same limited resources. Although there are areas of overlap of all minority groups, there are significant enough differences to necessitate a separate international group and resources to address the issues of this group. The extra academic tasks of trying to learn a new culture and wrestling with the issues of acculturation, alienation, loss of social support systems, language barriers, and a new workplace culture are unique challenges of this group (Heilberger & Vick, 1992). Those of us that identify as international educators have much in common with ethnic minority faculty in the United States and often get support to deal with these common issues;

however, people who have been raised in the United States as minorities still have a grasp of the majority culture that international faculty can only guess at. For us, being in a foreign country, a new culture, and a different educational system exacerbates the task of negotiating a new identity.

International Is a Very Diverse Category

The category of international is an attempt to find a "home" for international faculty and students in the U.S. landscape, and it includes heterogeneous people from countries outside of the United States. Currently the international faculty in the United States came from countries from around the world. This group is more diverse than any of the national minority groups, because its constituents come from different countries and cultures. The one "shared experience" that binds this truly divergent group of people together is that they are foreigners in a foreign land at the same time.

Internationals Often Find It Necessary to Develop a New Identity

New international faculty and students often have to do the challenging work of growing into a new identity. As seen in M.R.'s narrative above, people in the United States perceive the stereotypic features or phenotypic characteristics of an individual as salient in defining them. "Over time, race has acquired a social meaning" in this country, "in which these biological differences, via the mechanism of stereotyping, have become markers for status assignment within the social system" (Pinderhughes, 1989). International faculty may perceive themselves in a certain way in their countries of origin, then find that in the United States they have been assigned a different group membership. This may be a struggle for international faculty and students, for whom gender, SES, religion, or other factors may be more important in their self-identity than the physical characteristics Americans may focus on. This may also create additional difficulties as the newly assigned group membership rarely means more privilege and an elevation in social status.

Others May Lack Knowledge of an International's Country and Its People

We discovered that even in the academe, people are susceptible to the forces that one faces in everyday life. People's notions and stereotypes about other countries and their nationals are often pronounced. Faculty, staff, and students may see you as representing your entire country, quite literally, as you may be the only person from that country that they know well. It was for this reason that, as described above, M.R. fielded some interesting questions during an interview and people were confused by C.W.-H.'s appearance because they had associated her English accent with White skin.

New International Faculty Are Susceptible to Role Overload

Both of us faced multiple challenges in this area. The unwritten job description of supporting our institutions' minority populations made for a heavy workload, but given our commitments and passions, the work was hard to decline. We have discovered since that this is a very common occurrence for both ethnic minority and female faculty. Faculty belonging to any underrepresented group find that they are drawn into official and unofficial responsibilities to the institution, their students, and other, newer faculty. We wish to do the responsible thing, especially if declining would deprive a committee or a student of much-needed input; however, in the process, as C.W.-H. says, we become exhausted and depleted. In our experience, most institutions do not have the means to measure this contribution, so it remains invisible and unrewarded. M.R. knows of international (and ethnic minority) faculty who were encouraged to serve on countless committees and mentor dozens of minority students, only to be reminded later that these activities did not count toward tenure.

International Faculty May Be Isolated and Lack Role Models

International faculty frequently find themselves the "only one of a kind" in an academic department. It is extremely rare for them to find another international faculty member working on the same floor, much less someone else from their own country of origin. This can lead to a sense of isolation. M.R. is extremely lucky to have a research partner who shares her identity as an international educator, and C.W.-H. counts herself fortunate to have a few international faculty as friends from whom she can gain support. However, many new international faculty do not have these sources of support. In the world of academia, as in other professional spheres, to be without a mentor or support network is, in our minds, a serious stumbling block (Lee, 2000).

International Faculty May Find
Their Course Content Selected for Them

International faculty in the mental health field bring with them rich data. This leads to students reaping the benefits in the form of interesting and enriching case examples, innovative viewpoints, new literature and research, and stimulating class discussions. However, international faculty face a dual burden. As M.R. noted, faculty that were minorities themselves taught most of the classes on diversity. This leads to a situation where issues of diversity become narrow and marginalized, and the faculty who teach these issues are marginalized, in that they are seen as having expertise only in this area. In addition, and ironically, if there are sensitive institutional issues around ethnicity, they frequently emerge in classes taught by minority faculty. While moderating difficult discussions is extremely rewarding for teachers, it can also become a burden, especially if other faculty are not doing the same in their own classes. All the processing and meditating then fall on the few faculty that make themselves accessible to discuss these issues.

International Faculty May Be Expected to
Support Students From All World Cultures

As was illustrated by M.R.'s experience with the Asian student's family, international faculty are often expected to be knowledgeable about all world cultures and people so that they can provide support and guidance to diverse international student bodies. In addition to this monumental task, international faculty also negotiate the stereotypes that the students (U.S. and international) may have about people from the international faculty's country of origin.

Institutions Need to Make Formal
Changes to Support Diverse Students

In our increasingly diverse academic world, there is often a push to recruit diverse faculty and students since they add something unique to the academic environment. However, institutions are often resistant to making the institutional changes needed to adequately support this solicited diversity. Our experiences attending to the needs of international students within academic settings illustrate the struggle of institutions to make formal changes to support diverse students.

Reflections, Questions, and Exercises

Helpful Hints for International Faculty

We have compiled a list of ideas to help international faculty cope with the challenges of teaching in the mental health field in the United States. You might wish to add to this list. Our top three suggestions are networking, networking, and networking. In our experience, and that of our colleagues, we have found that a natural antidote to isolation and culturally challenging situations is to seek out other faculty of international origin and support each other (Rastogi, Fitzpatrick, Feng, & Shi, 1999). This support is enormously helpful when you need to process difficult issues and hear another's interpretation of culturally challenging situations. A support dyad or group may be formed face-to-face or electronically. New advances in technology have made it possible to continue mutually supportive relationships with like-minded individuals without being anywhere near them physically. We highly recommend that international faculty join professional organizations, and particularly the chapters of these organizations that focus on the interests of international or ethnic minority professionals. These relationships can also help faculty pursue professional interests such as working on research on cross-national or cross-cultural issues. You may be able to find other people from your own cultural background and engage in peer mentoring. Some professional organizations will match junior faculty with senior faculty of color to facilitate the mentoring process; organizations can be contacted directly about whether they offer this option. We also suggest seeking out another type of mentor. Find a senior colleague in your own school, particularly in your department. This might be someone who has been with the university for a number of years and/or is tenured. In our experience, international faculty and faculty of color often feel as if they have to go it alone. This may be a reservation borne out of cultural norms, or a result of negative experiences in the past. We recommend stepping out of your comfort zone to invite this senior colleague to lunch. Ask if she or he is willing to act as your mentor, and specify the areas in which you need information and feedback. Most people are flattered to serve in this role. Nurture this relationship, and learn the history, politics, and unwritten rules of the department. This faculty member may help you decide how to handle committee overload, and teaching and advising issues. Also, try to get to know all faculty and administrators. Offering to visit their classes and do a guest lecture on your area of expertise or your own culture is a great way to "win friends and influence people."

In your classes, it is helpful to share your background with your students (Rastogi et al., 1999). Most course material in the mental health field naturally lends itself to discussions of culture. You might bring in case studies or papers (written by you or by others) to illustrate the significance of culture, or talk about the differences and similarities between your culture of origin and that of your students. Learn about your students' backgrounds, too. We have found that this models openness to learning about differences and teaches students how to incorporate intergroup differences in interventions with clients. M.R. also found that talking about her cross-cultural research kindled the interest of a number of students in working with South Asian families.

Prevention is also better than cure. When you interview for an academic job, pay attention to details. Speak with international and U.S. minority faculty and students to get an idea of what it is like for them to be in that institution. Ask all administrators about their vision of diversity and how they implement it. Review faculty teaching and syllabi focus to judge the institution's support for international issues and other diversity issues.

Tips for Administrators

If you are an ethnic minority or international administrator, we refer you to the section above. Administrators will benefit from being sensitized to the enormous pressures facing new international faculty. The biggest challenge for the former is making themselves aware of the "invisible" problems and contributions of the latter. We recommend setting up a friendly meeting with the incoming international faculty member to find out what she or he needs in terms of both professional and personal support. In addition, some international faculty need legal help with their visa and work permit papers. This is a very convoluted, expensive, and time-consuming process. We believe that the institution should be at least partially responsible for providing financial and legal resources to international faculty in this process, and administrators can serve as advocates for them during this time.

One way to help new faculty get to know the other faculty and students is to set up a seminar early on in the academic year and invite all the new faculty to talk about their cultures of origin and life experiences. This works as an icebreaker in the department, and it also introduces students and faculty to mutual areas of scholarly interest. It is important to recognize that singling out faculty of color or international faculty for such exercises could unintentionally mark them as "exotic" and lead to the assumption that White people do not need to explore their ethnic heritage (Wieling & Rastogi, 2003). Therefore, we hope that academic mental health programs will encourage *all* persons to be aware of their ethnicity and culture and the impact of these on a person's overall identity.

Along these lines, we also recommend that administrators encourage more faculty, particularly those belonging to the *majority* group, to gain expertise and teach the diversity courses in the program. Administrators can use a variety of incentives and support structures to ensure that all the faculty shoulder this area of responsibility. This does not preclude the idea that all course syllabi must take into account issues of diversity, including cross-national differences.

Committee and advising overload is a big challenge for international faculty and faculty of color. This is an important area where administrators can serve as gatekeepers. We recommend protecting new faculty until they have settled in and are caught up with their teaching preparation and research obligations. In our opinion, this process takes 1 to 3 years. In the interim, administrators may choose to have all committee membership requests for new faculty routed through them. Also, as mentioned above, administrators can help new faculty find a mentor by suggesting names of senior faculty to choose from. Implementing these suggestions will go a long way to enriching the department and keeping morale high, burnout low, and faculty turnover to a minimum. This is a win-win situation for all.

References

Almanac 97–98. (1997). *Chronicle of Higher Education.* Retrieved March 22, 2004, from http//www.chronicle.com

Lee, E. E. (2000). *Nurturing success: Successful women of color and their daughters.* Westport, CT: Praeger.

National Center for Education Statistics. (2001). *Background characteristics, work activities and compensation of faculty and instructional staff in postsecondary institutions: Fall 1998.* Washington, DC: Author.

Pinderhughes, E. (1989). *Understanding race, ethnicity and power: The key to efficacy in clinical practice.* New York: Free Press.

Rastogi, M., Fitzpatrick, J., Feng, D., & Shi, L. (1999). Becoming a professor: A survival guide for international students and new faculty. *Family Science Review, 12,* 257–274.

Smith, R., Byrd, P., Nelson, G., Barrett, R., & Constantides, J. (1992). *Crossing pedagogical oceans: International teaching assistants in U.S. undergraduate education.* (ASHE-ERIC Higher Education Report no. 8). Washington, DC: George Washington University, School of Education and Human Development.

Wieling, E., & Rastogi, M. (2003). Voices of marriage and family therapists of color: An exploratory survey. *Journal of Feminist Family Therapy, 15*(1), 1–20.

SECTION III

Theory- and Research-Based Interventions and Approaches

13

South Asians
in the United States*

Developing a Systemic and
Empirically Based Mental
Health Assessment Model

Azmaira H. Maker,
Mona Mittal, and Mudita Rastogi

This chapter comes out of our experiences as South Asian women, academicians, and mental health practitioners in the United States. Even though there has been a substantial increase in the South Asian population in this country, there is sparse literature on the unique mental health needs, assessment issues, and practice-based interventions for the many subgroups that comprise this population. The term *South Asian* refers to those from India, Pakistan, Sri Lanka, Bangladesh, and Nepal. While not homogenous, this group has common characteristics that set it apart from other ethnic groups. These include cultural factors, immigration experiences, individual and family needs, and beliefs about mental health issues. Given the significance of family and community relationships in this population (Almeida,

---

*The authors contributed equally to this chapter.

1996; Rastogi, 2002; Rastogi & Wampler, 1999), we have grounded our model in general system theory and taken a multicultural perspective (Falicov, 1995) to assessment and intervention. We have also relied heavily on Bronfenbrenner's Ecological Model (Bronfenbrenner, 1992) to capture a multilayered approach to assessing clients (see our Systemic Multicultural Assessment Model in Figure 13.1). Utilizing an ecological approach enabled us to frame this model in a systemic and sociopolitical context, thus the model is potentially more dynamic and effective than a model with a unilateral structure. Our aim for this chapter is to provide practitioners with (a) a summary of the empirical mental health literature on South Asian immigrants, (b) an overview of this population's mental health needs derived from the literature, and (c) a systemic assessment model for working with South Asians.

Personal Backgrounds

As the three of us reflected on our interests and experiences, we decided it was important to share some of these experiences so as to provide the reader with a context for understanding our positions and for evaluating the context of our writing. Our backgrounds have given us certain perspectives on this subject matter and ourselves. Our work and writings reflect these perspectives, and thus this chapter is framed by a degree of subjectivity. The following accounts regarding our backgrounds will help the reader remain aware of the biases and experiences we bring to our work.

Mudita Rastogi (M.R.)

I was raised in India in an upper middle-class family that valued education and liberal values. While I enjoyed a privileged and comfortable life, I was also acutely aware of being less privileged due to my female gender. As a teenager, I lived in Hong Kong for 3 years and attended an ethnically diverse British school. This was a consciousness raising experience that gave me a taste of being the "other" in terms of culture. It also taught me about prejudice and stereotypes. In college, I became interested in working with economically disadvantaged Indian rural communities around environmental and social issues, which further helped me tune into issues of power, privilege, and difference.

While working on my Ph.D. in marriage and family therapy, I developed a passion for studying gender and ethnicity. I especially care about ethnic minorities having access to culturally sensitive mental health services. In the classroom, I attempt to foster self-reflection in students about working with cultural groups other than their own. Not a month goes by when I don't get calls from people seeking referrals to therapists that are sensitive to specific ethnic issues. Even in a diverse city like Chicago, South Asian clients often do not have too many choices; therapists that are knowledgeable and trained to work with this population are few and far between. It is my hope that this chapter will be a step toward increasing the choices for South Asian clients.

Azmaira H. Maker (A.H.M.)

I am a first-generation South Asian, Muslim, immigrant woman from Pakistan living in the Midwest. My mother is from East Africa and my father is from India; they have very different religious backgrounds. My parents now reside as permanent immigrants in Pakistan. As a legacy of colonialism, my parents studied in England, I went to a British school, and my family sways comfortably in the suspended realm of East meets West, with our core rooted in a tricultural identity of East African, English, and South Asian. This is particularly evident in our language, as family discussions frequently integrate English, Urdu, Gujrati, Katchi, and Swahili, all in the same conversation. My immigration to the United States added yet another valuable dimension to my worldview, as feminism and psychology entered my schooling.

I completed my doctorate in clinical psychology under the Boulder-Colorado model, with much of my training and clinical experience from a systems and psychodynamic orientation, working extensively with children and adolescents. Given my own cultural blend and coming from a rather oppressive society, my passion lies in the cross-sections of gender, culture, and family violence. When I went to Pakistan for a time, I practiced and taught in hospital, outpatient, and educational settings and struggled to transfer my Western techniques to an enormously different psyche and community. I have felt a similar conflict in working with immigrants in the United States. Thus, I feel it is essential to question the notion that Western models of psycho-pathology and psychotherapy can be effectively transporting to vastly different cultures, and to encourage higher educational institutions, clinicians, and researchers to carefully gauge the application of these models.

Mona Mittal (M.M.)

I was born in India into a middle-class family and grew up in the nation's capital of Delhi. I enjoyed the privileges that people from my socioeconomic class experienced. During my growing years, I did not think much about my liberties and simply took them for granted. It was not until I was in my master's program that I began to think about the wide differences among people in India and throughout the rest of the world. It was also then that I confronted questions about my identity and the position I held in society by virtue of my birth into my family.

After completing my master's degree, I decided to pursue a doctoral degree in marriage and family therapy in the United States. My personal and academic journeys in this country, which has such a different culture from my own, have made me acutely aware of different dimensions of diversity and their impact on people. My interest in and passion for working with culturally diverse families is fueled by my own experiences of privilege in one context and of struggling to make meaning of my differences (physical attributes, accent, culture, etc.) and connecting with people in another context.

Challenge to Psychotherapy of Increase in U.S. South Asian Population

The national origins quota system in the United States was abolished under the Immigration Act of 1965. Since then, immigrants from South Asia have ranged from a highly trained professional class to a blue-collar working class. According to the 2000 U.S. Census, South Asians number 1.7 million (14% of the Asian population), making them the fourth biggest Asian group in the United States. The rapidly changing demographics present challenges to mental health professionals and researchers. In the last decade, the literature has explored differences in attitudes, modality and ethnicity preferences, acculturation, utilization, duration, and drop-out rates in psychotherapy for different racial groups in the United States (Paniagua, 1996, 1998; Sue, 1988; Sue & Sue, 1990; Tharp, 1991; Yamamoto, Silva, Justice, Chang, & Leong, 1993). However, South Asian clients have been neglected in the majority of the literature.

It is imperative to critically examine and include South Asians in our investigations on the effectiveness of Eurocentric models of treatment, and to rethink the applicability of such models to people with a different value and cultural system (Rastogi, 2002; Rastogi & Wampler, 1999). This is particularly important since the process of therapy varies for different ethnic groups (Paniagua, 1998), along with treatment modalities, attitudes, and acculturation.

Acculturation and Ethnic Identity Issues Affecting South Asians

Acculturation

Acculturation, which is defined as adapting to a new culture based on contact with the majority group in the new country, is a long-term process. Sodowsky and Carey (1988), using Berry's (1980) classic bidirectional model of acculturation, found that Asian Indians could be divided up into three distinct groups, namely, traditional, bicultural, and "Americanized." They found that the size of the last group was very small and its composition was not influenced by individuals' length of stay in the United States.

Acculturative stress is associated with difficulties in making the transition to a new culture (Krishnan & Berry, 1992). Sodowsky and Lai (1997) divided up acculturative distress of Asians into general stress (e.g., anxiety) and cultural stress (e.g., anger toward the majority culture). They also discussed the importance of intercultural competence, including areas like career and social relationships. Low-income clients report perceiving more prejudice, and this produces further difficulties for them in the area of cultural adjustment. Other findings include the centrality of family support and networks in reducing acculturative distress. Current age and age at the time of immigration are also important factors in determining acculturative distress. The literature indicates that the older people are when they immigrate, the more likely they are to experience acculuturative stress, while people who immigrated at a younger age score lower due to having a bicultural orientation (Sodowsky & Lai, 1997). Mehta (1998) found that Asian Indians who perceived greater acceptance in the United States, and formed deeper social and cultural ties in the majority community, experienced lower levels of psychological distress. To summarize the literature (Berry, 1980; Mehta, 1998; Sodowsky & Lai, 1997), the major factors impacting acculturation for South Asians are the following:

1. Contact with and acceptance by the dominant culture. This provides individuals with a foundation for positive feelings about the new culture.

2. Cultural orientation and involvement. This helps provide opportunities for individuals to learn about the new culture.

3. Language usage and cultural skills. These help individuals navigate easily in the new culture.

4. Demographic variables. As discussed above, age and income are important factors affecting individuals' acculturation.

One limitation of the literature on acculturation is that there are a limited number of studies that use a South Asian sample. These studies primarily rely on highly educated samples, and thus have a narrow generalizability of results. This limitation is critical, given what we know about the relationship between income, perceived prejudice, and acculturative difficulties. In addition, with the exception of a few general statements, most empirically based articles do not discuss the psychotherapy needs of South Asians in any depth. This is especially important given the significant underutilization of mental health services by this group (Das & Kemp, 1997). Finally, most South Asians in the United States do not live in homogenous communities (Durvasula & Mylvaganam, 1994). Thus, their experiences with acculturation happen in the context of their families. Differential acculturation among family members can add to acculturative stress. However, there is virtually no literature on how to work with South Asian families in therapy in the United States (for an exception, see Almeida, 1996).

Ethnic Identity

People's ethnic identity involves defining their ethnic membership, and it is central to how people see themselves. This makes it necessary to regard people's ethnic identity along with their acculturation while considering their mental health needs. Most models see ethnic identity as a stage-based process that is sequential and fluid and as a multidimensional construct (e.g., see Atkinson, Morten, & Sue, 1989; Phinney, 1989).

There are two components of ethnic identity (Sodowsky, Kwan, & Pannu, 1995). These are (a) the external component, which consists of a person's language or languages, friends, and so on; and (b) the internal component, which includes cognitive, moral, and affective dimensions. These dimensions vary independently, leading to four possible outcomes of ethnic identity based on whether a person is high or low on these two dimensions (Sodowsky et al., 1995). This conceptualization is helpful when considering how acculturation impacts both the external behavior of a family and the family's internal functioning. For example, Sodowsky and colleagues indicate that a family might more easily change in one area (e.g., language usage at home) than in another area (e.g., core values such as views on dating the opposite sex). Their research also shows that individuals' ethnic identity is not related to their family functioning (i.e., the core patterns of the family's relationships). However, Sodowsky and colleagues found that Asian Indians who had greater interest in exploring their own ethnicity also perceived that their family was more "Indian." This points to the central importance of South Asians' ethnic identity going hand in hand with their views about their family.

The limitations of this literature include that there are very few studies in the area of ethnic identity among South Asians. These studies do not examine critical variables like socioeconomic status (SES), which could impact ethnic identity. Furthermore, both acculturation and ethnic identity experiences of South Asians are very closely tied to their sense of self as part of a family (Durvasula & Mylvaganam, 1994). Thus, effective intervention with this group must include an assessment of acculturation, ethnic identity, SES, immigration history, demographic variables, and their family and community (Das & Kemp, 1997; Durvasula & Mylvaganam, 1994; Moy, 1992). These factors may impact South Asians' cultural attitudes toward psychotherapy. Therefore, in the next section we review literature on South Asians' attitudes and preferences regarding mental health services, as well as the utilization of such services among the South Asian population in the United States.

Clinical Issues: A Summary of the Literature

South Asians' Attitudes Toward Therapy

There is significant underutilization of mental health services among South Asians (Das & Kemp, 1997). South Asians experience a powerful division between the private and public self, and disclosure to an outsider involves an intense degree of exposure and vulnerability for this group. Shame, the cultural stigma of mental illness, guilt, and family loyalty further inhibit South Asians from seeking mental health services (Chandarana & Pellizari, 2001; Das & Kemp, 1997). South Asians may also perceive mental illness as punishment for immoral acts (Ellinger, 1996), as spirit possession, or as a physical problem (London, 1986; Malik, 2000; Ramakrishna & Weiss, 1992; Steiner & Bansil, 1989; Uba, 1994), thereby seeking atonement, spiritual healers, and/or physicians rather than psychotherapy for relief.

The label of "model minority" that has been applied to South Asians implies that this group performs "better" compared to other ethnic and racial minorities in the United States. This label pressures many South Asians to either deny their mental health issues or face the fear of losing their status in American society (Abraham, 2000; Das & Kemp, 1997). They also underutilize mental health services because they lack awareness of these services (Beliappa, 1991).

The South Asian view of the purpose of therapy may differ from the Western view as well. Given South Asians' perception of mental illness as a medical, spiritual, or religious predicament, they may view therapy only as a problem-solving tool. In addition, South Asians are more likely to value and relate to a systemic process of intervention (Beliappa, 1991; Das & Kemp, 1997; Parikh & Garg, 1989). Roland's (1988) clinical work with people of Indian origin led him to the construct of the *familial self*, in which the individual does not see himself or herself as separate from the family. In contrast, in most North American and Western European societies, the *individualized self* reflects the inner psychological makeup of people (Roland, 1988). The familial self allows people of South Asian origin to coexist in familial and community relationships with a deep sense of emotional connectedness, permeable boundaries, and a high degree of receptivity to others. This impacts the South Asian family structure and communication patterns (Das & Kemp, 1997). The Eurocentric model of healing, which centers on individuality, autonomy, independence, achievement motivation, identity, and a linear process (Guisinger & Blatt, 1994), is diametrically opposed to the South Asian worldview of interdependence (Rastogi, 2002; Rastogi & Wampler, 1999), circularity, the primacy of family welfare, and pluralism (Sue & Sue, 1990). Thus, with regard to psychotherapy, South Asians' attitudes, use, modality, and therapist ethnicity preferences may be starkly different from the norm for White populations.

Existing Literature

There is paucity of research on South Asians' attitudes towards psychotherapy. In a sample of high SES Asian Indian immigrants, Sharma (1995) identified acculturation and education as predictors of this group's attitudes toward help-seeking behaviors, with a positive correlation between the former and the latter factors. Similarly, Sheikh (2001) showed that acculturation level, but not gender, was predictive of attitudes toward seeking professional psychological help in a sample of Indian and Pakistani immigrants.

A study on support and mental health needs by Wadhwani (2001) suggested that Asian Indian college students felt that their current support system of family and friends could meet their needs, and they were unaware of services available at the college counseling center and did not feel a need for them. This suggests that perceptions of social support and being an integral part of the family might play a role in determining attitudes and help-seeking behaviors among South Asians. In contrast, a recent study by Maker (2003) showed that college and graduate South Asian women felt that existing psychological services could meet their mental health needs, and many of the women had actually been in therapy. Maker's (2003) findings also showed that the South Asian women studied were significantly more comfortable discussing their problems with a therapist than with a physician. The mixed results across these two studies indicate the importance of conducting large cross-sectional research to better identify attitudes toward mental health among first- and second-generation educated South Asians residing in the United States. The impact of gender differences also needs to be examined further, as a review of the literature indicates that Sheikh's (2001) study is the only survey that includes gender as a predictive variable. With respect to client-therapist ethnicity match and preferences regarding treatment modality, Wadhwani's (2001) analysis indicated that Asian Indian college students did not express a specific preference for an Asian Indian therapist. Instead, the students identified therapist characteristics such as "caring, understanding, empathic, and a good listener" as most important, regardless of ethnicity. However, Gomes (2000) found a significant preference for an Asian psychologist over other ethnic groups in a community sample of Asian Indians. The difference between Gomes's (2000) findings and Wadhwani's (2000) findings perhaps reflects acculturation differences between first- and second-generation Indian family members living in the United States, which implies that we need to examine this as a mediating factor. In fact, Panganamala and Plummer (1998) found that Asian Indians who immigrated to the United States before they were 10 years old showed more positive attitudes toward counseling than those who immigrated at a later age. Only one study could be located that explored treatment modality among South Asians. Gomes (2000) found no preference for family versus individual treatment in his study, as might have been predicted for South Asians (Das & Kemp, 1997). This area needs further exploration.

Limitations of Existing Research

This body of research has important limitations. The samples are small and include a narrow range of people in terms of age, education, socioeconomic status, and nationality (individuals from Sri Lanka, Nepal, and Bangladesh are often excluded). The studies also do not control for mediating factors such as number of years in the United States and generational and gender differences. A cross-sectional study with a large sample of both men and women from an array of SES and regional backgrounds is needed. The questions of therapist-client ethnicity match and modality preference also need to be studied further so that mental health services in this country better serve the South Asian community.

Mental Health Needs of
South Asians Across the Diaspora

No national level epidemiological surveys have been conducted with South Asians in the United States (Sue, Sue, Sue, & Takeuchi, 1998). Given the sparse literature on South Asians in this country, we also looked at studies conducted with South Asian immigrants and their families across the globe. We hoped to compare this body of literature to the one that has evolved in the United States, and to perhaps extrapolate from the findings. A search of mental health literature found only a small number of studies on the prevalence of psychopathology among this population in the United Kingdom.

There is considerable debate in Britain around statistics related to the presence of psychological disorders and symptom levels in South Asians living there. Examination of depression in British Asian Indians and Pakistanis reveal lower rates than in the indigenous population (Cochrane & Bal, 1989; Cochrane & Stopes-Roe, 1977). Furnham and Malik (1994) also found that British South Asians had low rates of psychiatric illnesses, particularly affective disorders. Even though similar studies have not been conducted in the United States, we hypothesize that the findings might be similar.

Several researchers have emphasized the need for understanding culturally specific verbal expressions of psychological distress (Mumford, Bavington, Bhatnagar, & Hussain, 1991; Wilson & MacCarthy, 1994). Hussain and Cochrane (2002) highlighted the role of religion and spirituality in the construction, understanding, and treatment of mental health problems among South Asians in addition to the above. They recommend the use of traditional healers in conjunction with mental health services. Other studies focus on specific causes of depression among South Asian women in the United Kingdom, including the impact of migration (Nazroo, 1998), levels of acculturation (Furnham & Malik, 1994), racism and hostility (Currer, 1984), and social isolation (Jervis, 1986). While practitioners working with South Asians in the United States must use caution in drawing parallels about South Asians' mental health based on epidemiological studies in the United Kingdom, similar results can be expected here.

An area of mental health that has received much attention in the United Kingdom, but not in the United States, is suicide among South Asians. Patel and Gaw (1996) conducted a review of the literature and concluded that suicide rates of young women immigrants from the Indian subcontinent were higher than those of their male counterparts and of young indigenous women of their immigrant country. The reasons for this include underreported levels of mental illness; marital and family conflict (especially with in-laws); moving to another country, which is experienced as an unfamiliar, lonely, and hostile environment; domestic violence; childlessness; and cross-cultural conflict with parents about sex roles.

Das and Kemp (1997) highlighted similar factors as precipitating the need for mental health services among South Asians in the United States. Such factors include social isolation and increased stress levels due to minority status, negative stereotyping and social rejection of immigrant children at school, generational tensions experienced due to conflicts between ethnic and dominant American values, racial discrimination, and being treated as foreigners. Domestic violence has been identified as another important factor influencing the need for mental health services in this population in the United States (Abraham, 2000; Krishnan, Baig-Amin, Gilbert, El-Bassel, & Waters, 1998).

An Empirically Based Systemic Assessment Model for South Asians

We have developed the Systemic Multicultural Assessment Model in Figure 13.1 based on a review of the literature, our personal and professional experiences, and Bronfenbrenner's Ecological Model (1992), which we used as a lens to frame the model. Below, we elaborate on the various domains and techniques used to conduct an effective assessment and treatment plan with South Asian families.

Structure of the Systemic Multicultural Assessment Model

The inspiration for the conceptual layout of this model came from Bronfenbrenner's Ecological Model (1992). The structure of the Systemic Multicultural Assessment Model provides guidelines for systemic assessment and treatment planning when working with South Asian clients. The model depicts a dynamic and fluid process, with interactions across its various dimensions. This is reflected in the model by the use of arrows and dotted lines between the various circles.

Explanation of the Model

Circle 1 encompasses help-seeking attitudes, therapist's ethnicity, and therapy modality preferences. This circle also includes consideration of larger sys-

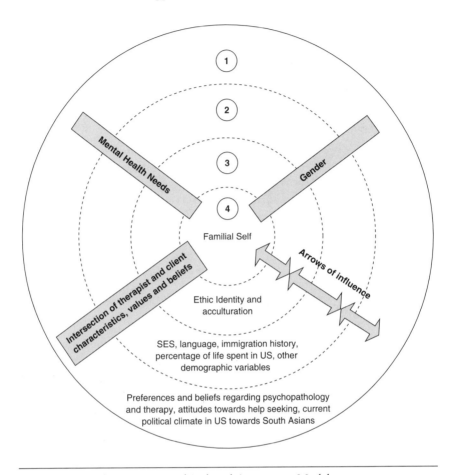

Figure 13.1   The Systemic Multicultural Assessment Model

tems issues like the current political climate and attitudes in the nation regarding South Asians, as political factors may have a powerful impact on South Asians' interactions with professionals outside of the family.

Circle 2 consists of demographic variables like language preference, SES, the percentage of the client's life spent in the United States, immigration history, and so on. These factors determine important within-group differences that are linked with differences in mental health needs.

Circle 3 consists of the client's identity in the context of the immediate environment. This circle includes the client's ethnic identity and acculturation, as well as self-definition within familial experiences and the external world.

The inner-most circle, Circle 4, consists of the "familial self" (Roland, 1988) defined earlier in the chapter.

Gender is a global variable that slices across and influences the contents of all the circles in turn; the client's views of and beliefs about her or his gender are impacted by each circle.

Similarly, mental health needs span all four circles. The various circles can influence the same mental health issue differentially. For example, if a child is not doing well at school, the therapist's assessment could encompass Circle 4 (family hierarchy), Circle 3 (level of acculturation), Circle 2 (unfamiliarity with language), and/or Circle 1(the family being suspicious of unfamiliar systems).

The intersection of therapist-client characteristics, values, and beliefs cuts across all the circles. At each level of assessment, therapist and client variables have an impact on the nature and content of therapy. For example, if the therapist and client are from different religious groups (e.g., Hindu and Muslim), tensions might develop in their relationship based on the political relations of these groups in the therapist's and client's countries of origin.

Instructions for Use of the Model

1. As we go from the outer circle (Circle 1) to the inner circle (Circle 4), we go from (a) the public sphere, easy to alter behaviors, external characteristics, and attributes that are easier to assess to (b) the private sphere, stable behaviors those are harder to alter, core characteristics, and attributes that are relatively difficult to gauge. We thus recommend that an assessment begin with Circle 1, proceed to Circle 4, and cover all four circles.

2. The impact of each circle on all other circles needs to be considered.

3. The issues of gender, mental health needs, and intersection of therapist-client characteristics relative to each circle should be assessed.

Questions to Guide Use of the Model

To help therapists use the Systemic Multicultural Assessment Model most effectively, we have listed some key questions. Please keep in mind that these questions are meant only to serve as guidelines and do not preclude other questions. Also, they should not *all* be asked if the presenting problem warrants a different track of questioning. It is important to remember that although the process of therapy with South Asians may look similar to that with other Asian and ethnic groups in the United States, the assessment model focuses on areas that are significant and unique to South Asian immigrants.

Circle 1 Assessment: Attitudes, Beliefs, and
Preferences Regarding Psychopathology and Therapy

Factors such as cultural values, religious beliefs, gender, first- versus second-generation issues, familial loyalty, and feelings of shame and stigma can all significantly contribute to determining clients' attitudes, goals, and preferences regarding psychotherapy. It is critical to pay attention to these variables and conduct a culturally sensitive interview early in the assessment phase to secure the initial alliance with the family. It is also essential to remember that not all family members will share the same attitudes and preferences; in fact, there may be significant variations based on gender, age, life stage, and acculturation differences. Here are some questions to consider asking clients during a Circle 1 assessment:

1. Tell me in your own words what brings you to therapy? Have you been to therapy before? What does therapy mean to you?

2. Would you be willing to share with me your religious and spiritual beliefs about your problems?

3. Whom do you go to for help with your mental, emotional, and family problems?

4. What if any concerns do you have about coming to therapy, particularly as related to the rest of your family and community?

5. Do you want other people included in therapy? Whom would you like to invite?

6. How will it be for you to work with me given (the same or different ethnicity)? What are the potential benefits or problem areas in us working together?

Circle 2 Assessment: Demographic Variables Like
Language Preference, SES, Immigration History, and so on

This assessment should gather information on clients' immigration history and experiences, their economic status, community network, and language preferences. In order to gain a deeper understanding and appreciation for the experiences and problems faced by South Asian clients, it is important to contextualize their economic and social standing before and after immigration. Some questions to consider asking clients during a Circle 2 assessment are as follows:

1. What language do you feel most comfortable speaking? Would you mind my asking what language you dream in? (This can lead to a discussion of what

language the client is most comfortable with. At this time, the focus is not on interpreting the dreams.)

2. Will having someone in session that can communicate in both languages help? Who can that person be? (The therapist should *not* pick this person.)

3. Who in the family first immigrated to the United States? When did they immigrate? What were their reasons for immigration?

4. How long have each of you been here? How does your life here compare to your life at home?

5. Can you please tell me about the work that you do? What kind of work do other family members do?

6. What is the role of religion and/or caste in you life? How important are they to you?

7. Do you have friends where you work and in the community that you live? Do you have any relatives in the United States? What is your relationship with them like?

Circle 3 Assessment: Acculturation and Ethnic Identity

Because of the South Asian cultural norm of deference to the professional, it would be more effective for the therapist to ask direct questions about acculturation and ethnic identity than to wait for opinions to emerge or to ask in more indirect ways. A direct exploratory stance gives the clients permission to share their thoughts without offending the therapist. If the therapist has limited knowledge of the family's culture, he or she should express this in order to place the clients in an empowered and educational role. Further exploratory, nonjudgmental questions will highlight each family member's unique psychosocial position as an immigrant or a second-generation South Asian residing in the United States. Important questions for a Circle 3 assessment are the following:

1. What has the process of living in the United States been like? What do you like about it? What are the things that you do not like or struggle with?

2. Have you encountered any significant racial and/or hostile comments or experiences so far?

3. Do you see yourself as "South Asian," a specific nationality (Indian, Pakistani, Bengali, etc.), "Americanized," or somewhere in between? Please explain.

4. What are some American values or beliefs that you have endorsed that may be in conflict with your cultural identity? What are some American values you have rejected and why?

5. What are some of your ethnic, religious, and spiritual values you feel you have lost or had to give up to integrate into the society here?

6. In your family, if there are differences in ethnic identity, acculturation, and values among family members, how do these differences impact each of you?

Circle 4 Assessment: Familial Self

Differences and similarities between the therapist's sense of individuality and family and the family's sense of the familial self is a critical factor. The racial, ethnic, religious, and language differences that determine the familial self can impede the therapeutic alliance, particularly if the family feels that the therapist is ignorant, judgmental, or misinformed about their unique family system. Creating a space and a language for a bridge between the differences can greatly facilitate the therapist's understanding of the clients. This is equally true if the therapist is from the same racial, ethnic, religious, or regional background as the family, as there are many variations in acculturation, identity, immigration history, and education levels among South Asians. Questions to ask clients during a Circle 4 assessment include the following:

1. What are the family and individual value differences between your culture and the dominant U.S. culture?

2. How do the different generations of your family get along? What are some areas of concern or conflict? What are some areas you agree on?

3. What role does each family member play in the family? How does your family's role conflict or coincide with your ethnic identity and role in society? How do you cope with this conflict?

4. How are intrafamily relationships experienced? (Ask questions about each set of relationships.)

Gender

South Asian cultures place importance not only on age but also on gender in assigning roles and power in families (Rastogi & Wampler, 1998, 1999). This factor interacts with each of the four circles in different ways and should be explored across each domain in the model. It would be an error to assume that all family members share similar gender role beliefs or that the family's beliefs parallel the therapist's. For instance, a more traditional father may feel his powerful role as head of the family being threatened by an unfamiliar therapist, whereas a member of the second generation in this country, such as the highly acculturated daughter, may identify with the therapist as a catalyst for change. Consequently, it would be important to not assume that one voice portrays all opinions. Gauging gender differences through observations of individual clients' attitudes toward therapy, degree of Americanization as expressed through their clothing and language usage, and structural factors like seating arrangements in the therapy room is also possible. Some of the questions on gender are as listed below.

1. What is it like to be male/female in your family?

2. What are the differences in expectations, duties, and privileges for the two genders? What messages does one get in your family about being a boy or a girl?

3. Do you feel any conflict between your gender role in the family and your gender role in the larger society?

4. What are some intergenerational conflicts between the women and men in the family regarding gender role expectations? What are some intergenerational conflicts between members of the same gender?

Mental Health Needs

Researchers have recommended a supportive treatment approach with South Asians that incorporates a psychoeducational component, along with respecting clients' interpretation of their problems (Hoch, 1990; Sharma, Dev Triguna, & Chopra, 1991). The family may prefer short-term, active, and unidirectional interventions because of cultural biases toward a problem-solving, medical model, "fix it" approach, with high precedence given to family loyalty, privacy and shame, and the hierarchical role assigned to the "doctor." Immediate symptom relief, concrete guidance, and incorporating holistic and spiritual approaches may also be greatly valued by the clients. It is crucial to explore individual goals and understanding of therapy, as there may be vast differences between genders and generations. Naturally, conflicts in therapy goals and modality will have to be further explored and negotiated between the family members and the therapist if an effective treatment plan is to be developed. Some important questions to consider asking clients so as to assess their mental health needs are as follows:

1. What are your goals for therapy and modality preference? (Discuss the options, as well as their benefits, and drawbacks.)

2. How often do you feel you need to come to therapy? What is the length of time you are hoping to resolve these problems in (duration of therapy sessions)?

3. Are there indigenous medicines or spiritual approaches that you value in taking care of yourself and your family members? How can we try and include some of those methods or people in our work together?

4. What is your understanding of the situation that you are in right now, and what are your ideas for resolving your problems?

Implications and Conclusion

We have constructed a comprehensive Systemic Multicultural Assessment Model to assess the mental health needs of South Asians based on the literature in this area and our own personal and professional experiences. This model is unique in that it draws from North American and British literature; thus it can speak to the needs of a range of South Asian immigrants and their offspring. The model is grounded in systems theory and Bronfenbrenner's Ecological Model, and it focuses on relationships, the familial self, and the community. As suggested by the literature, our model addresses such factors as acculturation, ethnic identity, attitudes toward therapy, and demographics, which impact therapy effectiveness and outcome. Other unique features of this model include gender, mental health needs, and intersection of therapist-client characteristics, values, and beliefs as slicing across all four levels of assessment. We have delineated the various issues relevant to assessing South Asians and listed specific questions to guide the assessment process. This model is a work in progress, and we will continue to refine it. In a future publication, we plan to use case studies to illustrate its use for assessment, treatment planning, and interventions. It is also our hope that this model will lead to more empirical work on the effectiveness of therapy with South Asians. To this end, this Systemic Multicultural Assessment Model will need to be used in pilot studies with a clinical population and tested for both efficacy and effectiveness. This may lead to further modifications and testing of the model. Integration of clinically based feedback and research will help the field to develop an empirically tested, effective approach. This will eventually enable South Asians to receive more culturally appropriate and effective psychotherapy.

Reflections, Questions, and Exercises

Educators may use this chapter in multiple ways. Our suggestions are listed below.

1. Students may be required to read English translations of South Asian fiction and/or watch South Asian films to become familiar with the complexities of the culture. Alternately, supervisors may utilize cases described in the clinical

literature (see, e.g., Almeida, 1996) to provide students with "hands-on" clinical exercises. Students should be required to use the Systemic Multicultural Assessment Model to assess the family or client in the case study. This exercise may be done in a written format or as a role-play, and it should be critiqued by the supervisor and other students.

2. Supervisors can demonstrate through role-plays how to create a dialogue around topics such as cross-cultural issues, immigration, beliefs, values, and racial and ethnic identity. Creating a dialogue around these sensitive issues will provide a model for students to internalize and will facilitate culturally sensitive and effective interventions.

3. Educators, supervisors, and students can engage in discussions of how to become aware of their own blind spots regarding their diversity and their clients' diversity. It would be particularly helpful to talk about their personal limitations when working with South Asian clients and ways to handle these differences in the therapy room.

4. Practitioners, students, educators, and supervisors may choose to reflect on how the approach presented in the Systemic Multicultural Assessment Model is similar to and different from their approach to working with other ethnic groups. Ideas for adapting the model may be generated to create flexible working models of assessment when working with clients from diverse backgrounds.

References

Abraham, M. (2000). *Speaking the unspeakable: Marital violence among South Asian immigrants in the United States.* New Brunswick, NJ: Rutgers University Press.

Almeida, R. (1996). Hindu, Christian, and Muslim families. In M. McGoldrick, J. Giordano, & J. K. Pearce (Eds.), *Ethnicity and family therapy* (2nd ed., pp. 395–423). New York: Guilford.

Atkinson, D. R., Morten, G., & Sue, D. W. (1989). A minority identity development model. In D. R. Atkinson, G. Morten, & D. W. Sue (Eds.), *Counseling American minorities* (3rd ed., pp. 35–52). Dubuque, IA: William C Brown.

Beliappa, J. (1991). *Illness or distress? Alternative methods of mental health.* London: Confederation of Indian Organizations.

Berry, J. W. (1980). Acculturation as varieties of adaptation. In A. M. Padilla (Ed.), *Acculturation: Theory, model, and some new findings* (pp. 9–25). Boulder, CO: Westview.

Bronfenbrenner, U. (1992). Ecological systems theory. Six theories of child development: Revised formulations and current issues. In R. Vasta (Ed.), *Annals of Child Development* (Vol. 6, pp. 187–251). Greenwich, CT: JAI.

Chandarana, P., & Pellizzari, J. R. (2001). Health psychology: South Asian perspectives. In S. S. Kazarian & D. R. Evans (Eds.), *Handbook of cultural health psychology* (pp. 411–444). San Diego, CA: Academic Press.

Cochrane, R., & Bal, S. (1989). Mental hospital admission rates of immigrants to England: A comparison of 1971 and 1981. *Social Psychiatry and Psychiatric Epidemiology, 24*, 2–12.

Cochrane, R., & Stopes-Roe, M. (1977). Psychological and social adjustment of Asian immigrants to Britain: A community survey. *Journal of Social Psychiatry, 12*, 195–206.

Currer, C. (1984). Pathan women in Bradford: Factors affecting mental health with particular reference to the effects of racism. *International Journal of Psychiatry, 30*, 72–76.

Das, A. K., & Kemp, S. F. (1997). Between two worlds: Counseling South Asian Americans. *Journal of Multicultural Counseling and Development, 25*, 23–33.

Durvasula, R. S., & Mylvaganam, G. A. (1994). Mental health of Asian Indians: Relevant issues and community implications. *Journal of Community Psychology, 22*, 97–108.

Ellinger, H. (1996). *Hinduism*. Valley Forge, PA: Trinity Press International.

Falicov, C. J. (1995). Training to think culturally. *Family Process, 34*, 373–388.

Furnham, A., & Malik, R. (1994). Cross-cultural beliefs about depression. *International Journal of Social Psychology, 40*, 106–123.

Gomes, S. L. (2000). Factors affecting Asian Indian selection of psychotherapy: Therapist ethnicity and therapy modality. *Dissertation Abstracts International, 61*(2), 1081B.

Guisinger, S., & Blatt, S. J. (1994). Individuality and relatedness. *American Psychologist, 49*(2), 104–111.

Hoch, E. M. (1990). Experiences with psychotherapy training in India. *Psychotherapy & Psychosomatics, 53*, 14–20.

Hussain, F. A., & Cochrane, R. (2002). Depression in South Asian women: Asian women's beliefs on causes and cures. *Mental Health, Religion, & Culture, 5*(3), 287–311.

Jervis, M. (1986). Female, Asian, and isolated. *Openmind, 20*, 10–12.

Krishnan, A., & Berry, J.W. (1992). Acculturative stress and accultuation attitudes among Indian immigrants to the United States. *Psychology and Developing Societies, 4*, 187–212.

Krishnan, S. P., Baig-Amin, M., Gilbert, N., El-Bassel, N., & Waters, A. (1998). Lifting the veil of secrecy: Domestic violence among South Asian women in the U.S. In S. D. Dasgupta (Ed.), *A patchwork shawl: Chronicles of South Asian Women in America*. New Brunswick, NJ: Rutgers University Press.

London, M. (1986). Mental illness among immigrant minorities in the United Kingdom. *British Journal of Psychiatry, 149*, 265–273.

Maker, A. (2003). *Attitudes and utilization of mental health services by college and graduate South Asian women in the United States*. Unpublished manuscript.

Malik, R. (2000). Culture and emotions: Depression among Pakistanis. Squire, Corinne (Ed.), *Culture in psychology* (pp. 147–162).

Mehta, S. (1998). Relationship between acculturation and mental health for Asian Indian immigrants in the United States. *Genetic, Social, and General Psychology Monographs, 124,* 61–77.

Moy, S. (1992). A culturally sensitive, psycho-educational model for understanding and treating Asian-American clients. *Journal of Psychology and Christianity, 11,* 358–367.

Mumford, D. B., Bavington, T., Bhatnagar, K. S., & Hussain, T. (1991). The Bradford somatic inventory: A multi-ethnic inventory of somatic symptoms. *British Journal of Psychiatry, 150,* 379–386.

Nazroo, J. Y. (1998). Rethinking the relationship between ethnicity and mental health: The British fourth national survey of ethnic minorities. *Social Psychiatry, 33* (4), 145–148.

Panganamala, D. R., & Plummer, D. L. (1998). Attitudes toward counseling among Asian Indians in the United States. *Cultural Diversity and Mental Health, 4*(1), 55–63.

Paniagua, F. (1996). Cross-cultural guidelines in family therapy practice. *Family Journal: Counseling and Therapy for Couples and Families, 4,* 127–138.

Paniagua, F. (1998). *Assessing and treating culturally diverse clients: A practical guide* (2nd ed.). Thousand Oaks, CA: Sage.

Parikh, I. J., & Garg, P. K. (1989). *Indian women: An inner dialogue.* New Delhi: Sage.

Patel, S. P., & Gaw, A. C. (1996). Suicide among immigrants from the Indian subcontinent: A review. *Psychiatric Services 47*(5), 517–521.

Phinney, J. S. (1989). Stages of ethnic identity in minority group adolescents. *Journal of Early Adolescence, 9,* 34–49.

Ramakrishna, J., & Weiss, M. G. (1992). Health, illness, and immigration: East Indians in the United States. *Western Journal of Medicine, 157,* 265–270.

Rastogi, M. (2002). Mother-Adult Daughter questionnaire (MAD): Developing a culturally sensitive instrument. *Family Journal, 10*(2), 145–155.

Rastogi, M., & Wampler, K. S. (1998). Couples and family therapy with Indian families: Some structural and intergenerational considerations. In U. P. Gielen & A. L. Comunian (Eds.), *Family and family therapy in international perspective* (pp. 257–274). Milan: Marinelli Editrice.

Rastogi, M., & Wampler, K. S. (1999). Adult daughters' perceptions of the mother-daughter relationship: A cross cultural comparison. *Family Relations, 48,* 327–336.

Roland, A. (1988). *In search of self in India and Japan: Toward a cross-cultural psychology.* Princeton, NJ: Princeton University Press.

Sharma, H. M., Dev Triguna, B., & Chopra, D. (1991). Maharishi Ayur-Veda: Modern insights into ancient medicine. *Journal of the American Medical Association, 265,* 2633–2637.

Sharma, P. (1995). Asian Indian attitudes toward seeking professional psychological help. *Dissertation Abstracts International, 55*(10), 4614B.

Sheikh, A. J. (2001). Gender and levels of acculturation as predictors of attitudes toward seeking professional psychological help and attitudes toward women among Indian and Pakistanis in America. *Dissertation Abstracts International, 61*(10), 5581B.

Sodowsky, G. R., & Carey, J. C. (1988). Relationships between acculturation-related demographics and cultural attitudes of an Asian Indian immigrant group. *Journal of Multicultural Counseling and Development, 16,* 117–136.

Sodowsky, G. R., Kwan, K. K., & Pannu, R. (1995). Ethnic identity of Asians in the United States. In J. G. Ponterotto (Ed.), *Handbook of multicultural counseling* (pp. 123–154). Thousand Oaks, CA: Sage.

Sodowsky, G. R., & Lai, E.W. M. (1997). Asian immigrant variables and structural models of cross-cultural distress. In A. Booth, A. C. Crouter, & N. Landale (Eds.), *Immigration and the family: Research and policy on U.S. immigrants* (pp. 211–234). Mahwah, NJ: Lawrence Erlbaum.

Steiner, G. L., & Bansil, R. K. (1989). Cultural patterns and the family system in Asian Indians: Implications for psychotherapy. *Journal of Comparative Family Studies, 20*(3), 371–375.

Sue, D. N., & Sue, S. C. (1990). *Counseling the culturally different: Theory and practice* (2nd ed.). Toronto: John Wiley.

Sue, S. (1988). Psychotherapeutic services for ethnic minorities: Two decades of research findings. *American Psychologist, 43*(4), 301–308.

Sue, S., Sue, D. W., Sue, L., & Takeuchi, D. T. (1998). Psychopathology among Asian Americans: A model minority? In P. B. Organista, K. M. Chun, & G. Marin (Eds.), *Readings in ethnic psychology* (pp. 270–282). Florence, KY: Taylor & Francis/Routledge.

Tharp, R. G. (1991). Cultural diversity and treatment of children. *Journal of Consulting and Clinical Psychology, 59*(6), 799–812.

Uba, L. (1994). *Asian Americans.* New York: Guilford.

U.S. Bureau of Census. (2000). *Statistical abstract of the United States, 1998.* Washington, DC: U.S. Government Printing Office.

Wadhwani, S. M. (2001). As assessment of the concerns and service needs of Asian Indian college students. *Dissertation Abstracts International, 62*(1), 567B.

Wilson, M., & MacCarthy, B. (1994). Consultation as a factor in the low rate of mental health service use by Asians. *Journal of Psychological Medicine, 20,* 113–119.

Yamamoto, J., Silva, J. A., Justice, L. R., Chang, C. Y., & Leong, G. B. (1993). Cross-cultural psychotherapy. In A. C. Gaw (Ed.), *Culture, ethnicity, and mental illness* (pp. 101–124). Washington, DC: American Psychiatric Press.

14

Black Women Victims and Perpetrators of Domestic Violence

A Therapeutic Model Incorporating Racism and Black History

Denise D. McAdory

The focus of this chapter is on working with Black women initiators of family domestic violence who are married to or in long-term relationships with Black men. For the past 8 years, I have provided treatment for Black women referred by the Domestic Violence Court for alternative sentencing instead of serving time in the county jail. I developed the group family violence system therapy concept in an effort to encourage Black women victims who had become perpetrators to bond, empathize, understand the dynamics of family domestic violence from a multigenerational perspective, examine the systems that developed within the generations, and acquire the skills necessary to support themselves and each other.

A key element that enables me to provide this type of treatment is that I am a survivor of domestic violence. The question that always puzzled me earlier was why I "selected" a man with the propensity for violence. I now realize that power, control, the need to be loved, low self-esteem, rage in the Black male subliminally fed by racism, and a lack of Black history and pride are a few of the underlying factors in such violence. The impetus for the group family violence system therapy program is to create a sense of hope. This sense of hope is a desire to succeed by overcoming violence through knowledge of the history of our ancestors. It is accomplished by taking small steps to obtain reasonable solutions to problems.

Professional and Personal Background

I am a Black woman and the oldest of five children. I had a controlling father who expected excellence, and a submissive mother. My mother took the position of accepting my father's leadership at the sacrifice of her "self." This was a family pattern passed down by her mother and by her mother's mother (McAdoo, 1997). Through the eyes of a child, I saw a domineering man and a docile woman. However, put in a historical context, I can now understand my father's and my mother's behaviors. Being the oldest, I had to excel academically, my dating and socializing were limited, and my church participation was mandatory. I graduated from high school in 1965 in the top 10% of the class. I attended college on an academic scholarship and graduated with a bachelor's degree in psychology. During my junior year in college, I met a man, my first boyfriend, who appeared suave and debonair and made exciting promises to me. I saw this man as a method of escape from the control of my father and the pressure of being the oldest. Little did I realize that he was not honest and that underneath his smooth nature lived a violent man. I discovered this the day we eloped. On that day, I experienced the first of many beatings, insults, and name-calling. The violence continued through my pregnancies and the births of our children, along with the cycle of my leaving and returning. However, in 1974, after he severely beat me and threatened our children, I left for the final time. The children and I lived with my parents for the 2 years it took me to obtain my master's degree in counseling.

In 1993, after working for over 20 years at a local agency and at a hospital, I obtained my second master's degree, this one in marriage and family therapy with a theology background. Being in school helped me cope with the death of my oldest son from heart complications. Shortly after his death, I began working part time as a family therapist and entered the doctoral program in family gerontology. In spite of my academic and job accomplishments, racism and discrimination were ever present in my life. Several times I wanted to lash out verbally against insults supposedly said in jest and against reprimands for not smiling at the joke and so not being a team player, but I had to control my feelings of rage because of my sons (Welsing, 1991).

While my father was controlling, was there a method to the madness of his parenting and providing for his family? Was his behavior positive or negative? I can now see that it was both, because for him, the end justified the means. Moreover, society did not give him too many options or role models. My father overcame daily confrontations with racism and excelled by educating his children and demanding his wife's support. My parents lived to see all of their children become successful. I too was propelled to educate my sons and myself. Initially, I was angry because of the unwritten pressure of having to stay several steps ahead of Whites, but my father always said that "more is better," that they can never discount or deny education, certification, and experience. My unwritten goal has been to survive in the waters of racism using my rich cultural and family history. I want my clients to do the same.

A Case of Domestic Violence

At this point in their lives, Harry, a 55-year-old Black male laborer, and Betty, a quiet but submissive Black female executive, had been married for 30 years. Over the course of the marriage, he controlled the finances. The latest episode of violence occurred when he cursed at her for failing to close the garage door properly. Her explanations pushed him to a state of extreme rage and he stated, "If you continue to talk, I will knock your damn head from here to kingdom come." This was followed by an hour of insults about her family. He then drove off in her car and shouted that his dinner had better be ready when he got back.

Normally, he would return, promise to change his behavior, and apologize, and she would accept it. This time, however, in the early morning after the violent incident, Betty was arrested for awakening Harry at gunpoint and threatening to blow his head off if he ever insulted or humiliated her again. Before bail could be posted, she had to spend 12 hours in lockup with other women who were victims of family domestic violence. During that period, it was determined that Betty (a victim) had become a perpetrator. Shortly after her release, she appeared in domestic court and was given the alternative sentence of group family system therapy instead of 6 months in the county jail.

The Initial Stages of Therapy

During 10 weeks of intensive group therapy and psychoeducation about violence, Betty learned the principles of and reasons for family domestic violence. She reported that Harry perceived her submissive demeanor as a sign of weakness, and she discussed what pushed her to the point of wanting to kill him. In spite of work-related accomplishments, she did not feel good about herself as a Black woman because of unfair expectations established by her mother while growing up.

The group cohesiveness and insights led Betty to start the journey of developing a plan of action for her life and marriage (Yalom, 1985). The primary core of the group family violence system therapy is the client's learning how to regain mental freedom, make healthy choices, and examine the past and the systems that developed over a three-generation period. How clients understand "love" is also explored in the therapy. Betty learned that key reasons many Black women remain in a violent situation are fear of the perpetrator and of being alone, the need for love, and the belief that life is better with a partner, even if he is abusive. In addition, she realized that there were other Black women who, like her, believed they were the cause of the abuse. The women believed that if they had sex as often as their partners wanted, prepared meals in the fashion demanded, dressed a certain way, and/or relinquished contact with family and/or friends, their partners would not be abusive. For many Black women, believing that they are the cause of the abuse is related to their being caretakers at the expense of the "self" (McAdoo, 1997). Betty vowed never to live in an abusive situation again. At the completion of 10 weeks of 1-hour weekly sessions, she accepted that she loved Harry, but that it was important to love her "self" more. Betty and Harry decided to make one last attempt to salvage their marriage with my assistance.

An Outline of the Therapy Approach

In the approach that I follow, I first insist on safety and ask that the couple remove all weapons from easy access. The couple is asked to exhibit respect at all times and to refrain from using insults. Also, when I am conducting therapy, I have to continually examine my own personal issues related to the presenting problem. Before providing therapy for victims of abuse, I find it helpful to meditate and relinquish personal concerns associated with my own history of abuse.

When my thoughts and feelings reached a neutral state of being, we began the journey to assist this couple. I asked the clients about their present conflict, and during the course of therapy I determined when to discuss past events (Minuchin, 1974). Then I presented historical accounts about the behavior, attitude, and/or family life of Blacks, which I followed by giving them homework assignments.

To assist this couple, I had to explore the historical causes of their problem. A key element of Bowen's (1978) theory is to gather family history across three generations. Using this format afforded us the opportunity to examine the possible causes of Harry's rage. He admitted to feeling anger and rage over having completed 3 years of college only to end up being expelled for selling and using drugs. He wanted to blame others for this incident, as well as for other unhealthy choices he'd made during the course of his life. It was critical for me to gain Harry's respect and overcome his resistance to mental health treatment because of his pride and unwillingness to share personal issues (Boyd-Franklin, 1989). To establish rapport, I spent time with Harry exploring 18th-century slaveholder Willie Lynch's ideas on how to keep Blacks in bondage mentally and physically (Lynch, 1712, cited in Johnson, 1999). Lynch's long-range goal was to teach Blacks to distrust one another by pitting female against male and light skinned against dark skinned, and thus to distinguish status and create divisions on the plantations. Female offspring were raised to be independent, and male offspring, because of their mothers' subconscious fear for their lives, were raised to be emotionally dependent but physically strong.

This discussion got Harry's attention. In a subsequent session, he processed the dynamics of his family of origin in relationship to his abusive behavior and personal fears. Betty listened as he released years of fears, concerns, and rage associated with his perception of his mother as weak and his father as unavailable. When he rebelled against them, he used drugs to help him cope. Before the session concluded, it was as if a light suddenly appeared. Harry looked at Betty and said through tears that he was sorry for the years of abuse and the lack of emotional support, and that he was glad he'd entered treatment with a Black therapist. Their assignment for the next session was to talk with one another and to develop two questions pertinent to their family of origin and marriage, especially if they wanted to remain a couple.

In the next session, Betty wanted to discuss her insights about her family of origin issues before sharing their questions. From her perspective, Harry's feelings in many ways coincided with the rage and anger she experienced as a child and in her current job. Rather than experiment with drugs, she pushed herself to excel academically and professionally. She realized that she married a man who was confrontational because she perceived her own father as weak for not standing up to her mother. Betty found her management position rewarding, but she was unable to handle the subtle racism she encountered at work and wanted Harry's support. When she did not receive it, she performed above expectations at work, but at home she would quietly insult Harry for not being supportive (Cose, 1993).

At this point, I instructed the couple to analyze their positive and negative feelings at two critical points during the preceding 2 months of their marriage (Minuchin, 1974). This exercise enabled them to see how the baggage from the past had affected their self-esteem as individuals, their respect for one another, and the ways in which they were threatened by one another. They also came up with the following questions and concerns:

Betty and Harry:	Why are we afraid of asking our parents questions about their marriage and early childhood experiences?
Harry:	Why didn't I realize that fussing, cursing, and threatening Betty is considered abuse? I believed that as long as I didn't hit Betty, it would be okay to exhibit those behaviors.
Betty:	I love Harry, but I do not understand why I am afraid of living without him in the event therapy does not work.

I will return to this case study at the end of the chapter, but at this point I want to explore the issues the case has raised thus far and to discuss their implications.

Additional Interventions

It is important for therapists to gain the respect of Black males and to thank them for taking the risk to enter therapy. I tell them that I am assisting them with adjustment issues, not treating them for a "mental disorder." This relabeling helps them with continuing to seek therapy. I assist the Black women in understanding why they, the "victims," evolved into perpetrators. Therapists can use role-play to demonstrate positive methods for expressing anger, rage, and frustration in the absence of violence. Other beneficial techniques for clients involve practicing taking turns speaking, taking at least 10 deep breaths before speaking, thinking calmly before speaking to avoid shouting matches, not speaking negatively about family members, and only discussing information relevant to the primary complaint. If the Black man is willing to continue with therapy (when marital therapy is implicated), it is critical to prohibit the Black woman from sabotaging the process by putting him down, cursing at him, or hitting him in the therapist's presence (a source of embarrassment and devaluation of his self-esteem). In the event that the man or woman feels rage during a session, I address it immediately by teaching the couple how to understand its cause.

Black Family Domestic Violence and Its Treatment

The Link Between Violence and Oppression

For Blacks, family domestic violence is partially related to the collective experiences of oppression. These experiences during the formative stages of development can lead to unresolved rage and various levels of violence. To make healthy choices, Blacks must understand that family domestic violence is deeper than an examination of the "Cycle of Violence" (Walker, 1979). To become free of the effects of violence, Blacks need to recognize the multigenerational and systemic effects of oppression, underemployment, and racism. For Blacks, freeing the self involves overcoming the most destructive psychological consequences of slavery, including the loss of identity. During slavery, oppressors tried to obliterate, diminish, or disregard the African individuals' sense of self and collective identity as a people. Hence, Black people have had to wrestle with the self-identifications they created during slavery, in addition to the identifications attributed to them by Whites. The issue of self-identification versus the attributions made about them have continued to create psychological and ideological dilemmas for Blacks in America (Anderson, 1993).

These psychological and ideological conflicts coupled with present day overt and covert racism can lead Black women to rage against Black men, many of whom are raging against self and society. Willie Lynch's goal of keeping Blacks down by pitting them against each other has become a reality (Lynch, 1712, cited in Johnson, 1999). When Blacks decide to confront the problems perpetrated by society, some Black men inadvertently turn against themselves and their families. This position has resulted in many Black women fighting back by releasing the demon of rage. Rage, after gaining power and control over mind, body, and soul, leads to the ultimate demise of self. We Blacks are fighting and killing one another when we should be joining to provide healthy family lives for our children, who could break the Cycle of Violence (Walker, 1979).

Systems Thinking and the Role of the Therapist

To understand the dynamics of family domestic violence and how Black women move from the position of victim to that of perpetrator, it is necessary to look at the systems involved from a multigenerational perspective and to understand a family's response to stress (McHenry, 1994). A focus on the social systems approach allows the therapist to look beyond the family and the individual to the wider social system, as families do not live in isolation but are part of the larger social context. This external environment in which the family is embedded is referred to as the *ecosystem* (Boss, 1988). The ecosystem consists of historical, cultural, economic, and developmental influences. These influences must be considered for clients undergoing group family violence system therapy.

A therapist working with this population should avoid common pitfalls. One frequent challenge for a therapist from another culture is to receive training in multiculturalism and Black family dynamics. Familiarity with the relevant literature is crucial, especially in the areas of Black culture, religion, family, history, and hope. Therapists must understand the influence of these areas, and the link between their absence in the lives of clients and clients' rage. Another critical component to therapy is therapists' passion to work with these clients—therapists must exhibit a sincere interest in guiding Black couples and women who abuse through the therapeutic process.

A Case of Domestic Violence: Conclusion

After a close examination of the couple's families of origin and history of abuse, we worked on their differentiation of self (Bowen, 1978). This process permitted Betty and Harry to start letting go of negative parental and family influences and move toward accepting their own respective contributions to the marital problems. The realization of what those contributions were really hit them when the picture of numerous triangles emerged. It became clear that when they were at odds, Harry and Betty would make a third person or situation a part of the conflict. With the involvement of the third entity, the conflict would escalate to chaos, name-calling, blaming, and finally violence. At this point in therapy, they made a conscious decision to avoid triangulating others in their personal life. Also, if there were problems at work, Betty decided to discuss them with Harry, but not to attack him if his emotional support did not reach her level of expectation. In essence, she would have to let him offer support in a manner comfortable for him and compliment his efforts. He was to do the same for her and they were not to end the day in anger. The key element of the therapy was to establish that a *situation* was the cause of their distress and not blame the entire relationship.

Harry and Betty did not cut-off from their families emotionally, and they eventually met with their parents to discuss how their early lives had affected them. They also began visualizing how society has a tendency to reinforce what goes on at an emotional level between couples, and vice versa. They concluded that Blacks would like to have a piece of the American pie, but because the rules of the game are constantly changing, many are thrust into a pit of rage, despair, depression, and, for some, violence (Cose, 1993).

The impetus for a chapter of this nature is to encourage therapists to consider delving deeper than the presenting complaint. For most Blacks, violence is a direct result of the past history of slavery, the psychological scars of the 20th century, and the aftereffects of integration (Johnson, 1991). Many Blacks are educated and employed for years in atmospheres that are neither friendly nor supportive. If the Black male is unable to verbalize feelings associated with societal oppression, the end result may be verbal, emotional, and physical attacks on his loved ones. The Black female, in an effort to be supportive, believes she has to function as a superwoman at the expense of her "self" (Boyd-Franklin, 1989). This, too, backfires.

In conclusion, family domestic violence is a compilation of societal issues, power dynamics, and emotions that have run amuck. The therapist should take the clients from that end of the pendulum to the opposite end by stimulating Black women and/or couples to be excited about academic and employment successes, parenting thoughtfully, and discussing relational and societal concerns calmly. Clients can learn to use the power of differentiation to overcome these concerns. In other words, processing and thinking can lead to success, and negative behaviors can lead to abuse, incarceration, and/or death. To guide Black women who are victims and initiators of domestic violence, therapists must exhibit passion for the work and positive regard for their clients, provide hope, build self-esteem, develop an interest in Black history, examine multigenerational family dynamics of violence, and assist in creating survival plans for victims.

Reflections, Questions, and Exercises

1. List and discuss the causes of family domestic violence for Black clients, based on the case study.

2. Willie Lynch was a slave owner who taught Southern slavers how to maintain control and guaranteed it would last 300 years. Explain the long-term effect of that methodology on Blacks during the 20th century and entering the 21st century.

3. The historical context of violence against Blacks is critical to understanding the dynamics of family domestic violence in the Black community. What is the role of the history of slavery as a contributing factor to Black domestic violence?

4. For therapists and students: What would be some of the challenges you would personally face, should you ever provide family domestic violence therapy in group or couple format to Black clients?

References

Anderson, T. (1993). *Introduction to African American studies: Cultural concepts.* Dubuque, IA: Kendell/Hunt.

Boss, P. G. (1988). *Family stress management.* Newbury Park, CA: Sage.

Bowen, M. (1978). *Family therapy in clinical practice.* Northvale, NJ: Jason Aronson.

Boyd-Franklin, N. (1989). *Black families in therapy.* New York: Guilford.

Cose, E. (1993). *Rage of a privileged class.* New York: Harper & Row.

Freud, S. (1961). On narcissism: An introduction. In J. Strachey (Ed. & Trans.), *The standard edition of the complete psychological works of Sigmund Freud* (Vol. 14, pp. 69–102). London: Hogarth. (Original work published 1914)

Johnson, C. (1999). *The Willie Lynch letter and the making of a slave.* Chicago: Lushena Books.

Johnson, R. (1991). *Black psychology.* Berkeley, CA: Cobb & Henry.

McAdoo, H. (1997). *Black families* (3rd ed.). Thousand Oaks, CA: Sage.

McHenry, P. (1994). *Families and change: Coping with stressful events.* Thousand Oaks, CA: Sage.

Minuchin, S. (1974). *Families and family therapy.* Cambridge, MA: Harvard University Press.

Walker, L. (1979). *The battered woman.* New York: Harper & Row.

Welsing, F. C. (1991). *The Isis papers: The keys to the colors.* Chicago: Third World.

Yalom, I. (1985). *Theory and practice of group psychotherapy.* New York: Basic Books.

15

From Polarization to Pluralization

The Japanese Sense
of Self and Bowen Theory

Narumi Taniguchi

As a person who was born and raised in Japan, in my 9 years in the United States I have felt like I am walking upside-down. Although there are many similarities between Japan and the United States, the cultures in the two countries are poles apart in some areas of life. For example, silence, reading others' minds, and accepting and accommodating are valued in Japanese culture, whereas the direct expression of ideas and feelings, thinking critically, and assertiveness are valued in U.S. culture. I have struggled to develop a family therapy approach that holds well in both Japan and the United States.

In the midst of experiencing this clash of cultures, I realized that the Japanese sense of self, represented by the Japanese word *jibun*, is quite different from the American sense of self. *Jibun* consists of two Chinese characters: *ji*, which implies self, and *bun*, which implies portion. That is, *self* in Japanese culture means "one's portion," which suggests that the self is only a part of the group (Rosenberger, 1992). In other words, in Japanese culture, the self does not exist without the group to which it belongs, whereas in American culture, the self seems to exist by itself. In describing this distinct Japanese psychological structure and contrasting it with the American individual self, Roland (1988) used the term *familial-group self,* which entails an extremely high level of interpersonal sensitivity and fosters the "we-self" that results from individuals' strong identification with the family or other groups.

My excitement about *jibun* doubled as I learned about Western post-modernism and social constructionist philosophies. Social constructionists' relational view of self-conception (Gergen, 1994) is amazingly similar to the Japanese sense of self. However, as I became more interested in social constructionism, I found myself going back and forth between the postmodernist and modernist worlds and facing another challenge, which was to find a way to hold together the two clashing philosophies.

I found a path to reconciling these philosophies when I discovered that the key assumptions of postmodernism and social constructionism, including no absolute realities and no essential self, are innate in Japanese Zen Buddhist culture. In Buddhism, there is no absolute existence like that of God in Christianity, and all humans have the potential to be a Buddha. Like Buddhism, the Shinto religion has had a tremendous influence on Japanese culture. In Shinto, numerous goddesses and gods exist in a manner incompatible with the nontheism of Buddhism. This incompatibility mirrors the clash between modernism and postmodernism. However, Japan has not been polarized by the two religions; in fact, Buddhism and Shinto have blended together very well and filtered into the lives of Japanese people. My excitement tripled as I started searching for an answer to what has made this pluralism possible in Japan. Uryu and Shibuya (1996) argued that the receptive character of Japanese people is one of the main reasons for this pluralism. I believe that this receptivity exists because the self is developed in a group along with other members' selves and group harmony is highly valued. Roland (1988) also expressed this view.

Although my struggle still continues, I now believe that *jibun* is an essential tool for bridging the gap between two worlds—of therapy and life, of the United States and Japan, of modernism and postmodernism. It is beyond the scope of this chapter to discuss the Japanese sense of self in detail, but throughout the chapter I will attempt to elaborate on how by using *jibun* in therapy I make sense of the seemingly incompatible cultures and worldviews of the United States and Japan.

My family has influenced me enormously. It is the first group that I belonged to, and it is the group in which my self developed. As the eldest of three children, I was expected to take care of my brothers and guide them. As a daughter, I was expected to help my mother with the housework and keep everyone happy, especially my father, who was a lonely, angry man. I strongly resented the roles that were imposed on me, but I was not allowed to express my anger. It was only after I left home and came to the United States that my relationship with my parents, especially with my father, started to change. It was the 6,000 miles of distance from my home and family, and Bowen's concepts of triangles and differentiation of self, that helped me in the process of developing *jibun*.

A Family Therapy Approach Using *Jibun*

The Epistemological and Theoretical Base of the Approach

The family therapy approach presented here has been influenced by social constructionist epistemology, systems theory, and Bowen theory. Social constructionism is often seen as incompatible with systems theory and Bowen theory, because it is based on postmodernism, a completely different world-view from the modernism of these theories. However, using the concept of *jibun*, one can hold these polarized epistemologies and theories together. In what follows, I describe what each of these theories contributed to my approach.

Social constructionism asserts that realities are constructed socially, in other words, through interaction.[1] Gergen (1994) challenged the notion of an independent core self and proposed instead that self emerges through inter-actions. This view of self is compatible with *jibun*, which is seen as develop-ing in groups. The following assumptions emerged in my approach: (1) a universal reality does not exist, so we all have our own realities that may be different from the realities of others, and (2) the self develops in relationships.

In *systems theory*, the concepts of system and subsystem are very similar to *jibun*. *Jibun* exists only as a part of a group, and group harmony is regarded as most important. A Japanese group consists of multiple small groups that are embedded within a large group, and the large group belongs to an even larger group (Takahashi, 1991). In second-order cybernetics (i.e., cybernetics of cybernetics) the observer is a part of the system; thus, the observer influences and is influenced by that system (Becvar & Becvar, 2002; Goldenberg & Goldenberg, 2000). This supports the postmodern assumption of the existence of points of view instead of reality. This view fits the concept of *jibun*, in that self and group are inseparable. Systems theory contributed the following concepts to my approach: (1) looking at the whole is vital, (2) the individual cannot *not* interact, and (3) the individual is always a part of the system.

Among the theoretical concepts in *Bowen theory*, the differentiation of self, triangles, and multigenerational transmission process have guided me the most in my self-development and in my work as a therapist. Kerr and Bowen (1988) stated, "Differentiation describes the process by which individuality and togetherness are managed by a person and within a relationship system" (p. 95). A concept similar to this is seen in *jibun*. In Japanese culture, those who are seen as being selfish and who disturb the harmony are excluded from the group. For fear of this, people sometimes bury themselves completely in the group and have no *jibun* (Doi, 1971).[2] Lebra (1992) explained this phenomenon as "self saturated in the interactional world." When a person is able to develop a self that is not rejected by the group, that person is considered to have *jibun* (Doi, 1971). This process of having *jibun* is similar to differentiation. Differentiation is "saying 'I' when others are demanding 'we'" (Friedman, 1991, p. 141). Triangles form when, due to heightened anxiety, two people draw a third person into the system to stabilize it (Friedman, 1991; Kerr & Bowen, 1988). If the third party maintains differentiation, a change can be induced in the two-person relationship (Friedman, 1991).

In both social constructionist epistemology and systemic thinking, the therapist cannot be an outside observer. In the approach using the concept of *jibun*, the therapist's use of self is also considered crucial and inevitable because the therapist's self, as well as the client's self, develops in the client-therapist group. Friedman (1991) stated that "the differentiation of the therapist is technique" and "promoting differentiation in others is connected to the *being* of the therapist" (p. 138). I use this concept broadly in my approach; both differentiation of the therapist within the therapeutic system and from the therapist's family of origin are important. Clients often present high levels of anxiety and reactivity. It is crucial for the therapist to remain differentiated (i.e., to be less reactive) in order for change to occur. In the approach using *jibun*, not only clients but the therapist too develops self in the client-therapist group. By having *jibun* in the group, the therapist can become receptive to the client's self without being afraid of becoming saturated in the group. In other words, the therapist opens up space for the client's self to develop in the client-therapist group. This is similar to one of the premises in narrative therapy, in which therapists facilitate the development of conversational space by using therapeutic questions (Anderson & Goolishian, 1992).

Multigenerational transmission is defined as the passing down of emotional responses through multiple generations (Friedman, 1991; Kerr & Bowen, 1988). This multigenerational perspective is innate in the concept of *jibun* because the child's self and the parents' selves develop within the family, and the parents' selves have developed in their respective families of origin, and so on. In my work, I use genograms (McGoldrick & Gerson, 1985) to gather family information, engage the family, and invite clients to bring in their selves that have been developed in their families of origin.

Finally, an assumption generated through my life experience and expressed in Bowen theory is that people can change and develop a different self.

What Brings People Into Therapy?

As an overarching principle, I believe that people come to therapy because of group disharmony and/or the issue of saturated self. I think behavioral problems in children or issues with couple relationships have to do with the former. Many psychiatric symptoms have to do with issues of saturated self; that is, having no *jibun* in the group to which the person belongs.

What Leads People to Change?

Change provokes anxiety in the whole system, and so the system develops homeostatic reactions. When people come to therapy, a new group and relationships are formed with the therapist. I believe that relationships produce change in people. In the client-therapist group, one of the goals for both the clients and the therapist is to integrate the new self with the self that developed in other groups (e.g., their families of origin). For that reason, it is important that the therapist develop *jibun* in the client-therapist group and create space for the client's self to develop. In this process, it is crucial for the therapist to maintain differentiation because this automatically contributes to differentiation in the client (Friedman, 1991). When this happens, the therapist's having *jibun* contributes to the change in the client's self. On the other hand, if the therapist gets drawn into the client's old relationship patterns (triangles), the system appears to get stuck.

What Is the Role of the Therapist?

When clients first come to therapy, they are often in crisis and full of anxiety. I believe that the first role of the therapist is to soak up their anxiety (Ball, 1996). Like a sponge that can absorb water and hold it, I listen to clients' problems while trying to be aware of my own reactions and not acting on them. In Bowen theory, this process is described as creating a therapeutic triangle in which the therapist attempts to remain a nonanxious presence, which automatically leads to a change in the relationship of the other two sides of the triangle (Friedman, 1991). In the Japanese sense of self, being a sponge implies that the therapist is receptive to the clients' selves.

The second role of the therapist is to be respectful of the clients. This is something my culture taught me, and most of the time it is the natural thing for me to do. Mutual respect is essential in forming a group and maintaining group harmony. This is as true for the therapy group as for any other group.

The third role of the therapist is to be an expert. People often come to therapy seeking professional help, and I believe therapists should attend to that expectation. This role is particularly important in Japanese culture because therapists are often called by the title *sensei,* which is also used for teachers, doctors, lawyers, and those who have special skills and/or knowledge. I share my knowledge and techniques with my clients. However, I am tentative, respecting the client's choice of what information to adopt and which technique to respond to. It is important to make sure that my clients can disagree with me. I attempt to create enough space for the client's self to develop in therapy. Anderson (1997) stated, "Tentativeness does not equal vagueness but being open to the other person and leaving room for his or her participation" (p. 146).

The fourth role of the therapist is to be an inquirer. Because I do not know the client's particular family, I ask questions. Even if we use the same words, I do not assume we both mean the same thing. I believe that things have different meanings for different people. By asking questions, I believe I am creating space for the client's self to develop. This is similar to Anderson and Goolishian's (1992) concept of the therapeutic question, which is "the primary instrument to facilitate the development of conversational space" (p. 27). As the clients try to answer the questions, they experience their selves (Freeman & Combs, 1996), which means they develop their selves.

The fifth role of a therapist is to differentiate and have *jibun.* In Bowen theory, the therapist's differentiation is crucial for change to occur (Friedman, 1991). The therapist's maintaining differentiation within the group, having *jibun,* means that he or she does not get caught up in the emotional system. By having *jibun,* the therapist creates space for each client's self to develop. In this sense, I think that therapists must use their selves in conducting therapy.

The following case study illustrates how I applied this approach and used the concept of *jibun* in therapy with an intercultural couple and in supervision with White supervisors.

Case Study

Background

Gloria, a 43-year-old White woman from Spain who had been living in the United States for more than 20 years, had been married for 4 years to John, a 43-year-old White professional. This was a second marriage for both of them. A few days after a violent incident, during which John had pulled Gloria's hair and thrown her against a wall, John made the initial contact with a family therapy clinic and requested couple therapy.[3]

Their presenting problem was not just the violence but their communication as well. Gloria and John wanted to communicate with each other without arguing. In the initial interview, they could not agree on anything while describing what had happened. Their group harmony was disturbed, and they were both afraid of losing their relationship. They felt lonely and angry when they perceived the other person distancing. Although they wanted to feel closer to each other, John spent a lot of time with his computer, and Gloria had become less intimate with him.

While neither of them was very differentiated, both had distanced themselves from their families of origin. Gloria's family had barely been able to maintain group harmony, with everybody trying to develop their respective selves around the alcoholic, abusive father. In other words, nobody in her family was really allowed to have *jibun*. Gloria left Spain more than 20 years ago, and her self no longer belonged to either her family of origin or her cultural group. John's family of origin and especially his mother were very religious. The mother's self seemed saturated in her religious group. John wanted to be accepted by his mother, but she did not accept him because they had religious differences. These differences prevented John from having *jibun* in his family of origin, and he eventually became religiously inactive. John's self belonged to neither his family of origin nor his religious group anymore. Gloria and John were very reactive to each other. Gloria wanted respect from John, and John desired physical intimacy from Gloria. They were both afraid that if they gave in to their partner's preferences, they would lose control over their lives and their selves would be saturated. They were no longer able to develop their respective selves in this relationship, and the more one of them tried to do it, the angrier the other one became. Thus each partner was discouraged from trying to have *jibun*.

As the therapist, I tried to develop my self in this client-therapist group. This case was particularly challenging for me because of my background: I tend to get intimidated by older men due to experiences with my angry, dominant father; I tend to see women as powerless, like my mother. I am also angry at the patriarchal nature of Japanese society.

Interventions

When John called the clinic, he requested a session immediately, so I expected the couple to be in crisis and focused my efforts on being the "sponge" in the first session. They started arguing with each other over who was telling the truth. Since I believe that one person's truth can be different from another's, I emphasized that they would both have a chance to tell me their own version. By doing so, I invited them to bring in the selves that had developed in the marriage. I also changed my focus to their feelings and created space for their new selves to be developed in the client-therapist group. John was able to talk about his loneliness and his fear of losing control, and he expressed his new self through tears. Gloria was angry and said that she did not want anyone to control her because of her experiences with her controlling ex-husband. I helped her get in touch with her fear, and she expressed her new self through tears as well.

I used the genogram with this couple to help them experience their own and each other's selves. Gloria cried while talking about her brother, who was killed in a car accident. John turned toward her and looked very serious. When questioned, he said that he was feeling sorry for her, and then asked Gloria if she wanted a hug. She accepted his offer. This took courage for John because he thought he would be rejected, but instead Gloria allowed him to connect with her.

Through the course of therapy, I used my self to avoid being triangulated. I paid attention to my physiological reactions. When I became aware of my emotional reactivity, I deliberately did something different. For example, I often found myself in disagreement with John over who said what, which was the same pattern that he had with Gloria. When I noticed myself occupying Gloria's place, I inquired if he felt I had misunderstood him as Gloria had misunderstood him, and then I empathized with his feelings.

Supervision

I received supervision for this case from more than one supervisor, all of whom were White men. There was a time when the entire team behind the mirror, including my supervisor, thought that John was disrespecting me. My supervisor said that he wanted to come into the therapy room and rescue me, although he resisted the temptation. I was shocked and felt belittled by the team because my experience with John was that he did respect me. My usual reaction in such a case is to not talk about it and to withdraw to preserve group harmony. This was how I dealt with anger in my family of origin. With the help of my supervisor and my team members, who created space for my self to develop, I was able to talk about how I felt. This was a differentiation experience for me; I was able to have *jibun* in my supervision group. In a subsequent session, I brought up the issue of respect by sharing with the couple what my team had observed. After this, Gloria began to develop her self by demanding respect from John.

There was a time when this couple recycled their interaction patterns and I felt stuck. My supervisor suggested that I focus on positives; this was a significant shift for me in terms of my reactivity in session. In the approach using *jibun*, maintaining group harmony is as important as developing self, but I had been caught up in the couple's negativities and had forgotten about maintaining group harmony. As soon as I switched my focus to increasing the positives in their relationship, they started to make some changes. Subsequently, they reported several incidents during which John became upset with Gloria but did not become hostile, and she recognized her overreaction and apologized. Both started to develop their new selves in their relationship.

Gloria and John were different in the areas of culture, gender, and education, all of which were related to their power differential. Both desperately wanted not only to connect with each other but also to have a self in this relationship. However, because of this power differential, they had been unable to have both connection and self. John brought his self (developed in his family of origin) into the marriage and demanded that Gloria accept it. However, he was unable to connect with her because he did not open up space for her to develop her own self. Gloria tried to maintain her self around John for the sake of harmony. When Gloria sought *jibun* in the relationship, the system shook. John was no longer able to push her back to where she was before, unless he used physical force. As I invited Gloria to talk about the power differential, she verbalized her need for respect. She understood that when she felt disrespected, she became angry and distanced herself from John, both emotionally and physically. Although John struggled with acknowledging his power, he understood how much his angry reactions affected Gloria. It took them over 10 sessions to identify one thing each of them was willing to do differently: For Gloria it was to avoid overreacting, and for John it was to remain calm. Their new selves began to develop. It was the first step toward their goal of having *jibun*—having their individual selves and still connecting with each other. Gradually the severity and frequency of their arguments decreased, and there was no more violence.

Conclusion

When individuals face differences, their natural reaction is to polarize. By doing so, they often feel a sense of relief. It is a challenge for us all, therapists and clients, to get out of our comfort zones and try to make sense of all the differences around us. Pluralization to me is not about being indecisive, but about tolerating differences while holding our anxiety. Although the Japanese sense of self facilitated my transition from polarization to pluralization, this idea of self is not limited to Japanese culture. Roland (1988) suggests that people who come from a culture where the predominant self is individually based do have a familial self in the background, and vice versa. In the United States, I struggled because I wanted to have *jibun*, yet I could not and did not want to lose my self as a Japanese person. In the beginning I tried to act "American," thinking that this was expected of me and that it would give me a sense of relief. However, I found not only that this was impossible but that my Japanese self was too important to give up. From that moment on, I asked other people to create space for my self to develop in the United States. I was very fortunate to be surrounded by the people who were willing to open up space for me, some without being asked. I was able to develop this therapy approach because of people—faculty members, supervisors, and colleagues at both Texas Tech and Syracuse University and my family and friends—who were willing to tolerate and accept differences. By describing the concept of *jibun*, I hope that I have given readers of this chapter more options to use in working to develop their new selves and in helping their clients and students develop new selves as well.

Reflections, Questions, and Exercises

The following exercise will help students, clinicians, and faculty to better understand *jibun* (i.e., one's portion of the group self) and to be able to utilize this concept in clinical work, in supervision, and in relationships with their family members, friends, and colleagues.

Jibun Pie Exercise

1. Draw a circle that represents a group to which you belong. The group can be your family, your intimate relationship, your friends, your work group, your therapy group (i.e., you as a therapist with your clients), your supervision group, or some other group.

2. Divide this pie between the members of the group, in which each piece represents one member's *jibun*. You can be as creative as you want to be by using different colors to represent different members, different shapes, different types of lines, and so forth. Be aware of the size of each member's piece of pie and whose piece is next to whose.

3. After finishing the drawing, answer the following questions:
   a. How do you feel about the size and the position of your piece and of the other members' pieces?
   b. How large a piece would you like to have, and where would you like your piece to be placed?
   c. What would it take for you to get your ideal pie, and what would it look like?
   d. How do you feel about seeing yourself as a piece of the pie, rather than as a whole pie?
   e. How is the concept of *jibun* different from or similar to your own cultural beliefs about self?

Notes

1. To illustrate social constructionism, terms like *language, conversation, discourse, story,* and *narrative* are often used. Although they all include words and verbal expressions, they also include other forms of communication such as nonverbal communication, art, music, dance, silence, and so forth. It is very important to recognize this in considering the Japanese sense of self, because both Shinto and Buddhism value experiences, actions, transmitting ideas from mind to mind, silence, and blank spaces over words.

2. Roland (1988) used the term *onionlike self* to describe this state of self, meaning that there is very little sense of self and the presented self is a false self.

3. When there is ongoing violence in a relationship, conjoint therapy is not recommended because of the safety concerns. In this case, it was only after I had done a thorough assessment of their safety that I agreed to do couple therapy. I also used a no-violence contract to ensure their commitment to safety.

References

Anderson, H. (1997). *Conversation, language, and possibilities: A postmodern approach to therapy.* New York: Basic Books.

Anderson, H., & Goolishian, H. (1992). The client in the expert: A not-knowing approach to therapy. In S. McNamee & K. J. Gergen (Eds.), *Therapy as social construction* (pp. 25–39). Newbury Park, CA: Sage.

Ball, J. S. (1996). Consultant as sponge: An evolutionary journey. In P. A. Comella, J. Bader, J. S. Ball, K. K. Wiseman, & R. R. Sagar (Eds.), *The emotional side of organizations: Applications of Bowen Theory.* Washington, DC: Georgetown Family Center.

Becvar, D. S., & Becvar, R. J. (2002). *Family therapy: A systemic integration* (5th ed.). Needham Heights, MA: Allyn & Bacon.

Doi, T. (1971). *Amae no kozo* [The anatomy of dependence]. Tokyo: Kobundo.

Freeman, J., & Combs, G. (1996). *Narrative therapy.* New York: Norton.

Friedman, E. H. (1991). Bowen theory and therapy. In A. S. Gurman & D. P. Kniskern (Eds.), *Handbook of family therapy* (Vol. 2, pp. 134–170). New York: Brunner/Mazel.

Gergen, K. J. (1994). *Realities and relationships: Soundings in social construction.* Cambridge, MA: Harvard University Press.

Goldenberg, I., & Goldenberg, H. (2000). *Family therapy: An overview* (5th ed.). Belmont, CA: Brooks/Cole.

Kerr, M. E., & Bowen, M. (1988). *Family evaluation.* New York: Norton.

Lebra, T. S. (1992). Self in Japanese culture. In N. R. Rosenberger. (Ed.), *Japanese sense of self* (pp. 105–120). New York: Cambridge University Press.

McGoldrick, M., & Gerson, R. (1985). *Genograms in family assessment.* New York: Norton.

Roland, A. (1988). *In search of self in India and Japan.* Princeton, NJ: Princeton University Press.

Rosenberger, N. R. (Ed.). (1992). *Japanese sense of self.* New York: Cambridge University Press.

Takahashi, T. (1991). A comparative study of Japanese and American group dynamics. *Psychoanalytic Review, 78,* 49–62.

Uryu, N., & Shibuya, N. (1996). *Nihon Syukyo no Subete* [All about Japanese religions]. Tokyo: Nihon Bungei.

16

Kum Ba Yah[1]

The Relevance of Family Systems Theory for Clinicians and Clients of African Descent

Martha Adams Sullivan

Family systems therapy offers a culturally syntonic approach for intervention with clients of African descent and for therapists of African descent working cross-culturally. Yet, Black therapists are underrepresented in the field. Clearly, this is attributable to macro systems issues such as institutional racism and class privilege. The current discourse and debate regarding the best means to address greater diversity in education, particularly higher education, is applicable to family systems training as well. Furthermore, Black clinicians who might be candidates for family systems training have little opportunity to benefit from the experience and perspectives of experienced Black clinicians regarding family systems practice. I am a Black woman (I use the term *woman* rather than *female* here to deliberately reference the cultural context of Black womanness) family systems therapist, and I have written this chapter primarily for the clinician trainee *and* to describe the goodness of fit of family systems theory with the Black therapist's cultural orientation.

Two assumptions underpin this work. First, people of African descent, despite ethnic and individual differences, retain "Africanisms" derived from traditional African culture to some extent. Second, the culture of the therapist is a salient component of the therapeutic context.

It is a given that the professional development of those of African descent may include structural barriers. Trainees will have their own history of dealing with these barriers more or less successfully. However, the emphasis here is not on those obstacles but on the goal of selecting a practice approach that is congruent with the Black clinician. This discussion will also include a discussion of feminist principles, as the writer is a feminist.

Personal and Professional Background

Being of African descent and born in the United States, I am comfortable identifying as an African American. However, I prefer to identify as Black, or as a Black woman. For me, using the term *Black* is a political and aesthetic statement. It is through Black identity that I am connected with the diaspora; for example, when I encounter people of African descent from the Continent and the Islands, we all refer to ourselves as Black. My womanness is also essential to my identity. Gender, for me, needs to be understood in the context of race; to know me as a woman is also to know that I am Black, a Black woman. I identify as a feminist (although I rather like Alice Walker's (1984) term *womanist*), and I challenge White feminists to prioritize racism. With regard to class, I distinguish class identification from income. As many people do, I identify with the working class background of my family of origin. I do not identify with many middle-class values, despite having the education, occupation, and income generally thought to denote middle-class status. This is not uncommon in the Black community. A within-group conceptualization of class in the Black community reflects different indicators and more gradations of class than exist in the dominant society.

I am not considered bilingual, as not everyone believes, as I do, that Black English is a dialect, with its own syntax. (I have witnessed numerous occasions where clinicians unfamiliar with the dialect have misinterpreted what was communicated to them.) I am certainly bicultural, although the terms *bilingual* and *bicultural* have become blurred so that the assumption in practice is that biculturalism applies only to those who are bilingual. The discussion below of African retentions or "Africanity" (Nobles, 1974) should not be interpreted to mean that Black families do not espouse Western cultural values. To the contrary, managing their lives in the West requires that Black people understand Western culture in order to navigate their environment more or less successfully. Nevertheless, many people simultaneously hold values and beliefs that stem from traditional African culture.

Unfortunately, Western culture often overlooks Black culture. Du Bois (1903) spoke of this phenomenon in the early 20th century. Later, Chestang (1976) wrote of "cultural duality," that is, understanding and being agile at navigating different cultural realities, as an important means of coping. My own heritage has readied me for this, in that I am fortunate to have had the nurturing and preparation that my extended family provided for coping with life, including coping in an oppressive environment. This background also enables me to assist others who are "different."

I was born and raised Roman Catholic, a significant factor in my life. Like many Black Catholics in the United States, my family's Catholic roots are tied to the extremely high value Black families place on education. Racism has ignored this value. Yet, education is typically seen as the most important means to upward mobility, respect, and the liberation of the Black community. It is "the one thing they can't take away from you." My maternal grandmother converted from the African Methodist Episcopal faith to Catholicism so that she could place her 6 children in Catholic school where they would receive a better education. Although educating her children was apparently her original motivation to convert, my grandmother became a very devout Catholic. Her children were very involved in the church, and in turn, raised us Catholic and educated all 24 of us, her grandchildren, in Catholic schools from elementary school through secondary school. My Catholic school experience provided me with excellent academic preparation; it was also one factor in my preparation for living in a racist world. It was an important, yet complex and imperfect experience of community. I am proud to be a Black Catholic. I also question and challenge the Catholic Church on issues of racism and sexism within the church, just as I challenge these in general. I belong to a Black Catholic church congregation. I reject people's using "the Black church" to refer only to Black Protestant churches of various denominations as much as I reject using "the church" to refer only to White Catholic experience. These perspectives ignore the roots of Christianity on the African continent and in the Black Southern United States.

Currently I hold an executive position at a local government agency. I am a social worker, and I teach on an adjunct basis at the Hunter College School of Social Work as well as the Minuchin Center for the Family. Twenty years ago I developed the Center for Older Adults and their Families in the New York City public hospital system to bridge aging and family systems practice. My specialization in aging, and in Later Life Families, is a clear outgrowth of my experience in my family of origin, as I am part of a large extended family in which the elders are central. The Center for Older Adults and their Families serves a multiethnic, multiracial population reflective of the diversity that is New York City, and particularly the Lower East

Side of Manhattan. I also retain a small private practice treating ethnically diverse clients of all ages.

Personal Experience

My path has been at once deliberate and seemingly filled with detours due to obstacles related to institutional racism and classism. Like water, continually seeking its destination despite barriers here and there, I do believe, in retrospect, that I have come at each point to where I needed to be. This is not to excuse the discrimination and prejudice I experienced but to place such experiences in context, viewing them as systemic in origin rather than merely as individual acts of malice. A critical factor here is that as I became clearer as to what I was seeking, the obstacles became detours, not dead ends. By no means do I wish to minimize these experiences, as they present an added burden to the role of merely being a student, a burden that middle-class White students do not have. I trust that sharing my experiences and my perspective on family systems will be beneficial to trainees and will inspire those who encounter such obstacles to stay on course.

An example of an obstacle I faced was when I was shut out of an opportunity for family training in graduate school. My budding interest in working with families had led me to seek out a little known fieldwork placement at a prestigious family therapy institute. However, my "advisor" made it clear that I would not be assigned to this placement because "their clients are middle class." At the age of 20-something, I handled this situation very differently from how I would handle it today. I was hurt and disappointed, but I did not have the confidence to fight this decision alone. The larger context of the graduate school environment was, for me and for most new students, intimidating. Nevertheless, I was acutely aware that this was a systemic exclusion, that I was not deemed to be of the proper race and class to obtain this select placement. I also understood that my advisor, a person of color as well, was likely handing down a decision that she could not or would not fight, and that perhaps the institute also put pressure on the school regarding the type of students to be placed. This angered and saddened me. Not to be totally defeated, I insisted on a mental health placement and was prepared to fight this time, to have my request granted. I was assigned to a clinic in a settlement house. I agreed to go to check it out, assuring the school that if it were not to my liking, I would not accept the placement.

The clinic was in many ways a traditional mental health clinic, where clinicians relied on psychodynamic approaches to treat individuals. It was a clinic truly rooted in the community, which was partly a function of its settlement house sponsorship. In many instances, entire families were seen in the clinic, with each member having her or his own individual therapist. Periodically, clinicians would determine that it was necessary to hold a conference so that each of the therapists involved could better understand the progress of the others. Typically, these conferences occurred when some conflict related to the treatment arose between the therapists. I asked my supervisor "Doesn't anyone ever sit down with the whole family together?" This was met with a quizzical look that seemed to say, "Why on earth would you do that?" Even without background or training in working with families, it just naturally made sense to me that these family members were living together and interacting with each other all the time, so why not intervene with them as a unit?

Two events converged to create a turning point in the orientation of the clinic: The long-time director resigned and a new supervisor was hired who happened to be a Bowenian family therapist. This supervisor encouraged the new director to engage in family training. The process of organizational change was at times painful, but it nevertheless provided a very rich learning experience. The leading candidates for the directorship were internal— supervisors with longevity in the clinic and connections to the community. The clinic converted to a family approach and invited me to join the staff upon graduation, which I was pleased to do. I remained at the clinic for several years, during which the clinic moved from the Bowenian to the Milan systemic approach.

Thus, being discriminated against and not being assigned the placement I'd sought at the prestigious family therapy institute led me to a placement that ultimately became pivotal in my career. However, that was not the last time I was to experience discrimination, as later my attempts to further my training were again thwarted at another institution. I was supervising a family treatment team when I decided to pursue an institute certificate program. I had a rather unique background in that I'd had several years of expert supervision, as well as on-the-job training and some external training in family systems work. The institute was ready to offer me admission but first inquired as to whether I would be "comfortable in classes with people [I] could supervise." Since I was thought to be overqualified for the entry level, I asked why, then, the institute didn't simply place me with peers at a more advanced level in the training program. They refused. I was left with questions about the reasons for this refusal.

By this time, I had left the first clinic I worked in and begun developing and directing a geriatric mental health program in the mental health department of a public health-care facility. I was passionately pursuing work with the elderly using a family systems approach. This was over 20 years ago and I already had nearly a decade of experience working with families and supervising. When I thought about it, I didn't really need to devote significant time to seeing institute patients. I began advanced training with Salvador Minuchin, which was perfectly suited to my needs for a number of reasons. Sal Minuchin's institute required trainees to bring their own cases for live and videotaped supervision. I brought the families I was working with— multiethnic, poor, working poor, and middle-class later life families, many with serious mental illness—for consultation with Sal Minuchin. Training at the Minuchin Center for the Family (then Family Studies, Inc.) also focused on developing the trainee as a family therapy supervisor. Sal Minuchin made it clear that he was not teaching structural family therapy but "family therapy." Nevertheless, his own background in working with the poor and families of color was important. He once said "I developed my theory with Black families." Sal Minuchin had become an elder himself and was able to stimulate my understanding of this stage of life for individuals and families. Coming out of retirement for the second or third time, his interest was not to develop a family therapy clinic but to develop clinicians who could make a difference in the field and continue the work of advancing family therapy. The institute was clearly organized around this goal. Admission to the institute was based upon an individual interview with Sal Minuchin at his home. What could be more intimidating? He began challenging me on the telephone and continued to do so in the interview. Although he never said so directly, I felt for the first time that my own ethnic and racial background was recognized as a professional asset, not a liability, and that Sal Minuchin welcomed a Black student to the institute to be "kicked and coddled" with the rest of them.

Relevant Literature

There is considerable literature on the influence of culture and gender in family therapy. McGoldrick and Carter (1998) are among those most known for pioneering and continuing to add to knowledge ethnicity and race within the field. Sociologists such as Billingsley (1988), Frasier (1939), Ladner (1971), and many others have written on Black families in the United States. Boyd-Franklin's (1988) seminal work focuses on treatment of Black families. Ault-Riche (1986), Bograd (1986), and the "Women's Project," consisting of Walters, Carter, Papp, and Silverstein (1988), are among those who have drawn attention to the issue of gender in family treatment. Aponte (1997) has written considerably on the person of the family therapist and continues to teach from this viewpoint. Cantor (1990) directly addresses issues related to women as therapists. Good supervision and training programs often focus on the therapist's reactions as information regarding the system and how it functions.

In what follows, I identify the basic tenets of systems theory and demonstrate their congruence with the cultural perspectives of people of African descent. I incorporate into the discussion the works of Mbiti (1969, 1990) and Karenga (2000) on African tradition, as well as the basic principles of feminist practice. A couple of points are worthy of note here. First, I do not assume that Black clinicians will work exclusively with Black families. In this discussion, the focus on Black families is a means to understand the Black therapist's own worldview as well as that of some of the families she or he may treat. Second, given that African philosophy is an Eastern philosophy, families of other cultures (e.g., Asian cultures) may recognize similarities between their cultures and the African culture described here. Finally, Black families have commonalities with other groups based upon class, agrarian roots, and so on. The pointed discussion below does not intend to deny the diversity of Black families nor the important aspects they share with others. It is intended, however, to highlight for Black clinicians and clinicians working with Black families the aspects of Black family existence that relate to their African heritage. One may note that discussion of slavery is largely absent from this discussion, for in my view that would be a different discussion altogether. That Black people survived slavery in numbers, wounds and all, is a testament to the resilience of the human spirit in general and to our African heritage in particular. I believe that slavery attempted to obliterate us culturally, hence the need for the following discussion.

Family Systems Theory and African Philosophy

Lewin (1997) is often quoted as saying that "there's nothing so practical as a good theory." A theory is good to the extent it is useful, helping the therapist to understand behaviors, feelings, and attitudes and to intervene in the clinical situations presented to her or him. Theory, then, is the lens through which the therapist gains a perspective on the client. Yet, theory is useless without a therapist. The therapist's ability to form a therapeutic relationship is the most important factor in the therapeutic process. The therapist, however, comes to the clinical encounter not with brand new eyes but with a perspective born of her or his own experience. This perspective or worldview is the result of sociocultural experience and unique individual experiences. Ideally, there should be a good fit between the therapist's own eyes or worldview and the theoretical lens she or he chooses. For purposes of our discussion, the lens is that of principles derived from family systems theory.

There are, of course, a variety of family systems theories. Yet, it is possible to identify principles that are germane to family systems theory in general (Herr & Weakland, 1979; Papp, 1994). People of African descent represent many ethnic groups throughout the diaspora. It is a premise of this work that despite ethnic distinctions, these groups tend to retain Africanisms to a greater or lesser extent. Africanisms are philosophical worldviews, that is, the "understanding, attitude of mind, logic and perceptions [that underlie] the manner in which . . . peoples think, act or speak in different situations of life" (Mbiti, 1969, p. 2).

Systems Theory and Communitarianism

General systems theory describes a *system* as being comprised of interrelated parts such that the whole is greater than the sum of those parts. Applied to families, this means that the interrelatedness of family members defines behavior and that larger systems issues impact family functioning. By extension, as the therapist engages with a family, the therapist becomes part of that context and of a therapeutic or professional system such that the therapist can impact family behavior. In fact, the family's pull on the therapist becomes useful information for understanding what it is like to be in a particular family. Clearly, this requires focusing on how the system functions and how individuals function within their family system. Family systems therapists understand individual pathology but do not seek to treat it; rather, they seek to help the family system function optimally, even given the limitations of individual members. For example, a therapist might ask, Is the family system able to see that the schizophrenic family member takes medication, works, and is listened to and respected in the family? If there is another crisis in the family, such as an acute illness, is the family, including the schizophrenic member, able to organize themselves to meet the demands of this crisis and appropriately care for the ill member?

Group orientation and family centeredness is an African retention that is apparent in many Black families. This communitarian philosophy emphasizes the individual as an integral part of the whole such that "I am because we are and since we are, therefore I am" (Mbiti, 1969, quoted in Martin & Martin, 1985, p. 12). This "cardinal point of African philosophy . . . means that traditional Africans did not see themselves as individuals with a concern for self over the group but see that group as a corporate part of the individual personality" (Martin & Martin, 1985, p. 12). This worldview and way of being is distinct from Western values, which emphasize empowering the individual for the individual's sake. Even the Black family who points to the identified patient and say that "the problem is him" often feel on a deeper level that "we have a problem." Similarly, their definition of family not only is extended in nature but includes the living and the deceased and also may include blood and nonblood kin, that is, is a system. One of the most important sets of questions to ask a Black family are those designed to identify who is in the target system. For example, Who else should probably be here? Who helps you or advises you about this? Who do you wish was here to help? and so on. Do not overlook the role of the deceased in the family system. Deceased members may even visit the living through dreams in order to give advice. Traditional African societies considered the deceased to still be members of the community as long as there were people alive who remembered them by name.

Kwanzaa is a perfect example of communitarianism. An African American cultural celebration developed by Maulana Ron Karenga, Kwanzaa focuses on seven principles, the Nguzu Saba, which reflect the needs of the entire community and challenge members of the community to behave in the community's best interest, not their own:

- UMOJA. Unity. To strive for and maintain unity in the family and community.
- KUJICHAGULIA. Self-Determination. As a community, to define ourselves, name ourselves and speak for ourselves. The "self" here is the community.
- UJIMA. Collective Work and Responsibility. To build and maintain the community together and to make each other's problems our own and do our problem solving together.
- UJAMAA. Cooperative Economics. To build and maintain commerce from which the community can profit.
- NIA. Purpose. To make the development of the community a priority.
- KUUMBA. Creativity. To continuously contribute to the beauty of the community and the community's capacity to grow and develop.
- IMANI. Faith. To believe in the Creator and the community's capacity to endure (Karenga, 2002, p. 2).

Communitarianism is inherently about connectedness and interdependence more than individual independence. The practical principles of Kwanzaa, for example, are intended to be integrated into daily life. Kwanzaa celebrations can be elaborate or simple. A family or group can light a candle each day at the dinner table and discuss the principle for that day. Alternatively, guests may be invited for a large gathering or community organizations such as schools may conduct Kwanzaa celebrations with culturally relevant dancing, recitations, songs, and so on. The lighting of the candle and discussion of the principle are the essential part of the celebration. It is decidedly not an individual experience. Remarkably, the celebration of Kwanzaa, which was derived from traditional East African cultures, is now spreading not only throughout the West but back to the African continent as well. This speaks loudly and clearly of the relevance of these traditional principles and to the lasting and continued commonalities among the people of the African diaspora with the Motherland. Apparently, our brothers and sisters on the continent also relate to the need to elucidate and deepen our connection to the traditional values of our heritage apart from Western traditions imposed by colonialism.

The fact that family systems therapy de-emphasizes pathology is also important in working with Black families, because the experience of racial oppression has denigrated Black individuals and families. It allows for the strengths of Black families to become useful tools in therapy. Several authors have delineated the following strengths of Black families: strong kinship bonds and extended structure, strong achievement and work ethic, high value placed on education, flexible roles, strong religious orientation, development of survival strategies (Billingsley, 1988; Boyd-Franklin, 1988; Frasier, 1939; Pinderhughes, 1986).

Circularity and Dualism

Circularity is a key family systems concept that speaks directly to the development and maintenance of problems by asserting that they are maintained by the reciprocal influence of multiple behaviors or causes. This model differs from the linear model of causality in that it does not seek to determine a single cause of the problem. Family systems therapists use this model to understand the reciprocal patterns that maintain clients' problem behaviors and to intervene by altering or disrupting them such that the problem behaviors must change.

Just as the family's problem cannot be understood apart from the multiple behaviors and influences of the family system, similarly, African thought places the individual being in reciprocal relationship with the community context. In the traditional African way of being,

> to be whole is to belong to the whole community. . . . A person cannot detach himself from the . . . group for to do so is to be severed from his roots, his foundation, his context of security, his kinship, and the entire group of those who make him aware of his own existence. (Mbiti, 1969, p. 2)

The individual and the community have a "symbiotic empathy and investment in each other's happiness" (Mbiti, 1969, p. 33).

Furthermore, the concept of *dualism* means that seeming

> polarities or opposites, e.g. day and night or dead and living are viewed as having a reciprocal and unifying function rather than a dichotomous one, which dynamically unites them such that they create a whole maintaining equilibrium by adjusting each to the other. For example, death, while it represents the soul leaving the body, is not simply the opposite of life but is inherently related to life; it is another dimension or phase of the same phenomenon. (Sullivan, 1994, p. 161)

Admittedly, these are highly abstract ideas. However, they speak to a worldview that is, in its essence, holistic and systemic, in which all are integrally parts of the whole in the most basic way. These ideas also speak to why Black family therapists recognize that to be separated from others, to be cut off or isolated, is *the* most painful existence for Black people. Conversely, attempts to cope with adversity typically involve taking in, including, extending, or sharing in some way. Informal adoption, extended family structure, and the incorporation of nonkin as family are obvious examples of this. However, there are countless ways in which people's efforts to strengthen connections and ties to others are part of managing their daily lives.

Present Experience

While family systems approaches vary with regard to their focus on the past, in general, such approaches focus on seeking change in the present, understanding that the past cannot be changed. Exploration of the past is generally more limited in systems approaches than it is in individual approaches, and it is intended to assist the therapist in targeting a change of behavior or perception of behavior in the present—through, for example, identifying generational patterns, challenging perceptions of current problems, developing a language for discussing problems that is congruent with the family's—or in motivating change in the present. The underlying principle here is that despite past occurrences, it is chiefly present organization that supports problematic behavior. Therefore, efforts to change behavior must, ultimately, focus on the present.

The notion of time as being defined more by events and experience than by the calendar is very foreign to the Western mentality. Many indigenous African languages do not have a future tense that extends beyond the immediate future (i.e., 6 months or so). This is because history was handed down orally and extended back only as far as could be remembered and passed down. In this context, Mbiti (1969) said, "Time is simply a compilation of events which have occurred, those which are taking place now and those which are inevitably or immediately to occur" (pp. 16–17). Events that have not been experienced or are expected to be experienced at some point beyond the immediate future, then, are cast into "no time" or at best potential time, as there is no guarantee that they will actually occur (Mbiti, 1999, pp. 16–17). This is a very difficult concept for the Western mind, which views time as very divorced from experience, almost as if it were a concrete entity to which experience must be subject.

The oft-quoted example of the way the African time sense is manifested by Black people in the West is "CP Time," colored people's time. The term is used somewhat tongue in cheek by Black families to denote what in Western culture amounts to late, very late. Families themselves may not fully know the roots of this behavior. If the time of the wedding is when the wedding or the party or the get-together actually occurs, it is not really late. Other examples include "having church," as opposed to going to church, which means not only that worship is an inherently active, creative, and deeply participatory experience but also that the mass ends when the spirit indicates that it is over. There is no rush to end "on [clock] time." This distinction is one of the more discernable cultural differences between those of African descent and those in the dominant culture. It is not uncommon to have a party where all of the White guests arrive exactly at the time on the invitation and begin to leave as soon as the speeches are over or the cake is cut. Those of African heritage will mostly arrive later and stay a long time, as long as they are enjoying themselves. Annually, I host a large Kwanzaa gathering to which guests generally arrive within an hour or so of the time stated on the invitation. Many of the same guests come each year. One year, practically everyone came at nearly the same time—about 3 hours after the time on the invitation. I responded that obviously I had selected the wrong time, and my Kwanzaa community had a different sense of when this gathering should occur. I felt good about the fact that there was that sense of connectedness between us and that that connection was the main force here, not the clock, which often feels artificial.

Of course, the obvious corollary to this is the therapeutic appointment time. Western clinics have to run according to clocked appointments. Perhaps what is more significant, though, is the realization that to the family, the notion of getting their fully allotted time may pale next to their experience of the therapist and the therapy. This experience is partly determined by the extent to which the family feels connected to the therapist and comfortable with focusing on the present.

Persistence and Fatalism

Rooted in psychoanalytic theory, *resistance* is understood as a transference reaction. Individually oriented therapists speak as if the individual is resisting them or (more accurately) resisting the therapy. Systemically oriented therapists recognize (1) the system's natural tendency toward homeostasis and (2) that this homeostasis also pertains to the therapeutic system (i.e., the interaction between family and therapist). Thus, the notion of *persistence* is more useful, such that the therapist is challenged to understand and respect the family's tendency to stay the same while figuring out her or his role in perpetuating the situation. Restraint from change interventions, for example, is one method of responding to persistence (Papp, 1994).

Similarly, African philosophy accommodates the tendency of situations to respond to other than human intervention. *Fatalism* is "a world view in which it is believed that humans do not have the power to cause events and that their intellects are not such that they can understand or predict the future with any degree of confidence" (Pennington, 1985, p. 128). However, fatalism does not imply futility or promote inactivity; it does allow for action while simultaneously recognizing that life is unpredictable despite our attempts to affect it, that the Creator is ultimately in control. Therefore, people are able to maintain a sense of dignity in the face of adversity, which may occur despite their best attempts to avert it.

Traditional African thought, then, understood that situations could sometimes persist even as people work on trying to change them. A person can "let go and let God," which implies that the change is possible—although perhaps not in the time or manner that that person might expect. Ironically, this is not a hopeless posture, but one that views change contextually. It allows for greater possibilities for change, including changes not of the person's own design, while simultaneously fostering patience in the process of change. Knowing this is essential for the therapist who is trying to understand a family's view of the possibility for change and their expectations of the process of change. It is important for the therapist to ask the family, Do you think this situation can change? What or who do you think can change it? Then, if the family has placed the situation "in God's hands," the therapist can ask, What do you think God may want you to do? and Who do you think God could work through? Finally, the therapist can ask the family, What do you think will happen if this change occurs?

The African retention of faith and the place of religion in daily life (discussed below) have been the most important coping mechanisms for Blacks in the United States. During Kwanzaa, faith is the principle for the last day, when there is a big feast. This highlights the importance of the faith that will be needed to sustain the community throughout the year to come. The ability to work toward change while placing our troubles in God's hands brought Black people through slavery and continues to support us through contemporary forms of racial oppression.

Systems and Social Institutions

Systems theory has been referred to as an "elastic paradigm" (Small, 1995), since principles of general systems theory apply to all forms of social organization by focusing on the interrelatedness of individuals, families, social groups, communities, and societies (Greene & Ephross, 1991). For this reason, systems theory is well suited to incorporating tension and conflict at the societal level as part of the family's context. Understanding the interrelationship of the family with social institutions (e.g., education, religion, and patriarchy) and thus with institutional racism is germane to the therapist's understanding of the functioning of the family system and how to direct efforts toward change. Such understanding is a clear asset in working with Black families, as issues of religion and spirituality, racism, sexism, and oppression, for example, are part and parcel of our life experience.

I cannot leave the subject of families of African descent without focusing on their religion and spirituality directly, although I have touched on both all along. These concepts of African thought are derived from the study of traditional African religions. All of the concepts discussed above have been artificially extricated for examination, but they are more facets of the same lens, so I hope that the reader will come away from this chapter with an appreciation of the essential and central notion of holism in African thought.

Studying the religions is studying the community, and by extension the family, the individual. Predominantly Black church congregations, regardless of denomination, are communities. Predominantly Black church congregations have become an important vehicle for maintaining this critical sense of belongingness, which tends to be eroded by a number of factors, including urbanization.

To understand the place of religion in Black life means looking way beyond Black people's involvement in organized religion. A White Catholic priest assigned to a Black parish commented once that Black people are "the most religious people" he had ever known. He was witnessing the fact that religion is part of the fabric of life for Black people and that he too had become a part of their lives in a way he had not experienced with other congregations. This ability of Black people to "take in" reflects the discussion earlier in this chapter of community reciprocity. Meaning is assigned from within the community—once you have meaning, you are inside. This is true regardless of the nature of Black people's religious affiliation or whether there is a religious affiliation at all. Even those who may identify as not religious are often referring to their not participating in organized religion. A closer examination of their worldview, their explanations of life situations, and so on will often reveal an inherent religious or spiritual perspective, wherein there is an acknowledgement of the Creator who has a meaning in daily life.

When they are involved in organized religion, Black people exert a mutual and reciprocal influence on religious practice. Some obvious examples of this are the integration of spirituals and gospel music, call and response liturgy, the role of the church mother, and referring to congregants as brother and sister. Less obvious, though, is Black people's seamless incorporation of religion in all of life, beyond religious ritual. Black vernacular is loaded with references to the involvement of the Creator in everyday life. "He will not give you more than you can bear." "God didn't bring me this far to leave me." "God don't like ugly." "Not your time, but God's time." "God works in mysterious ways." Rather than "I got lucky," a Black person might say, "I am blessed." Other sayings include: "Too blessed to be stressed" and "Thank God, [who is] good all the time." Family members may be considered to be embodiments of deceased members, at least in certain aspects of their behavior or personality. The therapist may even be viewed as an answer to someone's prayers. It is often in times of trouble that these deep-seeded beliefs become evident.

The notion of joining the family system is most appropriate for working with Black families; the therapist knows when he or she has been allowed in and should manage that relationship appropriately. Over the years, I have become a member of many families. Years after therapy ends, I receive postcards, photos of new babies, wedding pictures, and news. Upon terminating therapy, I assure the family that they can call on me in the future should the need arise, much as they would their family physician. I am like the lawyer on retainer, without the retaining fee. I also give families permission to contact me, apart from a major problem, for a consultation or even to share good news. Moreover, families see me participating in the life of the community. Other family members or members of their community are referred to me, as I am considered an insider with a special role in the community. It is important to manage this relationship so as to continue to be able to be a resource to the family. To become too much family eradicates one's role as therapist; to remain too distant is to offend or betray. Supervision is critical here, particularly for the beginning therapist.

No discussion of Black families is complete without reference to the impact of racism, sexism, and other forms of oppression on Black families. In fact, volumes have been written in the literature of family therapy as well as of many other disciplines—with divergent views. My purpose here is not to detail the impact of oppression but to validate that Black family functioning cannot be understood without taking into account the role, often a destructive role, of larger systems upon that functioning. Ecological family systems approaches and multisystems approaches speak to this most directly. Forces outside of the family exert a powerful influence on the family system, including differentially empowering members within the family system. For the most part, Black families understand this intuitively; their survival in hostile environments has required and developed this capacity to understand power. The therapist needs to understand that, for example, institutional racism in one educational system may define the Black male child as a problem when he would not be considered a problem in another educational system.

Black families do not escape the influence of patriarchy in American society. While Black families are often thought to demonstrate more egalitarian gender role expectations, this should not be assumed to mean that power differences are not an issue. Domestic violence, for example, is no less prevalent in Black families than it is in other families, and overwhelmingly, when violence occurs, males are batterers and women are victims. Gender role flexibility in Black families was reinforced during slavery in this country. Black women were never placed on a pedestal with White women; they were viewed as chattel, as were Black men. The intersection of racism and sexism in this society makes for a very complex and difficult situation for Black men and women in families. Gender expectations can lead Black men to seek the gender privilege afforded to White men and place Black women in the position of being the emotional center of Black families, while racism denies them the privileges and supports to fulfill these questionable roles (Ladner, 1971; Pinderhughes, 1986).

A case can be made that feminist principles are congruent in many ways with the principles of African philosophy described above. Feminist theorists studying women's development from an individual perspective have elucidated the salience of connectedness and relationship, and of care and sensitivity to others, in women's development (Chodorow, 1978; Gilligan, 1982). In this sense, African philosophical thought as outlined here might be cast as "feminine," inasmuch as it emphasizes interdependence and mutuality. Feminist principles are not necessarily systemic. However, inherent in feminist practice is the expansion of the view of the individual to include sociocultural forces such as patriarchy and sexism, and feminist practice cautions against pathologizing behavior that may be a function of external forces that are beyond a woman's control. Similarly, feminist therapists stress the importance of the person of the therapist to the therapeutic process. For example, while acknowledging that there is a power dynamic in the therapeutic relationship, feminists insist that therapists should consciously manage this relationship in a way that empowers clients.

Conclusion

Black family systems therapists are underrepresented in the field of family therapy. While the structural barriers that promote this status quo need to be explored, trainees would benefit from an analysis of the relevance of family systems theory to them and to the families they may treat. Seasoned Black family therapists can and should articulate this for prospective trainees. Students, educators, and administrators should take deliberate steps toward this end. Obviously, training programs should prioritize the inclusion of Black therapists on their faculty. Black therapists should also be involved in training programs as consultants, visiting faculty, and guest presenters. Where this experiential content is lacking and/or where Black faculty is not sufficiently represented, Black and non-Black students and faculty need to advocate.

Reflections, Questions, and Exercises

1. Clinicians can try to identify the impact of their own heritage-based world-view on their clinical approach.

2. Students and clinicians can explore and discuss their own sense of their identity and family of origin, and how these relate to their perspective on families in general and particular families they encounter.

3. Clinicians, supervisors, and trainees can discern their attitudes and feelings toward Black clients, taking into consideration class, ethnicity, age, and gender differences. They might also try to identify how bicultural they and their clients are.

4. Educators, supervisors, and administrators can discuss how best to support students and therapists of color in the institution. (They need to be mindful that some minority students may feel separated from other minorities and/or have ambivalent feelings about their own heritage. This can be very painful and may require processing in an individual supervisory session instead of the trainee group.)

Note

1. *Kum Ba Yah* is the title of a traditional African American spiritual song, and the words mean "Come by here."

References

Aponte, H. (1997). *Bread and spirit: Therapy with the new poor.* New York: Norton.

Ault-Riche, M. (1986). A feminist critique of five schools of family therapy. In J. C. Hansen & M. Ault-Riche (Eds.), *Women and family therapy* (pp. 1–15). Rockville, MD: Aspen.

Billingsley, A. (1988). *Black Families in White America.* New York: Simon & Schuster.

Bograd, M. (1986). A feminist examination of family systems models of violence against women in the family. In J. C. Hansen & M. Ault-Riche (Eds.), *Women and family therapy* (pp. 34–50). Rockville, MD: Aspen.

Boyd-Franklin, N. (1988). *Black families in therapy.* New York: Guilford.

Cantor, D. (1990). *Women as therapists.* New York: Springer.

Chestang, L. (1976). Environmental influences on social functioning: The Black experience. *The diverse society: Implications for social policy* (pp. 59–74). Washington, DC: NASW.

Chodorow, N. (1978). *The reproduction of mothering.* Berkeley: University of California Press.

Du Bois, W. E. B. (1903). *The souls of black folk.* Chicago: A.C. McClurg.

Frasier, E. F. (1939). *The Negro family in the United States.* Chicago: University of Chicago Press.

Gilligan, C. (1982). *In a different voice: Psychological theory and women's development.* Cambridge, MA: Harvard University Press.

Greene, R., & Ephross, P. (1991). *Human behavior theory and social work practice.* New York: Aldine De Gruyter.

Herr, J., & Weakland, J. (1979). *Counseling elders and their families.* New York: Springer.

Karenga, M. R. (2000). About Kwanzaa. *MelaNews.* Retrieved March 9, 2004, from www.melanet.com/kwansaa/whatis.html#history

Ladner, J. (1971). *Tomorrow's tomorrow.* New York: Doubleday.

Lewin, K. (1997). Problems of research in social psychology. *Resolving social conflicts and field theory in social science.* Washington, DC: APA Books.

Martin, J., & Martin, E. (1985). *The helping tradition in the Black family and community.* Silver Spring, MD: NASW.

Mbiti, J. (1969). *African religions and philosophy.* New York: Doubleday.

Mbiti, J. (1990). *African religions and philosophy* (2nd ed.). Oxford, UK: Heinemann.

McGoldrick, M., & Carter, E. (1998). *Ethnicity and family therapy* (2nd ed.). New York: Guilford.

McGoldrick, M., & Carter, E. (Eds.). (1999). *The expanded family life cycle.* Boston: Allyn & Bacon.

Nobles, W. (1974). Africanity: Its role in Black families. *Black Scholar, 5*(9), 10–17.

Papp, P. (1994). *The process of change.* New York: Guilford.

Pennington, D. (1985). Time in African culture. In M. K. Asante & K. W. Asante (Eds.), *African culture: The rhythms of unity.* Westport, CT: Greenwood.

Pinderhughes, E. (1986). Minority women: A nodal position in the functioning of the social system. In J. C. Hansen & M. Ault-Riche (Eds.), *Women and family therapy* (pp. 51–63). Rockville, MD: Aspen.

Small, S. (1995, April). *Family systems and Black families.* Paper presented at the annual meeting of the National Association of Black Social Workers, New York.

Sullivan, M. A. (1994). May the circle be unbroken: The African-American experience of death, dying and spirituality. In J. Parry (Ed.), *A cross-cultural look at death dying and religion.* Chicago: Nelson Hall.

Walker, A. (1984). *In search of our mother's gardens.* New York: Harvest Books.

Walters, M., Carter, B., Papp, P., & Silverstein, O. (1988). *The invisible web: Gender patterns in family relationships.* New York: Guilford.

17

Family Therapy From a Hindu Indian Worldview*

*Nithyakala Karuppaswamy
and Rajeswari Natrajan*

L et us begin with a story. A passenger was completely lost between the decks of a great Atlantic liner. He finally ran into a steward and asked for help in finding his cabin. The steward asked, "What is the number of your cabin, sir?" "I couldn't tell you, but I'd know it at once, because it has a lighthouse outside the porthole." This wry excerpt expresses our struggle as Hindu women from India who came to the United States to be trained as marriage and family therapists. In an environment that is primarily Eurocentric, dealing predominantly with American clients, our reference points changed and landscapes shifted as we searched for a cohesive unity of Indian and U.S. cultures to use in conceptualizing our clients' world and our interventions. We had to reexamine our philosophies of change, which had hitherto been rooted in our culture of origin. We also had to become mindful of the assumptions about human nature, self, family, and health that we had taken for granted in India but seemed inapplicable in this culture.

When we were first confronted with this new culture, we found ourselves challenging our beliefs and assumptions. There was a sense of disorientation

---

*The authors shared equally in the writing of this chapter.

and confusion. What we were talking about made sense to us, but it did not quite make sense to others, such as our colleagues and teachers—often it seemed like we were on parallel roads, missing each other's points of view. In the process of being trained as family therapists, we experienced the scary feeling that in order to be good therapists we might have to change our ways of being. This chapter is the result of our interactions in U.S. culture, and it is a way of reaffirming our beliefs and our ways of being. Our purpose is not to pass judgment on any worldview; rather, it is to describe how we were able to affirm our cultural beliefs and ourselves so that we could function well as Hindu Indian family therapists within a Eurocentric culture.

We believe that no matter which worldview we come from, Eurocentric or Hindu Indian, we eventually walk some of the same paths and reach similar goals. In this chapter, we explain the process we went through in defining our cultural assumptions and contrasting them with the assumptions of Eurocentric culture. Clarifying the differences in the worldviews of the two cultures helped us to understand how our Hindu Indian worldview could help us work effectively with our clients, as well as why it felt like we were traveling parallel paths with our colleagues and teachers. We have found that in reaffirming our beliefs, we can be open to challenges from others and challenge ourselves without the fear of having to give up our way of being and lose our identities.

Personal Backgrounds

Nithyakala Karuppaswamy (N.K.)

I am a woman from the city of Chennai in southern India. I was born a Hindu and have been deeply influenced by the spiritual philosophy of Hinduism rather than its religiosity. Currently I live in Indiana. I am a person with a disability, am the eldest of five, and wrestle constantly to maintain my sense of self and still be nested in a close-knit web of family. By the standards of Western family therapy models, my family might be described as enmeshed. My professional identity has shifted from that of a counseling psychologist with an individual perspective to a family therapist struggling to become more systemic in my therapeutic approaches. I see myself chiefly as a therapist and a teacher who is currently adorning new layers of identity as an international student in America, a minority, a woman of color, a social constructivist, and a feminist. All these multiple experiences and identities have shaped my specific worldview. They have resulted in my becoming more sensitized to issues such as emergence of the individual self in all of its facets, balancing the individualistic *I-ness* with a collective *we-ness,* searching for the meaning of existence in the face of adversities, expanding choices, and balancing wants with responsibilities. While I understand the pursuit for acceptance and happiness, I also sense the paradoxical value of pain and alienation as stimulants for growth. I appreciate the costs and benefits of inequities in gender, status, culture, ethnicity, and power. These sensitizing issues have a remarkable impact on the way I conceptualize my self, the world, relationships, and therapy. As my contexts change, the person I am changes also, and there are modifications to my worldview.

Rajeswari Natrajan (R.N.)

I am a 27-year-old woman, and I am also from Chennai. I belong to the Brahmin caste, a privileged caste in the Hindu community. I am the youngest of three in a family that is very traditional and conservative in values but prides itself on being highly educated (Western style) and progressive, technologically and materially. Among the many significant events in my life, the one that has had the most recent and a deep influence on me is meeting and committing to my fiancé, who belongs to another caste. This has been a bitter pill for my family to swallow, as they have to step down the social ladder to accept someone of a lower caste into the fold of the family. This event has opened a Pandora's box of caste prejudices and discrimination. Over the past 2 years we have been dealing with this painful issue. My impatience to resolve the issue with my family has not been rewarded. I realize now that healing cannot happen in haste, and that I have to find the intimacy in the process of having dialogues with the significant people in my life. I carry into my therapy these lessons that I have learned from life.

Being a Hindu in the spiritual sense, the Advaita (nondual) philosophy of the Hindu religion (Warrier, 1983) has impacted the way I see systems and relationships. I do not see myself as separate from my teachers, students, and clients. I see myself as a person and self who, under the garbs of a student, teacher, partner, relative, and therapist, witnesses the journeys of other people and selves. I walk the paths with those I encounter and try to understand and validate our journeys in life.

Our Relationship

It is important at this juncture to acknowledge the role of our relationship in shaping this chapter. Our constant dialogues over the years have been instrumental not only in locating the long-disappeared lighthouse but also in validating each other in our confusion, quests, and visions. Our relationship has also helped us challenge our worldviews and deal with our questions when our worldviews and therapeutic philosophies collided with those of our Eurocentric peers, mentors, and clients. We have served as each other's mirror, and we have each tried to grapple with our own image represented in the other. It is therefore fitting to say that the thoughts and ideas presented in this chapter were nurtured within and owe their existence to our relationship.

Worldviews and Views of Self in Western and Hindu Contexts

The cultures of the West and the East have been dichotomized by researchers within such broad labels as *individualist* versus *collectivist, independent* versus *interdependent, egocentric* versus *sociocentric, individuated* or *differentiated* versus *diffuse* or *collateral* (Dhawan, Roseman, Naidu, Thapa, & Rettek, 1995; Miller, 1994). These differences have a profound impact on the evolution of one's worldview. *Worldview* is a person's most comprehensive idea of nature, self, time, and society. It represents the cognitive and existential aspects of a given ethnic group (Ibrahim, 1991). It can be described as the way clients and therapists frame all information and the situations that occur in their lives.

Many theorists have presented models of worldview. Kluckhohn (1951, 1959) proposed a broad framework for understanding worldview that consists of five universal or existential categories: human nature, social relationship, nature, time orientation, and action orientation. For the purpose of this chapter, we have used the worldview model of Kluckhohn to explore the differences in the worldviews we have experienced as Hindu Indian family therapists in our encounter with our Eurocentric peers, instructors, and clients. Our exploration is by no means exhaustive and should be seen as a work in progress.

Western and Hindu Indian worldviews differ in their assumptions about the following:

1. Human nature, the nature of social relationships (Eurocentric worldview - individualistic; Hindu worldview - hierarchical and mutual),

2. Locus of control (Eurocentric worldview - internal locus of control; Hindu worldview - external locus of control), and

3. The concept of *action* (Eurocentric worldview - doing; Hindu worldview - being) (Ibrahim, 1991).

Based on these differences in conceptualization, which we explore in more detail below, the two cultures may offer distinctive solutions to universal human dilemmas.

Assumptions About Human Nature

We explore this assumption using three interconnected themes: (1) self as divine, (2) coexistence of good and evil, and (3) isomorphism.

Self as Divine

In Hindu philosophy, each element in this universe, the human self included, is considered part of the divine, variously called "the Infinite," "the Absolute," "the Godhead," or "the Brahman" (Isherwood, 1961). The self-realization that "I am Divine," or *Aham Brahmasmi,* or "the Absolute is within me" is perhaps most challenging for the Christian world to accept. At a certain level, this appears extraordinarily self-inflationary. Hindus believe that what we search for in the outside ultimately lies within us. So, the individual self is essentially considered to have the same nature as the divine self. In the words of Joseph Campbell (1988), "You are god in your deepest identity." According to this worldview, all life, no matter what its form, is part of the divine and has its rightful place and function to perform. From this point of view, one senses the importance of not only the self but also the other. The Hindu philosophy of considering the core self of an individual as divine is in conflict with the Christian beliefs about sin and how individuals have to redeem themselves of their sins.

Clinical application of the assumption. I (R.N.) was working with Fanny, a woman in her late 40s. (Names and some identifying information have been changed in this chapter to protect client confidentiality.) She was going through her second divorce and losing her eyesight due to a degenerative disease. The divorce was turning out to be a long drawn-out process, and Fanny said that she was feeling stuck. Her grief was deep, and she was very tearful during the majority of our sessions. She was trying to get back to school and work on a doctoral degree. During therapy, she revealed how she was back to a place where she was asking herself, "What am I going to do when I grow up?" My client drew an image of this long journey that she had to undertake before she could consider herself as "having arrived" or "feeling accomplished."

Given the circumstances, I saw my client as a very resilient woman who, with hope and help, could get control of her life again. I could have encouraged her to rebuild her life and helped her in the process by making concrete action plans. However, from my Hindu Indian theoretical persuasion that propounds "God is not other than oneself," I considered my client already a perfected human being. From this point of view, she did not have to travel any further in search of her pot of gold. The pot of gold was within her at that moment and she just had to realize it. In my work with her, then, my emphasis was less on what she needed to "do" to reach her goal and more on helping her understand that she had already "arrived," that she had her pot of gold and just needed to realize it.

Coexistence of Good and Evil

At this juncture, it would be fitting to explore the meaning of the word *divine* further. The word *divine* in the West has positive connotations associated with it. It is good, sacred, pure, gentle, powerful, merciful, and filled with grace. The *divine* or *good* is considered distinct and opposite *evil* in the Judeo-Christian belief system. However, for Hindus, the divine is a fusion of good and evil, creation and destruction, chaos and order. Advaita philosophy propounds that opposites coexist (e.g., joy and misery, high and low). In essence, the opposites are considered to be in the nature of each other, for example, *good* is considered to be in the nature of *evil* and vice versa. One has no meaning without the other, like light has no meaning without dark. Therefore, in therapy we believe in acknowledging and normalizing the unmentionable parts of human existence that are considered bad. For example, feeling aggressive toward your children, having sexual fantasies about someone other than your spouse or partner, and having a sexual orientation toward members of your sex are some of the unmentionables that we have to acknowledge in any relationship, as the following case example highlights.

Clinical application of the assumption. I (R.N.) was working with Mark and Dena, who had been together for 6 years. They started coming to therapy because Dena had had an affair. In therapy, Dena reported that she had been unhappy and resentful in the relationship for a long time. A theme that came up repeatedly in our sessions was their belief that healthy relationships are those in which people don't hurt each other so badly. The couple expressed their doubts about staying in the relationship. After much discussion, I explained to the couple how unhappiness, discontent, hurtfulness, and so on are an inherent part of every relationship, even the good ones, and how affairs and the fear of affairs are the unmentionable realities of every couple's life and do not necessarily make a relationship good or bad. This seemed to calm the couple quite a bit and normalized their fears, which in turn helped us continue with the therapy process.

Isomorphism

Another primary doctrine of Hinduism regarding human nature is unity (Woodroffe, 1966). In this philosophy, the collective consciousness (also called God) is said to be like a river, and the individual self to be small scoops of water being temporarily separated from the river. The nature of the water in the scoop is similar or isomorphic to the water in the river, which is again isomorphic to the nature of water in another scoop. In essence, the *I* is not considered to be different from *you* or *we*. A story that eloquently brings out this idea follows.

> The master was strolling with some of his disciples along the bank of a river. He said, "See how the fish keep darting about wherever they please. That's what they really enjoy." A stranger overhearing that remark said, "How do you know what fish enjoy—you're not a fish?" The disciples gasped at what they took for impudence. The master smiled at what he recognized as a fearless spirit of enquiry. He replied affably, "And you, my friend, how do you know I am not a fish—you are not I?" The disciples laughed, taking this to be a well-deserved rebuff. Only the stranger was struck by its depth. All day he pondered it, then came to the monastery to say, "Maybe you are not as different from the fish as I thought. Or I from you." (Mello, 1996, p. 28)

Clinical application of the assumption. I (N.K.) was working with Ben, who had come from a strong Catholic background. His parents had repressed any talk about sexuality, as well as insisted on careful avoidance of thoughts, feelings, and behaviors that were considered "sinful" according to the Catholic faith. In time, my client rebelled and, in his words, "left the church." He had not been a practicing Catholic for almost 15 years when, during a session, he shared a dream in which he was taking a ride with the Pope and there was an attempt to assassinate the Pope. In Ben's dream, he was the chauffer whose split-second decision would result in the life or death of the Pope. The dream and what it revealed led us to a dialogue regarding his denial and reexamination of a deeply ingrained part of his "religious self." He asked me numerous questions about my own faith, and how I saw good and evil. I explained that as a Hindu I had a tendency to see human nature as having the potential for both good and evil. Hitler and Buddha show us the range on the spectrum within which humanity can function. I shared with my client that as I try to realize my positive potential, I also need to acknowledge my shadowy, negative side and struggle with it just as he does in his life. The fact that the client and I were from different faiths gave us the opportunity to have a dialogue about our religious and spiritual beliefs and struggles, while providing space for the client to examine his rebellious stage and his current need to reconnect to his spiritual self. We come from different parts of the globe, are of different genders, and have different religious orientations, yet our search to find a meaningful holistic synthesis of our biopsychosocial, familial, and spiritual self was isomorphic. In fact, our differences provided me with a not-knowing stance in his eyes that enhanced his ability to deconstruct this deep spiritual struggle and come to a resolution.

Assumptions About the Nature of Social Relationships

In this section, as family therapy trainees, we have decided to focus specifically on the nature of familial relationships.

I (N.K.) was 34 years old when I first came to this country for my clinical training. Until that time I had lived with my parents and siblings in India. It is usual for both men and women to live with their family of origin until the time they marry (and even after marriage some might set up homes with their family of origin or other extended families). However, it was understandable that my White American instructor and peers, coming from a culture that expects young adults to leave home at 18 to set up an independent and autonomous life for themselves, asked me, "Why were you so dependent on your parents? Don't you think it's time for you to become differentiated from your family of origin?" This left me feeling confused. I was already mindful of having left my aging parents alone back in India at a time when I felt I should be providing support and care for them. I was struggling to balance my individual need to focus on my career development with my desire to be a supportive daughter. At this juncture, the reactions and questions of my American instructor and peers made me wonder whether there was something wrong with my life. I asked myself, "Am I too dependent?" Slowly, my confusion gave way to comprehension. What can be regarded as dysfunctional and functional in families and individuals is intrinsically rooted in the cultural contexts in which we live. It was not a question of whether I was right or they were—it was a question of whether I could balance gaining greater independence with maintaining interdependence with my family.

As mentioned above, perceptions of the self in the two worldviews are significantly different. In Western culture, the idea of separateness is considered central, contrary to the connectedness that is more usual for members of a system in Hindu culture. Roland (1987) wrote of the difference between the familial and the individualized self. Roland (1989) defined the *individualized self* as an "individualistic I-ness with relatively self-contained outer ego boundaries, sharp differentiation between inner images of self and other, and considerable social individuation orienting the person toward relatively autonomous functioning, inner separateness, and initiative" (p. 240). The *familial self* he defined as an individual attaining a sense of self-identity within the context of his or her relationship with the family. Contrary to the *I-ness* that is characteristic of the individualized self, Indian families experience a predominant sense of what Roland (1989) termed *we-ness*.

A metaphor helps explain the difference between the individualized self of U.S. culture and the familial self of Hindu Indian culture. The family is seen as a Banyan tree in Hindu culture. The main tree gives ropelike offshoots from its branches. When these offshoots touch the ground, they take root and become a supportive trunk balancing the tree. Slowly, as the tree grows, more and more second- and third-generation trunks become the anchor for the aging parent tree. Thus, the whole banyan family are intricately connected to each other. The banyan family are nurtured by the parent tree and depend on each other for sustenance. They are never completely free, yet they are able to withstand the elements of nature through their combined strength. On the other hand, the majestic redwoods can be seen as representing families in the American culture. The redwood personifies individualistic values—autonomous, strong, self-sufficient, nurturing itself, and withstanding the forces of nature for decades by its own individual strength.

Clinical application of the assumption. Jen, a single mother, was referred to me (R.N.) by the school system. The school counselor related to me that the family was extremely close knit, to the point that it was dysfunctional. Jen confirmed the counselor's diagnosis and reported that she was taking care of not just her son but also her mother and sister in the same household. She reported that her mother had her own house, but she refused to stay there. Jen stated that she was extremely close to her mother but needed some space and peace of mind. She was in tears as she related how she had to fight for time with her son. Jen reported that her mother got involved in activities that she (Jen) considered special between her and her son. Jen's goal was to convince her mother to return to her own house, so that they could relate to and interact with each other better.

I worked with Jen to help her develop appropriate boundaries with her mother. I acknowledged Jen's desire to stay close to her mother while at the same time maintaining some level of exclusivity in the parent-child bond with her son. From my philosophical background, my work with her included helping her see that it is an honor and privilege to have her mother involved in her son's upbringing. In Hindu Indian families, as in families of many ethnic groups (such as African Americans, Native Americans, and Hispanics), no one person or couple has exclusive rights to the child. A child's upbringing is everybody's responsibility, and the extended family has an equal involvement in shaping the child. From this perspective, the son had much to gain through the shared nurturing from his grandmother and his mother.

Assumptions About Action and Change

Change is the only constant in this universe, and it is the main focus of therapy. However, "change" is a double-edged sword. There is both a positive and a negative connotation to the word *change*. It can be seen as a leap into the unknown. There is risk involved and an element of fear, and, yes, there are rewards.

Certain conditions exist in life that are beyond our human ability to change, no matter how painful and debilitating they are. I will use the example of my disability to explore this characteristic of change. I (N.K.) began developing my theory of change here, because the first realization of my conscious life was that no matter how much I wished or how hard I worked, I could not change some realities of my life. In Hindu culture, part of the conceptualization of change and action is the acknowledgment and acceptance of life as it is. Hindus are often seen as having a rather fatalistic perception of life, because of the Hindu belief in destiny and the acceptance of life as given. Parallel to this concept of accepting life as given is Kluckhohn's (1959) paradigm of "being" versus "doing." While the Eurocentric worldview places great value on doing, taking concerted efforts to bring about change in life by controlling life and taking the initiative to change, Hindu Indian culture places greater emphasis on being. However, this state of being is not a passive acceptance that results in effortlessness. A Hindu has different choices in how to react to a specific life condition. For example, I could hate my disability. I could let it destroy me and become a victim of it. I could feel inadequate because of it and respond by overcompensating. Or I could accept it as my friend and constant companion. This friend could open doors of experiences for me that would otherwise remain beyond the realms of my awareness. In reality, I have been through all these stages in my ongoing relationship with my disability. However, this process of accommodation is not a linear one. Each new phase of my life brings new challenges and a new awareness of what I have lost or can never be. However, these phases also give me hope and make me aware that my disability opens me up to new experiences.

The idea of free will is at the core of an individualized society, like U.S. society, that prizes autonomy. Free will places the responsibility for change in the hands of the person who makes the attempt to change. The more interdependent Hindu society does not support this idea. Hindu philosophy suggests that all of us have conditions that cannot be changed no matter how much we wish them to change. In executing free will, Hindus have to be exquisitely aware of interconnections and how their actions have consequences for the whole system. The repercussions or consequences of all individual actions are believed to be felt somewhere and at some time. The Bhagavad Gita, a sacred Hindu text, talks about the concept of *karma-palan* (Munshi, 1978). According to this concept, it is nature's law that individuals inevitably experience the consequences of their actions, both good and bad.

This brings up an important question for us as Hindu Indian therapists in training and working within a Eurocentric society. What should be the focus of therapy? Should the focus of therapy be how best to manage what cannot be changed? Or should it be change per se? We realized that it is a question not of either/or but of both/and. If we focus on change per se, it is important to caution our clients about the inevitability of consequences. We believe in providing a context within which clients can encounter some unchangeable realities of their lives. Some of these realities need to have their existence acknowledged, some need celebration, some need grief and homage, some need acceptance, and some need a concerted effort made to modify them.

Clinical application of the assumption. I (N.K.) saw Sharon and John, who were parents of two preteen children. Sharon had been a stay-at-home-mom throughout the marriage. Three years before they came to see me, she had gone back to school to obtain a master's degree in school counseling. She attended evening classes 4 days a week. Most nights, Sharon returned home late, after the children were in bed and John had completed most of the housework. The children complained about never seeing their mother. John was struggling to cope with the additional family responsibilities along with his work demands. Sharon felt torn between the stresses of school and missing her children's childhood. She also felt left out of the close tie that was forming between the children and their dad.

In this case example, through the changes she made in her life, Sharon was gaining greater autonomy, power, and resources that in the long run would benefit not only her but also her family, as well as lead to a more equitable relationship with her husband. However, these apparent positive changes were not without some negative consequences. These consequences included seeing less of her children, missing parts of their childhood, watching her husband replace her as the nurturing parent, increasing stress in her marital relationship due to changing roles, and so on. Thus, one change made by Sharon produced consequences through out the family system. I (N.K.) worked with this couple to help them understand that choices are made in the context of relationships, families, and the society at large. It was important for this family to be aware of the consequences of their choices and take responsibility for them. From the Hindu perspective, an important message for clients is knowing that no matter what people choose, there will be consequences.

An important assumption about change in Hindu Indian philosophy, which follows from the above discussion about consequences, is the inevitability of pain and the value of sitting with anxiety and pain. Existentialism recognizes that all life is marked by suffering and loss, which mock our attempts to achieve a full and happy life (Moon, 1990). In this worldview, pain, frustration, guilt, and anxiety are seen as unavoidable in our journey through life (Moon, 1990). However, one of the characteristics we have observed in our Eurocentric peers and clients in the United States is the concerted effort they make in the pursuit of happiness. They see pain, discomfort, and anxiety as anathema and to be avoided and replaced by pleasure. As therapists with a Hindu Indian worldview, we believe that when anxiety and pain increase, the system should not be hasty to resolve the problem. We believe that sitting with anxiety and pain helps the person to attain clarity and resolution and prevents destructive actions. A biological metaphor for this principle of "sitting with anxiety" is cells dividing. When cells undergo division, the initial stage involves a period of intense activity. This would be analogous to the rise of anxiety in the client system when a problem comes up. The final stage, which is cell division, does not occur immediately after the build-up stage. Cells go through a phase called the S-Phase or the synthesis phase. During this time, they are neither dormant nor dividing. It is a period of synthesis for the cells, and they spend the longest period of their being in this phase before they start to express themselves and to divide. Similarly, we believe that the client system should spend time sitting with anxiety and pain and resist premature resolution of a problem for the sake of ending discomfort. Our belief in this principle is based on the fact that in confronting their anxieties, pain, and discomfort, clients gain greater clarity, understanding, and validation regarding the depth and nuances of their problem and how it affects their system.

In order for the client system to be able to hold anxiety and pain, we believe that the therapist should facilitate a safe environment. In Hindu mythology there is a story about the *devas* (celestial beings). The *devas*, in the pursuit of the nectar that gave immortality, began churning the ocean (Chandrasekhar, 2001). During the process of churning the ocean, among the several things that emerged were noxious gases and poison. Unable to stand the noxious gases, the *devas* ran to God. They told God that they wanted to stop churning the ocean so that they could stop the pain and breathe again. God asked them to continue churning the ocean because the nectar that gave immortality could not be obtained without some endurance of pain. And God offered to hold the poison in his throat so that the *devas* could have some relief from the intolerable noxious fumes. The story ends with the *devas* obtaining the pot of nectar after prolonged churning of the ocean. This story serves as a metaphor for what the therapeutic environment has to be. The therapist must be a crucible for the clients, to help them hold their anxiety and pain. Before resolution or expression of affect, the self or the system must learn to hold its anxiety and tolerate it so that it will give information and clarity about what is going on (Keiley, 1991).

Clinical application of the assumption. As I (R.N.) worked with Dena and Mark, there were very intense sessions. Mark wanted Dena to move in with him, but Dena was still not ready to do so. This situation continued for a long time. Mark expressed feeling helpless and insecure because he was not sure whether Dena really wanted him. He was haunted by the fact that Dena had had an affair in the past. Dena was tearful and said that she was very scared and confused about what she wanted and that she hated herself for making Mark go through pain. Coming from my Hindu Indian perspective, I did not see this intense pain as negative. I believed that I should not move the couple into resolution too soon. I decided to let myself and the couple stay in that place of helplessness and not knowing. I narrated the Hindu myth about the *devas* to them, and I said that it is scary when you are churning and noxious gases are coming out of the ocean. Meaningful facets of their relationship and their conflicted feelings for each other were being churned out during this stage of sitting with anxiety. During this difficult phase of therapy, I assured them that I would support them to hold the toxicity of the issues they were revealing. I said that I did not know when the nectar was going to come out, however, and that they had to keep churning, trust the process, and believe that they were going to get the nectar. This story seemed not only to validate their fear and confusion but also to calm them down.

Reflections, Questions, and Exercises

1. We would like to first suggest the implications—for all international students of marriage and family therapy—of our working to incorporate our Hindu Indian worldview into our practice of therapy. We believe that it is important to acknowledge how our assumptions have affected our functioning in the Eurocentric culture. We need not only to be aware of but also to clarify our assumptions and juxtapose these assumptions with those of the dominant culture. Often, in search of our identity, we as international students may be

too quick to either accept or reject one worldview at the cost of the other. In the short run, it may alleviate our anxiety and help us define ourselves as part of either the in-group or the out-group. However, this may not be true synthesis or integration of our experiences. In the process of defining our identity as therapists it may be important for us to sit with our anxieties and struggle with the ambiguities that come with handling different worldviews at the same time. We believe that doing so will help us be more flexible and provide us with more tools to work with diverse clienteles. We also believe that it will help us accept the "good" and the "bad" of each culture and truly be multicultural in our work.

2. In research that I (N.K.) conducted, I asked Hindu Indian women to come up with a metaphor for themselves. One participant described herself as "water" taking the shape of the container in which it is kept or the terrain in which it is found. She said,

> Water takes the shape of whatever container you pour it in. And that's how I see myself. Coming here [to the United States] has been a big thing, but I have adapted to it. . . . The emphasis is on adapting and I would also like to say the ease of adapting. . . . I did not have to force myself to adapt. Water is the only thing I could see that expresses . . . the fluidity of my adaptation.

These words mirror our experiences as therapists adapting to a primarily Eurocentric program and its social milieu. Sometimes our White peers and counterparts see this ease of adaptation and tendency to merge with the environment as an indication of low self-esteem or lack of assertiveness. What this implies for trainers and supervisors in these circumstances is the wisdom of not making quick assumptions about international students. Instead, trainers and supervisors might sit with their discomfort while encouraging international students to articulate the aspects of their worldview that lead to their "nonassertive" behavior. The students might need time, space, and safety for this articulation, which the supervisor can provide. This may help students struggle with the conflicts they experience in synthesizing contradictory worldviews. In such a dialogue, a richer, more complex integration of the different worldviews of the training program and the trainee may occur, benefiting both.

References

Campbell, J. (1988). *The power of myth: Mask of eternity.* (Video recording with Bill Moyer). New York: Mystic Fire Video.

Chandrasekhar, H. R. (2001). *Tales from Indian epics.* Columbia, MO: South Asia Books.

Dhawan, N., Roseman, I., Naidu, R. K., Thapa, K., & Rettek, S. I. (1995). Self-concept across two cultures: India and the United States. *Journal of Cross-Cultural Psychology, 26*(6), 606–621.

Ibrahim, F. (1991). Contribution of cultural worldview to generic counseling and development. *Journal of Counseling and Development, 70,* 13–19.

Isherwood, C. (1961). *Vedanta for the Western world*. Hollywood, CA: Vedanta.

Keiley, M. K. (1991). *The role of affect and agency in addiction and recovery*. Manuscript submitted for publication.

Kluckhohn, C. (1951). Values and value orientation in the theory of action. In T. Parsons & F. A. Shields (Eds.), *Toward a general theory of action* (pp. 388–433). Cambridge, MA: Harvard University Press.

Kluckhohn, C. (1959). Toward a comparison of value emphasis in different cultures. In D. L. White (Ed.), *The state of social sciences* (pp. 116–132). Chicago: University of Chicago Press.

Mello, A. de (1996). *Song of the bird*. Anand, Gujarat, India: Gujarat Sahitya Prakash.

Miller, J. G. (1994). Cultural diversity in the morality of caring: Individually oriented versus duty-based interpersonal moral code. *Cross-cultural Research, 28*(1), 3–39.

Moon, B. (1990). *Existential art therapy: The canvas mirror*. Springfield, IL: Charles C. Thomas.

Munshi, K. M. (1978). *Krishnaavatara: The magic flute*. New Delhi: Sage.

Roland, A. (1987). The familial self, individualized self, and the transcendent self: Psychoanalytic reflections on India and America. *Psychoanalytic Review, 74*(2), 237–250.

Roland, A. (1989). *In search of self in India and Japan: Towards cross-cultural psychology*. Princeton, NJ: Princeton University Press.

Warrier, A. G. K. (1983). Bhagavad Gita Bhasya of Sankara. Madras, India: Sri Ramakrishna Math.

Woodroffe, J. (1966). *The world as power*. Madras, India: Ganesh.

18

Developing Culturally Appropriate, Evidence-Based Treatments for Interventions With Ethnic Minority Populations

Melanie Domenech-Rodríguez
and Elizabeth Wieling

There is a lack of conceptual, theoretical, and methodological frameworks that appropriately position families and communities of color within a historical, political, and socioeconomic context that accounts for their experiences. This has led to gross disparities in mental health services. The neglect of families of color—whether or not it is overt—has contributed to the perpetuation of misunderstandings, oppressive attitudes, and, ultimately, poorly designed programs of intervention and psychotherapy. Historically, race, culture, and ethnicity have not been seriously addressed in clinical and scientific literature.

Authors' Note: The authors would like to acknowledge the dedicated mentoring of Dr. Marion Forgatch, without whom this work would not have been possible. We would also like to acknowledge Dr. Guillermo Bernal for his mentorship and suggestions on the collaborative model. The preparation of this chapter was supported by NIMH grant 1-K01-MH066297-1A1 to Dr. Domenech-Rodríguez, and NIMH grant 1-K01-MH64506-01A2 to Dr. Wieling.

A report published by the National Institute of Mental Health (NIMH) addressing race and ethnicity in a multicultural society identified several factors as primary contributors to the current disparities in mental health services. Among the factors listed were: (a) the scarcity of empirically tested preventive interventions and psychotherapy treatments available for use with ethnic minority families; (b) no psychotherapy research meeting the basic criteria for demonstrating efficacy for ethnic minority populations; and (c) the use of inadequate or irrelevant research questions that will affect mental health care delivery for the country's increasingly diverse population (National Institute of Mental Health, 1999).

Conducting culturally sensitive and responsive research in a multicultural context is a monumental undertaking. The layers of complexity are almost endless as one considers potential factors influencing the research study. The historical and political context, sources of funding, institutional affiliation, research bias, individual and community bias, research focus, and specific research methods being employed are only a few of these factors. Decisions ranging from which research topics and populations merit investigation to which systems of communication should be employed in a study have profound implications on outcome. As researchers struggle to define the parameters around language in research studies, all too often *culture, ethnicity, race,* and *minority status* are used interchangeably. These terms are seldom well defined or placed within a conceptual framework, and the methodological consequences of this neglect are rarely considered. Because these terms are socially constructed—rather than biologically fixed—it is crucial that researchers be clear on how they are employing these terms when conducting research involving communities of color. It is beyond the scope of this chapter to include an in-depth discussion on the various domains influencing research with populations of color. However, we hope to introduce some of the issues involved in developing evidence-based treatments with ethnic minority groups and will use examples from our current work to illustrate this process. This chapter addresses some of the etiological and methodological issues associated with planning, conducting, and disseminating family-based prevention and intervention research programs with ethnic minority communities.

Personal Backgrounds

Melanie Domenech Rodríguez (M.D.R.)

I was born in Puerto Rico, the daughter of a graduate student father and a high school-educated mother. During those early years, money was tight, but over time my father became a college professor, and my mother went to college, then law school, and ultimately became a judge and a high ranking official in the Puerto Rican government. My mother's achievements are particularly noteworthy given her status as a Cuban immigrant in Puerto Rico. It is fair to say that I experienced multiple social strata during my childhood, and again as I struggled through college, graduate school, and finally a placement in an academic post. I am the daughter of activists, and as such, was well versed at a very early age in politics, especially Marxism, and social injustices. However, I had much to learn.

I remember vividly the precise moment when I learned about differences in the conception of race in Puerto Rico and the United States. I was a first-year college student dealing with a difficult schedule, my newfound independence, and the famous "freshman 15" (i.e., the number of pounds many students gain in their first year of college). As is typical on college campuses, intellectual discussions were commonplace. I lived in the "ethnic minority" campus of my undergraduate institution, and thus it was not unusual for the intellectual discussions to turn to issues of race and ethnicity. It was during one of these conversations with two African American women (one of whom was my roommate) and a Latina (whom Puerto Ricans from the island would have derogatorily labeled a "Nuyorican"[1]) that I learned I was not White. We were talking about privilege, and I was acknowledging my privilege due to the color of my skin. After I asserted that I was "White," a silence befell the room and I could almost touch the hurt and anger emanating from my peers. I asked out loud, "What exactly just happened?" They informed me that I was not White and would never be White. This is when I learned that Whiteness in the United States is not linked to the literal color of your skin, as it is in Puerto Rico, but rather to the ethnic and cultural background a person of any given color possesses. This incident led me to reexamine my place in U.S. society and to observe people and their interactions in a different way.

Since this incident, I have continued to examine the role of culture and ethnicity in my personal and professional contexts. I have been sensitized to recognize people's comments regarding race and ethnicity in a different light, and I have come to realize the profound impact that overt and covert racism has on the lives of others. Both forms of racism affect the people targeted and the people targeting. While the effect of racism on those being targeted is readily apparent, those doing the targeting are also affected; for example, what opportunities are parents taking away from their children when they discourage their children from playing with "dark" children? I have come full circle from that conversation in the dormitory room to realize that I have quite a large amount of privilege that comes from the lightness of my skin and the nearly unaccented English that often leads people in the western United States where I live to ask if I am from "back East." I have come to realize that this privilege puts me in a unique position to effect change for people with whom I share a similar national and/or ethnic background and who have not been as privileged as I am to be undetectable and thus unthreatening in many professional and personal contexts.

As I continue to move along in my professional development, I continually struggle and grow with issues of race and ethnicity. One such issue is how my race and ethnicity are perceived by others as my professional status changes (from first-year college student to professor), as I live in the United States for longer periods of time (as a recent immigrant versus a 15-year veteran), and as I work with Latino/a populations that have a different national origin than my own. Where I live, the majority of Latino/as are of Mexican origin. I recognize that different national origins represent differences in cultural values, beliefs, and practices. I see the hesitation in the eyes of my clients and research participants who are of Mexican origin, and the question—sometimes explicitly stated—of why am I interested in working with *Mexicanos?* My answer has evolved over time, and presently I would say that I recognize that our needs as Latino/as are homogeneous in certain contexts. I would not venture to use an ethnic gloss[2] across contexts, but I do assert that there are common experiences among Latino/as in the United States, both for recent immigrants and long-term or U.S.-born residents; for example: the exposure to racism and prejudice, poverty, low levels of utilization of mental health services, to name a few. The combination of understanding my privilege, maximizing my skills, and feeling fellowship with others of Latino origin fuel my desire to continue working with Latino/a populations. My personal goal of positively impacting as many people as possible in my efforts has shaped my specific interest in preventive interventions.

Elizabeth Wieling (E.W.)

I am a multiethnic woman with dual citizenship—in the United States and Brazil. I was born here but raised in the Amazon region of Brazil, and I returned to the United States at age 16 to pursue my college education. Growing up in one of the most economically and socially polarized countries in the world made me aware at a very young age of issues of social injustice, prejudice, and discrimination. I soon realized that even having access to education privileged me over a large sector of the population. I also became aware of the deep-rooted gender discrimination that existed in most institutional, cultural, and religious aspects of my life growing up.

My ethnic identity was the source of another conundrum. Even though I have brown skin and have relatives who are of African and Indigenous heritage, I was told I was White like my father. In Brazil, social status and wealth often have the power to override the disadvantages associated with the color of people's skin and deem them "White." When I moved to the United States, being White was no longer an option, despite my economic position and the fact that biologically I am half White. It was then that I had to rediscover my identity as a multiethnic woman. Interestingly, I was not fully accepted by Whites or by other ethnic minority groups. I often felt pressured by other minorities to identify as Latina or Black but not as a multiethnic or multiracial person, which meant a denial of my White heritage.

I believe these experiences with ethnicity, gender, and nationality have helped sensitize me to broader diversity issues. I developed a passion for under-standing the experiences of marginalized groups and pursued a doctoral degree in marriage and family therapy with the specific intent of using systems theory, and later postmodern, social constructionist, feminist, and multicultural frame-works to reach out to families that I saw as being systematically neglected and oppressed. I strongly believe in the importance of recognizing my privilege, as well as my position as a woman and a multiethnic individual, and being an agent of change at personal, social, and political levels.

My clinical and research experiences with populations and communities of color in the United States have had a profound impact on my identity. One of the most significant challenges I have encountered is related to the intersection of multiple aspects of "myself" as multiethnic, feminist, teacher, activist, interventionist, researcher, clinician, community member, and so on. I continue to learn about political posturing and the articulation of each of these domains across personal and professional arenas. For example, I have become increasingly aware of what might motivate me to identify as "multi-ethnic" as opposed to "Latina" in different contexts, as well as the repercus-sions of openly claiming a feminist, antihomophobic, anticapitalist ideology. This is relevant because owning my privilege and voicing "who I am and what I stand for" is isomorphically related to free expression, civil rights, and what I hope is attainable for populations of diverse backgrounds who have been systematically disenfranchised. The development of preventive and clin-ical interventions demonstrating efficacy and effectiveness is not likely to be accomplished without first obtaining a deep understanding of the multiple voices and experiences of groups at the margins of the dominant discourse. These gender, racial, ethnic, and broader cultural issues are complex and can-not be easily resolved with the "right" prevention or clinical intervention models. Rather, these issues demand a commitment on the part of clinicians and interventionists to continually challenge themselves and their contexts from a multisystemic perspective, which includes political, socioeconomic, cultural, and ecological spheres.

Literature Review on Evidence-Based Treatments With Minority Populations

A surgeon general's report on mental health (U.S. Department of Health and Human Services, 1999) stated that to be effective, the diagnosis and treatment of mental illness must be tailored to all the characteristics that shape a person's image and identity. In addition, the consequences of mental health professionals' not understanding such influences can be profoundly deleterious to those they seek to help. However, programmatic strategies have only been recently implemented at institutional research levels to ensure that research is relevant to ethnic minority groups. This relevance refers to both the research focus and the diversity of populations included in the investigation. In due time, these institutional changes are intended to lead to the development of a body of evidence-based preventive and clinical intervention programs that can better serve the needs of various cultural groups.

For the sake of clarity, we are defining *evidence-based research* as meeting the following criteria proposed by Chambless and colleagues (1996): (1) pre- and posttreatment status is assessed for clients from one or more ethnic minority group; (2) clients are blocked according to their particular ethnic group membership and randomly assigned to different treatments or to treatment and control groups; (3) multiple, culturally cross-validated assessment instruments are employed; and (4) findings are replicated. In a report documenting updates on empirically validated treatments, Chambless and colleagues (1996) stated that they were aware of no psychotherapy treatment demonstrating treatment efficacy for ethnic minority populations. Furthermore, most studies they reviewed either did not specify the ethnicity of their subjects or used only White subjects.

Although preventive and clinical research addressing these concerns is currently under way with support from federal agencies as well as private foundations, evidence-based research with ethnic minority populations is clearly in its infancy. The following recommendations were proposed by Chambless and colleagues (1996) to ameliorate research concerns involving populations of color: (1) specify the ethnic group membership of participants in all studies (as is now required by most funding agencies); (2) give incentives to investigators for studies of ethnicity and treatment; (3) encourage researchers to report effect sizes on major outcome variables by ethnicity; (4) report barriers preventing researchers from conducting research on diverse populations, thereby presenting an opportunity to learn from other researchers and populations; and (5) continue to use knowledge derived from this research to provide services to diverse populations to the best of our ability.

Ethnic minority children and their families are at increased risk of poverty and the risk factors commonly associated with poverty—such as additional stressful life conditions, living in communities with poor social infrastructures, exposure to high crime, language barriers, teenage pregnancy, school drop out, and racial and cultural discrimination—have been well documented. Yet despite the overrepresentation of ethnic minorities among those living in poverty and engaged in prevention programs developed for high risk groups, serious efforts to examine preventive and clinical intervention issues relevant to the experiences of minority groups have not taken place until recent years (Roosa & Gonzales, 2000).

Researchers are only now beginning to understand the dimensions involved in developing sound methodological approaches to investigating the efficacy and effectiveness of mental health and social interventions targeting different cultural groups. Cauce, Coronado, and Watson (1998) proposed two broad models often employed by researchers studying different ethnic minority or cultural groups. The first model is referred to as the Cultural Equivalence Model, which assumes mostly similarities across groups except for differences due to life circumstances. This framework is typically used in studies examining macro-level or "universal" processes across groups and is reminiscent of an etic or universalist perspective. Under this model, the researcher controls for differences in potentially confounding variables, such as SES (socioeconomic status), and differences in attitudes, values, and behaviors are thought to be minimized or to disappear altogether. The second approach, referred to as the Cultural Variance Model, presupposes that the unique struggles of various ethnic and cultural groups lead to variations in culture specific values, beliefs, histories, and life experiences. Studies using this approach are typically conducted without a comparison group, as it is believed that due to unique backgrounds, each ethnic group develops fundamentally different adaptation and/or resilience processes. Therefore, the risk and protective factors associated with a particular cultural group are not necessarily shared by other dominant or minority populations and therefore cannot be compared (Roosa & Gonzales, 2000). This approach is consistent with an emic perspective. Both approaches have their merits and shortcomings, and their usefulness must be understood within the context of the research aim.

A Conceptual Model

Although the literature is clear about the need for culturally sensitive interventions for ethnic minorities, how such interventions are arrived at is less clear. Some authors and researchers may approach this task from a purely emic perspective, choosing to develop interventions for each group they intend to target. Others might choose an etic perspective, wherein an existing intervention is used in its original form with all groups targeted. We suggest that an alternative approach is to combine the emic and etic approaches and use existing interventions that are carefully tailored and adapted for use with ethnically diverse groups. The combination of perspectives we espouse assumes that while the behaviors targeted by the intervention (e.g., oppositional or defiant behaviors) are exhibited across cultures, how persons understand those behaviors and how willing they are to engage in the process of therapy to change the problematic behaviors may differ by cultural groups. An approach for combining the etic and emic perspectives is presented in the Cultural Framework section of this chapter.

Prior to engaging in the cultural adaptation of an intervention, because it is such an enormous undertaking, we collaborated with leading experts in the field to identify some of the processes involved in model adaptation in consultation. We hope that this will result in an end product that is greater than the sum of its parts. An iterative model has emerged out of our collaboration for approaching the adaptation of empirically validated interventions for use with ethnically diverse populations. The model uses what Rogers (1995) referred to as a "diffusion of innovations" framework and incorporates existing theoretical frameworks into a comprehensive model. The outline for the Cultural Adaptation Process Model, shown in Figure 18.1, has three general phases and ten specific target areas.

The three phases outline the general process of adapting an intervention. Phase One outlines the iterative process among all those involved in the adaptation process. During this phase, a balance between community needs and scientific integrity is sought. Phase Two involves the selection and adaptation of evaluation measures, as well as the parallel process of adaptation evolution in light of the process of reinvention. Phase Three focuses on integrating the observations and data gathered in Phase Two into a packaged, new intervention. This phase also involves continued collaborations with the change agent for potential decentering of the original intervention. Each phase involves specific actions and people. Figure 18.1 provides a visual representation of the phases. Overall, the process is intended to move science forward, using existing knowledge derived from research on Whites to impact

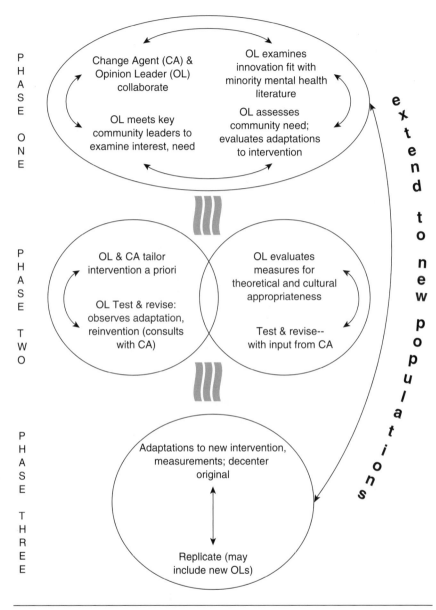

Figure 18.1   Cultural Adaptation Process Model

research on ethnic minorities, *as well as using ethnic minority-focused research to impact majority-focused research and practice.* This latter is perhaps the more challenging, as research on ethnic minorities has often resided on the opposite side of the science tracks.

In Phase One of the model, the players are identified and begin interacting. There are three players who are important: the change agent, the opinion leader, and members of the focal community. The change agent is the person who spearheads the process of diffusing an innovation. A change agent is often a university-degreed professional who has the technical expertise on the innovation (e.g., the person who originally developed the intervention to be adapted). The opinion leader is a community member who, by virtue of her or his conformity to the social norms of the community, has a unique position of strength in modeling the use of an innovation. How the "community" is defined may vary depending on the level of analysis. Within an academic context, the change agent might be a senior scientist who has developed an intervention, and the opinion leader might be a Latino/a scholar who wants to work with Latino/a populations. The Latino/a scholar has a better sense than the senior scholar of how to work with the Latino/a community, but the senior scholar holds the innovation (i.e., intervention). According to Rogers, opinion leaders tend to be linked to many forms of external communication, have a slightly higher status than others in the group, and are more innovative than others. Indeed, Rogers's (1995) diffusion of innovations research shows that there is a tendency for more effective communication among people with similar characteristics (e.g., SES, race), which is why change agents often have to exert their influence via opinion leaders, and why the Latino/a-scholar opinion leader would actually play the role of the change agent within the Latino/a community and would have to identify another person who would be the opinion leader (e.g., a local, admired teacher).

Another important player during Phase One, and throughout the process, is the target community. It is imperative to approach a community not from a colonizing perspective but from a collaborative one. From our experiences in the field, we have noted that our work is more likely to be perceived positively when we approach others in our capacity as members of our communities instead of as detached scientists. Rather than perceiving us as potentially "using" the community and moving on, we are seen as community members who have a stake in the outcome of the community. This does not entirely eliminate some members' suspicions, but it does help. In addition, approaching the community as community members gives researchers the opportunity to experience more fully the family, social, and political issues that a specific community faces. While some objectivity might be compromised, such active involvement in the community will allow researchers to "construct theories of psychotherapy and evaluate treatment grounded in the realities and experiences of ethnic minority populations" (Bernal & Scharrón-del-Río, 2001, p. 337).

During Phase Two, two parallel processes occur: the selection and adaptation of evaluation measures and the adaptation and revision of the intervention. The selection and adaptation of evaluation measures is a complex process that involves identifying appropriate measures. The appropriateness of measures involves (1) identifying measures that can quantify the process and outcome constructs targeted in the intervention (e.g., if one is intervening to improve parents' skills encouragement, then finding a measure of skills encouragement), and (2) identifying measures that have been associated with the areas that are being intervened upon (e.g., if discipline is targeted in the intervention and discipline is related to maternal depression, then measuring maternal depression). When working with ethnically diverse populations, finding appropriate measures also includes finding measures that have been normed with the population under study or submitting existing measures to the rigors of adaptation.[3]

The other part of the parallel process is the adaptation and revision of the intervention. This involves adapting the intervention a priori, testing it, and observing the process of *reinvention*, which is "the degree to which an innovation is changed or modified by the user in the process of its adoption and implementation" (Rogers, 1995, p. 175). Careful consideration of how participants in an intervention actually use the intervention and modify it can give the researcher critical information for further research and/or adapting the intervention, as well as another channel to use in listening for feedback from the community with which the researcher is involved.

Finally, Phase Three focuses on integrating the observations and data gathered in Phase Two into a "new" intervention, so that the intervention can be taken to scale and tested in a wider context. This phase also involves continued collaborations between the change agent and the opinion leader turned changed agent for potential decentering of the original intervention. Decentering is a concept born of the literature on translation of instruments and initially referred to changing an original instrument based on the issues that arose during the translation process (Marín & VanOss Marín, 1991). Here, the concept of decentering is expanded to mean the incorporation of new knowledge (e.g., gained in ethnic minority research) into the existing frameworks (e.g., ethnic majority research), so that the original product is impacted by the new findings.

The process of the proposed model is iterative, meaning that it is ongoing and repeats itself. However, iterations are not static repetitions, and with every cycle a new level of knowledge is gained that will help strengthen the intervention for use with a multitude of cultural groups. Each iteration provides additional information that may inform changes to previous versions of the intervention.

A Cultural Framework

In addition to having a plan for how to collaborate, having a cultural framework is pivotal for proceeding with cultural adaptation. Because we both work with Latino/a populations, the following framework is illustrated with this population in mind. We will first summarize the cultural framework and then provide a specific example for how it could be applied. The model we are using was developed by Guillermo Bernal and his colleagues at the University of Puerto Rico. This is the only framework we could identify for culturally sensitive adaptation of existing interventions. The purpose of the framework is to provide a structure for adaptation that can strengthen the ecological validity of interventions used in clinical and research settings. The framework developed by Bernal, Bonilla, and Bellido (1995) specifies eight major areas for adaptation—language, persons, metaphors, content, concepts, goals, methods, and context—among which there is some overlap.

Bernal and colleagues' (1995) framework to adapt an intervention considers structural as well as conceptual issues in intervention delivery. The authors are particularly concerned with *ecological validity,* or the degree to which the environment as experienced by the participant is the same as the environment the investigator assumes it to be. In the case of treatment research, the intervention is the environment, and as such ecological validity refers to the intervention having the properties that the investigator assumes it has (Bernal et al., 1995). Ecological validity is of particular importance in culturally adapting empirically derived interventions, given that one will take an intervention from the laboratory to the real world and add further complexity by taking it to a population that is likely different than the cultural group with which it was developed in the laboratory. The question, "Does the intervention work in the real world?" (ecological validity) is thus expanded to "Does the intervention work in the real world for people with different cultural contexts?"

Research-Based Case Study

In this section, we will provide a specific example of how we have conceptualized the process of adapting an EBT (evidence-based treatment) to better meet the cultural characteristics of Latino/a subsamples in the Midwest and West Coast of the United States. It is also relevant to note that we are part of a group of scholars that has been gathering at the Oregon Social Learning Center (OSLC) since 2000 to learn the empirically validated intervention techniques and the theoretical model underlying their parenting intervention. The scholars involved are all working towards adapting the Parent Management Training model developed at OSLC (hereafter referred to as the PMT-O) for use with ethnically and economically diverse communities across the country.

The common vision of this group of scholars is twofold: to make a difference in our communities of color and to learn the PMT-O theory and intervention well so we can appropriately adapt it to diverse populations, paying special attention to model fidelity, cultural adaptation, and rigorous research methods. We (the coauthors of this chapter) were both independently awarded 5-year Career Development Awards that started in the summer of 2003. A primary focus of our studies is to culturally adapt the PMT-O and to develop methodological frameworks and instruments that are culturally relevant. We are collaborating throughout this process as consultants on each other's projects. Although our research studies have different aims, a common objective is to culturally adapt, manualize, and test the PMT-O model. We will briefly describe the main tenants of the PMT-O model to provide a context for how we plan to adapt the intervention.

Parent Management
Training-Oregon Social Learning Center

The PMT-O intervention is the basis of several OSLC interventions that have been demonstrated effective. The interventions are all rooted in Social Interaction Learning (SIL) theory, which is the combination of two complimentary theoretical traditions, social interaction and social learning. *Social interaction* or *coercion* theory refers to the negative cycle of interactions between parents and their children (Patterson, 1982). It assumes that coercive parent-child interactions are learned, rather than conscious, and that they escalate as a result of previous reinforcement. The *social learning* perspective contributes the more global understanding of how patterns are ingrained within systems (Forgatch & Knutson, 2002), and it informs the positive parenting practices portion of the theoretical model.

Social Interaction Learning theory places the parent-child relationship in context (Patterson, Reid, & Dishion, 1992). It takes into account proximal and distal factors, as well as bidirectional influences on behavior. SIL posits that parents use both positive and coercive parenting practices that directly impact child adjustment. These practices are also affected by contextual factors in the parenting environment that affect youth to the degree that they affect the quality of parenting (Forgatch & Knutson, 2002; Forgatch & Martinez, 1999). There are five basic positive parenting practices that form the core of the OSLC model: skills encouragement, discipline, monitoring, problem solving, and positive involvement. There are three negative processes: negative reciprocity, escalation, and negative reinforcement.

The PMT-O intervention developed at the OLSC is particularly well suited to cultural adaptation. The intervention is theory based and has been hailed as one of the most promising available treatments for children, given its proven efficacy with White American youngsters (Kazdin & Wiesz, 1998). PMT-O's efficacy has been proven in preventive interventions, as well as in treatment interventions for severely behaviorally disordered youth (Kazdin & Wiesz, 1998). Further, the intervention teaches effective parenting practices, which have the potential of generalizing to all children in the family. The benefits for children of parents who are participating in a PMT-O program are wide ranging, including prevention of noncompliance (Martinez & Forgatch, 2001), reduction of problem behaviors at school (Forgatch & DeGarmo, 1999), reduction in physical aggression (Reid, Eddy, Fetrow, & Stoolmiller, 1999), lower likelihood of police contacts and fewer days institutionalized (Chamberlain, 1990), and, among divorced mothers, accelerated recovery from poverty (Forgatch & DeGarmo, 2002). Finally, the interventions have been mainly developed for and used with low-income, hard to reach White families. Low-income White families present challenges similar to those of Latino/a families, such as negative experiences with service sectors (e.g., schools, mental health), high illiteracy, multiple social stressors, and difficulties accessing services.

Research Plan for Culturally Adapting the PMT-O Intervention

An essential aspect of any study involving communities of color is that researchers, whether or not they are people of color, take the necessary time to effectively engage with the communities they plan to work with and ascertain that their area of study is indeed of interest and benefit to potential research participants. The process we have proposed for culturally adapting an intervention involves several phases. However, we will only elaborate on the aspects related to gathering initial focus group data and using that information to prepare a manual on the adapted treatment. The research steps to translate this new intervention into an EBT must involve the implementation of a solid research design to test the adapted intervention. It is critical to be mindful that the cultural adaptation of an intervention is not static. Therefore, we must allow for an evolving iterative process to emerge throughout the life of the research endeavor.

Gathering Focus Group Data

In our work, the purpose of conducting focus groups is to assess Latinos/as cultural values and attitudes toward parenting as the primary source of information used to guide the adaptations made to the model (e.g., parenting practices, developmental expectations). Focus group participants will also be asked about what factors they believe would facilitate and increase or decrease the likelihood of successful recruitment and retention for participation in such a study with Latinos/as. We are seeking to obtain attitudes and perceptions related to the core components of an intervention program. In addition to meeting this objective, critical theorists often recommend that studies with ethnic minority populations be conducted in such a way that offers the group or community an element of empowerment, collaboration, and emancipation. Having parents discuss their parenting practices and attitudes may have such an effect by helping them to normalize their experiences and to network with other parents.

Toward Developing Ecological Validity and Cultural Sensitivity: The Cultural Grid Approach

The eight elements proposed by Bernal and colleagues (1995) will be used as a theoretical framework for making cultural adaptations. The elements—language, persons, metaphors, content, concepts, goals, methods, and context—will be integrated into the interview schedule in order to help inform how each of the five core PMT-O components may be adapted. An example would be to ask about limit setting in such a way that it would explore the dimensions of each of Bernal and colleagues' (1995) elements. The first question will always be open-ended and broad, for example, "How do you manage your children?" "How do you set limits in your culture and in your family?" Additional questions might be: "What language do you use when you set limits with your child or children?" "What types of things do you say?" (exploring language and content elements) and "When you set limits with your child or children, do you associate this with a family saying or with a story?" (exploring metaphors and *dichos,* which are Spanish-language idioms). Particular attention will be given to new categories that may emerge or categories that should be deleted as core PMT-O components for Latino/a families.

The qualitative data obtained from parents during the focus groups will be placed on a 5 × 8 cell matrix containing information about the five topics introduced each week and the eight elements that will be used as a framework for increasing ecological validity and cultural sensitivity with Latino/a families. This system of categorizing data will allow for a systematic way to develop each section of the PMT-O model using Bernal's cultural framework. Table 18.1 illustrates how the cultural grid might be depicted.

Part II: Manualizing Adaptations to the Intervention

After in-depth data has been collected and analyzed to provide a rich description of how the PMT-O core components may be modified and extended, the process of manualizing these changes begins. It is anticipated that the manual will address several of the dimensions included in Bernal and colleagues' model, such as more visual and culturally appropriate illustrations or stories to explain the five core components of the model, more local narratives, and traditional idioms expressing Latino/a family values. Particular attention will be given to areas of the existing model that may need to be eliminated or radically shifted. Also, there may be additional dimensions that need to be incorporated into the model. The focus group data will be the primary means of informing how the model will be adapted for local Latino/a families. Table 18.1 illustrates how the PMT-O components might intersect with different cultural domains.

Conclusion

Overall this chapter has addressed the need for venturing into the arena of empirically validated treatments for ethnic minority populations. There is a clear need for work on interventions with ethnic minority populations as evidenced by the gap in this knowledge area, as well as repeated calls for intervention research with ethnic minority populations by senior scholars and institutions alike. There is also growing support from major organizations to engage in this research (e.g., the National Institutes of Health). Once the need is established and the financial supports are in place, it is up to researchers to determine exactly how to go about filling this gap in our knowledge and practice regarding mental health services for ethnic minorities. That is what we are trying to accomplish. We have presented information on our personal backgrounds to give the reader a sense of where our approaches to research and our communities were formed, and we have provided a model for collaboration that could facilitate research for individuals wishing to pursue such partnerships. In addition to a model for collaboration, we have also presented a model for cultural adaptation that might be of use to researchers interested in similar work.

Table 18.1 PMT-O Components and Cultural Domains for Use by Therapists

	Skills Encouragement	Limit Setting	Monitoring	Problem Solving	Positive Involvement
Language	Aliento,* echar pa'lante[1]	Poner límites,* alentar respeto[2]	Monitorear,* echar el ojo,[3] velar[4]	Solucionar problemas,* tener maña[5]	Envolvimiento positivo*
Persons	Take a more informal approach	Take a more formal or expert role	Take a more formal or expert role	Take a more formal or expert role	Take a more informal approach
Metaphors	Un clavo saca otro clavo	Árbol que nace virado jamás se endereza	Camarón que se duerme, se lo lleva la corriente	El diablo sabe más por viejo que por diablo	Al que buen árbol se arrima, buena sombra le cobija
Content	Conceptualize respeto and what it entails (unquestioning compliance with authority)	Frame in terms of helping the child learn to respect parents as well as others	Monitor by making sure that both parents know where the child is and the culture the child is navigating	Frame a more democratic household rule, as in a benign dictatorship	Connect with monitoring and with teaching the child buena educación[6]
Concept	Theoretical underpinning: Social learning theory and coercion theory, which are compatible with Latino/a values and behaviors				
Goals	Increase encouragement: to increase respeto and buena educación	Set more effective limits: to increase respeto	Achieve appropriate parental monitoring: Make sure parents are present during teachable moments	Increase effective problem solving: Teach the child to valerse por sí mismo[7]	Increase positive involvement: Teach the child buena educación
Methods	Group therapy, role plays, practices[8]	Group therapy, role plays, practices	Group therapy, role plays, practices	Group therapy, role plays, practices	Group therapy, role plays, practices
Context	Consider lack of modeling from parents' parents	Consider parents' interactions with and fear of Child Protective Services	Be flexible and cautious, given parents' likely need to work long hours in exhausting jobs	Consider parents' level of education in presenting problem solving approaches	Consider parents' work and its impact; consider gender roles within parents' culture

Notes: An asterisk (*) denotes a literal translation.
1. This means "to get ahead" and is a popular expression of encouragement.
2. This means to encourage respect; respect is an important Latino value.
3. This is a popular expression meaning "keeping an eye on."
4. This is a popular way of saying "watch."
5. This is literally "to be skillful" at something; it is culturally syntonic language and framing for teaching a child to problem solve.
6. This literally translates as "good education." It is important to note that the concept of educación for Latinos/as encompasses more than academic education. It also involves moral, social, and personal responsibility (Valenzuela, 1999).
7. This translates as "take care of himself or herself."
8. Homework is conceptualized as practice so as not to alienate participants who have had negative experiences with the educational system.

329

There are some important factors that we would like to highlight. We have only presented information on the initial steps of our work, which focus on gathering qualitative data to help inform potential changes to the theory driving aspects of our work and inform manual adaptation and/or development. However, our work uses a multiple methods approach. We believe that there are multiple ways of knowing and that qualitative and quantitative traditions provide information on different slices of reality. Our hope is that the process of combining the two approaches will give us a better knowledge base, and that the weaknesses and strengths of one approach will be balanced by the weaknesses and strengths of the other approach.

We also hope that by adding a multiple methods approach to our collaborative process, we can each learn from the other's experiences in our respective fields. Working together with different samples and having overlapping questions and objectives will, we hope, give us a greater depth of knowledge than we would have achieved by working independently. However, there are great limitations on what we will be able to learn given that we are spread over two geographical areas, neither of which has a burgeoning Latino/a population. The work that we are tackling is also being conducted by promising emerging scholars such as Esteban Cardemil (see, e.g., Cardemil, Reivich, & Seligman, 2002). The expansion of networks and evolving collaborations will be critical for the field to move forward as a whole. Continued use of multiple methods of research will also allow for researchers participating in expanding networks to bring in their areas of strength and make contributions to knowledge from their frame of reference while participating in an effort that values all ways of knowing.

Reflections, Questions, and Exercises

1. How does the researcher's background affect the kinds of questions that she or he asks and the approach to research that is taken?

2. What are the pros and cons of approaching research collaboratively rather than independently? Why is it important to outline a mindful collaborative process?

3. How much do we *need* to know about a particular population's values, behaviors, and outcomes before we can proceed with intervention research?

4. What are the pros and cons of culturally adapting an existing intervention versus developing a new intervention that emerges from a specific cultural context?

5. How does one arrive at a culturally sensitive adaptation of an intervention?

6. How does Bernal and colleagues' model help in culturally adapting an existing intervention? Are there other variables you would include in this model?

7. Consider your racial and ethnic background, economic and educational background, family influences, religious beliefs, and life experiences. How have these shaped you? Which factors seem to have had the greatest influence on you? Does the influence of these factors vary depending on context? How have these background variables shaped how you view the world and others in it? How do they shape how you conceptualize a "problem," and how you would go about solving that problem (including whether you would do so alone or with others, what tools you would use, how long you would persist, etc.)?

Notes

1. The term *Nuyorican* has undergone some changes and its valence is dependent on context. For example, in New York City, the Nuyorican Poet's Café is a center for cultural exchange, and Nuyoricanness is a source of pride. In Puerto Rico, as formerly in the United States, the Nuyorican is marginal. The Nuyorican often does not speak Spanish or speaks it very poorly (Seda Bonilla, 1974), and in Puerto Rico this symbolizes a departure from the Puerto Rican identity. The category has been compared to the cultural classification of the Mexican *pachuco* (Maldonado-Denis, 1980).

2. An *ethnic gloss* is the use of a single label to refer to a heterogeneous group of people (Trimble, 1991).

3. Finding appropriate measures is a colossal undertaking, as few measures are available. Existing measures may be outdated or have norms for groups other than those being studied (e.g., norms for Mexican Americans when Puerto Ricans are being studied). The following resources contain more information on measurement issues: on translating and back translating, see Brislin, Lonner, and Thorndike (1973) and Marín and VanOss Marín (1991), and for an excellent discussion on validity issues, see Knight and Hill (1998).

References

Bernal, G., Bonilla, J., & Bellido, C. (1995). Ecological validity and cultural sensitivity for outcome research: Issues for the cultural adaptation and development of psychosocial treatments with Hispanics. *Journal of Abnormal Child Psychology, 23*(1), 67–82.

Bernal, G., & Scharrón-del-Río, M. R. (2001). Are empirically supported treatments valid for ethnic minorities? Toward and alternative approach for treatment research. *Cultural Diversity and Ethnic Minority Psychology, 7,* 328–342.

Brislin, R. W., Lonner, W. J., & Thorndike, R. M. (1973). *Cross-cultural research methods: Comparative studies in behavioral science.* New York: John Wiley.

Cardemil, E. V., Reivich, K. J., & Seligman, M. E. P. (2002). The prevention of depressive symptoms in low-income minority middle school students. *Prevention & Treatment,* 5(8), http://www.journals.apa.org/prevention/volume5/pre0050008a.html

Cauce, A. M., Coronado, N., & Watson, J. (1998). Conceptual, methodological, and statistical issues in culturally competent research. In M. Hernandez & M. Isaacs (Eds.), *Promoting cultural competence in children's mental health services* (pp. 305–329). Baltimore, MD: Paul H. Brookes.

Chamberlain, P. (1990). Comparative evaluation of specialized foster care for seriously delinquent youths: A first step. *Community Alternatives: International Journal of Family Care,* 2(2), 21–36.

Chambless, D. L., Crits-Cristoph, P., Baker, M., Johnson, B., Woody, S. R., Sue, S., Beutler, L., Williams, D. A., & McCurry, S. (1996). An update on empirically validated therapies. *Clinical Psychologist,* 49, 5–18.

Forgatch, M. S., & DeGarmo, D. S. (1999). Parenting through change: An effective prevention program for single mothers. *Journal of Consulting and Clinical Psychology,* 67, 711–724.

Forgatch, M. S., & DeGarmo, D. S. (2002). Extending and testing the social interaction learning model with divorce samples. In J. B. Reid, G. R. Patterson, & J. Snyder (Eds.), *Antisocial behavior in children and adolescents: A developmental analysis and model for intervention* (pp. 235–256). Washington, DC: American Psychological Association.

Forgatch, M. S., & Knutson, N. M. (2002). Linking basic and applied research in a prevention science process. In H. A. Liddle, D. A. Santisteban, R. F. Levant, & J. H. Bray (Eds.), *Family psychology: Science based interventions* (pp. 239–257). Washington, DC: American Psychology Association.

Forgatch, M. S., & Martinez, C. (1999). Parent management training: A program linking basic research and practical application. *Tidsskrift for Norsk Psykologforening,* 36(10), 923–937.

Kazdin, A. E., & Weisz, J. R. (1998). Identifying and developing empirically supported child and adolescent treatments. *Journal of Consulting and Clinical Psychology,* 66, 19–36.

Knight, G. P., & Hill, N. E. (1998). Measurement equivalence in research involving minority adolescents. In V. C. McLoyd & L. Steinberg (Eds.), *Studying minority adolescents* (pp. 183–210). Mahwah, NJ: Lawrence Erlbaum.

Maldonado-Denis, M. (1980). *The emigration dialectic: Puerto Rico and the U.S.* New York: International Publishers.

Marín, G., & VanOss Marín, B. (1991). *Research with Hispanic populations* (Applied Social Research Methods Series, Vol. 23). Newbury Park, CA: Sage.

Martinez, C. R., Jr., & Forgatch, M. S. (2001). Preventing problems with boys' noncompliance: Effects of a parent training intervention for divorcing mothers. *Journal of Consulting and Clinical Psychology,* 69, 416–428.

National Institute of Mental Health. (1999). *Basic behavioral science research for mental health: A national investment.* (NIH Publication No. 96–3682). Retrieved March 31, 2004, from http://www.nimh.nih.gov/publicat/basbehav.cfm

Patterson, G. R. (1982). *Coercive family process.* Eugene, OR: Castalia.

Patterson, G. R., Reid, J. B., & Dishion, T. J. (1992). *Antisocial boys.* Eugene, OR: Castalia.

Reid, J. B., Eddy, J. M., Fetrow, R. A., & Stoolmiller, M. (1999). Description and immediate impacts of a preventive intervention for conduct problems. *American Journal of Community Psychology, 27,* 483–517.

Rogers, E. M. (1995). *Diffusion of innovations* (4th ed.). New York: Free Press.

Roosa, M. W., & Gonzales, N. A. (2000). Minority issues in prevention: Introduction to the special issue. *American Journal of Community Psychology, (28)2,* 145–148.

Seda Bonilla, E. (1974). *Requiem para una cultura.* Rio Piedras, Puerto Rico: Ediciones Bayoán.

Trimble, J. E. (1991). Ethnic specification, validation prospects, and the future of drug use research. *International Journal of the Addictions, 25,* 149–170.

U.S. Department of Health and Human Services. (1999). *Mental health: A report of the surgeon general.* Rockville, MD: U.S. Department of Health and Human Services, Substance Abuse and Mental Health Services Administration, Center for Mental Health Services, National Institutes of Health, National Institute of Mental Health.

Valenzuela, A. (1999). *Subtractive schooling: U.S.-Mexican youth and the politics of caring.* Albany: State University of New York Press.

19

Acculturation Versus Cultural Identity

The Need for New Cultural Lenses in the Mental Health Professions

J. Ruben Parra Cardona,
Richard S. Wampler, and Dean M. Busby

I (J.R.P.) was 18 years old when I came to the United States[1] for the first time as an exchange student. I still remember the words that the school counselor (in a predominantly White school) said to me on the first day of class, "Don't worry, you will acculturate fast to the U.S." I also remember saying to myself that day, "I don't want to acculturate, I just want to learn what is good about the U.S. What was that counselor talking about?"

Twelve years later I continue to be a student, but this time I am a student in a doctoral marriage and family therapy program. A significant part of my clinical work has been devoted to providing therapy for adolescents involved in the juvenile justice system. The majority of these adolescents are Latinos/as, and some of their parents or grandparents prefer to speak Spanish in sessions. As I was consulting with an Anglo probation officer on one of my cases, she seemed rather frustrated because the family and the adolescent were somewhat defensive toward her as a representative of the justice system and used Spanish expressions from time to time. At that point, the probation officer expressed to me, "How come it is so difficult for these people to acculturate? Everything would be easier for them!" As I recall these experiences, I connect with my feelings of frustration whenever "good people in the helping professions" want to "help" by inviting immigrants and minorities to become more American[2] through acculturating to majority U.S. societal norms and by implicitly expecting Latinos/as to give up pieces of or all of their cultural richness.

The purpose of this chapter is to revise and challenge the concept of *acculturation* and to introduce the concept of *cultural identity formation* as a way of understanding immigration and cultural identity experiences. In order to accomplish this, we briefly present our professional and personal backgrounds and the ways in which we have been able to cocreate a new model of cultural identity formation by combining our different life experiences and maintaining intercultural dialogues. We present the conceptual ideas that led us to the creation of the Transgenerational Cultural Identity Formation Model, along with relevant literature on this topic, and provide a case scenario of a concrete application of the model with a Latino family in the community. Finally, we offer suggestions for mental health professionals seeking to apply this model to the areas of academic training, clinical practice, and research.

Three Different Cultural Backgrounds

J. Ruben Parra Cardona

I came to the United States for the first time as an exchange student when I was 18 years old. I was so excited at that time because I was going to live in the most powerful country and I was going to be among *gringos* (Americans). My first day in an American high school was intimidating. I thought I was going to be greeted like gringos are treated whenever they go to Mexico. I was the international student, the new attraction at school! However, I experienced my first day feeling like a ghost. It was like I didn't exist for my classmates. Or if I did exist for some, I perceived unpleasant looks from them. I thought I was just being paranoid and my perceptions were just my imagination.

On the third school day, I had my first gym class. We were required to lift weights in teams. I was a little anxious because I had never lifted weights in my life. When my turn came, I lay down on the bench and was anxious, but I was trusting my team to take care of me if I needed help. As I was making a great effort to accomplish my sixth repetition of weight lifting, I realized that I didn't have any more strength. Slowly, the weights started to come closer and closer to me, and I was about to lose all my strength. I finally gave up and asked for help, but the help never came. As I was lying on that gym bench with all that weight on my chest, I heard someone whisper, "Pussy Mexican, you should have stayed in your country eating tequila worms." After this, my team members just walked away. Finally, the gym teacher came and helped me with the weights, assisted by other students. After catching my breath, I tried to process what I'd heard, but I just couldn't understand the anger that was directed at me. Why was that said to me? What's wrong with being Mexican? Why were the others angry at me?

That was when a process of self-hatred started to take place within me. I started to compare myself with all those tall, blond, blue-eyed Americans. I started to dislike myself, thinking, "I come from a bunch of Indians, and Americans come from Europe!" Gradually, I idealized America and the Americans and started to hate myself and my ethnic identity. I stopped being me because I wanted to be like them and thought, "Maybe they are right, maybe we Mexicans are not as good as they are." That was a painful year. Although I was able to learn English and to graduate with honors, I lost contact with my soul and my true heart. Academically successful but emotionally defeated, I returned to Mexico to pursue my college education.

After getting my bachelor's degree in psychology and working for a couple of years in community programs, I decided to return to America for my graduate education. I had the dream of becoming a family therapist, and although I was afraid of experiencing discrimination again, the best education and training in marriage and family therapy was in the United States, so I returned to this country to pursue my master's degree.

The feeling of inferiority that I had felt during high school but not since came back during the first class of my master's program. I remember looking at my teacher and comparing our skin colors and automatically thinking, "I wish I were White!"

One of the faculty members, Kenneth Hardy, was able to see my struggle with being a minority deep down in my heart. He became my mentor and also was the person who challenged me the most regarding my cultural identity. When he presented to our class the concepts of dynamics of oppression and White privilege, I felt new energy enter my heart. Everything started to make sense! Slowly, I started to be aware of the way in which skin color makes a difference. I was able to observe that in some places, people wouldn't talk to me, pretending that I was invisible. And although I suffered new experiences of discrimination, I started to realize that the reasons for such actions had nothing to do with me personally.

I gradually started to be in touch with my brownness and the beauty of my ethnicity. I read about slavery and the unfair Mexican-American War. I watched videos and read books written by Martin Luther King. I painfully witnessed some police abuse of African American people. Slowly, an understanding of the dynamics of racial oppression became clearer to me. It was time to nurture myself and to realize that those words said to me many years ago came from a group of people who supported a racist ideology.

At this time, I also became aware of the many ways in which immigrants in the United States feel the pressure to acculturate and blend in. I started to have challenging conversations with faculty and classmates around this topic and to be aware of my own process of cultural identity. I started to identify the traits from both cultures that I wanted to incorporate into my identity, as well as the ones that I wanted to challenge and reject. I embraced my Mexican values more than ever, I became proud of my color and heritage, and I also started to appreciate the beautiful gifts that the United States had to offer.

As a doctoral student, I have had the great opportunity to collaborate with faculty and classmates committed to social justice and willing to create a change in society. These supportive relationships have helped me to be more committed to my own journey in forming my cultural identity and my identity as an MFT. My awareness of racial discrimination, the dynamics of oppression, and the pressure immigrants feel to acculturate has shaped my clinical work in profound ways. I always try to be sensitive to and willing to explore the ways in which the dynamics of oppression and pressure to acculturate are part of my clients' presenting problems. I do not see myself as an MFT confined to the four walls of a consulting room. I believe that as a therapist I have a commitment to be an agent for social change, to identify and impact, if possible, the larger systems that affect the families I work with. Immigrant and minority families do not exist in a vacuum, and frequently they are affected by discrimination and cultural pressures to conform to an established norm. It is therefore my ethical and moral responsibility to be attentive to these overt and many times covert realities.

I believe that immigrant and minority families should experience culture in the United States as different stories, with different outcomes, without one story being the dominant one, and with the voices of those who have less power heard, respected, and celebrated. For these families, having this experience of U.S. culture depends on their individual cultural identity development. The Transgenerational Cultural Identity Model we have created, and which we discuss in detail below, will enable therapists to guide families toward this integrated cultural experience.

Richard S. Wampler

I never had a problem with acculturation or developing a cultural identity in the United States. I am "American culture" in many ways and my cultural identity is as "American" as the apple pies my 91-year-old mother can still make. My history is, in many ways, that of America. My Swiss-German

Wampler ancestors came to the German-speaking part of Pennsylvania in 1747 and moved into the Shenandoah Valley before the American Revolution, where they intermarried with other Swiss-German, German, Dutch, and a few French immigrants. Some of them stayed there, but my more immediate ancestors moved to Indiana shortly after the Indian treaties of 1810. My Irish Protestant Kilpatrick great-great-grandfather and mother came to Iowa in the 1850s, not because of the Potato Famine but for the cheap land. My father was born, truly, in a log cabin on a small Hoosier farm. My mother was born in a blizzard in a sod house on the plains of Colorado where her father and mother had homesteaded on 140 acres. My parents met at Indiana University, and they lived almost all their 56 years together within 15 miles of the homes of two of my great-grandfathers, a great-great grandfather, and a great-great-great grandfather. Raised in small town Indiana, I was almost unaware of any racial, ethnic, or cultural differences among people—my elementary school was all White, my church likewise, and I cannot remember seeing Black people, although there were a few hundred such residents out of the 20,000 or so people in my town.

Indiana has a reputation as the Mississippi of the North for a good reason. I was not aware of it as a child, but there was an all-Black elementary school across town, only two blocks from my father's all-White school. When I was in third grade, I remember being on the playground teeter-totter at school during recess and looking up at the outside staircase and seeing a Black girl—and being astounded. Who was she? What was she doing in my school? There was no answer to my questions; I do not recall ever seeing her at school again, but that one memory remains vivid. Later, I discovered the patterns of housing segregation that existed in my hometown, the history of Klan activity in Indiana, and the strong prejudices that many adults held about Blacks and Jews. Entering Indiana University in 1960, I learned that separate dorm suites were reserved for Jews and for Blacks, that Black students could not get a haircut in the barbershops around the university, and that the fraternities and sororities were closed to both Jews and Blacks.

Perhaps my only saving grace was that I was raised in a stiff-necked, conservative, Calvinist Protestant church that traced its history back to persecutions in Scotland by Catholics (whom we were taught to despise and fear) and, later, by English Episcopalians (ditto). Between the brave martyrs in the fires and the milkmaid who heaved her milking stool at an unworthy Anglican bishop when he took the pulpit, I learned what it meant to be different, to be a minority, and to be persecuted—mostly secondhand, but it turned out to be important learning for me. When I discovered the wider world in my teens, I used what I had learned to identify with other different, persecuted minorities. Of course, this did not happen overnight. I remember arguing with the minister over the place of Jews and Catholics in God's heaven, being appalled at a Sunday night sermon attacking Catholics, and encountering my first Black classmates in junior high and discovering that I liked them.

On reflection, I think I adopted pretty conventional liberal views by osmosis in college. I watched the Selma police attacks on television, I encountered open bigots and open liberals and liked the liberals better, and I worked alongside a sweet young woman, a member of the Fair Play for Cuba Committee, who faced a long jail term for her beliefs and words. Graduate school in Philadelphia introduced me to still more people who were not White, Midwestern, and Protestant, but my encounters with other ethnic groups were limited to those with my all-White classmates, some of whom were Jewish, and visits to the Italian market. One shock I had was being told by a female lab assistant, a graduate of one of the Seven Sisters colleges, that she and I had virtually identical records but that I had been admitted because I am a man and "would make something of [myself]."

My real learning about diversity and acculturation did not occur until I ran headlong into the feminist revolution of the early 1970s. The revolution began well before that, but it was late coming to Kansas where I was teaching. I finally understood that, for women, "acculturation" to male society meant invisibility and less power. It meant accommodation to the dominant White male culture (mine) in dress, aspirations, choices, behavior, and outlook. Failure to acculturate meant rejection, labeling, and being demeaned—"castrating bitch," "bra burner," and "ball buster" were among the milder epithets reserved for women who failed to meet the 1950s Barbie norms that many men (including myself) and women held. In my own marriage, I had to acknowledge that it was my choice of which graduate school to attend that reigned, although we both were admitted to three prestigious schools and my choice was the weakest of the three for Karen, my wife. In addition, I assumed that she would do the cooking, although neither one of us had much experience in cooking, and that, bizarrely enough, it was me who should call the president of the National Organization for Women to find out how to start a local chapter of women who were employed part-time at the university. I am somewhat embarrassed to acknowledge that my great concession to the women's movement at the time was to make a chocolate mousse, probably the first cooking I had done since our marriage.

With the help of good friends in the women's movement, I learned to do better than an occasional dessert. After we moved to Indiana, I was blessed with a colleague, Cathryn Adamsky, who took no nonsense from me and who led the charge both for women and for civil rights, taking me with her at times. Under her tutelage and with support from Karen, other women, and a men's group, I began a process of encountering my own training as a male chauvinist and ethnocentrist—a process that still goes on every day.

Once I grasped the issues of power and privilege that male oppression brings to women, I came to a much deeper understanding of the issues of power and privilege that my America brings to persons of color and to immigrants. For me, grappling with these issues and resolving them is the task my White America must undertake in this century, before we are no longer the numerical majority and the dominant culture. The myths of the melting pot and the American dream of success through hard work are ones my America loves because they allow us to require everyone to fit one mold. Those who have failed to "melt" and become one with the homogenized ideal citizens of my America can be blamed for their own exclusion from power and privilege. When we (I) give up that myth, we (I) must first acknowledge and then directly address the impacts of inequalities of birth, color, ethnicity, race, opportunity, education, access, and so on. Doing so is not painless or easy.

As a male, White, Protestant trainer of marriage and family therapists, I have many failings. My blindness to my own power, prestige, and privilege sets me up to diminish, discourage, and offend my students by ignoring their lack of power and privilege. I have been helped by courageous students who would not allow me to ignore the impact of that blindness on them, by Karen's refined sense of fairness that calls me to account periodically, and by my own ability to empathize, even if it is well after the offense. Given the dominance of Whites and males in our field, especially as trainers, I have an obligation to make persistent efforts to connect with students of color, international students, and students from religious minorities to bring these issues of power and privilege to the table for honest discussion *and action*. It is not enough for me to have had the epiphany that White and/or male privilege and power corrupt; my religious upbringing included "Faith without works is dead."

Dean M. Busby

Although I was born and raised in the United States and have always considered this country to be my primary nation and culture of origin, twice in my adult life I have lived outside the United States for a significant amount of time as a "foreigner." These experiences, along with my childhood experiences as a member of a religious minority in the Church of Jesus Christ of Latter-Day Saints (LDS), have indelibly impressed upon me the significance and salience of cultural identity in the health and well-being of individuals and families. Although, at times, I have been able to hide behind my White middle-class appearance and ignore the struggles that others had with living in the United States while simultaneously feeling culturally connected to other countries and ethnic groups, usually my ease has been broken within a short period of time by personal experiences that have reminded me what it feels like to be among others who do not see the world as I do, or by the experiences of my students and clients who do not have the luxury of hiding in the majority.

As Ruben and I started to explore models of cultural identity and the process of immigration, it became more and more apparent to me that the healing process of the therapeutic experience must be centered primarily around cultural identity. Bringing culture to the center of therapy, instead of allowing it to remain at the periphery, can be one of the most liberating and helpful experiences for clients.

This experience of centering cultural identity has coalesced for me, in part, as a result of introspection regarding my own background and my experiences in other countries. Raised in a religious culture that has a history of severe and sometimes violent oppression, I was told from the youngest age about the sacrifices and struggles of my ancestors to hold onto their beliefs in the midst of an environment of hostility. Some of my ancestors joined the LDS church in the first few years of its existence during the 1830s. These ancestors, themselves descended from some of the earliest English religious immigrants to New England in the 1600s, were exposed to harsh persecution. They were run out of their homes in New York, Ohio, Missouri, and Illinois. Some of my ancestors were shot, others were raped, many became ill and died from exposure and diseases such as cholera. All of them repeatedly lost their physical possessions because of their religious beliefs. It was not until they fled to Utah, then an unsettled area of the West, that they found a period of peace where they could live as they wanted. Some of my other ancestors joined the LDS church in the 1860s in Sweden and England and immigrated to Utah to find opportunities that were not available in their home countries and to escape persecution from their neighbors and other family members who rejected their change of religion. Several of these ancestors were ostracized by their families and forbidden to speak to their parents after they joined the LDS church. Almost all came to the United States in circumstances of abject poverty. While many of my ancestors immigrated here looking to find prosperity and peace in the mountains in the West, those from Sweden struggled for decades to feel at home in this new country while they scratched out a living on farms in an area of the country that nobody else wanted.

These stories of my ancestors and their struggles to immigrate and adapt to a new country that was not accepting of them are poignant. I developed a strong sense of identity as a result of the cultural transmission of this heritage across generations that made me feel unique, and I have felt a commitment to maintain the beliefs and perspectives of my family that have been so dearly held by my ancestors despite great odds. As I have interacted with families from Latin American cultures living in the Southwestern United States, I have recognized a similar struggle within families of Latin descent to maintain an identity with their way of life while trying to also fit into a new way of life. I have come to believe that the cultural heritage of each of us, whether conscious or not, has a significant influence on our interactional habits and our belief systems. It has been enjoyable for me to develop this new, more respectful model for cultural identity with Ruben and Richard.

Having shared our personal stories as well as our motivation to cocreate a new cultural narrative, in the next section we present a discussion on acculturation and the need to develop a new research agenda for the study of cultural identity.

Acculturation Versus Cultural Identity

Acculturation is understood as the way in which minorities gradually adapt to the dominant culture and change their beliefs, values, and behaviors as a result of the contact with a new culture (Banks, 1987). One of the possible results of acculturation is *assimilation,* in which individuals lose their original cultural identity as they fully identify with a second culture (LaFromboise, Hardin, Coleman, & Gerton, 1993). Therefore, acculturation refers to a process that can be identified as a continuum, and assimilation is at the extreme end of such a continuum, as it refers to a situation in which immigrants renounce their original cultural identity and become part of a new culture.

Some researchers have reached the conclusion that immigrants must sacrifice their ethnic identity to increase their social connectedness with American culture (Valentine, 2001). The concept of *psychological imperialism* (Ben-David, 1993) refers to the belief that assimilation is required in order to improve the economic and emotional well-being of immigrants.

Different voices in the mental health field have urged us to acknowledge the ways in which we have organized our theories and practice as a replication of the dominant value systems of U.S. society (McGoldrick, 1998). However, a significant part of the clinical and research work in our field continues to be informed by such dominant values (Roer Strier, 1996; Turner, 1991). For example, recent research designs rely on acculturation scales (reflecting an assimilationist viewpoint) to interpret relational functioning (Farver, Narang, & Bhadha, 2002; Negy & Snyder, 2000). Although such studies represent valuable efforts to have a deeper understanding of the role that immigration and cultural identity play in interpersonal relationships, there are dangers involved in using constructs and scales designed to reflect an assimilationist framework.

One of the dangers of such a framework lies in the assumption that the final goal is for immigrants to become identified with American culture while diminishing or discarding identification with their original culture. This view is consistent with the historic view of the United States as a melting pot into which each successive wave of immigrants must blend to become part of some homogenized whole. The melting pot concept is exemplified by this true story of a family of Italian immigrants who arrived in Georgia in the 1930s: The father of the family ordered his children and wife to speak English, to stop speaking Italian, to eat only traditional American dishes, and to join the Presbyterian Church. "We are Americans now!" was his motto.

Our use of the term *cultural identity* rather than *melting pot* expresses the perspective we are taking to understand immigration and cultural development by acknowledging difference rather than insisting on sameness. Cultural identity implies an encounter of different cultures with many possible outcomes. This view coincides with Falicov's (1995) call for the development of a more multidimensional position when addressing cultural identity. According to Falicov, individuals who are part of different cultures and acknowledge cultural differences have a more varied and fluid understanding of cultural identity than those who believe they must choose one culture. This multidimensionality allows movement away from the idea that groups, families, and individuals must give up their original culture and become assimilated into the host culture.

Based on this framework of cultural identity, we have developed a theoretical model of immigration and cultural identity formation that moves away from limited acculturation and/or assimilation models by integrating transgenerational processes into a wider context and retaining individual and family variables.

In the following section, we describe the basic principles of the model. Although we show the application of the model by illustrating experiences of Latino/a immigrants, it is important to keep in mind that the model can be applied to any immigrant group.

The Transgenerational Cultural Identity Model

The Transgenerational Cultural Identity Model explores the personal, familial, and sociological dimensions of the immigration and cultural identity experience. Since the main objective of this chapter is to explore applications of the model to the mental health field, the reader is referred to our earlier work (Parra Cardona, Busby, & Wampler, 2002) for a detailed explanation of all the elements of the model.

The first part of the model offers an explanation of the variables and dynamics usually experienced by an immigrant individual and/or family (see Figure 19.1).

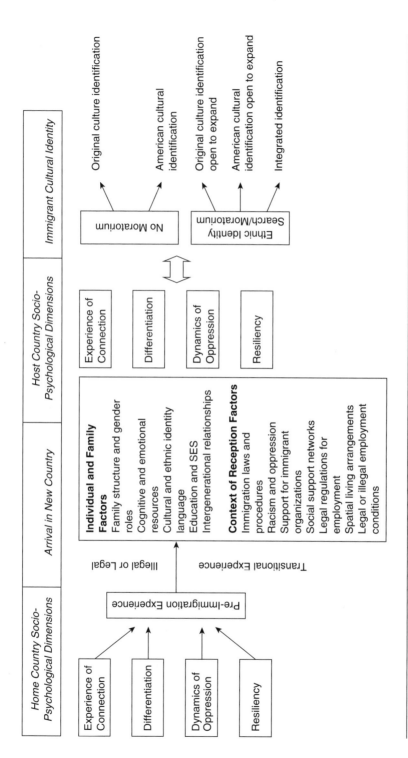

Figure 19.1 Transgenerational Culture Identity Model for the Immigrant Generation

345

To reach a better understanding of the family dynamics involved in immigration and cultural identity formation, it is essential to know the experiences of immigrants. The way in which such individuals and families integrate the cultural experience of immigration can serve as either a booster or a filter for subsequent generations of their families. For example, a Latin American family escaping economic difficulties by coming to the United States, but struggling with leaving behind family and friends, will most likely embrace and retain the values that they consider important from their culture. However, a Latin American family escaping trauma, persecution, and civil war might experience a more difficult time transmitting to future generations the values that they appreciate from their original country.

The resulting cultural identity for the generation that immigrated and subsequent generations of their families is the result of complex transgenerational processes and is influenced at all times by the context (see Figure 19.2). To apply and interpret this model, consideration must be given to the immigrant generation, as the dynamics of cultural identity of later generations are likely to be highly influenced by the experiences of their immigrant forebears.

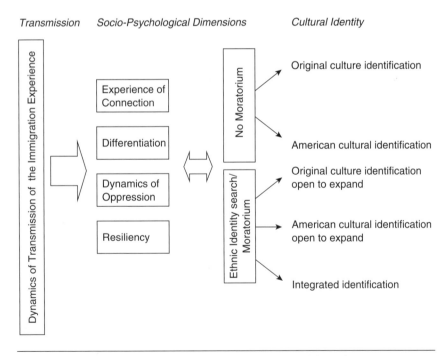

Figure 19.2   Transgenerational Cultural Identity Model for Subsequent Generations of Immigrants' Families

An important aspect of the Transgenerational Cultural Identity Model lies in its inclusion of specific socio-psychological dimensions (experience of connection, differentiation, dynamics of oppression, and resiliency) that are present throughout the process of the immigrant experience. The end result of the immigration experience is predicted to fall into one of the following five general categories of cultural identity formation: (1) Original culture identification, (2) American cultural identification, (3) Original culture identification open to expand, (4) American cultural identification open to expand, and (5) Integrated identification. A major emphasis is given in this chapter to two parts of the model—socio-psychological and relational dimensions and categories of cultural identity formation. It is our belief that an accurate understanding of such concepts is helpful for clinical work, training, and research in mental health fields.

Socio-Psychological and Relational Dimensions

The socio-psychological dimensions defined below play a major role in cultural identity formation by pushing individuals and families away from their home country and pulling them toward the new culture.

Experience of Connection

This dimension is drawn from the integration of attachment theory (Bowlby, 1988) and Bowenian theory (Donley, 1993). Under this combined theory, a child attaches not only to his or her primary caretaker but also through the primary caretaker to the wider emotional field and culture. It is essential for immigrants to establish meaningful relationships with members of the new country's minority and majority groups in order to have new experiences of connection, and through these relationships to achieve a connection with the larger society.

According to Suarez-Orozco, Todorova, and Louie (2002), "20% of children in the United States are growing up in immigrant families and a substantial number of these children are affected by issues of separation" (p. 637). New and meaningful relationships are vital to immigrants trying to cope with such losses. By establishing new and strong intimate relationships, immigrants might experience a new "secure base" where they can feel safe, loved, and accepted.

Differentiation

Differentiation refers to an individual's ability to have a sense of self as unique from the culture, social class, or family that surrounds him or her

(Kerr & Bowen, 1988). It is important for immigrants to differentiate from both their home and host countries if they are to achieve a clear sense of identity. Although the concept of differentiation is usually applied to individuals in their families, it can also be applied to families within immigrant communities. A family may be able to integrate both home and host country cultures when their immigrant group does not do so.

In the case of those descended from Mexican immigrants to this country, it is interesting to see the complex ways in which differentiation takes place across generations. For instance, in our community work with Mexican American families, we have found adults who do not speak Spanish and want to be identified only as "Americans," because being identified as Mexicans was linked to severe racism and oppression when they were growing up. When asked about their cultural heritage, many of them do not have knowledge about the way in which the first of their family to immigrate came to this country. It is clear that in these individuals a cultural cut-off is present. However, it is also common to find that later generations want to go back and resolve such cut-offs. Teenagers asking questions about their cultural heritage, choosing to learn Spanish, and feeling proud of finding their "Brown" identity represent examples of attempts at resolving such cultural cut-offs. It might be possible that Mexican American teenagers feel safer about reconnecting with their cultural heritage as the dynamics of racism in this community are not as oppressive as they were 30 years ago. Therefore, it is important to keep in mind that differentiation is not just an individual process but a family process across generations, and that it can be influenced by many contextual variables (e.g., dynamics of oppression).

Dynamics of Oppression

Oppression is unjust authority exercised over individuals that makes them feel confined and shaped by forces that seem to be beyond their control (Frye, 1996). Oppressive experiences can be found in individuals' home country as well as in their host country. For example, racism has been present in Mexico since the Aztec empire was conquered by Spain. A class system based on race and skin color was established, with the Native peoples as the least powerful group. According to Fortes de Leff (2002), "Skin color remains important in social and political relationships in Mexico today. It has been a principal symbolic organizer and identity model. Being 'White' or 'blonde' as Mexicans call white-skinned people, is associated with the people in power, belonging to a higher social class, deserving privileges. Being 'dark' relates to Indian origin, denoting an inferior social class and implying submission" (pp. 620–621). It is not uncommon to hear expressions from Mexicans and Mexican immigrants such as "Don't be an Indian!" (Don't be stupid). The dynamics of oppression can have powerful roots in the immigrants' home country if such immigrants were associated with the Indian race based on their skin color. Further, such oppression might continue and possibly become worse by coming to a country where prejudice based on skin color or appearance has been and continues to be present.

Other forms of oppression involve efforts to integrate a group into the mainstream society. The objective of assimilation is a homogenous society. There is a danger that total assimilation might erase the characteristics of the minority's culture and replace them with traits of the majority group (Yetman, 1999). For example, there is a danger that some Mexican values will be labeled as pathological. In the family therapy field, Mexicans' preference to remain close to family and maintain close contact with relatives might be considered an example of "enmeshment." Such judgment is discriminatory in the case of Mexicans, as emotional closeness, *familia,* is a very important Mexican value. However, such value does not correspond to the American value of independence.

Resiliency

McCubbin and McCubbin (1988) define *resilience* as "characteristics, dimensions, and properties of families which help them to be resistant to disruption in the face of change and adaptive in the face of crisis situation" (p. 247). In essence, *resiliency* is the capacity to rebound from adversity strengthened and more resourceful (Walsh, 1998). Although the concept of resiliency was developed as an individual one, resiliency can be viewed as a family-level construct as well (Hawley, 2000). In describing the family processes by which families face their challenges, Walsh (1998) has been a strong proponent of the relational nature of resiliency.

In working with immigrant families, it is crucial for mental health professionals to embrace a framework based on resiliency. Immigrants face a number of powerful stressors, and a strength-based approach is the best way to work with these families. Processes such as depression and anxiety, commonly present in any immigration experience, can mislead helping professionals into focusing on pathology, instead of focusing on the ways in which families can cope with such normal effects of immigration.

Having clarified these concepts, in the next section we will discuss the different ways in which cultural identity formation can take place and the role that the socio-psychological variables play in such a process.

Categories of Cultural Identity Formation

Once the arrival in the new country has been accomplished, immigrants will undergo a process of cultural identity formation. This process will be mediated by the socio-psychological and relational variables discussed above. The immigrant generation will start the process, setting the stage for the cultural identity formation of subsequent generations of their families. The force of "pushes" and "pulls" experienced by those who immigrate, along with their own cultural identity development, will determine the particular dynamics of transmission of the immigration and cultural experiences.

Roer Strier (1996) has described the way in which the relations between immigrant parents and their children are especially vulnerable to the risks associated with immigration. The generational clash, reflecting the culture clash, may skip the first generation in the new country and emerge in the second, depending on the rate of the family's adaptation. As a result of this complex process, five possible outcomes of cultural identity might result. It is important to clarify that the following dimensions of cultural identity do not describe a stage model, rather, this model is categorical. Individuals do not move in a sequence from Category 1 to Category 2 and so on. Individuals find themselves at a particular category at a specific moment in time based on lived experiences and the familial and societal variables present at such moments.

Category 1. Original Culture Identification

Individuals and families might live in the United States but consider themselves as nationals of their birth country. In this category, immigrants do not identify themselves with elements of the host culture and may actively resist identification with the new culture. To the extent possible, they retain the customs, language, dress, and foods of their native country. They try to affiliate with similar individuals and families.

Category 2. American Cultural Identification

Individuals and families consider themselves Americans and reject elements of their original culture. In this category, they spurn and demean their native culture. They minimize contact with the home country and other immigrants.

Category 3. Original Culture Identification Open to Expand

Individuals and families in this category continue to consider themselves nationals of their birth country, but they are open to incorporating elements of the host culture, especially those that they consider significant.

Category 4. American Cultural Identification Open to Expand

In this category, individuals and families consider themselves Americans, but they are willing to incorporate elements of a second culture.

Category 5. Integrated Identification

This category includes individuals and families that have been able to incorporate elements from both cultures and whose identity is based on such integration. For example, in the case of a Mexican American family this integration might include celebrating American holidays with traditional Mexican dishes mixed with new dishes or observing the Day of the Dead while also going trick-or-treating.

The final step in the process of cultural identity formation is recursive. Individuals who have identified themselves with a specific category will continue to be influenced by the different socio-psychological and relational dimensions, and as new experiences affect their cultural identity and trigger new processes. For instance, someone in the category of integrated identification who has an aggressive experience of racism might go back to the process of moratorium, reach the new cultural identity of original culture identification, and consequently refuse to incorporate the traits and values of American culture.

The descriptions of these categories make it clear that engaging in a process of cultural identity formation is a relevant developmental task. When cultural identity is unexamined, the individual or family will match some group chameleon-like—without developing a sense of true ethnic identity. Some individuals or families may achieve a "normative" identity by remaining wholly identified with the original culture or moving completely into the new culture. The individual with an achieved cultural identity has adopted an identity that could be located among the five possible cultural identity categories. It is characteristic of such an identity to remain relatively stable unless a major event impacts the cultural experience of the individual.

Next, we will illustrate the way in which this cultural model has been applied when working with a Mexican American family in the community.

Case Study

The Chavez family[3] were referred to the Parent Empowerment Project (PEP) by the juvenile probation department because Juan and Alicia Chavez's 14-year-old daughter, Jessica, was charged with shoplifting and theft. At the time, Juan was 50 years old and Alicia was 37. Juan, who was born and raised in the United States, maintained a close relationship with his family, and they resided in the same city where the family lived. He had a full-time position in a manufacturing company. Alicia was born and raised in Mexico. As a child, Alicia lived in a little town in a northern state of Mexico. When she was 18 years old, she moved to the border on the Mexican side, looking for better living and economic conditions. It was during this time that she met Juan and married him. She became an American citizen by naturalization and continued to maintain strong ties with her family in Mexico. Alicia had a part-time job and devoted the rest of the time to her family.

Even though we attempted to have family sessions with all family members, it was difficult to engage Juan in sessions because of his work schedule. We cannot rule out the possibility that Juan was reluctant to attend sessions, viewing his role as the traditional provider and protector, and Alicia's role as the parent responsible for dealing with the child and home. Alicia was present for all family sessions. During the initial sessions, Jessica seemed willing to collaborate with the treatment team; however, the more we explored the reasons for her behavior, the more she became defensive and stopped collaborating. It also was evident that Alicia became anxious with Jessica's reactions in session and, on many occasions, attempted to stop Jessica from sharing her thoughts and feelings.

As a treatment team, we began to experience frustration because we could not find a way to connect with Jessica, and she was not open to our feedback. After several conversations, we realized that we needed to apply a resilience and cultural framework in order to be effective. Obviously, this family was struggling with complex immigration and cultural issues. The family consisted of three individuals belonging to three different generations. Further, it was essential for us to see them not as being "pathologically defensive" but as "developmentally and culturally challenged." We decided to redirect our course of treatment and embrace a strength base and cultural perspective.

We started the eighth session by asking Jessica what it was like for her to be a daughter in her family. We asked her to think about the different ways in which she and her father and mother saw the world according to the different cultural contexts in which they had been raised. After asking this question, we witnessed a reaction of more disclosure from Jessica than ever before. She first expressed this opening up by saying, "It is so difficult to talk with my parents, and especially with my Mom about my stuff. She was born in a little *ranchito* (little village) where girls start having sex when they are 20. I just cannot connect with her and share my experiences with her because she doesn't want to listen to me and would start reading me the Bible just like the old women in that *ranchito* do to their daughters. It is so frustrating!"

After listening to this powerful disclosure, it was clear to us that the cultural component of therapy was the most essential element we had to address if we were to help the family improve their relationships with each other. We identified that we were working with two people holding two different cultural identities: Alicia (Mexican culture identification open to expand) and Jessica (American cultural identification open to expand). We encouraged both family members to share their cultural stories.

It turned out that although Alicia had become a dual citizen (Mexican and American), in her heart she felt Mexican because she highly valued traits of the Mexican culture, such as maintaining strong ties with family and showing solidarity whenever people are in need. Her ideal of a teenager is a child who decides not to have sex until marriage and does not even wonder about drugs or illegal behavior because that would cause pain to her parents and disgrace to the family. Jessica, on her side, reported that her mother's values are old fashioned because a lot of the people her age are experimenting with sex, drugs, and alcohol. Although she reported not engaging in such practices, at times she wondered how it would be to engage in such behaviors. Further, these themes were common topics of conversation at school, and she had been criticized by some of her cohort because she was not sexually active.

As a treatment team, we conceptualized this conflict as a cultural problem and labeled it as a family being challenged by cultural identity differences within the family. We were committed to providing an opportunity in sessions to allow each family member to share her or his own cultural story and, at the same time, to find ways to create a bridge to promote their reconnecting with each other.

We reframed Alicia's attempts to lecture Jessica as signs of her love and concern for her daughter. We explored how these attempts at protection were taught to Alicia by previous generations and how they were expected by mothers in Mexican culture. On the other hand, while reinforcing Alicia's place as parent, we explored with Jessica ways in which she would like her mother to exercise her authority and guidance, consistent with Jessica's cultural experiences. Jessica expressed that what she needed most was for her mother to listen to her stories without jumping in and lecturing, and to hear her mother's opinion after she felt understood by her mother.

We coached Alicia in empathic listening and in new ways to offer her guidance to Jessica. In a matter of weeks, the relationship between Alicia and Jessica started to improve in a significant way. Even though we observed Alicia's struggles when listening to her daughter's stories, she was able to validate whatever Jessica had to say (even when Jessica told her that a "Gothic" boy had approached her and invited her to participate in dark rituals!). As a result of this, Alicia increasingly became Jessica's confidante, and Jessica reported that she was feeling like she could share with her mother her own concerns about sex, drugs, and other themes. Alicia gained confidence in her abilities as a mother, reinforced her authority with Jessica, and was able to achieve a balance of discipline and guidance in a very effective way. She realized that her guidance was much more effective when Jessica felt understood and validated by her. Five months after we started treatment, Jessica was released from probation because of significant improvement in her behavior.

As a treatment team, we found that the Transgenerational Cultural Identity Model was extremely important in helping this family. By developing a strong framework based on resiliency, by identifying the role of the different sociopsychological variables, and by identifying and respecting the fact that family members had achieved different cultural identities, we were able to create a new cultural reality for this family. Our objective was not to acculturate Alicia into the American way by asking her to give up her Mexican values, nor to acculturate Jessica into the Mexican way and push her to see "reality" according to imposed Mexican values. Our objective was to identify the different cultural identity positions of the family members that had created a breach. In doing this, the family's cultural identities and experiences were valued and respected, and they were able to redefine their family by creating a new experience of cultural integration. The parental subsystem was reinforced, and the intimacy between Alicia and Jessica was increased.

Our self-awareness as individuals was important to our effectiveness as a treatment team. We had to be in tune with our own cultural values in order to prevent imposing our own values and expectations. More than once, we had to handle our own anxiety, just as Alicia did, whenever we wanted to impose our own cultural values on Jessica instead of listening to her experiences. We learned that by becoming aware of our own cultural identity, we were also able to identify the ways in which we could facilitate or obstruct the process of change when differences in cultural identity were so significant.

Reflections, Questions, and Exercises

The Transgenerational Cultural Identity Model offers a way of understanding the experiences of immigration and cultural identity formation by acknowledging and working with cultural differences, thus moving us away from models that assume acculturation and assimilation into the U.S. mainstream society as a norm. In an increasingly culturally diverse U.S. society, it is more essential than ever before to understand that cultural experiences cannot be reduced to one objective: assimilation. It is crucial to understand that cultural development can result in a number of different cultural identities. Although this chapter has been primarily focused on the influence of the process of immigration on individuals and families, it is also useful, when taking a systemic view of intervention, to consider the influence of immigration on the regions, states, and countries where it has been occurring for centuries. This may allow therapists and families to reinterpret certain dynamics in their communities that may seem baffling and confusing. Immigration forces everyone to change. By its very nature, it rubs together cultures, people, and behaviors that are very different, creating something entirely new. Genetic variation in animals creates greater resistance to disease and more physical flexibility; cultural variation in individuals and populations creates more resistance to cultural myopia.

The Transgenerational Cultural Identity Model needs to be tested across different settings and areas of practice to demonstrate its effectiveness and to refine it. In what follows, we reflect on the role of mental health professionals in supporting cultural identity formation and explore various applications of the model in clinical and training settings and research.

Clinical and Training Settings

As mental health professionals, it is important for us to examine the way in which relationships of dominance, submission, power, and privilege are embedded in social discourse (Hoffman, 1992). Regarding ethnic and cultural minority groups, the term *acculturation* has been used many times in company with an agenda of assimilation. Understanding the use of acculturation and assimilation as means of oppression and transmitting such knowledge to students are tasks that will contribute to creating our role as agents of social change.

The Theoretical Myth of Sameness (Hardy, 1990), which is the belief that all individuals and families of an ethnic group are virtually the same, can also be applied to each family regarding their cultural identity development. It is important that as supervisors and clinicians we understand that we are not working with just one cultural identity in a family, because every individual might be at a different place in his or her cultural development journey. Developing such sensitivity might enable us to identify ways in which family members have stopped communicating their cultural stories to each other because the stories are so different.

The socio-psychological variables of the model (experience of connection, differentiation, dynamics of oppression, and resiliency) are useful theoretical tools when working with clients, because these variables come from a focus on strengths. When studying cultural identity, it is important to keep in mind that it is not an isolated experience, but one that is embedded in larger sociological systems.

It is essential for us as mental health professionals to examine our cultural identity and journey of cultural development. Being aware of our own identity will enable us as supervisors and trainees to be attentive to potential biases or filters when working with families presenting multiple cultural identities.

Research

As researchers in a developing profession, it is important to realize that a crucial step in any research process is being able to identify the agenda that is guiding the research. There is a need to examine the agendas of the existing literature on cultural development and the way these impact our views of relationships, as well as being aware of our own agendas that guide our work. It is important to remember that research implies the possibility for maintaining a status quo or the opportunity to promote social change.

The distinction proposed by Hardy and Laszloffy (1998) regarding cultural sensitivity versus cultural awareness is particularly relevant when conducting research on cultural identity development. *Cultural awareness* is limited to the ability to cognitively identify differences in cultural identities; *cultural sensitivity* allows the researcher to develop an attitude of respect and appreciation for cultural differences when conducting research. Such cultural sensitivity has obviously been lacking in studies suggesting that ethnic minorities should give up their cultural identity in order to "fit in with" the larger and dominant culture.

Notes

1. The term *United States* is used across Latin America to refer to the country of the United States of America. Based on the fact that countries such as Mexico call themselves "Estados Unidos Mexicanos" (Mexican United States), it is important to use the term *United States* with sensitivity, since this name is not exclusive to just one country in the American continent.

2. The word *American* is commonly used by people in Latin America to describe people with a U.S. citizenship or legal residence. Based on this, the term *American* will be used in this chapter to make the distinction between an immigrant and a nonimmigrant. It is important to note, however, that the word *American* cannot fully describe the vast ethnic diversity present in the United States. Further, this term can be used mistakenly to refer exclusively to one country (the United States), when in reality, *America* refers to two continents, not just the United States. By considering that only U.S. citizens "are Americans," there is a risk of perpetuating a system of domination that excludes noncitizens of the United States who wish to be identified as Americans.

3. The names in this case have been altered to protect the clients' confidentiality. The in-home therapy was provided by Jose Ruben Parra Cardona, MFT, and Linda Flores Olguin, Parent Educator. The full treatment team included Richard Wampler and Maria Bermudez, PEP Co-Directors and Supervisors; Narumi Taniguchi, Hye-Sun Ro, and Neetu Arora, MFTs; Mary Ann Gutierrez and Thelma Garibay, Parent Educators; and Cullen Manny, PEP Coordinator.

References

Banks, J. A. (1987). *Teaching strategies for ethnic studies.* Boston: Allyn & Bacon.

Ben-David, A. (1993). Culture and gender in marital therapy with Ethiopian immigrants: A conversation in metaphors. *Contemporary Family Therapy, 15,* 327–339.

Bowlby, J. (1988). *A secure base.* New York: Basic Books.

Donley, M. G. (1993). Attachment and the emotional unit. *Family Process, 32,* 3–20.

Falicov, C. J. (1995). Training to think culturally: A multidimensional comparative framework. *Family Process, 34,* 373–388.

Farver, J. A. M., Narang, S. K., & Bhadha, B. R. (2002). East meets west: Ethnic identity, acculturation, and conflict in Asian Indian families. *Journal of Family Psychology, 16,* 338–350.

Fortes de Leff, J. (2002). Racism in Mexico: Some cultural and clinical aspects. *FamilyProcess, 41,* 619–624.

Frye, M. (1996). Oppression. In P. S. Rothenberg (Ed.), *Race, class and gender in the United States: An integrated study* (pp. 146–149). New York: St. Martin's.

Hardy, K. V. (1990). The theoretical myth of sameness: A critical issue in family therapy training and treatment. In G. W. Saba, B. M. Karrer, & K. V. Hardy (Eds.), *Minorities and family therapy* (pp. 17–34). Binghamton, NY: Haworth.

Hardy, K. V., & Laszloffy, T. A. (1998). The dynamics of a pro-racist ideology: Implications for family therapists. In M. McGoldrick (Ed.), *Re-visioning family therapy: Race, culture, and gender in clinical practice* (pp. 118–128). New York: Guilford.

Hawley, D. R. (2000). Clinical implications of family resilience. *American Journal of Family Therapy, 28,* 101–116.

Hoffman, L. (1992). A reflexive stance for family therapy. In S. McNamee & K. J. Gergen (Eds.), *Therapy as a social construction* (pp. 7–24). Newbury Park, CA: Sage.

Kerr, M. E., & Bowen, M. (1988). *Family evaluation: An approach based on Bowen Theory.* New York: Norton.

LaFromboise, T., Hardin, L., Coleman, K., & Gerton, J. (1993). Psychological impact of biculturalism: Evidence and theory. *Psychological Bulletin, 114,* 395–412.

McCubbin, H. I., & McCubbin, M. A. (1988). Typologies of resilient families: Emerging roles of social class and ethnicity. *Family Relations, 37,* 247–254.

McGoldrick, M. (1998). Introduction: Re-visioning family therapy through a cultural lens. In M. McGoldrick (Ed.), *Re-visioning family therapy: Race, culture, and gender in clinical practice* (pp. 3–19). New York: Guilford.

Negy, C., & Snyder, D. K. (2000). Relationship satisfaction of Mexican American and non-Hispanic White American interethnic couples: Issues of acculturation and clinical intervention. *Journal of Marital and Family Therapy, 26,* 293–304.

Parra Cardona, J. R., Busby, D. M., & Wampler, R. S. (2002, November). *No soy de aqui ni soy de alla?: Transgenerational cultural identity formation.* Workshop presented for the National Conference of Hispanic Association of Colleges and Universities, Denver, CO.

Roer Strier, D. (1996). Coping strategies of immigrant parents: Directions for family therapy. *Family Process, 35,* 363–376.

Suarez-Orozco, C., Todorova, I. L. G., & Louie, J. (2002). Making up for lost time: The experience of separation and reunification among immigrant families. *Family Process, 41,* 625–644.

Turner, J. E. (1991). Migrants and their therapists: A trans-context approach. *Family Process, 30,* 407–419.

Valentine, S. (2001). Self-esteem, cultural identity and generation status as determinants of Hispanic acculturation. *Hispanic Journal of Behavioral Sciences, 23,* 459–468.

Walsh, F. (1998). *Strengthening family resilience.* New York: Guilford.

Yetman, N. R. (1999). Patterns of ethnic integration in America. In N. R. Yetman (Ed.), *Majority and minority: The dynamics of race and ethnicity in American life* (pp. 227–271). Boston: Allyn & Bacon.

Index

About the Editors

Mudita Rastogi is an associate professor at the Illinois School of Professional Psychology, Argosy University, Chicago, and is in private practice in Arlington Heights, Illinois. She obtained her Ph.D. in marriage and family therapy from Texas Tech University, and her master's degree in psychology from the University of Bombay. Rastogi is a Licensed Marriage and Family Therapist, a Clinical Member of AAMFT, and an Approved Supervisor. She has published in the areas of family and couple therapy, cross-cultural and gender issues, intergenerational relationships, and practice issues and South Asian families. Her clinical interests also include adolescents, domestic violence, trauma, and EMDR. Rastogi serves on the editorial boards of the *Journal of Marital and Family Therapy* and *Journal of Systemic Therapies*. She frequently presents workshops nationally and internationally. Rastogi has over 15 years of clinical experience in both India and the United States with a highly diverse client population. She also has an interest in partnering with grassroots, nonprofit organizations.

Elizabeth Wieling is an associate professor in the Department of Family Social Science at the University of Minnesota. She obtained a Ph.D. in marriage and family therapy and human development and family studies from Iowa State University. Wieling is a Licensed Marriage and Family Therapist, a Clinical Member of AAMFT, and an Approved Supervisor. Her research and published work involve the development of culturally sensitive and effective clinical interventions, cross-cultural therapy and supervision, intercultural couple relationships, and status of women issues, including mental health, family relationships, education, economic well-being, and political influence in the United States and abroad. Wieling is investigating the cultural adaptation processes involved in modifying an evidence-based parenting treatment program to better fit the cultural characteristics of a sample of at-risk Latina single mothers and children. This study is being conducted as part of a 5-year Career Development Award funded by the National Institute on Mental Health. Wieling serves on the editorial boards of the *Journal of Marital and Family Therapy* and *The Journal of Feminist Family Therapy*. She frequently presents workshops nationally and internationally.

About the Contributors

Carmen Aguirre is a doctoral student in the marriage and family therapy program at Texas Tech University. She teaches undergraduate classes and is a residential therapist at an adolescent detention center. Her current research, on which her dissertation will be based, is on single Latina mothers and the effectiveness of a parenting program. She is also interested in developing interventions for incarcerated adolescent females. Aguirre developed and is currently implementing a model that integrates narrative therapy and art. She is also the founder of a Latino/a students' writing group that address issues of professional identity in MFT students of color.

Saba Rasheed Ali is an assistant professor in the counseling psychology program at the University of Iowa. She received her doctoral degree in counseling psychology from the University of Oregon. Prior to her hire as an assistant professor within the counseling psychology program at the University of Iowa, she was a postdoctoral fellow for 2 years in that program. Her research and scholarship interests are in the areas of career development of high schools students, poverty issues, and the integration of multiculturalism and feminism.

J. Maria Bermúdez is an assistant professor of marriage and family therapy and is on the Women's Studies Counsel at Texas Tech University. She is a Clinical Member and an Approved Supervisor of AAMFT and teaches MFT contemporary theories, clinical practicum, qualitative research methods, and gender and diversity. Bermúdez is originally from San Pedro Sula, Honduras. Currently, her research examines conflict resolution among Latino couples and the experiences of Mexican and Mexican American mothers parenting alone. She is especially interested in the social constructions of race, ethnicity, culture, religion, gender, language, and power.

Nancy Boyd-Franklin is a professor in the Graduate School of Applied and Professional Psychology at Rutgers University. An African American psychologist and family therapist, she is internationally known for her work with ethnic minority families and communities. She has published extensively on such topics as multicultural issues; cultural competency; ethnicity and family therapy; the treatment of African American families; multisystemic interventions with poor, inner city families; therapeutic support groups for African American women; home-based school and community interventions; and HIV/AIDS. The most recent of her five books is the second edition of her first book, *Black Families in Therapy: Understanding the African American Experience* (Guilford, 2003).

Dean M. Busby received his doctorate in marriage and family therapy from Brigham Young University. He is a professor and the chair of the Human Development and Family Studies Department at Texas Tech University in Lubbock, where he resides with his wife and three sons. His interests in culture and identity emerge from his family and cultural background, in which knowing his history was always emphasized, and from several experiences living outside the United States. These experiences in his family and abroad heightened his sense of the relevance and centrality of understanding who we are and how our cultures influence the way we make sense of the world. His research has most often focused on multiculturalism and on premarital and early marital relationships and their assessment, and it has been published and presented in a wide variety of settings, including professional conferences, journals, seminars, television programs, newspapers, and books. Busby's research has also won awards from professional and university entities and been funded by grants from university, business, and government agencies.

Laurie L. Charlés is an assistant professor of family therapy at the University of South Florida (USF) in Tampa. She is director of the Marriage and Family Therapy Certificate Program in the Department of Rehabilitation & Mental Health Counseling at USF and a Clinical Member and Approved Supervisor of AAMFT. She is also a Licensed Marriage and Family Therapist in Florida and Louisiana and a Licensed Mental Health Counselor in Florida. Charlés received her doctoral degree in family therapy from Nova Southeastern University in Ft. Lauderdale, Florida, and her master's degree in counseling psychology/marriage and family therapy from Our Lady of the Lake University in San Antonio, Texas. Her professional pursuits include gender issues in MFT training and supervision, the construction and deconstruction of language in the therapy room, and the role of systemic thinking in crisis management. Charlés is a Returned Peace Corps Volunteer and is currently working on a book about her experiences in the Peace Corps in Togo, West Africa.

Krista M. Chronister is an assistant professor in the counseling psychology program at the University of Oregon. Her research and published scholarship focus on a broad range of issues related to domestic violence, including battered women's economic and career development, community mental health interventions with ethnic minority and immigrant families experiencing domestic violence, and immigrant mental health. Chronister has experimentally tested the effectiveness of community career intervention programs with battered women and empirically examined ethnic differences in perceived career supports and barriers with American and immigrant battered women.

Edward A. Delgado-Romero is an assistant professor in counseling psychology at Indiana University, Bloomington. He is also adjunct faculty in Latino studies and on the board of the Institute for Latino/a Cultures ("La Casa"). Delgado-Romero is the past chair of the Section for Ethnic and Racial Diversity of the Society for Counseling Psychology (Division 17 of APA) and is now the treasurer for the National Latina/o Psychological Association. He is a licensed psychologist in Indiana and Florida. His research interests include Latino/a psychology, multicultural counseling competence, ethics, and investigating race and racism in the psychotherapy process and his research has been published in several prominent journals and in books. Delgado-Romero received his Ph.D. in counseling psychology from the University of Notre Dame. He then became a clinical assistant professor and the assistant director for clinical services at the University of Florida Counseling Center, where he was recognized several times for his service to students, including by the 1999 Superior Accomplishment Award.

Janet M. Derrick is in private practice as a Registered Family Therapist in Kamloops, British Columbia. She is a Clinical Member and Approved Supervisor in AAMFT and the Canadian Registry of Family Therapists and a member of the Canadian Psychological Association. She is also a mother and grandmother. Derrick has delivered workshops and trainings throughout Canada and internationally on Native trauma, Native families, and relationships between Natives and non-Natives. She did therapy work with residential school survivors, was clinical supervisor at a culturally based drug and alcohol treatment center, facilitated a national Aboriginal focus group that created a Code of Ethics for residential school healing projects, and currently provides therapy in Native trauma programs. Derrick has published articles about the box and circle systems and contributed to books on Native issues. She received the John Banmen Award for outstanding contribution to family therapy in British Columbia. Derrick is also President of the Interior Aboriginal Arts Society.

Jonathan R. Flojo is a research associate at the Instructional Research Group in Long Beach, California, and is a doctoral candidate in counseling psychology at the University of Oregon. He has been a special education teacher, behavior analyst, community college counselor, career counselor, and health educator. In addition, he is an independent consultant focusing on policy issues related to health disparities in minority communities. His primary professional interests include the mental and physical health consequences of stigma and social discrimination, cultural competence and professional training, LGBT health issues, HIV prevention in racial and ethnic minority and immigrant communities, and school-based academic and behavioral interventions.

Diane Hayashino is a staff psychologist at the University of California, Irvine Student Health Center. She teaches classes in cultural diversity and multicultural counseling and the Asian American experience. Hayashino received her doctorate in counseling psychology from the University of Oregon. She is a member of the American Psychological Association, the Asian American Psychological Association (and its Southern California Division on Women), and the American Counseling Association. Her professional interests include immigrant and refugee mental health issues, Asian American mental health, identity development, and multicultural counseling and training. Hayashino's research interests are parenting stress and adjustment and transition issues in immigrants and refugees and community prevention and intervention programming. At regional and national conferences, Hayashino has presented on community-based research, social advocacy and training, multicultural competency, parenting stress among immigrant refugee families, and culturally specific parenting programs.

Nithyakala Karuppaswamy is an international student from India currently doing her doctoral research in the MFT program at Purdue University in Indiana. She received her master's and M.Phil. (post master's) degrees in counseling psychology and applied psychology, respectively, from the University of Madras in India. She worked for 8 years in India as a consulting psychologist in drug and alcohol rehabilitation programs and also specialized in working with individuals with depression, anxiety, and academic under-achievement issues. Karuppaswamy also worked as a lecturer in the psychology department in Mother Teresa Women's University, Madras, for 2 years prior to coming to the United States. In this country, she earned a master's degree in human development counseling from the University of Illinois at Springfield. Her research interests are self-of-the-therapist issues and multicultural family therapy. Karuppaswamy is currently focusing her research on the factors that facilitate and hinder the cross-cultural therapeutic competencies of MFT therapists.

Shalonda Kelly is an assistant professor in the clinical department of the Graduate School of Applied and Professional Psychology at Rutgers University. She has a dual Ph.D. in clinical psychology and urban studies from Michigan State University. Kelly's research interests are racial, ethnic, and cultural issues and couple relationships. She has published articles on the effects of Afrocentricity and stereotypes on African Americans' couple relationships and on underlying pro- and anti-Black dimensions of African American's racial perspectives, among other subjects, and book chapters on assessment and treatment. Kelly obtained supplemental funding from the National Institute on Drug Abuse to develop the first observationally based measure of ethnicity related behaviors manifested in the couples therapy setting with a drug-abusing population. She has a cognitive behavioral and systems orientation and is a member of a number of important national psychological organizations. Kelly has created and/or participated in several community-based mentoring programs for African American youth.

Larry Jin (Kwok Hung) Lee is a Licensed Clinical Social Worker employed as a behavioral medicine specialist at Kaiser Permanente Medical Center in South San Francisco. Lee believes in the intersection of mind, body, spirit, and intuition, and he works closely with physicians in primary care. He has been part of the Kaiser Northern California Region Multicultural Task Force, planning cultural competence conferences and training for Kaiser employees and mental health clinicians. Lee has been a persistent advocate and voice for culturally literate and relevant mental health care and is a diversity consultant to many community agencies. His private practice focuses on the healing power of personal narrative and the ongoing mindful work of unlearning oppression and forming authentic relationships across cultures. He is married and the father of a son and a daughter. Lee envisions writing a casebook for clinicians on the art of being fully authentic and present across cultural differences.

Azmaira H. Maker is a visiting assistant professor in the Department of Psychology at Marquette University in Milwaukee, Wisconsin. She is from Pakistan and completed her doctorate in clinical psychology at University of Michigan, Ann Arbor. Her research interests are trauma and family violence, with a focus on cross-cultural risk and outcome models of child and woman abuse. These models include gender roles and beliefs about violence. She is also interested in investigating varying coping strategies, including religion and spirituality, among immigrant women and women of color. Her clinical experience and interests lie in children and families, with a specialization in child abuse and partner violence. She also has significant experience working with a diverse immigrant population and has worked extensively in Pakistan as a consultant for nongovernmental organizations, schools, and mental health institutes.

Denise D. McAdory is an assistant professor of sociology and anthropology at the University of South Alabama in Mobile. She teaches courses on marriage and family, African American issues, religion, and gerontology. She is also a part-time adjunct instructor at Spring Hill College teaching gerontology courses. McAdory holds a Ph.D. from Union Institute in family psychosocial gerontology, an M.A. in counseling from the University of South Alabama, and an M.A. in marriage and family therapy from Mobile College. She is a Licensed Professional Counselor, Licensed Marriage and Family Therapist, Licensed Gerontological Counselor, and a Licensed Domestic Violence Counselor. Coupled with academic responsibilities, she was a therapist/manager in community mental health for 20 years and is currently a marriage and family therapist for a local agency. McAdory is a consultant-speaker-trainer nationally and internationally on domestic violence, stress management, discipline, and elder care. She is also the coauthor of *Who Are You, Staking a Claim in This Land?* (2004, Trafford).

Ellen Hawley McWhirter is an associate professor in the counseling psychology program at the University of Oregon. McWhirter is the author of *Counseling for Empowerment* (1994, American Counseling Association) and coauthor of *At-Risk Youth: A Comprehensive Response* (3rd ed.; 2004, Brooks/Cole). She is a recipient of the Fritz and Lynn Kuder Early Career Scientist-Practitioner award from the Society for Counseling Psychology (2001) and received a Fulbright Scholar award to teach and conduct research in Santiago, Chile, from the U. S. Department of State (2004). Her scholarship areas include ethnic minority and female adolescent career development and promoting empowerment through counseling and counselor training.

Mona Mittal is currently an assistant professor and director of research in the department of marriage and family therapy at Syracuse University in New York. She is a clinical member of AAMFT. Her areas of interest include issues of diversity, in-home therapy, ethnic minority and immigrant populations, status of women and children, and international family therapy.

Rajeswari Natrajan is a doctoral student at Purdue University in Indiana. She is from India, where she received a master's degree in social work from Madras School of Social Work in Chennai, then worked as a clinical intern at TRY (a home for children of commercial sex workers) and at the YWCA Sahodari Project (a family counseling center and shelter for women). She did casework, group work, and psychoeducational programs with inpatients and outpatients at these centers. Her thesis was on the status of children of commercial sex workers in Chennai. Natrajan received a second master's degree, in marriage and family therapy, from Purdue University. Her research reflects her goal of taking marriage and family therapy, especially systems therapy, to India; as part of her MFT master's thesis, she conducted a needs assessment for family therapy with middle SES families in Chennai. For her doctoral study, she is training social workers and counselors in Chennai in systems perspective and specific modalities in family therapy. Her other interests are training and supervision, self-of-the-therapist, and play therapy.

Debra A. Nixon, a native of Dallas, Texas, is a licensed minister, author, and founder of Liberation Ministries. Nixon is also an assistant professor at Nova Southeastern University, Fort Lauderdale, Florida. She is married to Michael, a commercial realtor. They have two children, Jon-Michael, 15 and Micha Beth, 13.

Kelly Ramón Ozambela is a doctoral candidate in the counseling psychology program at Temple University in Philadelphia. He is a Future Faculty Fellow and adjunct instructor in the counseling psychology program at Temple University. He currently works as a therapist at Abbottsford Family Practice and Counseling Network in Philadelphia, serving a predominantly low-income public housing community. He received a master's degree in counseling from Northern Arizona University in Flagstaff, then worked in student affairs at the University of Delaware. He completed his predoctoral internship at the University of Florida Counseling Center. Ozambela is past co-chair elect of the Latino Network of the American College and Personnel Association Committee for Multicultural Affairs. He is a guest lecturer on multicultural and Latino/a issues in graduate courses and has often presented on multicultural issues at conferences of national organizations. Ozambela's research interests include multicultural counseling competence, Latino/a psychology, and counselor training and supervision.

J. Ruben Parra Cardona is a Mexican citizen and a doctoral candidate in the marriage and family therapy program at Texas Tech University. He was born in Mexico and worked in his country as a state coordinator for a government program offering therapeutic and social services to children living and/or working in the streets. After being awarded a Fulbright scholarship, he moved to Syracuse University to obtain his master's degree in MFT. Most of his current clinical work consists of providing in-home family therapy for juveniles involved in the justice system. He is also a clinician in the

Southwest Institute for Addictive Diseases, providing clinical services for adults on probation with a history of drug-related charges. His current research focuses on the design, implementation, and assessment of a parenting program for high-risk teen fathers. His interest in cultural diversity applied to clinical work originates from his experiences as an international student and the realization that culture is a central and permanent process of growth and enrichment.

Nenetzin Angelica Reyes is a student in the marriage and family therapy program at Texas Tech University and serves as the president-elect of the student association. She is currently working on further developing her research in the cultural identity of couples and children in Hispanic families—especially where there are interracial marriages and biracial children. She has participated in evaluating an established parenting program for its effectiveness with single, Hispanic mothers in the West Texas area through facilitating psychoeducational parenting groups and gathering research data. She is also a member of a writing group addressing professional identity and language at Texas Tech.

Luis Antonio Rivas is a staff psychologist at Seton Hall University Counseling Services in South Orange, New Jersey. He completed his master's and doctoral degrees in counseling psychology at Southern Illinois University at Carbondale. His dissertation was awarded the Donald E. Super Fellowship by the Division 17 of APA for outstanding research in the area of career development. As a graduate student, Rivas served on the executive council of the Division 17 Student Affiliate Group. Rivas's clinical interests include training and supervision, group therapy, working with student athletes, and multicultural counseling concerns. He is a certified alcohol and drug abuse counselor (CADC) in the state of Illinois and has worked with a substance-abusing population. He is also interested in bilingual counseling and Latino/a mental health concerns. He has presented on these topics at conferences and was one of the participants in the Culture and Communicative Competence for Mental Health Professionals Summer Institute at Our Lady of the Lake University in San Antonio, Texas.

Melanie Domenech Rodríguez is an assistant professor in the psychology department at Utah State University. Her research and clinical work focuses on Spanish-speaking Latino parents' parenting practices. Domenech Rodríguez is currently conducting research examining parenting practices for the presence of culturally specific and universal practices that could, in turn, inform intervention development and delivery. Domenech Rodríguez's work is currently supported by a Career Award from the National Institutes of Mental Health.

Monika Sharma currently provides services to adolescents with emotional difficulties at GlenOaks Therapeutic Day School in Glendale Heights, Illinois. In addition to this, Sharma is part-time faculty at Argosy University's Illinois School of Professional Psychology in Chicago. Sharma has been working with children and adolescents for more than 10 years. She also has a strong interest in women's issues and cultural differences. Toward this end, Sharma has been the founder and an active member of the Junior Board of Directors for Apna Ghar, an agency that provides services to South Asian women and children who are victims of domestic violence. She also volunteers as a therapist at the Chicago Women's Health Center.

Quincy R. Smiling is a doctoral student in the rehabilitation counselor education program at the University of Iowa. His minor is hospital administration. He worked as a vocational rehabilitation counselor for the Vocational Rehabilitation Department in the state of South Carolina prior to returning to graduate school. His career objective is to acquire a position as an executive director for a vocational or medical rehabilitation agency.

Martha Adams Sullivan is Deputy Commissioner for the New York City Department of Health and Mental Hygiene. Sullivan earned her doctoral and master's degrees at the CUNY Hunter College Graduate School of Social Work where she is adjunct faculty. Sullivan is also a visiting faculty member at the Minuchin Center for the Family, where she received advanced training with Salvador Minuchin, and an active member of the American Family Therapy Academy. Sullivan's work focuses on the needs of the elderly, women, people of color, and those who are homeless. Sullivan developed the Center for Older Adults and Their Families, a family systems-oriented multiservice mental health program of the Gouverneur Diagnostic and Treatment Center, and the Women's Comprehensive mental health program for mentally ill women and their families. She oversees the Bureau of Community Liaison and Training for constituents interested in meeting the needs of those with mental illness, chemical dependency, and mental retardation/ developmental disabilities and their families. She has also advanced grants development and mental hygiene promotion and prevention. Sullivan is the recipient of several awards for her leadership, advocacy, and community service.

Narumi Taniguchi is a doctoral candidate in marriage and family therapy at Texas Tech University. She graduated from Kobe University in Japan and came to the United States to study MFT. After earning her master's degree in MFT from Syracuse University in New York, she went back to Japan for a few years and worked as a marriage and family therapist at Matsuda Clinic in Osaka. Currently, she is a part-time therapist for the Employee Assistance Program and the Criminal Justice Services within the Southwest Institute for Addictive Diseases at the Texas Tech University Health Sciences Center. Her doctoral dissertation focuses on developing a Japanese version of a couple relationship assessment tool that is widely used in the United States. She is a clinical member of AAMFT and a member of the Japanese Association of Family Therapy.

Danielle Torres earned her master's degree in clinical psychology/marriage, child, and family therapy from Pepperdine University in California and her Ph.D. in counseling psychology from the University of Oregon. She is currently an assistant professor in the school counseling program at Pacific University. Her favorite aspect of teaching is mentoring students and providing a stimulating and inclusive place to learn. Torres's professional areas of interest include addressing educational and counseling issues affecting students of color (particularly Latinos/as), strengthening the home-school connection in K–12 schools, and career development issues.

Richard S. Wampler is a professor of marriage and family therapy at Texas Tech University. A licensed marriage and family therapist and psychologist, his interests are in developing, implementing, and evaluating community-based programs for high-risk families. His current research projects include evaluation of the Parent Empowerment Project for Latinos/as and the transfer of the Parenting Through Change Program to single Latina mothers. Wampler's other interests include training MFT students and training in supervision. He was awarded the American Association for Marriage and Family Therapy's Training Award in 2001.

Carole Woolford-Hunt is Associate Director of Training, Assistant Professor, and Faculty Director of International Student Services at the Illinois School of Professional Psychology, Chicago. She obtained her M.Ed. from Northeastern Massachusetts University and her Ph.D. from Western Michigan University. Dr. Woolford-Hunt has experience working in college counseling center settings in the United States and in community mental health in England. Her other areas of interest include psychodynamic and relational schools of therapy, clinical supervision and training, therapist development, cross-cultural mental health issues, and the treatment of racially and ethnically diverse clients.

Jorge Antonio Zamora is a graduate student in the marriage and family therapy program at Texas Tech University. He is a first-generation Mexican American from South Texas. His current activities include providing therapy to incarcerated juveniles and their families at a local juvenile justice center, as well as engaging and mentoring fathers to become proactive in their children's lives with the Texas Tech Fatherhood Initiative Program. While Zamora's professional pursuits include establishing his own clinical practice and completing his Ph.D., he also envisions himself providing a service to the underrepresented populations within and around South Texas.